The UWI Gender Journey

The UWI Gender Journey

RECOLLECTIONS AND REFLECTIONS

Joycelin Massiah
Elsa Leo-Rhynie
Barbara Bailey

THE UNIVERSITY OF THE WEST INDIES PRESS
Jamaica • Barbados • Trinidad and Tobago

The Institute for Gender and Development Studies
The University of the West Indies

To the women of the Caribbean

The University of the West Indies Press
7A Gibraltar Hall Road, Mona
Kingston 7, Jamaica
www.uwipress.com

and

The Institute for Gender and Development Studies,
The University of the West Indies

A catalogue record of this book is available from the
National Library of Jamaica.

ISBN: 978-976-640-582-3 (print)
978-976-640-583-0 (Kindle)
978-976-640-584-7 (ePub)

Cover illustration: Coyotito Bennett, *The Couple* (acrylic on canvas, 2014).
By kind permission of the artist.

Cover and book design by Robert Harris

Set in Minion Pro 10.5/14.2 x 27

Printed in the United States of America

CONTENTS

SECTION 4. CONSOLIDATION, 1996–2010 – *Barbara Bailey*

SECTION 5. CONTINUITY – *Joycelin Massiah, Elsa Leo-Rhynie and Barbara Bailey*

APPENDICES

ILLUSTRATIONS

Figure

Plates

Tables

MESSAGE FROM SIR ALISTER McINTYRE

Vice-Chancellor (1988–1998), The University of the West Indies

THE EVOLUTION AND GROWTH OF GENDER STUDIES AT the University of the West Indies, starting from humble beginnings almost four decades ago, is one of the epic stories of that institution. Though never endowed with sufficient resources to discharge its intellectual and policy mandate, the Institute for Gender and Development Studies is now spread over the three campuses of the University as well as the Open Campus, and its leaders have forged ahead to open up new areas for academic investigation, to distil the elements requiring societal action and to impressively disseminate those issues at the communal and national levels and beyond.

As we look towards the future, the task of the UWI, governments, and private benefactors and supporters – both regional and international – is to band together to support the institute's ongoing and future work, with respect to developments in areas such as teacher training, research and its dissemination, and community leadership. Among other things, this will require further institutional adaptation and growth, by the university gearing itself to innovate through new forms of governance and the development of teaching and research programmes. For its part, the leadership of the institute should continue and intensify the work that they have been doing by way of public education and of support for institutional development at communal and national levels. I am privileged to lend my endorsement to the ongoing tasks being pursued in these and other areas.

MESSAGE FROM PROFESSOR E. NIGEL HARRIS

Vice-Chancellor (2004–2015), The University of the West Indies

THIS HISTORY OF THE INSTITUTE FOR GENDER AND Development Studies by three eminent Caribbean scholars, Professors Joycelin Massiah, Elsa Leo-Rhynie and Barbara Bailey, will be an important contribution to the significant body of literature on the evolving dynamics of gender relationships and roles in the Caribbean. It will tell the story of achievement by a stellar group of scholars who, through the years, have inspired students, helped shape policy at the national, regional and international levels, and established the IGDS on the regional and global stage as a centre of excellence. The institute boasts among its founding mothers Caribbean greats Peggy Antrobus, Joycelin Massiah and Lucille Mathurin Mair. In more recent years, Elsa Leo-Rhynie, Barbara Bailey, Rhoda Reddock, Eudine Barriteau, Patricia Mohammed, Verene Shepherd (current university director of the institute) and a host of other dedicated researchers have kept the flame burning bright at home and abroad. It is significant that, to date, six of the ten recipients of the CARICOM Triennial Award for Women – Peggy Antrobus (1990), Lucille Mathurin Mair (1996), Joycelin Massiah (1999), Rhoda Reddock (2002), Barbara Bailey (2008) and Eudine Barriteau (2011) – were or are University of the West Indies faculty and have all had a role in the evolution of the institute.

The breadth and scope of research produced by the IGDS, in addition to their advocacy, outreach and community activism, fully supports the mission of the UWI – to propel the economic, social, political and cultural development of West Indian society through teaching, research, innovation, advisory and community services and intellectual leadership. The significant, integrated regional research agenda that underpins and drives the work of the IGDS is impressive and is to be highly commended. This includes areas such as the role and impact of gender on ideology, political economy, empowerment, education and popular culture, to name a few.

I recommend this telling of the evolution of the IGDS, from the perspective of three of its principal advocates, to scholars, students, policymakers and the wider community. Over its twenty years of service, the IGDS has made a significant contribution to development in the region, to the understanding and appreciation of evolving gender roles and of the need for all members of our community to work in harmony to achieve our development goals and objectives.

MESSAGE FROM PROFESSOR SIR HILARY McD. BECKLES

Vice-Chancellor (2015–), The University of the West Indies

THE UNIVERSITY OF THE WEST INDIES, LIKE THE many insular worlds that host it, has had good reasons, rooted in the history of its creation, to struggle with internally institutionalized gender injustices. It has done so in public, even if polite, ways and always with a view to re-engineering social relations and pedagogies. Many women, and a few good men, have had more than a career cause to rise up in support of a culture of equity that promotes political and policy emphasis upon the ideology of egalitarianism. I have witnessed many of these moments over nearly four decades that contained contests which were more often effectively brokered than allowed to crash upon the shores of belligerence.

Over the six decades that spanned the ending of the colonial era and the beginning of the national one, bridges have been built that have enabled the academy to cross over into a land where faces have turned against hegemonic, masculinist hubris. Such crossings have called upon women in academic faculties and other facilities to inspire, to be assertive and to provide institutional leadership. The Institute for Gender and Development Studies emerged as the fastidious custodian of this commitment to gender liberation and related intellectual engagements. It has been an effective leader in the interactive fields of teaching, research, policy formulation and institutional refashioning.

Finally, it is a force for good within the governance model that guides us as a university with a deep and determined opposition to social and academic injustice. In this regard, we value the institute's vision and centrality to our evolving identity, and we celebrate all those persons, carefully commemorated in the text, who have made these transformative moments and movements possible. Such efforts, the book indicates, have not been taken for granted. Rather, they are greatly respected and projected as standards to be sustained by the current leadership and beyond. The future we desire for our university depends upon the institute's continued success in fulfilling its mandate and delivering upon its mission.

FOREWORD

The Institute for Gender and Development Studies: A Sacred Inheritance

VERENE A. SHEPHERD
University Director, Institute for Gender and Development Studies, and Professor of Social History, University of the West Indies

I AM PLEASED TO HAVE BEEN INVITED TO write the foreword to this fascinating book which charts the history and evolution of the Institute for Gender and Development Studies from its beginnings as a loose grouping of women interested in uniting around issues of women and development, through its existence as the Women and Development Studies Unit and the Centre for Gender and Development Studies to becoming the IGDS. This necessary book, which should become required reading for all UWI/IGDS administrators, staff and students as well as non-governmental and civil society organizations working on gender, catalogues the promises, pitfalls and triumphs of the "gender journey", not only at the UWI, but, more broadly, in Caribbean society. In the process, the authors, who embarked on this project solely as a labour of love without any financial remuneration, sing praise songs to some of the men and women, including external stakeholders, who were either involved in the journey or facilitated it in some way. More importantly, they catalogue their own role in making the IGDS what it is today – lest we forget.

This writing project, only modestly supported financially by the IGDS, the campuses' Research and Publications Fund and the Office of the Pro Vice-Chancellor (Research), is intended to ensure that the authors' roles in the birth, formation and growth of the now mature IGDS are documented; that the present crop of staff in the IGDS do not forget what the "foremothers" had to go through to create the institute; and that, in a way, we realize our responsibility to carry on what could be termed a sacred inheritance. The passion and energy with which they embarked on their project and their obvious commitment to continued identification with it are admirable.

The three authors represent three distinct stages in the process of development of the IGDS. Joycelin Massiah initiated and coordinated the first regional research project, Women in the Caribbean Project, which, on its completion, gave rise to the Women and Development Studies Groups and the regional steering committee, which she chaired for several years; Elsa Leo-Rhynie was the first professor and regional coordinator of Women and Development Studies and was instrumental in establishing the CGDS; and Barbara Bailey led the process of transforming the centre into an institute.

Throughout the five sections and twelve chapters of the book, the authors remind us of the impetus for their interventions, the historical and sociopolitical context within which the pioneers and the staff laboured to create, maintain and upgrade "a unique interdisciplinary academic programme within a generally traditional discipline-based university" and to do so regionally, within a region whose components are geographically separated by hundreds of miles of sea. In the authors' words: "Having understood, lived and embraced the experience of regional cooperation during their student days, it was only natural for them to design and maintain a programme which has remained regional to its core. Together, they have lived through the thirty-odd years of evolution of a simple idea into a vibrant, some would say revolutionary, addition to the academic knowledge and offerings of the regional UWI."

The book demonstrates the truth in Marianne Marchand's observation that

> the area of gender and development has been a site of many debates and critical contributions to the field of development studies. It has also been characterized as bridging practice, policy and theory, addressing the concerns of practitioners in the field, policy makers and academics. Yet trying to find a balance has not always been easy – often leading to debates among the various groups and resulting in different perspectives within the field.[1]

But it is clear that the debates within the field did not result in permanent rupture at the IGDS; on the contrary, despite the occasional ideological divide, those who were and are still on that gender journey have been able to blend academia and activism to develop into scholar-activists who bridged practice, policy and academia, as in Marchand's formulation. Brick by brick, they and others built a solid body of data to provide the content of the academic programme, just as they had to do with the institutional structure that would act as the scaffolding for such content.

Enclosed within these pages, in one place, is a veritable repository of indigenous knowledge and feminist scholarship, and present and future generations of scholars and scholar-activists will benefit from this roadmap: a Sankofa-style[2] looking back, taking stock of the present, plotting the agenda for the future and, in the process, decoding the mysteries of the present by going back to the roots of that tree of gender.

The role of historical forces and international human rights actions in showing the need for serious attention to women's and gender issues, both inside the academy and out, has not escaped the notice of the authors; all three of them would have benefited from Lucille Mathurin Mair's monumental work of scholarship on slavery and the post-slavery period[3] and from accounts of women's struggle for rights and respect from 1865 to 1962 and beyond, and they would have been animated by these historical forces and knowledge. They, and other women, seized the opportunities created in the Caribbean to act on the possibilities to infuse the ideologies of self-determination, women's rights as human rights, and social justice – all ideologies of the 1960s and 1970s – into their scholar activism and organizing.

In examining the initiation, development, diffusion and institutionalization of a project of women/gender studies at the UWI, they rely heavily on personal experience, practical involvement and recollections – personal and those of others who were with them on this gender journey. But as we all know, after a certain stage of life, memory and recollection are unreliable as the only sources of books, and so, as true academics, they make ample use of published and unpublished sources – archival and those within the IGDS (incomplete as IGDS documentation is, as I have come to realize myself).

As I read this labour of love, I could not help but develop a new appreciation of what it must have taken the pioneers to persevere on this difficult, but obviously rewarding, journey. In fact, I can relate to many of the challenges that have been exposed in this book as the authors sought to outline the journey from its beginning to where their formal association ended in July 2010, when Barbara Bailey demitted office as university director and passed the baton to me. There are troubling aspects to this account, however: it reinforces the fact that, because top UWI administrators are mostly male, unless these powerful men are, or have been, on our side, gains made by the IGDS will continue to be tenuous. So, structural and institutional changes are needed to obviate such a necessity. This is what a gender policy can achieve.

Today, the regional IGDS continues to face some of the same challenges that the pioneers faced: space constraints; inadequate staff complement; lack of understanding and sympathy – even a hostility towards what we do; lack of understanding of the structure and independent nature of the IGDS after twenty years; and precarious funding. Indeed, the autonomy of the institute (like that of the previous centre) has been frequently challenged.

Indeed, the similarities between the environment of the 1980s, in which the foremothers struggled, and the current one are stark. Patriarchal ideologies and practices continue to try to invisibilize women and disempower young men, not only in the larger society, but within the walls of UWI. Our men and women – young and old – continue to embrace backward, gender-discriminatory ideologies and practices, with negative consequences for all. Despite the efforts to increase its visibility, the place of the university director of the IGDS is hardly understood outside of the IGDS; and administrators do not appear to be in any hurry to understand it. In addition, many IGDS students, especially the males, continue to complain that they are often asked why they have chosen such an option and are even ridiculed by those who regard gender studies as a soft and irrelevant option.

Questions asked decades ago continue to be asked, including: what has the shift from women's to gender issues really achieved? How can this difference and meaning be conveyed to society and to the university community in particular? Has institutionalization caused an abandonment of the on-campus activism and concern for campus women? What impact has the presence of the IGDS made on gender equity and equality at the UWI?

Carolyn Cooper is less than impressed, noting, according to our authors: "After three decades, women at UWI are no closer to gender equity than we were before we established the women's studies working groups in the 1980s." She has a point. To compound things, institutionalization may have increased our attention to teaching and project garnering and servicing; but it has also changed the relationships among the campus units, with each exercising a level of autonomy that has practically rendered the Regional Coordinating Unit impotent.

Nevertheless, despite these challenges, it is clear that the gender and development paradigm is now universally promoted in the Caribbean, as it is globally, as the means of integrating gender equality concerns in national, regional and international projects, programmes and policies. The IGDS, like its predecessor CGDS, has led the vanguard in this regard and has also, through its gender and development academic programmes, produced a small but significant cadre of persons throughout the region with the requisite skills to engage in this critical work.

We owe a debt of gratitude to these brave women, who surveyed the patriarchal inheritance and its continuing role in women's subordination and insisted not only that societal change should take place but that UWI should lead the transformation – inside itself and, ultimately, outside. The way they organized this book is a testament to the tradition of women uniting around projects, a tradition that must be preserved. But let us not fool ourselves. While the journey must continue, there are, no doubt, more twists and turns ahead. Change is also inevitable.

As all units seek to address some of the recommendations of the recent quality assurance review and align our activities and programmes with the UWI's overarching 2012–17 strategic plan, we will please some and disappoint others. The institute must take note of the gaps that are still to be filled and the challenges and threats that lie ahead, among them institutional uncertainties and continued sexism, patriarchy and unequal power relations that still affect the way it negotiates its place in the university. As the IGDS continues to take stock and complete the inventory, let us also be conscious that we are in a dynamic field that will be ever changing; and sometimes, it will be necessary to change the structure and programme preferred by some. The quality assurance review, the strategic operational review and the curriculum review that is due in the Regional Coordinating Unit this year will no doubt give us an opportunity to revamp old courses and programmes, and to introduce more relevant ones, as new blood will have new interests, and societal needs will make new demands of us. That is the nature of this and other journeys. But equally, change does not mean a departure from core values.

And to those who say that gender and development is dead, we say that it is not. On the contrary, as Marchand argues, "it is the site of innovative and critical thinking about development issues in a transformed and globalized world".[4] Where we need to focus now is on becoming more relevant to the campus and the rest of Caribbean society and on redoubling our efforts to reduce gender inequality on multiple fronts. While there have been some positive gains for gender equity in the years since the adoption of the Beijing Platform for Action, we can relate to the factors that several scholars have identified as contributing to the "overall failure of gender mainstreaming".[5] According to Aruna Rao, these include "the challenging policy environment within which gender mainstreaming processes operate, inadequate resources allocated to this work, institutional features that have blocked change, and the way in which gender mainstreaming processes have been implemented".[6]

She continues: "While advocates of gender mainstreaming envisioned both institutional and social transformation, in practice, bureaucracies have not proven to be effective agents of social transformation."[7] Rao argues, "Moving forward should involve strengthening the capacity of states and development bureaucracies to deliver on their own operational mandates and developing realistic strategies and workable alliances in light of the constrained institutional environment."[8]

Yes, overcoming these challenges to greater gender equity requires a stronger and diverse but unified voice for change; greater accountability; and increased, targeted resources. But I am confident that the IGDS will find that unified voice for change. The IGDS will stay independent; it will respect foundational culture; it will continue to increase our visibility; and it will continue to show our relevance inside and outside of the UWI.

Notes

1. Marianne Marchand, "The Future of Gender and Development after 9/11: Insights from Postcolonial Feminism and Transnationalism", *Third World Quarterly* 30, no. 5 (2009): 921–35.
2. The Sankofa bird, in Ghanaian philosophy, looks back to gain inspiration for planning the future.
3. Lucille Mathurin Mair, *A Historical Study of Women in Jamaica, 1655–1842* (Kingston: University of the West Indies Press/Centre for Gender and Development Studies, 2006).
4. Marchand, "The Future of Gender and Development after 9/11", 921, 931.
5. See, for example, Marchand's own perspective on this issue of gender mainstreaming, ibid., 925. See also Jane L Parpart, "Exploring the Transformative Potential of Gender Mainstreaming in International Development Institutions", *Journal of International Development* 26 (2014): 382–94; Jane L. Parpart, "Gender Mainstreaming in an Insecure and Unequal World", *Academic Council on the*

United Nations Sytem Informational Memorandum, no. 77 (Winter 2009); and Jane L. Parpart, "Fine Words, Failed Policies: Gender Mainstreaming in an Insecure and Unequal World", in *Development in an Insecure and Gendered World*, ed. Jacqui Leckie, 51–70 (Farnhem: Ashgate, 2009).

6. Aruna Rao, "Setting the Context: Approaches to Promoting Gender Equity – Gender at Work", in Elizabeth Bryan with Jessica Varat (eds.), *Strategies for Promoting Gender Equity in Developing Countries: Lessons, Challenges and Opportunities*, ed. Elizabeth Bryan with Jessica Varat (Washington, DC: Woodrow Wilson International Center for Scholars, 2008), 8.
7. Ibid.
8. Ibid.

ACKNOWLEDGEMENTS

THE RECOLLECTIONS AND REFLECTIONS WHICH ARE DOCUMENTED IN this book cover a journey of almost thirty years. For some time, Barbara Bailey had been trying to solicit funds to contract Joycelin Massiah to write the history of the Women and Development Studies Group/Centre for Gender and Development Studies/ Institute for Gender and Development Studies at the University of the West Indies, for the benefit of maintaining a record of this journey as well as to inform future generations. The project proposal remained shelved because of a lack of funding.

When the twentieth anniversary of the establishment of the CGDS/IGDS was imminent, in September 2013, Barbara and Elsa Leo-Rhynie decided that they would approach Joycelin with a view to collaborating to prepare a manuscript to celebrate this milestone. We felt that there were many lessons to be learned from our experience with this innovation and that these lessons could not only be an important guide to the future growth and development of the IGDS but also be a useful model for other similar initiatives. The idea was enthusiastically endorsed by Vice-Chancellor Nigel Harris and the university director of IGDS, Verene Shepherd, and we thank them both for their encouragement and support. Despite the fact that there was no funding available, we were greatly motivated by the vice-chancellor, who stated in a meeting on 26 July 2012 that "it is vital that experiences such as yours in the establishment of the IGDS are recorded so that others can learn from them" and also that "UWI owed a debt of gratitude to the IGDS in that it had produced women currently in leadership positions". Verene has been a constant source of support, and we thank her very much for this as well as for her insightful and comprehensive foreword to this volume.

The Regional Coordinating Unit of the IGDS submitted the proposal for the preparation of the manuscript to the University Research and Publications Committee, and the funds allocated have covered the cost of one meeting of the authors, some research assistance and most of the charges for publishing the manuscript. The St Augustine campus unit, through its Campus Research and Publications Fund, funded a second meeting of the authors and the services of a reader/editor. The Nita Barrow Unit, Cave Hill, also received funds from its Campus Research and Publications Fund, which were sent directly to the UWI Press to help defray costs associated with the publication of the manuscript.

The authors hope that the book will serve as a record of an innovation which has been unique in the UWI and which has been significant in both academic and activist scholarship. We have avoided using the word "history" in the title or in descriptors of the work; none of the three authors is a historian, and the research conducted may not fully satisfy the criteria of a historical manuscript. We have sought, however, to be as accurate as possible in reporting the events, achievements, implications and actions which have constituted the journey from WAND and the WICP to the WDSGs and the CGDS and ultimately to the IGDS. To paraphrase Linda Speth of the University of the West Indies Press, we have been involved in telling a story rather than producing a transcript.

In locating documents and other relevant sources of information, we were greatly helped by research assistance from the IGDS Regional Coordinating Unit and campus units: Dalea Bean, Gabrielle Hosein and Charmaine Crawford served as campus liaisons, and Nuncia Meghoo from the RCU provided preliminary research assistance. We acknowledge with thanks the ready availability of UWI and IGDS documents which facilitated our research. Lisa Herman-Davis deserves special mention because of the research assistance she provided during the period of the authors' meetings, when she did her best to satisfy the frequent demands for documents. She, along with Margaret Hunter, who has been with the IGDS for several years, took good care of us during these meetings. Thanks also to Dr Stanley Griffin and the staff of the University Archives, who provided us with a comfortable workspace on the several occasions when we needed one.

In telling our story, we have deliberately not used academic titles for our CGDS colleagues and associates – for convenience and also because some of their designations have changed over time. Special thanks and appreciation go out to them all and especially to our colleagues and friends who have been with us for almost the entire journey: Peggy Antrobus, Eudine Barriteau, Patricia

Mohammed and Rhoda Reddock. Their involvement, encouragement and input have certainly made the journey, and our recording of it, an enjoyable and productive experience. Pat's collection of photographs spans most of the period and treated us to many nostalgic moments as we pored over them and decided which ones to include. Those used in the book include several from her collection as well as others from the collections of the IGDS units.

We acknowledge also, with thanks, the help of Shakira Maxwell of the RCU; of the unit heads, Charmaine Crawford, Leith Dunn and Piyasuda Pangsapa, who were most accommodating of requests for information – documents and photographs – from a variety of sources. Paulette Bell-Kerr read through the manuscript and guided us in its preparation for submission to the UWI Press. Linda Speth, Shivaun Hearne and the team at the UWI Press have also been most helpful and very professional in the preparation for and during the publication process.

We are particularly indebted to the WDSG members and others like Sir Alister McIntyre, Professor E. Nigel Harris, Professor Hilary Beckles and Professor Edward Greene who responded positively to our request for testimonials by sharing their recollections and reflections of the journey. We purposely did not conduct interviews as we wanted the testimonials to reflect spontaneous and unique recollections or reflections rather than guided responses. This resulted in a range of very interesting reminiscences, anecdotes, thoughts and perspectives, which others may not have had and which added a personal touch to the text (see appendix 8 for a list of persons who submitted testimonials). We also tapped into the conversations recorded with some of our pioneers during the twentieth-anniversary conference of the IGDS in November 2013. These have all greatly enriched our own recollections and the documented information. We are disappointed that we did not receive testimonials requested from a number of other people who played significant roles in the UWI gender journey.

The authors undertook this assignment, without remuneration, as their contribution to ensuring that the legacy of the CGDS/IGDS is preserved for posterity. To all who contributed, in any way, to the completion and publication of the manuscript, we offer sincere thanks for allowing us to be involved in the wonderful experience of recollecting, reminiscing and reflecting on the many facets of the "gender journey", which has been a major initiative in the history of the UWI.

ABBREVIATIONS

AWOJA	Association of Women's Organizations of Jamaica
BUS	Board for Undergraduate Studies
CAFRA	Caribbean Association for Feminist Research and Action
CARICOM	Caribbean Community
CARIWA	Caribbean Women's Association
CCGEF	Canada/Caribbean Gender Equality Fund
CDB	Caribbean Development Bank
CEDAW	Convention on the Elimination of All Forms of Discrimination against Women
CGDS	Centre for Gender and Development Studies
CGSSS	Consortium Graduate School of the Social Sciences
CIDA	Canadian International Development Agency
DAWN	Development Alternatives with Women for a New Era
DSO	Direct Support to Training and Institutions in Developing Countries
F&GPC	Finance and General Purposes Committee
GBV	gender-based violence
GDS	Gender and Development Studies
HDI	Human Development Index
IGDS	Institute for Gender and Development Studies
IOP	Internationaal Onderwijs Programma (International Education Programme)
ISER	Institute of Social and Economic Research
ISER (EC)	Institute of Social and Economic Research (Eastern Caribbean)

ISLE	Island Sustainability, Livelihood and Equity Project
ISS	Institute of Social Studies
NBU	Nita Barrow Unit
NGO	non-governmental organization
OECS	Organisation of Eastern Caribbean States
PVC	pro vice-chancellor
RCH	regional clearing house
RCU	Regional Coordinating Unit
RSC	Regional Steering Committee
SCOR	Senate Committee on Ordinances and Regulations
UAC	University Academic Committee
UF&GPC	University Finance and General Purposes Committee
UN	United Nations
UNDP	United Nations Development Programme
UNESCO	United Nations Educational, Scientific and Cultural Organization
UNICEF	United Nations Children's Fund
UNIFEM	United Nations Development Fund for Women
UPEC	University Planning and Estimates Committee
UWI	University of the West Indies
WAD	Women and Development
WAND	Women and Development Unit
WCW	World Conference on Women
WDS	women and development studies
WDSG	Women and Development Studies Group
WICP	Women in the Caribbean Project
WID	Women in Development
WSG	Women's Studies Group

Section 1

CONTEXT

JOYCELIN MASSIAH

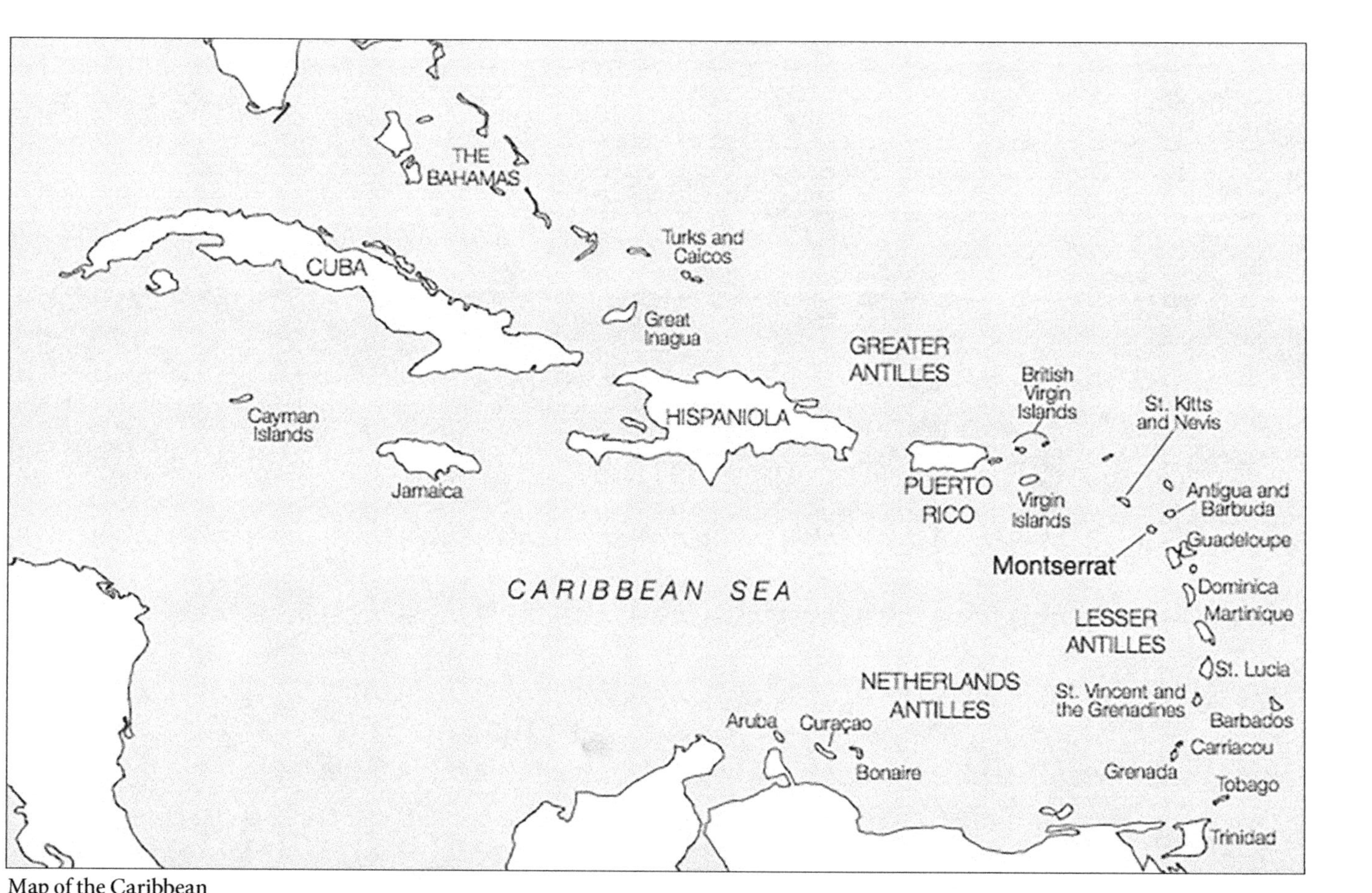

Map of the Caribbean

CHAPTER 1

SETTING THE STAGE

> The gains must be documented and disseminated and this is one very important way in which we of the twentieth century can give a legacy to the twenty-first century.
> —*Hermione McKenzie, "Shifting Centres and Moving Margins: The UWI Experience"*

THE OPPORTUNITY TO SHARE IN THE CREATING, MAINTAINING and upgrading of a unique interdisciplinary academic programme within a generally traditional, discipline-based university must surely be counted as special. To have been able to do so for a programme stretching across the three campuses of the regional University of the West Indies, geographically separated by hundreds of miles of sea, must surely count as remarkable. To have been able to keep that programme going for around thirty years and to have reached the point where a serious proposal could be made for the entity to be considered a centre of excellence, a clearing house on issues of gender and development studies regionally, must count as an unprecedented achievement in the life of the UWI, particularly as this possibility was endorsed by external reviewers. This programme has been the link which binds the three authors of this book, all of whom have played critical roles at different stages in its journey at the UWI. We count ourselves as exceptionally privileged to have shared in this inspiring experience.

The process did not take place in a vacuum. Rather, it was fuelled by historical events, by the activities of women's organizations and by events taking place both in the region as well as in the international arena. The West India Royal Commission,[1] better known as the Moyne Commission after the name of its chairman, reporting after the 1937–38 riots, drew attention to the unsatisfactory situation of women (Great Britain 1945a). But, even though the commission's perception of women's role in society was limited, the mere fact that it mentioned women served to give impetus to the efforts of women's organizations and increased their determination to improve the capacity of women, especially poor women, to perform their domestic duties. With that emphasis, it soon became evident that women needed to participate in the labour force in order to facilitate their domestic roles, and so training programmes aimed at providing income-earning skills became an important item on their agenda. Closer examination of the Moyne Commission Report revealed that the situation of women was much more complex and that they faced and endured discrimination within the prevailing political system. Political education therefore became yet another plank in the effort to improve the situation of women. Some of these women's organizations became integrally involved in the development of the major political parties of their countries, the shaping of the parties' ideological perspectives and the mapping of their party policies and programmes. Some of their key efforts were geared towards securing for women the right to vote, to sit on juries and to be appointed as magistrates, senior administrative officers or members of official boards and committees.

Much of this work was stimulated by events on the international level. In 1946, the United Nations had established the Commission on the Status of Women with a mandate to report annually to the Commission on Human Rights established in the same year. With these two Commissions and the Universal Declaration of Human Rights in 1948, the UN began its work on behalf of the women of the world. This meant that, at the highest levels, the status of women was now being seen as a human rights issue requiring the active involvement of national governments rather than dependence on the isolated efforts of women's organizations. At the same time, countries of the Caribbean region were emerging from a particularly traumatic period of history, characterized by the 1937–38 riots, but one which heralded the onset of a profound period of nationalism as well as regional integration. Following the demise of the federal experiment, the movement towards political independence intensified. It was a period filled with idealism, excitement and hope which encouraged experimentation and promoted tolerance and flexibility towards new ideas.

Women in the region understood these trends and quickly learned their implications. Women's organizations therefore became prevalent and influential, and through their operations women learned the skills of democratic organizing and management, of fundraising and disbursement, of mediation between government and civil society and of representation of the case for women's rights. They understood the need for banding together across the region and created the Caribbean Women's Association (CARIWA), which was important because it acknowledged that women were integral to the regional integration process. This was a major step forward. Second, the issues which they were addressing represented a move towards a Women and Development (WAD) approach. This was a departure from the women in development model and a move into an internationally accepted development paradigm strongly endorsed by women from the developing world, who were insisting that women's concerns were deeply intertwined with development agendas – and had ever been so, in their own historical experience. Third, the strategies which CARIWA used were essentially what is now being called gender mainstreaming; that is, they were targeting key policies (like political federation), key intergovernmental institutions (in particular, CARICOM) and key educational institutions such as the UWI in order to ensure not only attention but action on women's concerns in those places. Among other initiatives, CARIWA worked for the establishment of the WAND Unit within the UWI in 1978. This was indeed path-breaking thinking at the time and, in fact, marked the first tentative steps towards the introduction of women and development studies (WDS) into the regional academy.

As the international community moved towards the First World Conference on Women in 1975, Caribbean women's organizations had created a firm basis on which to move to the next level of women's development. They had created a solid foundation of discipline, commitment, dedication and caring on which the more development-oriented women's organizations of the next generation could build. They had created a climate conducive to the questioning of women's roles in society and to action designed to eliminate discrimination against women.

It was against the background of this maelstrom of activity that concrete action was taken towards the introduction of formal study of women and development into the UWI curriculum. The story of the origin, growth and development of the IGDS is one of the creativity, determination, collaboration, risk-taking and sheer hard work which mark the lives of Caribbean women throughout the region and which are demonstrated so clearly in the history of the women's organizations of earlier years. It was those early organizations which insisted on the establishment of the WAND Unit within the UWI to undertake outreach work on behalf of women of the region. Then, a single query from a single woman, Joycelin Massiah, on a single campus, Cave Hill, led, by turns, to the first regional research project on women, the Women in the Caribbean Project; to a series of informal discussion groups across three campuses, Women's Studies Group/Women and Development Studies Groups; to the design of a formal programme of teaching, research and outreach in WAD by those groups; to the creation of the CGDS; and, ultimately, to the IGDS emerging as a powerful and independent entity. The process attracted significant levels of funding from a wide variety of donors, including the Government of the Netherlands, through the Institute of Social Studies in The Hague, which carried the programme from 1986 to 2003. The relationships established among these partners and organizations are illustrated in appendix 1. The road was not easy, it was not smooth, but the women knew what they wanted and why. Kathleen Drayton, WDSG coordinator, describes it this way:

> When we started talking about Women's Studies in the University, we did not have a lot of theory but we had a lot of experience of male power and of social injustice which we could analyse. We lived and understood male power and women's unequal status. We knew that women had done and were doing a great deal, although to the books, men had done it all. History books still ignore women's roles in the development of their societies. The knowledge transmitted is that men did it all. (Drayton 2010, 15)

The journey, however, was followed with grit, and not a little humour, by a band of committed women. For women concerned with issues of gender inequality, this is an achievement to be celebrated.

Throughout its existence, the many scholars involved in this gender journey have been writing and publishing on a wide variety of issues related to women and gender in this region, providing, in the process, much new information and raising searching theoretical and methodological questions. Many scholars involved in the UWI gender journey, including these three authors, have written and addressed audiences across the region and beyond on various aspects of feminist scholarship and, indeed, on the centre itself (Bailey 2003, 2004; Leo-Rhynie 1992, 1999, 2003b, 2004; Massiah 1986a, 1993, 2004). Nowhere, however, is there a holistic assessment of the origin and evolution of the centre/institute. Hence this book, which seeks to trace the story of the initiatives over the 1978–93 period that gave rise to the centre, of the programmes which the centre designed and implemented after 1993, of the steps which marked its elevation to an institute, of some of the obstacles which it encountered and of some of the strategies employed to overcome those obstacles.

Each of the authors attended the UWI as an undergraduate during or immediately after the heady days of the Federation of the West Indies. Despite its failure, they were each inspired by the high spirit of regionalism which the federation had instilled in young people of the time and, indeed, which was the primary goal of the university itself. All three authors entered academic professions – demography in the one case, education in the other two – which brought them into direct contact not only with young women as students, but also with the issues affecting women throughout the region. As they analysed these issues, it became increasingly clear that, in their role as academics, their primary task was to offer young women students a new and valuable way of seeing themselves and their roles in their region and the wider world – not as objects or victims of patriarchy but as vibrant partners in development. For these three women, the way to do this was to ensure that students were exposed to theoretically and practically sound academic programmes addressing issues of women, gender and development, with particular reference to the Caribbean. Having understood, lived and embraced the experience of regional cooperation during their student days, it was only natural for them to design and maintain a programme which has remained regional to its core. Together, they have lived through the thirty-odd years of evolution of a simple idea into a vibrant, some would say revolutionary, addition to the academic knowledge and offerings of the regional UWI. The twentieth anniversary of the CGDS/IGDS therefore seemed an appropriate time for these three, all now retired, to pause and take stock of where the programme came from and where it should seek to go.

This book will present material depicting strategic points in the journey towards the present status of the IGDS, with a view to identifying lessons learned along the way and seeking opportunities for further advancement in the face of continuing challenges. Implicit in this is the aim of encouraging enhanced support for further development of the IGDS as a viable and respected entity within the UWI. Also integrally linked is the issue of the position of women in the UWI, bearing in mind that it is women who have pioneered and maintained the centre/institute. Additionally, there is the aim of charting a course for the pursuit of increased application of gender concepts to the development strategies of the region and, indeed, of the UWI itself.

Sources of material include personal recollections of the authors, documentary material, recordings, as well as testimonials from several persons who have been intimately involved at various stages of the process. The information collected is broadly located within a theoretical framework of innovation and change involving four distinct stages: initiation, development, diffusion and institutionalization, using the model proposed by Rogers and Shoemaker (1971) and further elaborated in Rogers (2003). The use of this innovation discourse was first introduced by Barbara Bailey (2003) as an analytical framework in an address delivered in Mexico. According to this theory, an innovation is diffused through several stages before it becomes acceptable in the community of which it is a part. The first stage is to identify and explain the innovative idea, paying attention to what makes it an innovation. The next stage involves the analysis of the innovation and putting its components into action, demonstrating the advantages, identifying potential pitfalls and designing measures to overcome them. The third stage relates to the measures to be taken in order to share information about the innovation, with a view to garnering support for the initiative and encouraging participation in the exercise. The fourth and final stage is when the innovation is accepted by the community or, at least, by critical groups within it. An important consideration in the process is the issue of time, since receptivity to a new idea depends on the way in which the new information is shared, the complexity of the new idea, the levels at which the idea is targeted and the compatibility with existing ideas and methods. Applying this framework to the UWI context reveals that, while the CGDS/IGDS programme represents an overall innovation which goes through these various stages towards acceptance, each phase within the overall innovation also goes through two or more of these four critical stages. Responding to these factors, therefore, takes time; thirty-odd years is what it took for the WDS/GDS programme to reach the point of becoming the IGDS.

In addition, Rowland (1982) identifies pragmatic and political issues related to the introduction of women's studies in the academy. *Pragmatic* refers to action both to strengthen the capacity of the innovative project to realize its objective and to anticipate and counter resistance. *Political* refers to issues pushing against the initiative both from within the group and from external forces as well as to pre-emptive strategies and action to forestall and counteract such forces. Attention to both sets of factors is important for successful institutionalization.

Against the above-mentioned background, the authors attempt to identify some key gender issues surrounding the situation of women, at the global level, in the region and at the UWI. They also highlight the positive factors which influenced the introduction of a programme of women/gender and development studies in the UWI and some of the negative factors which surfaced from time to time.

The book is organized in five sections, four of which provide an account of events and actions at various stages of the process of development of the programme, along with some highlights, while the fifth looks to the future. The first section addresses the socio-economic and political context which provided an enabling environment for the study of women's issues in the region as well as some of the conceptual and pedagogical challenges which influenced the origin and growth of the initiative.

Section 2 consists of chapters 3 and 4. The former provides an account of the pioneering efforts at introducing the idea of WAD into the academy through the mechanism of a regional outreach unit, on the one hand, and a large-scale regional research project, on the other. The first part of chapter 3 addresses the origins, philosophical approaches and some of the initial components of the outreach programme designed and run by the Women and Development Unit. The second part of chapter 3 examines the origins, strategies, achievements and outcomes of the WICP, paying particular attention to the importance of the link between the researchers, policymakers and women's organizations. This represents the *initiation* phase of the theoretical model being followed. Chapter 4 in the second section examines the establishment of WDSGs across the three campuses, provides a quick look at some of the initiatives of these groups, recounts how the WDS programme originated and grew into a full-fledged cross-campus programme, and hails the creation of the post of professor of WDS (later GDS). In effect, this may be construed as both the *development* and *diffusion* stages of the model – *development* in terms of the activities which centred on discussion of theories, concepts, issues and strategies, *diffusion* in terms of the outreach activities.

In section 3, chapters 5, 6 and 7 chronicle the emergence of the CGDS, its mission, challenges, actions and achievements. Here, the *development* and *diffusion* aspects of the process continue, but the *institutionalization* stage of the model may be perceived to have begun. Particular attention is paid to the role of regional and international agencies and to donors, especially the Government of the Netherlands, The Hague, through the ISS. An account is provided of the growth and strengthening of the teaching programme at both undergraduate and postgraduate levels.

Chapters 8 to 11 constitute section 4 and provide an account of the pursuit and further development of the tripartite mission of teaching, research and outreach as well as the transition from a centre to an institute, in what may well be the final stage of institutionalization of gender studies at the UWI. The final section of the book consists of the single chapter 12, which examines the achievements and lessons learned during this journey, identifies the current challenges and needs, and looks to the future, identifying emerging women/gender issues, challenges and opportunities for the IGDS and the possible transformational role for the institute in the UWI.

While this book cannot address every single aspect of the UWI gender journey, it can and does attempt to isolate some of the critical factors which have influenced its evolution. It offers perspectives and strategies for confronting the future, bearing in mind that it is a new generation with emerging concerns and ideas that will take forward the work. It is our hope that the contents of this book will encourage this generation of thinkers and inspire them to new heights of scholarship.

Note

1. The West India Royal Commission was established in 1938 by the colonial government to investigate causes of the 1937/38 riots and to recommend measures which could be taken to ameliorate conditions in the British West Indies. Chaired by Walter Guinness, first Baron Moyne, the commission consisted of ten members including two women, one an expert in tropical medicine, the other a social reformer. The commission's report, known as the Moyne Report, was presented in 1945 and gave rise to the Colonial Development and Welfare Fund, intended to assist in the reconstruction process in the West Indian colonies.

CHAPTER 2

GENDERSTANDING THE CONTEXT*

> I believe that the work of Women's and then Gender Studies provided valuable conceptual and policy frameworks, provided an institutional space for the exploration of critical issues in the social and economic space and an opportunity for academics and activists to work together.
>
> —*Hilary Robertson-Hickling, UWI lecturer and former WDSG (Mona) coordinator*

Historical Situation of Caribbean Women

Caribbean societies are a product of several waves of migration in the past; hence the resulting social mix includes indigenous Indians, European settlers, African slaves, and indentured servants from Asia, Africa and Europe. Each wave was marked by domination, subordination and violence between competing ethnic groups as well as between men and women within and across groups. Indeed, it has been said that these Caribbean countries have been subject to cultural forces as devastating as the earthquakes, hurricanes, even volcanic eruptions, to which they are often subject. Throughout each period of migration, women learned to accommodate to the prevailing unequal power relations. They developed survival skills for themselves and their children; they learned to build alliances, to negotiate space, to build and utilize leadership skills and to exercise those skills individually and collectively. Interestingly,

*We gratefully acknowledge the permission granted by our colleague Meryl James-Sebro for use of the term *genderstanding*, which she created.

they learned to do this with minimum dislocation and maximum peace. (See Anderson-Duncan 2012; Beckles 1988, 1989; Bush 1990; Mathurin Mair 1975, 2006; Shepherd, Brereton, and Bailey 1995.)

The particular historical heritage of slavery has also meant that the issue of political and civil rights, irrespective of religion, ethnicity or gender, is a deeply entrenched feature of Caribbean societies. The various slave revolts of the eighteenth and nineteenth centuries, under the leadership of slaves like Nanny of the Maroons in Jamaica, Nanny Grigg and Bussa in Barbados,[1] were an early signal of the thirst for these rights. The post-emancipation struggles and the 1937–38 riots were all designed to gain recognition and preservation of these rights. Of course, how these rights were observed is another story, but they were enshrined in constitutions throughout the region as countries attained political independence and the populations became quite aware of them. So, when women began to speak out about women's rights in the early years of the twentieth century, they were not trying to introduce a concept that was unfamiliar. What they were trying to do was to ensure that the notion of rights was applied unequivocally to women.

But what was the condition of the region's women in those early years? The region was essentially one of poverty, relying heavily on returns from the sugar industry, just as it did during the days of slavery. Evidence provided to the Moyne Commission, which was convened after the 1937–38 riots, pointed clearly not only to the severe poverty and substandard social conditions but also to the unsatisfactory situation of West Indian women. Influenced perhaps by the prevailing Victorian ideology in England, the report assumed West Indian women to be participating primarily in traditional nuclear-family units.[2] Not much recognition was given to the different family forms that prevailed, to the link between women's reproductive and productive lives, or to the fact that women may have had additional interests beyond home and family. There was certainly no analysis of the traditional family as an economic unit in which inequality between men and women was intrinsic; but the fact that the report paid any attention to women at all was path-breaking, as was the fact that the report gave rise to an entirely new feature of development praxis in the region – the community development approach, in which the contributions of women became significant.

Following the commission's report, governments embarked on several efforts to try to diversify the economy, improve social conditions and address the unacceptable situation of women. First, they promoted a strategy of "industrialization by invitation", based on the assumption that foreign investment would lead to economic development. The manufacturing industry became an important employer and contributor to the gross domestic product. This was supplemented by attempts to develop a tourism sector which, in time, became the lead sector in many of the economies. Increased provision for health and education services became important, if not critical, components of the development strategy. This was further supplemented by the introduction of social welfare departments charged with the responsibility of providing welfare services to the poor and needy. These efforts received key support from the women's NGOs, with their charitable work targeting poor and needy women, although their perception of women's roles did not, at first, vary materially from that of the commission. Their programmes included such initiatives as the creation of daycare centres; the provision of free food, clothing and other necessities; training in income-earning skills, mainly homemaking; and, in some cases, self-development skills. It was the classic WID approach, in which the traditional role of women was not questioned, the sexual division of labour was accepted and the non-domestic interests that women may have had were downplayed. The result was that, by focusing almost exclusively on what Moser called women's "practical needs" and not so much on their "strategic needs", the traditional hierarchical status quo seemed untouched (Moser 1989). That, at least, seemed to be the situation on the surface.

The emergence of women's institutes[3] may have been the catalyst which spurred women's NGOs to widen their horizons and to see the situation of women as being much more complex than was previously realized. They had seen official recognition from the Moyne Commission of the discrimination which women endured within the political system; and so, in the 1940s and 1950s, there emerged women's organizations concerned with the political education of women. The Jamaica Women's Liberal Club actively campaigned for women to sit on the Kingston and St Andrew parish council; the League of Women Voters in Trinidad and Tobago campaigned for the political and legal rights of women; the Women's Political and Educational Organisation of British Guiana (now Guyana) focused on political education and action. Together, these three women's organizations were integrally involved in the development of the major political parties of their countries, the shaping of their ideological perspectives and the mapping of their party policies and programmes. Also emerging at that time were women's professional associations – nurses, secretaries, and other professional and business women – concerned primarily with improving the skills of their members, but also providing a number of social services to the wider community.

By the 1960s and 1970s, the Commonwealth Caribbean had become a most exhilarating place. It was a period filled with idealism, excitement and hope. Following the immediate post-war years, equipped with a blueprint for future development provided by the Moyne Commission and brimming with new ideas, countries throughout the region began to explore avenues on how to collectively declare their political independence from Great Britain. At the same time, there emerged a desire for regional unity, which fostered the formation of a number of regional organizations in a range of areas and, ultimately, a movement towards the creation of a regional federation of territories within the English-speaking Caribbean. This entity existed for four years, 1958–1962, eventually succumbing to differences on a wide range of issues. The failed West Indies Federation seemed to create two opposing forces. On the one hand, there emerged a thrust towards political independence of individual territories, and, on the other, there was a great determination to build regional unity in whatever form necessary, although stopping short of another attempt at political unity. So territories began to negotiate for and declare their political independence. Jamaica along with Trinidad and Tobago started the ball rolling in August 1962. Guyana followed in May 1966 and Barbados in November of the same year. The territories of the Eastern Caribbean followed at a more leisurely pace, but follow they did. By the end of the 1990s, every country except Anguilla, Montserrat, the Turks and Caicos, the Cayman Islands and the British Virgin Islands had achieved political independence from Britain.

Even as these countries embraced their newly found independence with enthusiasm, they looked to the idea of regional integration as the framework around which issues of trade and functional cooperation in a wide range of areas could become the joint focus of participating governments. First came the Caribbean Free Trade Area in 1968. This was transformed into CARICOM with the signing of the Treaty of Chaguaramas on 4 July 1973. CARICOM was envisaged to function in three main areas – the common market, functional cooperation and the coordination of foreign policies.[4] The treaty served to produce a sense of togetherness, which took hold throughout the region, from Belize to Guyana. Slogans of "One Nation" and "One Community" became the mantras across the region.

This was really quite remarkable, given the geography of the region. Sitting as an archipelago between North and South America, the Caribbean occupies a strategic position as a port of entry between north and south in the Western Hemisphere and between east and west of the Atlantic Ocean. This means that the Caribbean can be, and has been, used as a trade and communications hub. That certainly was the case in the past and will undoubtedly continue to be so, even as the technological revolution is played out at ever higher levels. Further, the small physical size of Caribbean countries facilitates transport and communication, making it relatively easy to deliver programmes and messages across a single country and, indeed, across the entire region. It also makes it easier to create a sense of togetherness despite the complexity and disparity of resources; separation by sea; economic diversity; cleavages of race (especially in Guyana and Trinidad and Tobago), of class everywhere and, especially, of gender across and within all strata in every country. While similarities of history, geography and culture helped to keep the idea of regional integration alive, they also served to attach high importance to the individuality of each country, thus creating limitations on what can and should be done collectively.

This sense of independence linked to interdependence infected everyone in the region, including women, who recognized that kind of linkage in their personal lives. They now began in earnest to make their voices heard, in a number of arenas and on a number of subjects which they had previously avoided in public. So, for example, they lobbied to have included in the original Treaty of Chaguaramas an article protecting the rights of women and including responsibility of monitoring the position of women in the region among the duties of the CARICOM Secretariat. Interestingly, the text of the treaty, as outlined on the current official website, includes no such article. Nor is there the schedule setting out CARICOM's role in monitoring the position of women in the region.[5] Yet, on a previous edition of the same website, the following statement appears: "In 1983, CARICOM celebrated its tenth Anniversary and during a meeting of Ministers of Women's Affairs to commemorate this event it was recognized that the 1973 Treaty of Chaguaramus addresses the need to examine the position of women in the region" (CARICOM 1983). Further, in his address to that 1983 meeting, the then deputy secretary general had this to say: "in a fundamental sense, the mandate within CARICOM to pursue issues relating to women in development, is firmly entrenched as a basic provision in the Treaty of Chaguaramus itself; for that historic document clearly and expressly provides for the 'Position of Women in Caribbean Society' to be one of the 16 specific areas of Functional Cooperation within the Caribbean Community" (CARICOM 1983, 2, annex 2 to REP 83/2/38 WA). So the women may not have been successful in securing a specific article on women's rights in the treaty, but they did secure recognition of those rights by insisting on the identification of work in that area as a responsibility of a dedicated division of the secretariat.

In 1997, the heads of government in the CARICOM adopted a Charter of Civil Society for the Caribbean Community, agreeing to "pay due regard to its principles" and to ensure the widest circulation throughout the community. Included among the articles of the charter was one, article 12, on women's rights. According to that article:

> For the promotion of policies and measures aimed at strengthening gender equality, all women have equal rights with men in the political, civil, economic, social and cultural spheres. Such rights shall include the right
> (a) to be elected or appointed to Public Office and to be eligible for appointment to positions of decision-making bodies at all levels of their society;
> (b) to be afforded equal opportunities for employment and to receive equal remuneration with men for work of equal value;
> (c) not to be discriminated against by reason of marital status, pregnancy, lactation or health-related matters which affect older women;
> (d) to legal protection including just and effective remedies against domestic violence, sexual abuse and sexual harassment. (CARICOM Secretariat 1997a)

Despite this expansion of the idea of women's rights in a charter which was fully endorsed by the heads of government in 1997; when the original Treaty of Chaguaramus was revised in 2001, this principle of separately recognizing women's rights disappeared and was replaced by one which, in article 17, requires the Council for Human and Social Development to: "Establish policies and programmes to promote the development of youth and women in the community with a view to encouraging and enhancing their participation in social, cultural, political and economic activities" (www.caricom.org/jsp/community/regional_treaty-text.pdf).

Women's NGOs of the mid-1970s also lobbied for the establishment of a post of women's affairs officer within the secretariat. Initially, a part-time post of Nutritionist/Women's Affairs Officer, funded by United Nations Children's Fund, was created in October 1978. This post was subsequently upgraded to a full-time one with the designation "women's affairs officer", stationed at a women's desk, with effect from October 1980.[6] Women's NGOs also worked together and in concert with the CARICOM women's desk to design a plan of action for the English-speaking Caribbean, to be included in the UN Economic

Commission for Latin America and the Caribbean, for presentation at the UN mid-decade conference. They also worked together to effect the introduction of a WAD unit within the UWI, a unit to be discussed in chapter 3 of this volume.

So, from as early as the mid-1970s, the women of the region had a vision of an integrated region and of their place therein. They understood the necessity of linking women's NGOs with key institutions such as universities, the private sector and the major economic-development and political organizations of the region. Theirs was not the language of oppression, gender subordination, female solidarity or gender mainstreaming, terms which are common today, but their actions spoke loudly to those concepts. They never lost sight of their vision of a Caribbean-wide network of women working together in a spirit of non-partisan service towards the upliftment of the lives of all women of the region and towards their involvement in the structure and functioning of their governments. Ultimately, their goal was to secure recognition and protection of their rights. For the Caribbean women, the three parts of the theme of the 1975 World Conference of the International Women's Year held in Mexico – Equality, Development and Peace – were indivisible.

Contemporary Situation of Caribbean Women

Together, these initiatives by governments and women's NGOs helped to improve standards of living substantially, but not enough to move the region from, to use the terminology of the day, the category of "underdeveloped" countries in the world. Nor did these efforts do much to alter the subordinate position of women in the societies.

From the failed effort to realize a political federation of the region began the march towards political independence, and efforts at diversifying the economy began to intensify. This process continued throughout the 1970s, and by the end of that decade it was evident that, despite differences in pace and level of achievement among the various countries, the region as a whole was slowly becoming a "developing" region. Economic indicators were beginning to reflect general upward movement, with perhaps two exceptions. So, too, were social indicators.

Using the United Nations Development Programme Human Development Index[7] as a measure, one country, Barbados, was being classified during the 1980s as a very high-income country, while two – Trinidad and Tobago, and Jamaica – were numbered among the high-income countries of the world (see table 2.1). By the early twenty-first century (2005), there were five countries in the high-income bracket – Antigua, Barbados, Bahamas, Trinidad and Tobago, and St Kitts, while six were numbered among middle-income countries (UNDP 2007). Thereafter, the classification used by the UNDP was changed and values for the index recalculated. These new data indicate that by 2012 one country, Barbados, with an index of 0.825, was being cited among the very high-HDI countries of the world, nine countries were classified as high-HDI countries, three as medium and one as low (see table 2.1). In effect, this suggests that the region was demonstrating clear signs of improvement in levels of economic and social development, notwithstanding evidence of differences among countries. Yet, the period covered by these data was associated with the rising economic orthodoxy of the free market and structural adjustment programmes, which exacerbated income inequalities, levels of unemployment and levels of violence – in all of which, those suffering the worst effects were women.

Despite the country differences in economic achievements in the region, ideological perspectives on the role and status of women were uniformly limiting. Occupational opportunities for women were restricted essentially to nursing, teaching, clerical/secretarial work, services (such as sales, personal, domestic) and social work, with miniscule chances for physicians or lawyers, which were considered to be the plum occupations. Women enjoyed few political rights. In the absence of property ownership and age qualifications, they could not vote, hold public political office, sit on juries, or be appointed as magistrates, senior administrative officers or as members of official boards and committees. Where they were employed, their wages were significantly lower than those of men. By contrast, women were predominant in the domestic sphere, often bearing sole responsibility for their households. It was not until 1995 – with the introduction by UNDP of two measures of gender equality, the Gender Development Index and the Gender Empowerment Measure – that the inequality between women and men could be clearly demonstrated (UNDP 1995). The Gender Development Index measures the relative achievement of women and men in the areas of income, health and education. The Gender Empowerment Measure measures the relative participation of men and women in economic, political and professional spheres of activity. Table 2.2 shows the values for these two measures for those years and countries for which the data were available at the time of writing.

From this, it is evident that, while the relative position of women, as reflected

Table 2.1: Human Development Index, 1980–2012

Country	**Year**					
	1980	**1990**	**2000**	**2005**	**2010**	**2012**
Very High HDI						
Barbados	0.706	0.760	0.790	0.798	0.823	0.825
High HDI						
Bahamas	N/A	N/A	N/A	N/A	0.791	0.794
Grenada	N/A	N/A	N/A	N/A	0.768	0.770
Antigua	N/A	N/A	N/A	N/A	0.761	0.760
Trinidad & Tobago	0.680	0.685	0.707	0.741	0.758	0.760 **0.644**
Dominica	N/A	N/A	0.722	0.732	0.743	0.745
St Kitts	N/A	N/A	N/A	N/A	0.745	0.745
St Vincent	N/A	N/A	N/A	N/A	0.731	0.733
Jamaica	0.612	0.642	0.679	0.695	0.727	0.730 **0.591**
St Lucia	N/A	N/A	N/A	N/A	0.723	0.725
Medium HDI						
Belize	0.621	0.653	0.672	0.694	0.700	0.702
Suriname	N/A	N/A	0.666	0.672	0.679	0.684 **0.526**
Guyana	0.513	0.502	0.578	0.610	0.628	0.636 **0.514**
Low HDI						
Haiti	0.335	0.399	0.422	0.437	0.450	0.456 **0.273**

Source: UNDP 2013.
Note: N/A denotes no data available. Highlighted figures represent the HDI adjusted for gender inequality for the five countries for which the required data were available.

by the three defining variables of the Gender Development Index, has been improving over time compared to that of men, their empowerment levels have been lower and growing much more slowly. Thus, for example, the Gender Development Index for the Bahamas moved from 0.696 in 1970 – the highest value for the region at that time – to 0.841 in 2005, the second highest.

Table 2.2: Gender Development Index and Gender Empowerment Measure, 1970–2005

Country	Gender Development Index				Gender Empowerment Measure		
	1970	1992–94	1997	2005	1994	1997	2005
Bahamas	0.696	0.828	0.849	0.841	0.533*	0.544	0.696
Barbados	0.649	0.878	0.854	0.887	0.545*	0.602	0.649
Belize	0.517	N/A	N/A	0.814	0.369	0.470	0.517
Guyana	N/A	0.584	0.691	0.742	0.461	0.469	N/A
Haiti	N/A	0.354	0.426	N/A	0.349	N/A	N/A
Jamaica	0.685	0.710	0.731	0.732	N/A	N/A	N/A
Suriname	N/A	0.669	N/A	0.767	0.348	0.457	N/A
Trinidad & Tobago	0.555	0.786	0.790	0.808	0.533	0.571	0.685

Source: Gender Development Index – for 1970, UNDP 1995, 80, T.3.4; for 1992–94, UNDP 1995, 76–77, T.3.1; for 1997, UNDP 1999, 138–41, T.2; for 2005, UNDP 2007–8, 326–29, T.28; Gender Empowerment Measure – for 1994, UNDP 1995, 84–85, T.3.5; for 1997, UNDP 1997, 152–54, T.3; for 2005, UNP 2007–8, 330–33, T.29
Notes: * These two values are presented here as they appear in table 3.5 of the 1995 *Human Development Report*, however the 1997 report reverses the order.
N/A denotes no information available.

Barbados, with a value of 0.887, ranked number one in 2005. By contrast, the Gender Empowerment Measure values were much lower even for these two top-ranked territories. For Barbados, the Gender Empowerment Measure value for 1994 was 0.545, which placed it at number one, with an increase to 0.649 in 2005, which ranked it second. The Bahamas, with 0.696, ranked first. In other words, women may have been, and may be, doing relatively well in one sense, but not so well in another.

In 2010, the UNDP introduced yet another measure, the Gender Inequality Index, which is a composite measure intended to reflect inequality in achievements between women and men in three dimensions – reproductive health, empowerment and the labour market. Table 2.3 shows this measure for four selected years since the turn of the century.

According to table 2.3, the Gender Inequality Index seems to suggest that, since the turn of the twenty-first century, the level of inequality is declining

Table 2.3: Gender Inequality Index, 2000–2012

Country	2000	2005	2010	2012	2014
Bahamas	N/A	N/A	N/A	0.316	0.298
Barbados	0.314	0.336	0.347	0.343	0.357
Trinidad & Tobago	N/A	0.342	0.318	0.311	0.371
Jamaica	0.457	0.415	0.462	0.458	0.439
Belize	0.524	0.489	0.453	0.435	0.426
Suriname	N/A	N/A	N/A	0.467	0.463
Guyana	0.526	0.525	0.509	0.490	0.515
Haiti	N/A	0.514	0.596	0.592	0.603

Source: For years 2000–2012, UNDP 2013; for 2014, UNDP 2015, 224–27, T.5.
Notes: The Gender Inequality Index was first introduced in 2010 to replace the two previous measures of gender inequality, the Gender Development Index and the Gender Empowerment Measure. The new technique was applied to the available relevant data for some earlier years to produce the figures shown in this table which are reproduced from the cited source.
N/A denotes no data available.

in some territories (Trinidad and Tobago, Belize, and Guyana), but is showing signs of increasing among others (Barbados, Haiti), while it is fluctuating in Jamaica.

The impact of gender inequality on overall development may be depicted by relating the Gender Inequality Index to the HDI. Table 2.1 shows that whereas, in 2012, the HDI stands at 0.7 and over in the majority of cases, when the Gender Inequality Index is applied to these values, the HDI levels fall significantly. For example, in Trinidad and Tobago, the HDI in 2012 stood at 0.760, but when the Gender Inequality Index is applied, however, the HDI falls to 0.644. In other words, in the region, the level of overall development is considerably hampered by levels of gender inequality.

It is the contradictory situation portrayed by these various measures which undermines popular perceptions of Caribbean women as strong, powerful matriarchs. Women themselves have long understood this contradiction. They understood that, despite signs of upward trends in women's social and economic independence, their lived experience was a daily reminder of their subordinate position to men, whether in the home, the workplace or the community, regardless of race or class. So, women began not only to speak out but also to sing out.

Rex Nettleford has reminded us of the interconnection of society and the arts of the imagination. As he put it: "Social commentary by the calypsonians of the society's reaction to national policies, capitalism gone mad, political authority or the self-importance of the native inheritors of the colonial power is a form of action – expressed through art – that addresses problems of self-definition and gives critical clues about a people's perception of themselves" (Nettleford 1993, 51).

This is reflected in Trinidad and Tobago, for example, where, throughout the 1980s, a number of women turned to the calypso genre to draw attention to the negative portrayal of women by male calypsonians and to offer advice to women on how to respond to various forms of humiliation or brutality by men. In 1979, "Singing" Francine advised women experiencing domestic violence to "Put Some Wheels on Your Heels"; in 1980, "Singing" Diane announced: "Ah Done Wid Dat" in response to the same situation; also in 1980, Lady Jane prompted the authorities to "Send Those Raperman to Jail"; in 1984, "Singing" Sandra's "Die with My Dignity" provided powerful advice to women not to give in to sexual exploitation in the workplace; and in 1988, Denyse Plummer proudly proclaimed that "Woman Is Boss".[8] This trend has continued over the years, spreading to other countries. For example, Alison Hinds of Barbados speaks to the issue of women's independence in her popular song "Roll It Gal" (2005). These women became exceedingly popular during those years because of their positive messages to women to take control of their own lives and not to put up with unacceptable behaviour from men. Interestingly, some male calypsonians also provided positive images of women – for example, Adonijah of Barbados with his "Woman"; and indeed, many of the lyrics for songs sung by both women and men were actually written by men.

In Jamaica, there was the Sistren Collective,[9] a women's theatre collective which used popular theatre to raise public awareness about the concerns and needs of poor women. Similar groups existed in Dominica and Grenada. The interesting aspect of their methodology was their attempt to glean women's concerns directly from the women themselves, to transform those learnings into dramatic presentations and to engage the audience in the analysis of the problems identified and the designing of solutions. In the process, many aspects of government policies were critiqued, but equally important was the experience of organizational self-governance in the collective and the opportunity that gave for critical academic analysis.

What these artistes were doing was using what Nettleford (ibid.) calls their "creative imagination" to bring the reality of the lives of many Caribbean women to the attention of the wider society, giving, in the process, some measure of support to the affected women and a considerable measure of support to the messages being spread by the various women's organizations.

It was this kind of response from women across the region which generated the plethora of women's NGOs, the flurry of government activity from the mid-1970s and the entry of the UWI into the discourse on women and gender in the region (Mohammed n.d.).

Caribbean Women's Organizations

One of the important contributions of the first UN Decade for Women, 1975–85, was its reconfirmation of women's issues within a human rights context and the promotion of those issues as integral to the process of development and to the traditional concern with the guaranteed rights of the individual under national constitutions. In 1979, the Convention on the Elimination of All Forms of Discrimination against Women was adopted as the international standard for defining discrimination and establishing equality between women and men. By 1999, all countries of the Commonwealth Caribbean had signed and ratified the convention.[10] Another important contribution was the allocation to governments of responsibility for ensuring the advancement of women and for establishing institutional structures mandated for this purpose. From 1974 onwards, Caribbean governments began establishing some form of national mechanism for this purpose – desk, bureau, ministry, national commission, or national advisory council – singly or in combination.

On the political scene, several countries became independent, and many efforts were made to encourage the participation of women in politics. In a number of cases, there emerged "women's arms" or women's auxiliaries of the major parties. This was especially evident in Jamaica and Guyana in the 1970s, where these entities were particularly vocal in encouraging government initiatives in women's affairs. In 1972, Jamaica became the first country in the region to establish an advisory committee on the status of women. This was followed two years later by the appointment of an adviser to the prime minister on women's affairs, which post was first held by Lucille Mathurin Mair, and the establishment of a women's desk, with Peggy Antrobus as its first director. All of this was even before the UN Mid-decade Conference for Women in 1980. Trinidad and Tobago quickly followed in 1975, with a commission on the status of women and a parliamentary secretary in women's affairs. In November of that year, Barbados simultaneously appointed a national commission on the status of women and established a department of women's affairs. The commission was required to investigate the status of women and to make appropriate recommendations for governmental policy action. This enabled the Barbados attorney general to become the first such official to include mention of the status of women in his inaugural address to the UN General Assembly and to announce his government's plans to implement the UN recommendations emanating from the 1975 World Conference on Women (WCW). The commission made its report in 1978, and numerous meetings and national consultations, as well as legal reform in a number of areas, followed its presentation.

Recommendations from these various commissions prompted parliamentary debate across the region, which resulted initially in agreement to the creation of some form of national machinery concerned with women and development. By the mid-1980s, every territory in the region had done so. Some simply established a women's desk or bureau; others combined that action with some form of advisory/consultative body or policy directive. For example, in 1976, the government of Guyana produced a state (White) paper on equality for women, established a council on the affairs and status of women in Guyana, designated the Ministry of Cooperation as the ministry responsible for women's affairs and established a women's bureau. To seal the deal, as it were, on the move towards national machinery for women's affairs, the CARICOM Secretariat, in 1978, simultaneously appointed an adviser on women's affairs and established a women's desk. Interestingly, two countries established full ministries of women's affairs, Grenada in 1982, under the People's Revolutionary Government, and St Kitts and Nevis in 1984.

Women's NGOs also responded in a number of ways to the women's human rights issue. Some of the traditional NGOs attempted to link specific project activities to development needs as identified in national development plans. Others, new ones, focused on specific women's rights issues as particular incidents occurred. Yet others emerged using completely new strategies as the basis for their plans and programmes. Consciousness-raising of members became central. Research became linked with advocacy. Advocacy became linked with the media, popular theatre and culture, public demonstrations, and participation in international meetings. Trainees transformed the skills training received into small business enterprises. Also in the mix were women's professional associations, which worked towards transforming the practices within their professions and creating more spaces for the participation of women in their chosen profession. Networking with each other and critical partners became the primary tool of engagement of these various organizations. NGOs of this era became known as activists; that is, they were concerned not only with the situation of women per se but also with the context which gave rise to infelicities in their situation, as well as the sources of those infelicities which go beyond gender. Words like *subordination*, *oppression*, *struggle*, *liberation* became integral to their vocabulary. This was the era of the introduction of the concept of feminism into the dialogue. This was the era in which the idea of a women's movement began to take root.

Considerable ambivalence in the use of this term existed. There were those who wondered whether a movement actually existed, and others who wondered: If it did exist, precisely what was it? Antrobus (2004, 13–14) has provided a compelling catalogue of the characteristics of a women's movement, which is worth quoting in its entirety:

- A women's movement is a *political* movement – part of the broad array of social movements concerned with changing social conditions, rather than a network of women's organizations (although many women's organizations may be part of a women's movement).
- A women's movement is grounded in an understanding of women's relations to *social conditions* – an understanding of gender as an important relationship within the broad structure of social relationships of class, race and ethnicity, age and location.
- A women's movement is a *process,* discontinuous, flexible, responding to specific conditions of perceived gender inequality or gender-related injustice. Its focal points may be in women's organizations, but it embraces individual women in various locations who identify with the goals of feminism at a particular point of time.
- Awareness and *rejection of patriarchal privilege* and control are central to the politics of women's movements.
- In most instances, the "movement" is born at the moment in which individual women become aware of *their separateness as women,* their alienation, marginalization, isolation or even abandonment within a broader movement for social justice or social change. In other words, women's struggle for agency within the broader struggle is the catalyst for women's movements.

All of this was a far cry from the thinking of the older generation of women and the manner in which they had operated. Not surprisingly, therefore, there emerged something of a divide between the older, more traditional NGOs and the younger, more progressive ones. It was the catalytic role of WAND (the UWI unit for which the traditional NGOs had successfully lobbied and negotiated) that was crucial in binding the disparate forces into a concerted voice across the region. WAND recognized that, despite the diversity of objectives, strategies and political alliances among the women's NGOs, the common and binding elements were their promotion of women's rights and issues and their concern to create a just and fair society for all. WAND therefore became the nexus which linked the women's NGOs, policymakers, planners and the university. The UWI being the only regional body supported by the governments of the region for the express purpose of providing a common system of university education, the link also effectively reinforced these governments' commitment to the advancement of women.

An important, related development was the emergence of a new, regional entity, the Caribbean Association for Feminist Research and Action, dedicated to celebrating and channelling the creative power of women towards "individual and societal transformation thus creating a climate in which social justice is realized" ("CAFRA: Celebrating 17 Years", All Woman, *Jamaica Observer*, 8 April 2002). Conceived by WAND and a number of well-known Caribbean feminists, this organization represented all that was new among women's NGOs, embracing as it did the notion of feminism (which was relatively new in the region), the strategy of utilizing research and analysis of development issues as well as of linking women's strategic needs to the design and implementation of action. Membership covered all language areas of the region and included "feminists, individual researchers, activists and women's NGOs who define feminist politics as a matter of both consciousness and activism" (ibid.). The organization was launched in April 1985, and its new approach, reflective of the thinking of the newer generation of women's NGOs, was instrumental in furthering the work of the earlier generation in a number of important ways. For a start, the circle of networking was enlarged to include the poorest of the poor, the youth, the elderly, persons with disabilities, the indigenous and men. The new approach shifted from a focus on WAD to one on gender and development, creating appropriate strategic action in the process. This new approach also involved taking on board the discourse on the situation of men. All of this provided a welcoming environment for the entry of the university into the arena of gender and development studies, since it opened up new and potentially exciting areas for new research and action, with possibilities for impacting economic and political decision-making.

The University of the West Indies

The main impetus for the establishment of a university of the West Indies came from the British government, which, in 1943, had created a commission on higher education in the colonies under the chairmanship of high court judge Sir Cyril Asquith. The commission created several subcommittees, including one focusing on the West Indies under the chairmanship of Sir James Irvine, vice-chancellor of the University of St Andrews in Scotland. Following the recommendations of the Irvine Committee, the UWI began its journey towards the twenty-first century as an affiliate of the University of London, known as the University College of the West Indies in 1948 (Great Britain 1945b). Perhaps influenced by the precedent created by the Moyne Commission, which had included recommendations for improving the situation of women, the Irvine Committee gave high priority to the provision of higher education for women in the West Indies. At a time when women were routinely absent from English universities, which were considered the preserve of men, the Irvine recommendations were therefore path-breaking: "The women of the West Indies, though some of them are already showing their quality, do not yet make their full contribution to professional life or to public affairs. . . . With greater access to higher education, the influence of women, valuable in itself and perhaps especially requisite for the solution of the difficult social problems of the West Indies, would make itself felt." The report argued that, through the provision of residential accommodation within a regional university at a lower cost than overseas, "a gradually increasing number of daughters would be able to obtain higher education and play their part fully in the life of their communities" (Great Britain 1945b, 16–17).

Some have questioned the basis of this recommendation, suggesting that the residential provision facilitated the duplication of the collegiate environment of Oxford, Cambridge and St Andrew's in a tropical university and, further, enabled the university to retain an elitist image for several years. Be that as it may, the University College of the West Indies came into being as the recommendations envisaged.

Following acceptance of the Irvine Report, a royal charter was produced, which set out the conditions under which the college should operate, conditions which were repeated in the second charter, established in 2 April 1962 to mark the ascendancy of the college to full, degree-granting university status. Since then the university has expanded from a single campus, Mona in Jamaica, to two others, St Augustine in Trinidad and Tobago, and Cave Hill in Barbados. In addition, there is a single non-campus entity called the Open Campus, which services other countries of the region.[11] A new edition of the charter was produced in response to a report of the Chancellor's Commission on Governance (UWI Office of Administration 1998). All campuses are governed by this latest edition of the charter.

Among the various articles of the charter, there are two of particular relevance to this discourse:

> 4: Men and women shall be eligible for admission to and as students of the University and of appointment to any authority, office or employment of or under the University.
> 5 (1): No religious, political or racial test shall be imposed on or required of any person in order to entitle him to be a student or member of the University or to occupy any position in or on the staff of the University. (ibid.)

It is of interest that, while article 4 speaks directly to non-discrimination (in terms of eligibility) between women and men, it does not explicitly speak to equality, and this after a UN Decade for Women (1975–85) and five UN World Conferences on Women (1975, 1980, 1985, 1990, 1995) in which the theme of equality was prominent. Further, article 5 (1) speaks only of "him". Nevertheless, the spirit of these two articles suggests that discrimination against students or staff on any grounds would violate the conditions of the revised charter.

The Irvine Report had specially emphasized the importance of higher education for women as this would enable them to play their part fully in the life of their community. Consequently, when the first batch of students was admitted into the University College of the West Indies in 1948, there were twenty-three men and ten women, the latter thus accounting for 30.3 per cent of the total. It was not until 1982 that women comprised 50 per cent of total registration. Since then, the numbers have risen to 16,000 men and 36,000 women (2013/14), with the women comprising just over two-thirds of the total registrations, representing a complete reversal of the proportions obtaining sixty years previously, when the university came into existence (see table 2.4).

Further, an examination of the relative positions of men and women receiv-

Table 2.4: UWI Student Registration, by Gender, 1948/1949 to 2013/2014

Year	Student Registration				
	Male	**Female**	**Total**	**Female proportion of total registration**	**Female/ male ratio**
1948/49	23	10	33	30.3	0.44
1958/59	391	231	622	37.1	0.59
1968/69	2,657	1,559	4,216	37.0	0.59
1978/79	4,485	4,046	8,531	47.4	0.90
1988/89	5,336	6,560	11,896	55.1	1.23
1998/99	6,894	12,451	19,345	64.4	1.81
2008/9	13,426	30,153	43,579	69.2	2.25
2013/14	16,445	35,586	52,031	68.2	2.16

Source: For 2008/9, UWI Statistical Review, 2008/9; for 2013/14, UWI Statistical Review, 2013/14; for earlier years, see published UWI Official Statistics for relevant years.
Note: Registration figures include both undergraduate and graduate registrations.

Table 2.5: UWI Higher Degrees Awarded, by Sex, 1996/1997 to 2013/2014

Year	Higher Degrees Awarded				
	Male	**Female**	**Total**	**Female proportion**	**Female male ratio**
1996/97	205	337	542	62.2	1.64
2001/2	303	484	787	61.5	1.60
2006/7	450	831	1,281	64.9	1.85
2011/12*	N/A	N/A	1,896	N/A	N/A
2013/14*	N/A	N/A	2,083	N/A	N/A

Source: For years 1996/97 to 2006/7 figures, see Leo-Rhynie (2008, 9). For 2011/12 and 2013/14 see UWI Statistical Review 2013/14.
Note: *Data by sex not included in the reports for these years.

ing higher degrees, shown in table 2.5, reveals that, for the ten-year period 1996/97 to 2006/7, the number of female graduates was steadily increasing and outstripping that of male graduates. Data for 2011/12 were unavailable at the time of writing, but it is anticipated that, by that time, there would have been over two female graduates for every male one who received a higher degree. This demonstrates not only the importance which higher education has come to represent in the lives of young people of the region, but also the extent to which young women are seizing the opportunity of the availability of such education.

In an interesting article, Leo-Rhynie examined the extent to which this superiority in numbers of women had translated into increasing numbers of women in leadership positions in the various aspects of student government. Her conclusion suggested that not only was there no indication of such movement, but also that prospects for change did not seem favourable. On the one hand, there was "retention by young men of traditional concepts of patriarchy, power and dominance, and the use of psychological warfare to ensure the maintenance of a male-dominated power system of student leadership" (Leo-Rhynie 2003a, 290). On the other hand, there was "acceptance by young women of traditional concepts of patriarchy and dominance and a lack of motivation to effect change" (ibid., 291). We need to ask how and to what extent these findings apply to the world of work. Further, what is their impact on the movement towards gender equality in the society as a whole?

Turning to the staff situation (see table 2.6), we see that, among the academic staff, the number of women is consistently below that of men, except at the lower level of assistant lecturer. However, at the higher levels, there is evidence of increasing numbers of women, such that, by 2006/7, about one-fifth of professors were women, compared with less than 10 per cent in 1996/97. By 2011/12, this proportion had risen to over one-quarter. Among senior lecturers, just over one-third were women in 2006/7, as against one-quarter ten years earlier. At the lecturer level, the proportions were approaching one-half in 2006/7, and actually passed 56 per cent in 2011/12. It may, therefore, be argued that progress towards numerical parity among its staff is slowly being achieved within the university. We may ask what difference these increases have made in terms of programmes, approaches to delivery and quality of results (see Hamilton 1998; Leo-Rhynie 2008).

Table 2.6: Full-Time Academic and Senior Administrative Staff, 1996/1997 to 2011/2012

Level of Staff	1996/1997	2001/2002	2006/2007	2011/2012
	Female Proportion of Total			
Professor	6.8 (103)	16.9 (148)	21.8 (165)	27.8 (169)
Reader	10.5 (19)	*Category abolished*		
Senior lecturer	25.5 (267)	26.7 (300)	36.9 (293)	36.4 (332)
Lecturer	29.5 (597)	44.8 (696)	47.3 (822)	51.8 (966)
Assistant lecturer	56.2 (64)	64.3 (84)	52.8 (163)	57.4 (162)
Other	46.5 (43)	49.2 (130)	53.1 (98)	52.2 (67)
Total	33.8 (1093)	39.4 (1,358)	43.5 (1,541)	46.9 (1,696)

Source: UWI Official Statistics for years 1996/97 to 2006/7; UWI Statistical Review for Academic Year 2011/2012; for earlier years, see Leo-Rhynie (2008, 11).
Note: Figures in brackets reflect total staff in each category.

Women in the Public Sphere

Similarly, at the political level, numbers of women in both houses of parliament may have improved slightly, and the region can speak of having had, during the 1980s, a female prime minister, Dame Eugenia Charles in Dominica, and a female president, Janet Jagan, in Guyana; and at the time of writing in 2015 had two female prime ministers, Portia Simpson-Miller in Jamaica and Kamla Persad-Bissessar in Trinidad and Tobago. But the question exists as to what difference these increases have made in the body politic. In the private sector, there is significant evidence of increases in the involvement of women at the upper levels of management, but whether this has made a difference in the work environment for those at the lower levels, especially women, continues to be debated. In the public sector, women are to be found at the permanent secretary level throughout the region, but whether this has improved capacity and efficiency at all levels is yet to be determined. In other words, the issue is not only about numbers. If we are to be concerned about the progress of the region, of which its women are an integral part, then we have to investigate these related issues and how best to address them so that the contribution of women can be enhanced and recognized. It is these kinds of ideas which propelled a small group of women within the UWI to begin to explore the meaning of the concepts and frameworks which, at that time, the mid-1970s, were being used to analyse the situation of women around the world.

Concepts and Conceptual Frameworks

By the mid-1970s, the international community had begun not only to enter the development debate but also to take the lead in determining the issues to be debated. Having attained political independence during the late 1960s and early 1970s, many Caribbean countries had joined the UN and were participating in its democratization. They contributed to the discussions reviewing the first Development Decade, the 1970s, and offered suggestions for the second, the 1980s. It was a Jamaican woman, Lucille Mathurin Mair, who represented the Caribbean on the UN Commission on Social Development, which pushed for greater consideration of women's issues in its deliberations; and it was another Jamaican woman, Gloria Scott, who gave to the world the phrase "the full integration of women in the development effort" when she suggested an amendment to the resolution on the International Development Strategy for the second Development Decade. This allowed women to introduce the notion of equity, which was not, at that time, on the development agenda. The early work of the two 1946 UN commissions, one on human rights, the other on the status of women, linked as they were to the Universal Declaration of Human Rights, centred on women's human rights, with a particular focus on their legal rights. It soon became clear that such a focus required information on the content of the law, on paper and in practice, as well as the extent to which women were discriminated against in both. This was the impetus for the deluge of research which emanated from the various UN agencies, from universities and from private researchers. The findings of these various sources fuelled discussion which led to the designation of 1975 as International Women's Year and to the subsequent naming of the period 1975–85 as the Decade for Women. Major UN Conferences on Women in 1975, 1980 and 1985 provided opportunities for women to participate as part of their government delegations and, through the mechanism of the NGO forum, to share information from their research and community projects with an international audience. This process engendered considerable debate on a wide range of issues, concerns and concepts that went far beyond women's issues.

These debates also introduced a number of concepts which were initially unfamiliar, not only to the many Caribbean women who attended the gatherings and to women within the UWI who had not been exposed to the UN activity, but also to the women of the region generally. To list a few of the "unfamiliar" concepts:

- Status of women: What did this mean and how was it identified? How was it measured on its own and in relation to that of men? Could a single status of women apply to all women? How could such information affect women in their everyday lives?
- Equity: Was there a difference between equity and equality? How were they measured?
- Integration of WID: Were women not already integrated in a particular way which justified the type of development strategies being pursued?
- WAD: Could the use of this approach be a better way of signalling that a relationship did exist between women and development? How could this relationship be depicted?
- Feminism: What did this mean? Were there different types of feminism? Was this relevant to the study of women in this region?

These and many other concepts troubled those women in the UWI who had an interest in interrogating the realities of the lives of women in the region and promoting ideas to ameliorate their situation. The intuitive recognition that research had to be the starting point towards understanding was strengthened by the high priority given to research as a critical aspect of the first UN Decade for Women, 1975–85, along with its theme of equality, development and peace. Further, the decade reconfirmed women's issues within the human rights context, promoting those rights as integral to the process of development. The decade also allocated to governments responsibility for ensuring the advancement of women and for establishing structures mandated for this purpose. For the first time, women and women's organizations had a voice in the formulation of the work programme of the UN, and two women at the UWI were invited to prepare a background paper for a government delegation at the first UN conference concerned with women.[12] In effect, the recommendations emerging from the decade seemed to give validity to the question of whether or not women at the UWI should engage in research about women and advocacy on behalf of women regionally.

By 1995, a conceptual expansion of the themes of equality, development and peace began to emerge in the form of the introduction of the concepts of gender equality and women's empowerment. In addition, there emerged a recognition that it was also necessary to keep a sharp focus on men and their needs.

The increased awareness and focus on gender inequalities by both NGOs and university women encouraged an environment ripe for discussion of the possibility of introducing women's studies in UWI that were grounded in acceptable concepts. Discussion of the concepts mentioned earlier gave rise to the identification and discussion of yet other concepts, the following in particular:

- Gender: Was this simply a biological term? Or did it have sociological overtones/underpinnings?
- Gender and development: Would adopting this theme result in a loss of interest in the study of women's issues? Would women tend to lose whatever gains they may have made during the earlier WAD days? Would men be willing to engage in the study of men's issues? Would men be willing to link the study of men's issues to the study of gender and development?

These, in turn, gave rise to debates about how to design and execute a programme which would speak not only to the issue of academic rigour, but also to appropriateness and relevance to the Caribbean region. It was a time of learning, experimentation, risk-taking, disappointments and successes.

To Conclude

The factors which contributed to the growth and development of the GDS programme in the UWI were numerous and coalesced around a number of features of Caribbean society, each related to the other, all working together. Independent study of each factor leads inexorably to the fact of its links to the others. When the concept of development moved from economic growth to human development, it signalled recognition that development was intended to benefit men, women and children in an equitable way. Once that was understood and accepted, the trend towards the study of gender and development began. The UWI, with its mandate to conduct teaching and research programmes designed to improve the lives of Caribbean people, was hard pressed to ignore the introduction of a programme of GDS.

Notes

1. In a recent lecture, Verene Shepherd drew attention to a number of women leaders of slave revolts in other countries in the region.
2. Drayton has pointed out that "what has been called 'Victorian' is, however, of far more ancient lineage, dating back to the Middle Ages" (1982, x).
3. Women's institutes were established in several Caribbean territories during the 1940s to implement colonial development and welfare policies, based on the recommendations of the West India Royal Commission. According to Drayton, these institutes, patterned on British and Canadian models, were set up mainly in rural areas and ran classes for women in sewing, embroidery, tatting and crochet, baking, cake icing, cookery and handicraft. They also offered classes in childcare and occasional civic lectures. They were eventually overshadowed by various umbrella organizations, which continued the charitable work of the women's institutes and expanded activities into other areas relevant to women (Drayton 1997, 14).
4. The treaty was subsequently revised in 2001.
5. See www.caricom.org/jsp/community/regional_treaty-text.pdf.
6. This position, like the article supposedly included in the 1973 treaty, has also disappeared, so there is, at the time of writing, no dedicated unit or officer in the secretariat responsible for implementing and monitoring programmes on behalf of women of the region.
7. UNDP defines human development as a "process of enlarging people's choices" (Human Development Report 1990). The HDI seeks to offer a composite measurement by which progress in human development may be charted, through a combination of three indicators – life expectancy at birth, the adult literacy rate and the per capita gross domestic product.
8. I am indebted to Patricia Mohammed for sending me several of her papers, which led me to formulate this paragraph. Any errors in the passage are entirely mine. See Mohammed (1989, 2011 and n.d.) for a selection of the papers made available to me.
9. *Sistren* is a Jamaican term meaning sisters. For an account of their activities and achievements, see Ford-Smith 1989.
10. Most, however, have not signed the optional protocol granting the right of petition in individual cases, and the record on reporting to the CEDAW committee could use some improvement.
11. The UWI Open Campus was formally launched in Antigua and Barbuda in June 2008. Its origin was the School of Continuing Studies (formerly, the Department of Extra-Mural Studies), which carried a university centre in each of the fourteen

contributing countries, five special-purpose units at the Mona campus and one at the Cave Hill campus. The Open Campus is now an amalgam of the Board of the Non-campus Countries, the School of Continuing Studies, the UWI Distance Education Centre and the Tertiary Level Institutions Unit. At the time of writing, it had forty-two locations serving sixteen countries. These have since increased to almost fifty and seventeen, respectively. The Open Campus is headquartered on the Cave Hill campus. For more details, see www.open.uwi.edu/about/welcome-open-uwi.

12. They were Hermione McKenzie and Dorian Powell, lecturers in the Department of Sociology at the Mona campus, who prepared the background paper for the Jamaican delegation.

Section 2

INITIATION

JOYCELIN MASSIAH

CHAPTER 3

BUILDING A PRESENCE

WAND/WICP, 1976–1982

Learning to look and to listen.
—*Margaret Bernal, former WICP research assistant*

Introduction

Historical material suggests that gender inequality, unequal access to education, limited occupational opportunities, discriminatory wages and few political rights were embedded in general economic poverty throughout the Caribbean region. Certainly, those were the issues which the women's NGOs struggled with from the 1940s to the mid-1970s. During this period, the NGOs provided much that was positive. This included a climate conducive to the questioning of women's role in society, action designed to eliminate discrimination against women, and strategies to move towards a women-and-development approach in which women and their concerns were seen as being closely interwoven with the development issues of the day. The establishment of WAND was one such strategy.

The Women and Development Unit

WAND for me represented a team of women who shared strong bonds and a sense of commitment to the cause of gender equality despite our differing personalities and

> operating styles. There was a combination of leadership, team building, learning, sharing and I am sure we all grew in various ways as a result of the work we did.
> *—Jeanette Bell, former WAND project officer*

In 1977, the Jamaica Women's Bureau and the Social Welfare Training Centre of the UWI joined forces to organize the regional seminar "Integration of Women in Caribbean Development". Many of the women who attended that meeting were members of CARIWA, the only regional women's organization at that time. It was these women who insisted on including, among the several recommendations of the seminar, one for the establishment of a women's desk at the CARICOM Secretariat and another for the creation of a WAD unit in the UWI. They further recommended that this unit be located within the Extra-Mural Department, the outreach arm of the UWI, which was responsible for delivering a programme of continuing adult education. The broadly defined objectives of the proposed unit were

1. to build awareness of women-and-development issues;
2. to develop strategies and methodologies for the increased participation and integration of women in the development process;
3. to build the capabilities of women's programmes for integration;
4. to promote non-sexist approaches to curriculum development and training;
5. to develop cohesive and coordinated women-in-development programmes; and
6. to increase financial and technical support to women-in-development programmes. (WAND, n.d.)

Peggy Antrobus was included on a steering committee consisting mostly of members of CARIWA. The committee was charged with the responsibility of moving forward the recommendations of the seminar, including proposal-writing and fundraising for the fledgling unit, both tasks assigned to Peggy. After successfully completing these assignments, Peggy was offered the position of the first tutor-coordinator, a post she retained until her retirement in 1995. According to her:

> The Extra-Mural Department had been chosen by the participants of the Seminar because of its presence in all the non-campus territories, and also because of its history of being responsive to the needs and interests of the countries in which it operated . . .
>
> It is a tribute to Sybil Francis' clout with the director of Extra-Mural Studies,

> Rex Nettleford, his willingness to take risks, and the flexibility of the university administration that space was given to the establishment of WAND within the framework of the Extra-Mural Department. (Antrobus 2000, 11)

The story of WAND is truly a tribute to the vision of those pioneering women and to that of Rex Nettleford. It is also the story of the determination and dedication of one woman, Peggy Antrobus, who guided the unit from obscurity to become a dynamic leader of the women's movement in the region and beyond during the decades of the 1970s, 1980s and 1990s. Underpinning the work programme pursued by WAND was a strategy of development based on the participation of women in defining and resolving their own problems, with WAND as a facilitator providing consultancy, training, technical assistance and consciousness-raising (WAND, n.d.). This strategy served the unit exceedingly well, but key to its phenomenal growth was its capacity to raise substantial financial support from a wide variety of donors. As one observer from the Inter-American Foundation put it: "This level of support for a new organization with no track record attested not only to the interest of funders in supporting a regional women's programme in the Caribbean, but also to Antrobus' persuasive abilities" (Yudelman 1987, 80).

Antrobus says that, as part of the experience of fundraising to make WAND a reality, she learned a valuable lesson from Kristen Anderson of the Carnegie Corporation of New York. Anderson refused to fund the project until the steering committee had decided who would head the unit. It was a critical lesson on the importance of leadership, which should be remembered. It was also the lesson which persuaded Antrobus to accept the offer to head the unit: "It taught me something about projects which I never forgot: leadership is key. It doesn't matter how well written the proposal is, what matters is if someone is there to coax it along in its creation and development (Antrobus 2000, 10).

This lesson was so well learned that one donor, UNIFEM, observed that, after a while, WAND became "not only an executor of UNIFEM-financed projects but also the technical adviser to other groups that UNIFEM had assisted" (Snyder 1995, 144).

Equally important was that WAND saw its role, during those formative years, as being "to define a different relationship between the university and its constituency, a link between academia and activism" (Antrobus 2000, 11). Indeed, it was Antrobus who first began to think seriously about developing a strategy for introducing a formal programme of studies at UWI. WAND's engagement in that strategy would involve not only direct work with women's NGOs but also ongoing analysis of global trends, regional developments and critical assessments of its own activities.

During the period of Peggy Antrobus's leadership, 1978–95, the work programme of WAND moved through three phases. The first, 1978–81, was concerned with understanding and raising awareness about the situation of women in the region, and with identifying strategies and programmes for governmental and non-governmental entities which could encourage and upgrade women's participation in the region's development. During this stage, WAND provided project development assistance to NGOs in five countries, conducted several regional and national training activities, assisted four governments to establish women's bureaux, worked with women's NGOs to ensure the establishment of a women's desk at the CARICOM Secretariat and provided technical assistance to various ministries throughout the region. WAND also ensured that its staff attended regional gatherings concerned with women's issues. Norma Shorey-Bryan, former WAND project officer, now human resources management consultant, recalls her participation as WAND's representative at one such gathering:

> The first Caribbean "gender" workshop entitled "Women in Social Production" was held in Santo Domingo in the summer of 1980. . . . It was a phenomenal experience! We gained a deeper understanding of the historical experience of women's subordination, and grappled with some of the "new" concepts of gender linking it to the political, economic and social realities of our Caribbean.
>
> We laughed and we cried! We sang and danced! Through the inspiration of Joan and Honor from the SISTREN group in Jamaica, we enacted "our stories" and the experiences of our sisters in poignant and dramatic ways. We built enduring friendships that have woven their way through time – as we each have matured and used our talents to contribute to the fabric of the Caribbean women's movement. (Norma Shorey-Bryan, testimonial)

In effect, these early years marked WAND's efforts to promote "a strategy of development based on the participation of women in the identification and resolution of their problems" (WAND, n.d.). It was towards the end of that period that the famous Rose Hall project in St Vincent and the Grenadines was initiated. This was a community-level project designed to improve the community through a variety of activities. WAND provided technical assistance throughout the life of the project. After an initial training workshop in participatory approaches, needs assessment, programme planning and evaluation, a working group was formed which shared in the development of a number of activities. These included the creation of a farmers' group, a series of income-earning projects (sewing, fruit preservation, candy-making, a bakery), a pre-school and a workshop on the role of men. The project has been hailed as one of the marquee projects of WAND's strategy for enabling women to realize their own potential.

The key to the success of that project lay in its methodology. For WAND, it was important to begin the process of what later became known as "community empowerment" with a community-based workshop in participatory methodologies: "Needs Assessment, Programme Planning and Evaluation". It was the application of these skills that enabled the women of Rose Hall to carry out their own needs assessment, to plan and evaluate their many projects. Thus, from the very outset, the community "owned" the project and made all the decisions to move it forward. WAND simply continued to support their efforts. In doing so, WAND was able to demonstrate that it is possible for a university-based programme to respect and build the agency of women outside the walls of academia.

During the second stage, 1982–85, WAND upgraded its communications programme to enable it to expand its work in this area, by communicating more effectively with and about its constituency. The programme included several facets, including a regional quarterly newsletter, *Women Speak*; a monthly international news bulletin entitled *Woman Struggle* and a Caribbean resource book providing a resource guide and directory. In addition, there was a discussion series entitled "Issues Concerning Women and Development" as well as numerous addresses, lectures, radio/TV interviews and seminars/workshops. The importance attached to communications was reflected in the fact that the first regional workshop focused on the media. There was, in fact, a concerted attempt by WAND to reach out to its constituents, both to provide information on its ongoing activities and to deliver some element of consciousness-raising in keeping with the requirements of the original objectives of the 1977 seminar.

This second stage also saw WAND developing training in feminism for staff and representatives of NGOs. Regional workshops were held at the Barbados Labour College. Rhoda Reddock was a key resource person for those workshops. Then there was Andaiye's "school", which was the name given to the training sessions focusing on political theory for activists, provided for WAND staff, among others, during Andaiye's visits to WAND.[1] By the mid-1980s, the situation of women had worsened, primarily as a result of the adoption of the policy framework which demanded the introduction of structural adjustment programmes by CARICOM governments. This marked the turning point in WAND's orientation from 1984 onwards. While analysis based on the experience of Latin American women was critical for understanding the likely impact on CARICOM women, Andaiye's school linked the analysis to both the CARICOM context and WAND's programme. At this stage, after seven years of shaping the programme according to the changing context, WAND staff was ready for a deeper, theoretical understanding of the new policy framework. WAND's publications, especially the newsletter *Women Speak*, reflected the shift. Andaiye's school was the space in which a coherent approach – linking theory, practice and publications – coalesced.

Also developed during this stage was an evaluation system which enabled WAND to streamline its portfolio. It therefore instituted a number of community-level pilot projects, even as it furthered its work with the well-known Rose Hall project in St Vincent. Among the new pilot projects were: curriculum development for schools; a radio programme entitled *People of Tomorrow* targeting unemployed youth and encouraging them to turn their ideas into projects; and work with the faculty of Agriculture at St Augustine, UWI, in order to help them understand how to integrate women into their outreach projects.

The third stage, 1985–95, marked a shift from a mostly technical/professional approach to a more political/feminist one which sought to "empower women to promote changes in the system" (Snyder 1995, 150 quoted in WAND 1993). This stage was concerned with developing a new analytic framework more firmly grounded in the particular models which fuelled development praxis across time and regions and which determined the situation of both women and men. This was the period when, to counteract the effects of the then global economic recession, structural adjustment programmes were being introduced by various governments across the region and when it was becoming increasingly clear that it was women who were bearing the brunt of the effects of these programmes. This was the period of close collaboration with the Development Alternatives with Women for a New Era network, which had provided the analysis of what the new orthodoxy of structural adjustment meant for women's lives.[2] Antrobus was associated with this network from its inception, having been one of its founders and having served as general coordinator for six years, during which time the secretariat was located at WAND (see Antrobus 2000).

DAWN was concerned with developing an analytic framework which could change the course of the debate on women's issues by locating them within the macro-economic and socio-political context in which they originated and in which they were now located. Using this framework at a regional conference held in Barbados, in preparation for the third WCW, which was to be held in Nairobi in 1985, enabled participants to issue the "Bridgetown Statement" calling on the governments of the region to review the policy framework of structural adjustment. That the majority of participants were women, that they were in fact challenging their governments' flagship policy, that the charge was led by a unit within the university – all this carried huge implications for the future. It marked the turning point not only for women's organizing but especially for WAND itself. It was WAND which had introduced the women to the DAWN analysis, demonstrated how that analysis could be applied to advocacy, activism, skills in networking and negotiating at international meetings, and had grounded these efforts in a concern for social justice.

It was during this third stage that, in November 1988, WAND celebrated its tenth anniversary with a major regional consultation and symposium held in Barbados under the rubric "Crisis and Challenge". A selection of the papers presented was published in the journal of the then Department of Extra-Mural Studies, *Caribbean Quarterly*, volume 35, numbers 1 and 2 (1989). Participants at the consultation included representatives from regional and national organizations and the UWI. Their presentations were shared with the regional and international agencies invited to the symposium. This dual approach facilitated a frank and in-depth exchange on the key issues affecting women facing the challenges of the structural adjustment crisis which, at the time, was affecting the entire region. It drew from Rex Nettleford (1989, 12), who delivered the keynote address, the telling comment that "the very important issue of integrating women into the mainstream of development strategy, as it is now conceived and perceived, must be taken seriously. . . . Depriving workplaces of the maturity, imagination, compassion and that sense of process that our women have so long demonstrated to have in abundance, is tantamount to a crime against the social order."

This unequivocal support from one of the most senior male administrators in the system was indeed official recognition of the value of the work in which WAND was engaged. This influential endorsement from the university, coupled with the collaboration with and focus of DAWN on macro-economic issues, enabled WAND in 1993 to adopt a new goal "to seek to make a contribution towards building the human and institutional capacity for a model of development which is integrative, equitable, self-reliant and sustainable" (WAND 1993, 15).

WAND had therefore made the journey through three stages: from integration of women in the then existing WID model to the more active involvement of WID processes reflective of the global thrust towards the WAD model, and finally towards a model more effectively grounded in social transformation and justice. Since this movement and its maintenance would rely on increasing and improving levels of research and analysis, the process created a platform on which a formal women's studies programme could stand.

In a real sense, the WAND programme may be considered the start of WDS at UWI. For one thing, it was the only unit in the system which carried the word "women" in its name. For another, by grounding its primary outreach activities in research and analysis, it led the way in shifting the discourse on concepts in the region from WID to WAD. Then there was its insistence that working with women's issues was essentially a political activity and should be treated as such. However, there was no involvement in the creation and delivery of conventional academic teaching courses or research undertakings. Rather, the focus was on gaining and sharing an understanding of how women fitted into the development paradigm of the day and how that understanding could be used to improve their general situation. The work therefore engaged women directly in the formulation and execution of programmes on behalf of women in their own community and, ultimately, women of the region. Even as the work focused on women in communities, however, that work was used to train WAND's own staff as they explored what Peggy Antrobus described as "new strategies, methodologies and approaches to development" (Antrobus 2000, 15). Jeanette Bell recalls in her testimonial:

> I joined the staff of WAND in January 1983 at a special time in our history when attention started to be turned to the particular concerns/issues facing women in general and the women of our region in particular. It was a coming together of a team of women that brought a combination of skills and interests rooted in feminist awareness of the need for positive change in the English-speaking Caribbean. Not only did the work involve the staff of the unit, but the links were forged with a variety of talented and remarkable women who contributed as consultants and resource persons from across the region ranging from Belize/Jamaica in the north right down to Guyana and Suriname in the south. WAND facilitated encounters of various kinds with academics, activists, researchers, artists, writers and community leaders, etc. Activities of different kinds were always taking place, whether

> there were workshops in rural communities, seminars for activists who wanted to be more grounded in feminist theory/understandings, meetings of various kinds and events.

WAND also made special efforts to expose its staff and, indeed, other interested women in the region to regionally and internationally renowned women from whom Caribbean women could learn, but also who could themselves learn from Caribbean women. Bell recounts in her testimonial:

> There were some incredible times, many remarkable people. I recall meeting women like Clotil Walcott of Trinidad and Tobago, who led the Wages for Housework Campaign; Nawal El Saadawi, writer and activist from Egypt; the powerful work in feminist popular theatre of Sistren of Jamaica. For me, one of the many highlights was the visit to Barbados of Angela Y. Davis as a member of the National Black Women's Health Project out of Atlanta, USA. The event was hosted by WAND at the Barbados Workers Union Labour College at Mangrove, St Philip. Sitting among the group, without drawing any kind of attention to herself, she shared, only on request, her experiences growing up in the southern USA. The opportunity not only to attend her official lecture but to also hear her share her own experiences will always be very special to me.

The outreach work of WAND, in particular its small-scale empirical research and training courses, was especially valuable, in terms of increasing public awareness and raising the consciousness of women themselves. WAND continued to seek ways by which its work could be more closely linked with a formal academic programme. Peggy Antrobus, retired WAND tutor/coordinator, recalls in her testimonial that "after two years at WAND, I remember thinking: we are focusing on outreach, but there needs to be a teaching programme on WAD with the faculties. . . . I did not want a 'women's studies' programme patterned on US programmes that separated 'women's studies' (humanities/feminism, etc.) from 'WID' (social studies/economic development, etc.)".

Interestingly, at about the same time in the 1970s that WAND was seeking to establish itself, another initiative focusing on women was taking shape in another part of the UWI. At the Institute of Social and Economic Research (Eastern Caribbean) (ISER [EC]), a group of academic women was in the process of figuring out whether and how to design a multidisciplinary regional research project on the reality of women's lives, which could have the potential to strengthen the region's policymaking tools and enrich the region's intellectual heritage. Both of these efforts, WAND and WICP, were heavily influenced

Plate 3.1. Peggy Antrobus (*left*) receiving a gift of appreciation for her pioneering work in WAND from Rhoda Reddock

by the UN, with its slogan of "Equality, Development and Peace" that came into being in 1975, International Women's Year, which marked the start of the first UN Decade for Women.

Events within the region, sparked by the UN decade, were also influential. In 1975, Trinidad and Tobago established a standing commission on the status of women; in 1976, Barbados and Grenada each set up an ad hoc national commission on the status of women, while Guyana established a standing council on the affairs and status of women and issued a white paper on "Equality for Women". Between 1974 and 1984, at least ten countries had established some form of institutional mechanism within the government apparatus to monitor the situation of women and increase their participation in national development – variously termed desk, bureau, department, even a ministry (in Grenada). Jamaica took the lead here, establishing the first women's bureau in the CARICOM region, preceding and indeed leading directly to the establishment of WAND.

In 1981, CARICOM initiated the practice of hosting biennial meetings of ministers responsible for women's affairs, and, in 1983, Barbados and Dominica each appointed a standing advisory body to assist the desk in its operations. In 1978, women's NGOs campaigned successfully for the establishment of a women's desk at the CARICOM Secretariat. In addition, some government ministers were beginning to speak out on behalf of women. For example, in his inaugural address to the UN General Assembly in 1978, the minister of foreign affairs of Barbados made specific reference to his government's commitment to the inclusion of women's concerns on its agenda. It is generally accepted that this was the first time that a minister of any Caribbean country had ever made such statements at the assembly. If ratification and implementation of the CEDAW meant the establishment of formal institutional mechanisms for the execution of policy, then it could be said that, by the mid-1980s, most Caribbean governments were well on their way to achieving that objective. However, the translation of this activity into policy formulation and programmatic action was slow, hampered as it was by financial constraints, infrastructural deficiencies, the persistence of traditional patriarchal attitudes within the public services and the paucity of information about the reality of women's lives.

Issues of Caribbean women and the lessons learned from the existing women's NGOs were placed in the context of the maelstrom of women-focused activity which erupted in the region after the establishment of the UN Decade for Women (1975–85). The UN decade's high priority on research set the stage for the incorporation of information about Caribbean women into the regional and international discourse. The Caribbean region placed its own work collected from individual researchers, from NGOs, from international agencies and from the UWI, initially through WAND and the WICP, into the flow of research, information and data on women from around the world. One major outcome of the initiative was that it placed the issues of WAD firmly on the academic agenda of the UWI.

The Women in the Caribbean Project WICP

> The more the years pass, since that wonderful period of travel, research, discussion and documentation that characterized the WICP – the more clearly I see the many gifts we were given by those very varied groups of women, who patiently entertained our questionings.
>
> —*Margaret Bernal, testimonial*

Designing the Project: Initiation

In preparation for the 1975 WCW, which marked the beginning of the first UN Decade for Women, there was much discussion on the "status of women" around the world; but what did this phrase mean, especially in our Caribbean context? Joycelin Massiah's attendance at a conference on WAD at Wellesley

College and her membership of the National Commission on the Status of Women in Barbados helped to begin the process of unravelling the meaning of the phrase. It was not clear, however, whether anyone in the UWI was working on this at that time and, if so, what enlightenment they could provide on this matter. Searches through the annual UWI calendars, which listed completed and ongoing research, provided virtually no clues, but a few telephone calls yielded names of some persons across the three campuses who might have an interest. A short discussion paper entitled "Women in the Caribbean: Guidelines for Research" was prepared by Joycelin Massiah of the ISER (EC) and circulated to them. It turned out that, quite independently, two sociologists at Mona, Hermione McKenzie and Dorian Powell, were in the process of preparing a similar proposal. They had been involved in assisting the fledgling Women's Bureau of Jamaica with research and advice and were keen to take their work further. They suggested a third person, an anthropologist, Victoria Durant-Gonzalez. At Cave Hill, there were two interested persons – Christine Barrow, an anthropologist, and Joycelin Massiah, a demographer. A decision was taken to join forces. And so the nucleus of the WICP team was born, with three from Mona and two from Cave Hill – all full-time employees with responsibilities in their respective departments. All the parties were subsequently invited by Massiah to an initial meeting in May 1978 to explore suggestions for the design of a possible project. At that meeting, it was agreed to encourage potential participants from St Augustine and to invite a representative from the University of Guyana to future discussions and possible participation in any project which emerged from such discussions.

Agreement was reached on the overall objectives of the proposed project and on an initial draft. Five major objectives were identified:

1. Identify the subjective meaning of the social realities which women face, the way these realities are manifested and the consequences at the individual, community and societal level.
2. Devise a theoretical framework which would integrate the analysis of women's roles as they are affected by processes of social change from a multidisciplinary perspective and in different ecological settings.
3. Generate relevant data for elaborating a cohesive social policy directed towards women, which would readily be adapted for inclusion in development programmes of government and non-governmental organizations.
4. Identify appropriate mechanisms for the dissemination of research results and for incorporating those results into ongoing development programmes.

5. Produce a cadre of women who would be adequately equipped with the necessary research skills to conduct good research, in general, and good female-centred research, in particular. (Massiah 1986b, 1–2)

In sum, the project was conceived as being regional in its scope, multidisciplinary in its design and methodology, and participatory in its style. Four basic principles undergirded the participatory style of the project. The first was that every team member would be involved in all major decision-making. The second was that research assistants were to be treated as full team members and be involved at every stage of the design and execution of the project. The third was that members of staff, from across the three campuses, who expressed an interest in participating in the project would be invited to do so but would have to function within the framework of the project guidelines. The fourth was that relevant national, regional and international entities would be invited to be involved as interested stakeholders.

After several revisions and meetings, a final version of the proposal for a two-phase project was eventually completed for submission to funding agencies. The project benefited from two happy coincidences. Sir Arthur Lewis, Nobel Laureate in Economics and former vice-chancellor of UWI, happened to be visiting professor of economics at the Cave Hill campus and used to attend ISER (EC) staff meetings. At one of those meetings, when the lack of response to our funding efforts was reported, he suggested that a submission be made to the Leverhulme Trust Fund, where he was a director. As a result, funding for phase 1 of the project was received from that source. In the meantime, the phase 2 proposal was submitted to the Ministry of Development Administration at The Hague through the ISS, which acted on its behalf in these matters. The ISS had adopted the practice of asking its international students to assess proposals which came in from their part of the world. Rhoda Reddock, then a Caribbean student at the ISS, strongly endorsed the proposal, and, on that basis, the ISS recommended that the ministry support the project; thus phase 2 was supported by the ministry. Once the word was out that the project had attracted support from well-known, highly respected donors and was progressing satisfactorily, other donors followed suit at various points, thus enabling the project to meet most of its goals.

The interval between submission of the proposal to potential donors and the actual start of the project was utilized to develop links with researchers, both within and outside the region, who might be interested in the project and to develop a corps of research assistants who would be instrumental in the conduct of the work. Margaret Gill, former WICP research assistant, now UWI lecturer, Cave Hill, recalls her experience as the first assistant to be appointed:

> I took the WICP job as the first full-time officer on the project at the time, in 1979, after having to decide between it and an initially better paying job offered at the same time at the Barbados Development Bank. I literally worked out the pros and cons on a sheet of paper (I recommend it), even the benefits that were not quantitative, like "opportunity to grow intellectually". And WICP was it. After I returned to say I was in, ISER director Dr Joycelin Massiah offered me a more competitive salary. This good omen followed my involvement in the rest of the work. Joycelin said, "Here are three texts on women, the WICP proposal, and a box of several research instruments; we have to produce a questionnaire." I learned from the reading. I learned from the meetings with the researchers. I worked out the women's twenty-four-hour clock idea with a friend, Michael Small, who became a great economist at a university in the United States, and I learned about being an academic from Joycelin. At one meeting she told the researchers we worked together like characters in the play *The Boyfriend*. When she shared with me the writing of one of the monographs on work and put my name first on the credits, I also learned about raising up the next generation of academics. (Margaret Gill, testimonial)

The experience of Roberta Clarke, former WICP research assistant, currently UN Women regional director, South East Asia, was somewhat different:

> Generationally associated with the black power movement, the Grenada revolution, Caribbean regionalism, all my predispositions as a teenager were to the left and, yes, towards feminism. I bought "Sisterhood is Powerful" at fifteen from a bookstore, long closed down, in Bridgetown. The "personal is political" was my touchstone, giving me a way to judge internal coherence.
>
> In August 1981, having just graduated, I met Margaret Gill outside the Cave Hill Library, positively bouncing with joyful anticipation about her imminent commencement of graduate studies. She told me about the WICP with which she had been associated and encouraged me to apply for a research assistant position.
>
> I did, and then went for an interview in a sleeveless sundress, red and blue – my best dress and one only a twenty-one-year-old would wear to a job interview. Dr Massiah was, what I would come to understand, her constant self – direct, analytical, cool-headed and inquiring. She hired me that day and my life's course was set. (Roberta Clarke, testimonial)

Apart from recruiting staff during this waiting period, the opportunity was taken to develop a holding of relevant material in the ISER (EC) library. This activity included the production and distribution of a series of accession bulletins of relevant material arriving in the ISER (EC) library, as well as the production and publication of a comprehensive annotated bibliography of relevant material available in Barbados, where it had been previously decided that the project would be centred (Massiah 1979). A photocopying and book-loan service was introduced for the benefit of the researchers. As a public relations device, newsletters were issued periodically to supplement the personal contacts between the research team, individual researchers overseas and regional stakeholders such as the CARICOM Secretariat, WAND, CARIWA and the national administrative machinery for women's affairs operating in the project countries. It was also agreed that a representative of the project should attend the UN Mid-Decade WCW scheduled for Copenhagen in 1980 and that a special brochure on the project should be prepared for widespread distribution at the NGO Forum, which was due to run parallel to the governmental conference.

The primary aim of this activity was to create an enabling environment for the group of women who were about to undertake an exercise which had never before been attempted within the UWI. Once these various pieces were put in place, the core team of researchers began the task of identifying and inviting researchers who might be willing to undertake the task of assembling and collating data for writing a series of sector studies for phase 1. Six such researchers were identified, and they, together with six members of the project team, began preparing the manuscripts. These preparatory activities proceeded until funding for phase 1 of the project was received, and the project started officially on 1 October 1979.

As in any such undertaking, fundraising was a major task, occupying a considerable amount of time and effort. In addition to the funds received from the Leverhulme Trust Fund for the conduct of the documentary research of phase 1, funds were also secured from the Ford Foundation and the Carnegie Corporation; from CARICOM, MATCH[3] Canada, MUCIA (Midwest Universities Consortium for International Activities), OEF, and United Nations Educational, Scientific and Cultural Organization for attendance at various meetings; and from WAND and ISER (EC) for general support and the final workshop. Funds for the conduct of the empirical research in phase 2 came from the Ministry of Development Administration, The Hague, through the ISS, as well as the Carnegie Corporation, the Ford Foundation and the United States Agency for International Development. Funds for the regional conference which marked the end of the project came from the Ford Foundation, CARICOM, the Commonwealth Foundation and the Canadian High Commission, while support for the multimedia dissemination package came from the Caribbean Institute for Mass Communication, UWI. General administrative support was provided by WAND, ISER (Mona) and ISER (EC).

Development of the Project

The core team consisted of seven senior researchers, including the regional coordinator, Joycelin Massiah, and an equal number of research assistants, all female. Additional researchers, invited for specific tasks at different times during the project, increased the complement to twenty-eight, including some men. Members of the group were scattered across the region – in Jamaica, Barbados, Trinidad and Tobago and Guyana. Communication within the group was therefore paramount. Overseas telephone calls were numerous. Cables flowed freely – at that time, there was no Internet, no e-mail, no fax, no texting, no Skype. Colleagues attending meetings on other campuses were implored to carry packages by hand. Individual campus group meetings were constant. Inter-campus meetings of the research group were vital. Travel between project sites was critical. In effect, the team had to be constantly on the move while, at the same time, reserving time for reading and writing, not to mention their substantive departmental duties.

Table 3.1: WICP Researchers, by Campus

Level	Cave Hill	Mona	St Augustine	University of Guyana
Senior researchers (core)	2	4	N/A	1
Senior researchers (ad hoc)	5	1	N/A	N/A
Research assistants	6 (including 4 core)	2 (core)	1 (ad hoc)	1 (core)
Student assistants	5 (ad hoc)	N/A	N/A	N/A

Total: Twenty-eight, of whom fourteen were core and the remainder conducted specific short-term assignments.

Provision for travel was therefore an integral component of the arrangements. Between the first meeting of the original five in 1978 and the regional conference in 1982, there were eight formal project meetings. In the six months immediately before the conference, there were three country-wide workshops and twelve community-level workshops. This was not a small undertaking; nor was it inexpensive. It was certainly inconvenient for those coming from Jamaica, which, at the time, was experiencing severe economic problems. Hermione McKenzie recounts one experience of the Mona team on one of their return trips to Jamaica after attending a project meeting in Barbados:

> We from Jamaica travelled under financial constraints in this period because of Jamaican foreign exchange restrictions whereby each traveller could only take US$55 out of the country. Once we arrived at our destination we survived through sponsored hotel accommodation and per diem allowances. But we always had a narrow survival margin. Sometime near the end of the Women in the Caribbean Project, our Caribbean airline, BWIA, had a major strike of several weeks. Our Jamaican group travelled from Barbados to Trinidad, I think by British Airways, and then we were due to fly by ALM via Curaçao to Jamaica. We overnighted in the airport because we had no money left for a hotel. We had friends in Port of Spain who might have offered us a bed for the night, but at that period the Trinidad telephone system did not work well. The telephone produced numerous "wrong numbers". So at about 11:00 p.m., after calling our friends several times and each time getting a different sleepy, angry voice saying "Wrong number!" we gave up and decided to endure the night sitting on chairs at the airport. I think that Caribbean readers will understand what I mean when I talk about the bonds of "shipmates". (McKenzie 2004, 400)

Meetings were held mostly at Cave Hill, but the regional coordinator visited campus sites periodically, as did individual researchers, and the research assistants travelled regularly across the various project sites. For the research assistants, this meant actually residing in the project countries for the duration of the training and fieldwork aspects of the project.[4] One of the results of this strategy was that research assistants developed skills in encouraging cooperation from the women being interviewed. Margaret Bernal, who was based in Antigua, describes this process:

> These independent-minded and in-charge Barbadian grandmothers, Antiguan spinsters, Vincentian baby mothers and all the others presented in their life styles and stories a solid Caribbean tapestry of coping with unforeseen vicissitudes of life,

> surmounting with bravado and creativity the obstacles to family or community – and taking life on with an ironic and unfaltering audacity.
>
> In the field research, some respondents demurred at first, unnerved by the daunting and extensive questionnaire. There were always, however, accompanying hints of pride and approval – that such interest was being displayed in them, the ordinary women of the Caribbean. We learnt to wait, to relax into the warm island ambiance, observe the invariable open-air setting of that particular woman's life and work environment – and try again.
>
> Then the stories would come pouring out. (Margaret Bernal, testimonial)

Not unexpectedly, different locations generated different experiences for the different research assistants. There were also different lessons to be learned by each of them. Diane Cummins, now a gender consultant, who was then one of the two WICP research assistants based in St Vincent, recalls some experiences in coping with the physical conditions under which research interviewing was often conducted:

> It was the first time that we (Margaret and I) were living on our own. Neither of us knew how to cook, being spoiled by being at the end of large families. We had weathered managing the WICP data collection process in Barbados quite well, and we were now branching out to St Vincent. Mapping practically the whole country to set up the interviews – Windward, Leeward, Mesopotamia. Margaret even learned Owia and Fancy after sleeping in those two communities overnight to interview Black Caribs (as they called themselves then) over the Dry River. Not sure why I didn't go over the Dry River. Hiring staff went quite well – we both remember Alicia, our secretary/clerk with fondness. Were there challenges? The water went off in the first apartment and we could not bathe or cook for days! We eventually lived in three houses before we settled. We discovered that one of our interviewers was completing the questionnaires herself at home! Now we not only had to put additional checks in place to ensure the integrity of the survey, we had to fire her! But some joys too: We invited Eudine Barriteau to join us for Vincey Mas, and at the end of a long day jumping we realised that chemical toilets were not yet invented, all public places were on holiday, and we were far from home. (That was a joy and a challenge.) We learned how to drive on mountain roads and that was no easy test, coming as we did from Barbados. Vincentian friends treated us to food in the country by a river (cooked right there) off a leaf with a stick. And then there was the friendly priest who brought us huge containers of sliced mango, orange and apple medley for several weeks. Sweet! (Diane Cummins and Margaret Gill, testimonial)

Each campus had its own coordinator responsible for coordinating activities of the researchers on the particular campus, including supervision of junior staff, organizing regular discussion groups and liaising with the regional coordinator.[5] All levels of core staff were expected to be involved in the design of data-collection instruments, interviewer training and supervision, data analysis and report writing. This was a means of creating joint responsibility and ownership of the project as well as a sense of unity among the team. A high degree of flexibility was also introduced through the stress on individual initiative, the practice of participatory decision-making and the exploitation of every available avenue for communication. Thus, in a very short time, a strong sense of camaraderie was developed, and the research team was moulded into a group whose enthusiasm, dedication, level of commitment and capacity for sheer hard work were unsurpassed.

The project design consisted of two phases. The first was concerned with the collection and review of documentary material on women in a number of separate areas – law, family, politics, work, education and perceptions of women. The second phase focused on a multilevel interviewing strategy consisting of a standard, semi-structured questionnaire applied to women in three countries – Barbados, Antigua and St Vincent; detailed life histories of small numbers of women from the original samples; and in-depth, free-form interviewing around specific issues and/or groups of women – rural women in Guyana, unemployed women in Barbados, elderly women and their men in Jamaica, women in public life in the Eastern Caribbean, women's networks in Jamaica and men in Barbados. Data from these three levels of interviewing were integrated into a framework built around three themes – sources of livelihood, emotional support, and power and authority. Together, the two phases of data collection, both documentary and empirical, provided a rich source of information about women's lives in this region, which, it was hoped, could fuel further research as a possible precursor to a women's studies programme in the UWI and which could be used as a basis for policy and programme-planning.

There were some hurdles to overcome even before the interviewing could begin. While the intention was to conduct a multidisciplinary effort, the issues to be addressed cried out for the specialist skills of an economist, a data-processing specialist, a historian, a social psychologist and, towards the end of the project, even a media specialist. None of these skills was available through the existing staff of the project. To compensate for the absence of these skills or the availability of some only on a part-time consultancy basis, a number of alternatives were attempted. For example, phase 1 authors were encouraged to trace the history of their particular sector as part of their analysis. Phase 2 authors were asked to apply a cohort analysis as far as possible in order to address the issue of historical changes. A data-processing specialist was engaged as a consultant, initially on a part-time basis, but later converted to full-time for a short period. When the team experienced personnel problems, attempts were made to resolve them in a collaborative way. In other words, the team tried to be as practical as possible, while acknowledging the absence of key disciplinary representation.

Another concern was the absence of visible support from committed male colleagues. Campus principals and senior male staff within the ISER across the three campuses were a constant and reliable source of support. Beyond that, committed support was hard to find. Of the twenty-eight persons who contributed papers, technical advice and consultancy services, five were male, two of whom were senior researchers, one was the data-processing adviser, and the remaining two were research/student assistants. None of them was willing or able to join the project team on a full-time basis. One result was that the project was perceived to be a female-dominated activity, "a women's lib, male-bashing effort", designed, as one detractor put it, "to emasculate men". The project was accused of replicating irrelevant North American concepts. These and similar views may have worked to discourage significant male participation, but whether these sentiments were genuine or were being promoted to undermine the project the team never did discover, preferring to produce the results and let the record speak for itself.

The project ran from 1979 to 1982, during which time it produced and published six sector studies from phase 1, while phase 2 produced findings from 1,578 interviews and thirty-nine life histories across three countries as well as six small sector studies in a number of other countries. The results of the empirical studies were published in a variety of formats, and an extensive dissemination programme was initiated.

Sharing the Findings: Diffusion

In an insightful article reviewing the methodology and findings of the project, Patricia Anderson (1986, 291) draws attention to the deliberate absence of a prior theoretical framework to guide the project: "The WICP is distinguished by the largely inductive approach which it has taken to identify the key issues which affect women's lives and shape their consciousness. By insisting on 'letting women speak for themselves' instead of starting from a position of prior theoretical commitment, the project has produced a set of findings which are both consistent and contradictory." Indeed, her comment calls to mind a remark once made by Sir Arthur Lewis at an ISER (EC) staff meeting: "What can you do with a theory that you cannot do without it." Anderson sees the findings as consistent in that, despite the researchers' varying perspectives, their findings tended to converge, thereby pointing to the reliability of the data and the resultant theoretical and policy implications identified. The contradictions, as she saw them, pointed to the need for further theoretical analysis which could explicate the prevailing system of gender relations and the impact of that system on women (ibid.).

Perhaps the most significant aspect of the findings of the project was the apparently contradictory position between women's objective status and their subjective evaluations of that status. For example, they continued to rely on men's economic support but placed a high value on their own economic independence. Women in the study made full use of the educational opportunities available but seemed unable to translate their level of educational attainment into earning a comparable level of livelihood. Stereotypes about the role and function of both women and men continued to exist despite the changes in the societies towards a more egalitarian mode. Legal reform was ongoing, but in the absence of testing their legal rights in the courts, women's knowledge of these rights was limited. Women did not present themselves as leaders, but they dominated in domestic decision-making. Roberta Clarke, who prepared a paper for the regional conference which marked the end of the project, recalls:

> In preparing the paper entitled "Women's Organisations, Women's Interests" I met with women leaders from community and church groups as well as from political parties across the three countries. The women connected with political parties lamented the patriarchy that excluded women from representational politics. They recognized the exploitation inherent in the relationship between political leaders and women party members, the former depending on the latter for the sustenance of parties as fund raisers and campaigners. These women politicians spoke to the marginalisation of "women's arms" and the failure to position women in constituencies that were safer or in providing financing for campaigning. They spoke about misogyny and the sexual harassment which women faced on the hustings and about personal difficulties of getting partners and families to support their ambitions, including in the practical ways of sharing the reproductive care. But they were all hopeful that things would change. (Roberta Clarke, testimonial)

These and other contradictions led to the conclusion that investigating the operation of gender ideology in the region was the next step in the evolution of research concerned with relations between Caribbean women and men. To do so, however, required widespread dissemination and discussion of these findings, as well as a concerted move towards the enhanced research and study of women and gender issues.

The research group recognized that dissemination of the findings was not merely about sharing information, but also about packaging that information in different ways for different audiences. It was clear to the group that, in order to reach out to the varied audiences who might have an interest in the research results, it was necessary to devise a comprehensive communication strategy which would have greatest impact. Since both academic and non-academic audiences would have an interest, it was important to ensure that the strategy would be multifaceted and that the format and language would relate to the different groups. For the team, the aim of the strategy was not only to relay the results but also to facilitate understanding of what the research was seeking to do and why, and how the information could be used to further the overall goal of improving the situation of women in the region. Most importantly, it was designed to recognize and "give back" to the women who gave so generously of their time and information.

Accordingly, a multimedia dissemination package was designed, consisting of: the formal publications of the phase 1 and phase 2 material, generally targeting the academic audience (see appendix 2); national workshops in the project countries using detailed, country-specific reports and targeting key government personnel and women's NGOs; community-level workshops in the project countries, targeting the women in those communities who were respondents in the surveys; and country-specific brochures summarizing the main findings and recommendations for each country and providing useful information about facilities available in the respective countries. About those country reports, Roberta Clarke recalls in her testimonial:

> Reading those booklets from women in St Vincent and the Grenadines, Barbados and Antigua and Barbuda gave me insights, an inside track into the everyday lives of women across their diversities in the Eastern Caribbean. The booklets told the stories of women struggling with single parenting and economic marginalization; women living joyfully or not in extended, matrifocal families. Most of the women had no history and little expectation of public leadership or influence in their communities. But most of all, the responses in those questionnaires transmitted the

strength of Caribbean women, surviving and making difficult choices all along the way.

There was also a synchro-slide presentation, produced in collaboration with WAND, featuring a selection of the women originally interviewed and highlighting the major findings of the project; and a video presentation produced in collaboration with the Caribbean Institute of Mass Communications. It was entitled "Statements" and featured selected individual women who had been reinterviewed on the second round of interviews as well as women in non-traditional occupations. This video was used during the country- and community-level workshops and proved to be very popular. Margaret Bernal describes it in her testimonial:

> My special joy was the making of "Statements – Lives of Caribbean Women". Across the islands, women put aside their shyness of the strangers with camera – and relished their importance, their achievements, their beauty. There were unforgettable vignettes of real women, in their own voices, speaking against their green familiar backdrop, of cane fields, of driftwood beaches, of solitary hillsides.
>
> When the Antiguan coal-burner told her story – all her long-worn beauty flared again – in her flashing eyes, her tossing head. With her ramrod-straight back and a shrug – Coolie Gal defied her own life of marginalization and toil, spoke rather of a lifelong, defiant, independent spirit. Threw back her head. Laughed!

The final items in the dissemination programme were: a regional conference which brought together policymakers, administrators of women's programmes, regional and international academics and activists to assess the project, discuss its findings and advise on further activity (Massiah 1983); and a general reader which linked the project findings with material from literature, popular and folk culture and other sources (Senior 1991).

Each of these instruments reached out to a different audience, thus spreading the word not only about the existence of the project but of its findings and recommendations for action. In this way, it was hoped that the line between academic and "non-academic" research would be blurred, that the need for more research about women, by women and for women would be illustrated and that the need for the translation of the research into a formal programme of women's studies would be apparent.

But, beyond what the project planned and delivered in terms of dissemination of the results, project personnel were frequently invited to make presentations on one or other aspect of the project. For example, in 1983, the CARICOM

Secretariat invited the project coordinator to attend the Second Meeting of Ministers with Responsibility for the Integration of Women in Development to present a report on the findings of the project. Among the recommendations made by the meeting was one to monitor progress on implementation of the recommendations offered by the project so as "to enable structuring of a regional programme of action" (CARICOM Secretariat 1983, paragraph 124 [vii]). That regional programme was developed for the period 1986–2000 and was endorsed, with a number of amendments, by the ministers at their meeting in 1988. In effect, access to the relevant ministers was a critical avenue not only for disseminating information about the project but also for encouraging appropriate action at the ministerial level.

A related CARICOM initiative which drew on the experience of the project began with an invitation to the project coordinator to attend, as a resource person, a special workshop titled "Training Women for Effective Participation in Conference Diplomacy". This exercise was part of the secretariat's programme to prepare prospective delegates for effective representation at the UN Women's conference slated for Nairobi in 1985.[6] Here again was an opportunity to draw on the project's findings to assist representatives of the national machinery for women's affairs to improve their research presentations on the situation of women in the region, and to identify strategies at the regional level which could be incorporated into the recommendations for a regional approach at the conference.

An important aspect of this process of diffusion related to the element of time. The project itself ran from October 1979, with the start of the phase 1 component, to the regional conference in September 1982, a relatively short period for such a wide-ranging effort. Publication of the findings took longer. The annotated bibliography of relevant material available in Barbados appeared in 1979. The phase 1 papers appeared between 1981 and 1984. The combined findings of the two phases appeared in 1986 in a special issue of *Social and Economic Studies*, the academic journal of ISER, and the general reader was published in 1991. In all of that time, information from the project was being, and continues to be, used by researchers in their individual teaching and research efforts within the university and in their work in regional and international agencies, where some of them have been employed. In 1982, six months before the regional conference, women academics began discussing the possibility of a formal programme of WDS. Even before the final publication of the general reader, *Working Miracles*, by Olive Senior, women in the academy had developed an interdisciplinary course, Introduction to Women's Studies, which was introduced on all three campuses between 1986 and 1989.

The apparent success of the project, however, exposed both the work and those involved to further negativity, even hostility, described by Keith Hunte, then deputy principal of the Cave Hill campus, at the opening ceremony of the regional conference as "carping criticism". This speaks to the "prejudice in our higher education institutions which are usually hierarchical, autocratic and male-dominated", as Rowland (1982, 489) asserts. In the case of the WICP, it was interesting that, although no attempt was yet being made to introduce women's studies courses, the extent and level of criticism echoed much of what Rowland describes. However, most of this kind of criticism was subterranean and not expressed directly to team members, most of whom were not even aware of what was being said behind their backs. Some of those who were aware chose to engage the detractors in vigorous exchanges. Others chose to ignore the remarks, treating them as part of the journey to engage in and introduce research on women into the academy, and to simply get on with the work. Perhaps this was because the principal researchers on the project understood instinctively the contradictory nature of some critics – support of individual women on a personal and professional level but abrasive criticism of the idea of women's studies. Perhaps the principal researchers also understood instinctively that any questioning of women's situations would inevitably lead to questioning of the patriarchal nature of the university itself, and this could have been perceived as potentially threatening to entrenched positions. Or perhaps it was simply an instinctive understanding of the point made by Hunte at the opening ceremony of the regional conference:

> I suggest that the persistence of a negative attitude to the development of women's studies serves to remind us that those of us in the Caribbean who are employed as professional academics need to be aware that institutionalized scholarship is new to the region. The place of academic pursuits in helping policy makers solve problems, and to be in the forefront of an implementation strategy, is still not universally recognized. I think that if we understand this point, as academics we will be more patient with this carping criticism. (Keith Hunte, quoted in Massiah 1983, 118)

The conference did, however, provide an opportunity for those who wished to make valid critiques of the work, primarily about the absence of a theoretical framework. This was notwithstanding the fact that, as Anderson pointed out, the project had deliberately been allowed to proceed on the basis of "letting the women speak for themselves" rather than starting with a specific theoretical orientation into which the findings would be pushed.

There were several other critiques, most of which would have required either an entirely different focus for the project, or a detailed, immediate follow-up project. The former was not possible and the latter never materialized. Among the suggestions were a series of follow-up studies, workshops and seminars and the creation of a comprehensive data retrieval system. Funds for none of these were forthcoming. Despite this, the project team could claim a number of achievements. They had developed a strong and extensive database which could influence future research and contribute to the WDS programme. They had boldly created a methodological model which, to date, has not been replicated, and which has influenced women to undertake research in non-traditional ways. By doing so, they were not only being innovative but were also staying true to their cultural context of creativity and difference. The project produced a number of policy and action recommendations, some of which have been implemented in various arenas. The career paths of a number of the team members proved to be heavily influenced by the rigorous training received during the life of the project. Roberta Clarke's testimonial confirms this:

> I could say many things about that first year of working on the WICP. But first, it deepened my understanding of the mechanics of sociological enquiry. I made friends, and I met or came to know better women scholars from across the region. I learnt new and interesting things, like "ethnographic eyeballing", a phrase that Eudine (a colleague in ISER but not yet on the project), Diane and I spent many a humorous moment analysing. . . . I came back to the WICP project for another year's stint, but that first year will remain with me as a moment of defining direction. Everything that I have been able to do since then is built on this experience, on the opportunity given to me by others and, most importantly, on the relationships of scholarship and activism that were triggered by this year. The sisterhood was and remains powerful.

The impact of the project on interviewers, respondents, stakeholders and the general public continued to be felt by all team members long after the project had ended. Margaret Gill reports in her testimonial:

> Those of us who worked on the WICP could not help but be influenced by what the project was attempting. It was new and necessary and spoke to our ordinary lives and those of the many women and men whose lives the project touched. The project even attempted to bridge the gap with WAND, which, up to then, was not

> making the impact it could because it did not share the prestige that an ISER had in the intellectual community. That bridge was vital to the continued success of both the WICP and WAND till Peggy left.
>
> Perhaps the WICP had more impact on the creation of CAFRA than is admitted. It certainly brought me into the moment when CAFRA was created, a moment I would not have entertained outside of my involvement with WICP. And then I became, years later, an unopposed chairwoman of that regional body for six years. Of course, I brought with me all of WICP, and I continue to see the structural concepts and contributions of WICP working in so many places.

A major achievement of the project has been the basis it laid for the introduction of WDS in the UWI. WICP brought together three streams of the 1980s women's movement – women in academia, women in government and women's NGOs. This was possible because of the position of the UWI in Caribbean life, the personal and professional networking among the project personnel and the volume and quality of the material produced. Buoyed by the strong links created by the work of WAND and WICP, by the strong collaborative ties and by focused commitment to the goal of gender equality, Caribbean women worked together on the basis of a more profound understanding of the situation of women.

A few months before the WICP Regional Conference which marked the official end of the project, a meeting was convened by WAND and chaired by ISER (EC) "to discuss how a programme of Women's Studies might be formally instituted within the UWI" (WAND 1982, 6). Out of those discussions, the idea of WSGs (later, WDSGs) emerged, and three such groups were created, one per campus, with a regional steering committee operating out of the Cave Hill campus under the leadership of ISER (EC): "We had a large vision of the potential of UWI to make a significant contribution to the advancement of women in the region, along with the autonomy, funding and flexibility that made it possible for us to get the funding from Ford for the meetings of the steering committee that allowed us to follow up the 1982 meeting at the Caribbee Hotel" (Peggy Antrobus, testimonial). It is to the realization of that vision that the next chapter turns.

Notes

1. Andaiye, a well-known Guyanese feminist, political activist and educator, was one of the most ardent supporters of WAND. One among her many activities and roles was being co-founder of the Guyanese women's NGO, Red Thread.
2. DAWN was a network of women, researchers and activists across the developing world who were proposing "development alternatives with women for a new era", hence the acronym.
3. An NGO – MATCH International Women's Fund – which provides grants to women's rights organizations in the global South.
4. There were Margaret Bernal and Jean Jackson in Antigua and Barbuda; Diane Cummins, Margaret Gill and Averille White in Barbados; Diane Cummins and Margaret Gill in St Vincent and the Grenadines; and Stella Odie-Ali in Guyana.
5. The coordinators were Dorian Powell for Mona, Christine Barrow for Cave Hill and Sybil Patterson for University of Guyana. There was no team from St Augustine, just individuals involved occasionally, and therefore no need for a coordinator.
6. The full title of the conference was the "World Conference to Review and Appraise the Achievements of the United Nations Decade for Women: Equality, Development and Peace".

CHAPTER 4

BUILDING A TEAM

Women and Development Studies Groups, 1982–1992

> The WDSGs facilitated participation in and opportunities to contribute to the national, regional and global women's movement. They also contributed to the development of critical consciousness, awareness of gender as a philosophical tool of analysis; instilled passion and commitment to gender mainstreaming as a tool for participatory sustainable development and the hope for a better future for diverse groups of ordinary citizens.
>
> —*Leith Dunn, IGDS head, Mona unit*

THE UN MID-DECADE CONFERENCE ON WOMEN HAD TAKEN place in Copenhagen in 1980. A Caribbean woman, Lucille Mathurin Mair, had been appointed secretary general of the conference, and the opportunity had been taken to ensure Caribbean participation, especially at the NGO forum. There, Caribbean women provided information on what was taking place in their region, showcased material on the various projects and their outcomes, and participated in panels and discussion groups. In effect, there was a concerted effort to place Caribbean women and their concerns in the international arena and on the international agenda. Several persons who later became involved in the formation of WDS campus groups attended that conference and therefore had an opportunity to appreciate what had been achieved so far and to see how much more needed to be done. As a result of this and other UN initiatives during the decade, a number of governmental and non-governmental actions took place in the region (see chapter 2).

Throughout the region, therefore, experience had been gained in elucidating the concerns of women at the governmental level and advocating on their behalf within governmental structures. Further, as these women sought to improve the effectiveness of their efforts, they had also been gaining experience in interacting with women's NGOs.

Another interesting governmental initiative was that the CARICOM ministers of women's affairs, at their meeting in 1983 in celebration of the tenth anniversary of CARICOM, made a recommendation "to confer an award to an outstanding CARICOM woman whose work had made a significant contribution to the socio-economic development of the Caribbean" (CARICOM 1983).

In response, the CARICOM Secretariat introduced the CARICOM Triennial Award for Women. In 1984, around the time when the campus groups were just about one year old, the inaugural award was presented to a Trinidadian woman, Nesta Patrick, who had been involved in pioneering work with and for women for many years. Through the medium of social work, she had uncovered numerous infelicities in the condition of women of the region and had been engaged in remedial work to facilitate improvement in their lives. Further, she was making her information available to women in the university, through lectures and seminars and through membership of the St Augustine WDSG, thus strengthening the links between academia and activism. In addition, the reach of her work across the region to territories outside of Trinidad and Tobago signalled the importance of regionalism in a non-political format. Her selection as the inaugural awardee could only have been an inspiration to those within the university, especially members of the WDSG at St Augustine, who were striving to make their ideas about improving the lives of women in the region acceptable. In recognition of her work and its relation to the work of the UWI, Nesta Patrick was awarded, in 2001, an honorary degree of doctor of laws – again an acknowledgement of the relevance of women's issues to the work of the university.

The upsurge of action by governments in the region was not entirely of their own volition. Rather, it was a response to the increasing lobbying efforts of the women's NGOs, which had grown in numbers, strength and sophistication during the decade. Traditional women's NGOs were becoming more activist in orientation and, in fact, collaborated across the region to form a regional group, known as the CARIWA, dedicated to the promotion of women's rights and social justice. It was CARIWA which negotiated for the inclusion of an item on women's human rights in an article on functional cooperation in the original

Plate 4.1. Nesta Patrick (*third from left*), first recipient of CARICOM Triennial Award for Women, with CGDS campus unit heads (*left to right*) Pat Mohammed (Mona), Eudine Barriteau (Cave Hill) and Rhoda Reddock (St Augustine)

Treaty of Chaguaramas that created CARICOM. It was CARIWA which led the charge for the establishment of the women's affairs desk at the CARICOM Secretariat, as mentioned above. CARIWA also successfully campaigned for the creation of a WAD unit within the UWI.

Another regional group chose a different path. The CAFRA chose the medium of research to identify needs, mount advocacy campaigns and develop and implement problem-solving action programmes. At the national level, the 1980s also witnessed the emergence of a number of women's NGOs which focused on consciousness-raising among its members as well as the general public, using what could be defined as non-traditional means. Research became linked with advocacy, and advocacy became linked with the media, popular theatre and culture as well as public demonstrations.

The excitement produced by the wealth of information provided by the WICP, and the highly collaborative spirit created by that project, generated interest among female academics to explore how best the UWI could be involved in the regional and global thrust towards better understanding of how women fit into ongoing development theory and praxis. In some respects, the UWI was behind many areas of the developing world, including parts of Africa, across Asia (especially India) and Latin America, all of which had embarked on research, training and publications in women's studies since the early 1970s, though much of this work was outside of academia (Mathurin Mair 1988b). This view was echoed by Bridget Brereton in an interview some years later (cited in Kaminjolo 1993). The challenge in this region was to find ways to introduce the knowledge being gained through research and activism throughout the region into the curricula of the UWI.

Responding to this challenge was the trigger for the establishment of WDS groups across the three campuses. WAND was the catalyst. In March 1982, WAND secured funding from the Ford Foundation to convene a meeting to discuss the possible introduction of a women's studies programme in the UWI. The meeting was arranged by WAND in collaboration with ISER (EC) and chaired by Joycelin Massiah. The seventeen participants included staff members from across the three UWI campuses, the University of Guyana, the St Vincent Teacher Training College and the Caribbean Examinations Council. Each of the invitees had been involved in teaching and researching women's issues. Present at that meeting was Florence Howe of the New York State University and the Feminist Press, New York, who was a key figure in the establishment of *Women's Studies International*, a journal which grew out of the UN mid-decade conference on women in 1980. She shared her considerable experience of women's studies programmes in the USA. Also at that meeting was Rhoda Reddock, then a graduate student at the ISS, The Hague, who prepared the working paper for the meeting. Many of her valuable insights and suggestions were eventually incorporated into the final document of the meeting and, indeed, into the shaping of the proposed programme (WAND 1982).

> I was also present at the historic regional meeting called by Peggy in March 1982, which was chaired by Joycelin, that launched the WDSGs. That was truly a historic event and I had prepared the discussion paper (I still have a copy of the original) which was developed based on contributions from different persons in the UWI as well as my own research. Also present were Marlene Hamilton and Marjorie Thorpe, among others. (Rhoda Reddock, testimonial)

The women at that meeting were full of enthusiasm, and the discussions were rich and lively with new ideas around objectives, topics and target groups which should inform the three areas of teaching, research and outreach of the proposed programme. They were also concerned that issues of documentation and publication should be integral to the programme.

The meeting agreed on four main objectives:

1. To identify and build support for a women's studies programme through a cross-campus women's studies network
2. To establish a women's studies programme in the UWI system
3. To prepare a proposal for funding
4. To establish a regional steering committee to raise funds and build support through individual campus groups

To achieve these objectives, the meeting designed a three-phased plan for the gradual introduction of women's studies at various levels within the university system. It was the hope that this would culminate in an integrated and interdisciplinary programme of teaching, research and action. The first phase would establish individual campus WSGs to lay the foundation for the programme on their respective campuses. Also in this phase, it was recommended, activities of the campus groups should be coordinated by a regional steering committee comprising the three campus coordinators; the tutor/coordinator, WAND; and the director, ISER (EC), as chair. The second phase was to strengthen the Extra-Mural Department (which became the School of Continuing Studies, now the Open Campus) through training and sensitization, links with community groups, research and publications, and courses on women's issues targeting specific groups. The third and final phase, during the three-year period, was to be one of consolidation and institution of a formal programme with the establishment of a regional coordinating unit.

The First Steps: Initiation

The first Regional Steering Committee meeting was held in March 1982, immediately following the WAND/ISER (EC) meeting (WAND 1982), and the campus groups became operational between 1982 and 1984. The RSC functioned essentially in two basic areas. On the one hand, it coordinated the activities of the campus groups. To this end, from time to time, individual members of campus groups were invited to attend committee meetings dealing with specific issues. On the other hand, it functioned as a focal point for the UWI administration in the formal aspect of introducing a programme of WDS into the curricula of the university. In that regard, the RSC appeared before a subcommittee of the University Planning and Estimates Committee (UPEC), both in person and on the University of the West Indies Distance Teaching Experiment teleconference system, and were able to respond to queries about the proposed programme. The activities of the RSC coalesced around fund seeking, project development, inter-campus linkages, sponsorship of lectures and expanding and maintaining international contacts. On the basis of a proposal submitted by ISER (EC), Ford Foundation had assisted with funds to facilitate the work of the RSC from November 1983 to April 1986, to enable preparation of the project proposal to the ISS and to offset the salary of a full-time regional coordinator. Prior to that, funding for administrative support, office supplies and the like had come to WDS through ISER (EC) and WAND, primarily from their own budgets.

There was much interest in the formation of the campus groups when staff, both academic and non-academic, and students were invited to an inaugural meeting to announce the formation of the respective groups and to issue invitations to join. However, the process of transforming attendance at the launch into the act of actual joining, and thence into participating in the activities, witnessed a sharp drop-off in numbers. At Cave Hill, for example, that inaugural meeting attracted twenty-four persons, including a number of male colleagues; but the task of maintaining the group and carrying out its activities revolved around only nine members. By contrast, at St Augustine, the inaugural meeting included only a very small group, but that group eventually expanded as time progressed, though attendance fluctuated substantially. Some persons joined as a result of their personal research interests, others to educate themselves on women's issues, others to solidify ideas of women's independence and integrity learned during their formative years. All of them were concerned with how to persuade the university that women's studies was a legitimate field of study and that the time had come to begin the introduction of courses and modules in the teaching curricula. In addition, as Bridget Brereton (quoted in Kaminjolo 1993) pointed out during the tenth-anniversary celebrations at St Augustine: "In our teaching programme what we are mainly trying to do is to sensitize the students to the fact that women's issues and women's experiences are an extremely important part of the total sum of knowledge that universities are supposed to convey."

The steering committee had the task of defining the objectives, structure and content of the programme for the WDS groups and setting policy in cooperation with the coordinators of these groups. This was not always an easy or straightforward task, since the groups varied considerably in size, operated in different ways and engaged in different activities. The Mona group, which started in December 1982, called itself the Women's Studies Working Group, Mona; it functioned as a collective with a fifteen-member committee, "with everyone taking on whatever tasks were necessary" (McKenzie 2004, 403). This resulted in there being at least eight coordinators at Mona over the ten-year period (see appendix 3 for the names of coordinators of the three WDSGs), and their enthusiasm never waned. Veronica "Ronnie" Salter, UWI lecturer and former WDSG coordinator (Mona), recalls:

> My earliest memory of involvement with WDS was after the landmark conference held at the Social Welfare Training Centre shortly after the *Social and Economic Studies* publication of articles from the WICP. In those days, at Mona, most of the work on women was coming out of the social sciences, to which I was attached. Also, WDS was housed in the ISER in two rooms offered by Professor Eddie Greene. He not only housed the unit but ensured that we were very much involved in the ISER Thursday-afternoon seminars.
>
> How I remember the impact of Professor Errol Miller's controversial paper on male marginalization. There was standing room only, and then the room erupted with vociferous shouts from passionate female teachers about a remark made by the said author, when president of JTA, that, on a salary issue, teachers should: "Vote with their feet!" And the males *did* – they responded, thus leading to the feminization of teaching. To me, this marked the commitment of the Faculty of Education to the Unit; Arts and Natural Sciences were already on board. (Veronica Salter, testimonial)

The St Augustine and Cave Hill groups preferred a more structured approach. At Cave Hill, the smallest of the groups, which was launched in January 1983, there were a total of five coordinators over the same period, and the group functioned with just the coordinator to guide its work and a secretary/administrative assistant to deal with the routine administrative tasks. By contrast, the St Augustine group, launched in April 1982, had six coordinators over the same period, a deputy coordinator, a secretary/administrative assistant, and its members divided into a variety of committees and subcommittees. This group created its own constitution, based on the recommendations of a constitution committee. Other committees included a steering committee and committees or subcommittees on a range of issues including friendship, counselling and support, newsletter, fundraising, PhD/MPhil selection, arts, building fund, teachers, and sexual harassment. In addition, there was a "group under the tree", which met literally under a flowering Samaan tree and organized a series of annual management training workshops.[1] Rhoda Reddock, UWI professor, first head of CGDS St Augustine unit, now deputy principal of St Augustine campus, UWI, fondly recalls those days in her testimonial:

> I remember the St Augustine WDSG as very empowering for that generation of academic and administrative women. There was a common purpose – the establishment of the programme of teaching and research – but the groups also served as a kind of support group for women at that time. The famous "group under the tree", which came out of a workshop held at the Jamaican North Coast, continued to be an extremely strong bond for the women – many of whom were administrators – in this process. At St Augustine, at one time, as well, I recall an actual support group of senior women was set up to advise and support more junior women in their navigation of the system. I recall some of the members were Bridget Brereton, Desirée Wilson and Maureen Cain. I think many women benefited from this advice and support, and there is still need for such a group today.

Despite this variety of arrangements, all three of the groups were consistent in their desire to further the role of building support for activities in teaching, research and outreach on women's issues. According to Hermione McKenzie (2004, 406): "We were dynamic and innovative, inspired by a vision. We were very highly respected as a pioneering group bringing gender perspectives and gender scholarship to the academy and to the wider community."

One of the major undertakings of the regional steering committee and campus groups was the critique and elaboration of a variety of theoretical issues, including the prevailing notion of "integrating women in development". After much discussion, it was agreed that women were already integrated in development and that what we needed to be concerned about was what kind of development and how, at what points, and with what impact women related to development. It was felt that inclusion of the word *development* in the title of the programme would force women's studies enthusiasts to look critically at the concept of development, examine how particular connotations of the word and its practice affected women, and explore how some of the negative aspects could be reversed. The groups finally agreed that the name WSGs did not fully embrace what they professed to be about and that there was need to find a name which better reflected what the programme was seeking to achieve. Much lively discussion focused on this issue. Should the word *development* be added? Should the word *gender* replace the word *women*? Rhoda Reddock describes it very well:

> Some felt that the words woman and women were limiting, in that it gives the impression that men are excluded, whereas gender included relations between women and men. Others felt also that, to win support of a largely male hierarchy, the word gender might be more acceptable. Those opposed to gender argued that the area of studies had emerged out of a women's movement that had recognized the subordination and oppression of women and had worked to end women's invisibility. To remove the word women from the title of the programme would be a step backward. (Reddock 1994, 111–12)

The discussion proceeded for quite a while, until agreement was eventually reached that the name of the groups should be changed to WDSGs, and this is the name which went forward. It is worthy of note that the amicable settlement of this debate demonstrated the spirit of cooperation and compromise which has marked relations among the groups from their inception and which continues today. Once this decision was made, the RSC, with the support of the campus groups, moved forward, in 1983, to approach the ISS, The Hague, for assistance to implement the proposed programme on WDS. The ISS had supported the WICP generously, and it was hoped that they would be just as supportive of a formal academic programme.

In late 1983, Peggy Antrobus, Kathleen Drayton of Cave Hill, Elsa Leo-Rhynie of Mona, Joycelin Massiah of ISER, Hermione McKenzie of Mona, Marjorie Thorpe of St Augustine and others from the groups were named as representatives on a thirty-member UWI team to attend an Association of Atlantic Universities/UWI conference in Halifax, Nova Scotia, from 30 October to 5 November 1983.[2] The conference was intended to identify potential areas of cooperation between Atlantic Canada and the West Indies. Five topics had been identified, including women's studies. The WSG members on the team set out to gather information on a similar initiative which had been launched there. A paper detailing progress in discussions at UWI, prepared and presented by Massiah (see Massiah 1986a for the revised version of the presented paper), formed the basis of the conference discussions on possible cooperation between the Association of Atlantic Universities and UWI in the area of women's studies. A report of the conference was prepared by the UWI registrar and presented to UPEC at its meeting of 12 January 1984 as UPEC P. 16, 1983/84. The final report of that Halifax conference served to heighten interest in the issues of WAD and to draw attention to the role which administrators would be required to play in assisting any formal programme designed to bring those issues into academia. In a status report dated 7 September 1984,

Plate 4.2. Animated discussion: (*left to right*) Marjorie Thorpe (first head of WDSG, St Augustine), Peggy Antrobus and Joycelin Massiah

to the vice-chancellor on the programme in WDS being proposed for UWI, Zaffar Ali, Senior Project Officer, drew reference to the report of the Halifax conference, which was presented by the registrar to UPEC at its meeting of 12 January 1984. Ali revealed that, in that report, the registrar had noted "that in some areas, notably Women's Studies, the University of the West Indies was taking the lead".

Following the favourable report of the conference, two members of the RSC, Elsa Leo-Rhynie and Joycelin Massiah, sought and obtained an appointment with the then vice-chancellor of the UWI, A.Z. Preston, to seek his approval of the proposed initiatives of the RSC and the campus groups and to invite him to formalize his support for the project with the ISS. Around that time, Lucille Mathurin Mair had been visiting the Mona campus, at the invitation of the RSC, to deliver a lecture, conduct a departmental seminar and hold meetings with senior administration personnel.[3] Cognizant of her exceptional diplomatic skills, Leo-Rhynie and Massiah invited her to join them for the meeting with Vice-Chancellor Preston. By the end of the meeting, he had become a firm supporter of the project. With the assurance of his support, the prospects of success in mounting the WSG effort seemed bright. Indeed, he signed the statement of intent on 6 June 1985, three months after that meeting. Within a year, Lucille Mathurin Mair had been appointed regional coordinator of the WDS project funded by the Government of the Netherlands in collaboration with the ISS in The Hague.

Plate 4.3. Lucille Mathurin Mair, first regional coordinator, IOP/UWI/ISS Project

By 1985 WAND was already mounting courses on WDS among its constituents (WAND 1988). These courses began in October 1985 with an in-house orientation seminar designed to clarify for staff the relationship between women's studies and the work of the unit as well as to introduce discussions on gender at a theoretical level. A second seminar, mounted in March 1986, was regional, involved community development workers and others, and was aimed at introducing critical discussions on the prevailing development model and to expose participants to an understanding of a gender perspective to various aspects of their own work. A third seminar, also regional, was held in October 1987 and was conducted in collaboration with CAFRA. It was entitled "Making History, Making Change", with the aim of demonstrating the application of a feminist perspective to issues of social and economic development, using the medium of research. WAND was, in effect, demonstrating the relevance of women's studies in a variety of fora, mostly outside the academy, and thus stressing the necessity for the academy to accept this new area of scholarship.

WAND was involved in the deliberations and activities of the campus groups, and it was WAND which convened the meeting at which the framework of a formal WDS teaching programme was designed. For all practical purposes, therefore, it could be argued that the women's movement, through its links with WAND, exerted significant influence on the work of the WDSGs, just as it may be argued that the converse was equally true. The WDSGs became a resource for information and training for national and regional administrative machinery for women's affairs, on the one hand, and national and regional women's NGOs, on the other, with WAND as an essential partner in the collaborative process.

Creating the Programme: Development

The WDS groups had a vision and set of objectives which mandated the establishment of an academic programme in WDS at the UWI. However, for years, the groups functioned outside the mainstream of the academy, establishing and using links with lecturers and other staff members in furtherance of their objectives. Group members disseminated the findings of the WICP and also initiated action which resulted in the inclusion of those findings in relevant disciplinary courses. Some also developed courses in their own faculties, even before the groups acted. For example, in 1984/85, a master's course on sex roles and education was introduced in the Faculty of Education by Marlene Hamilton and Elsa Leo-Rhynie at Mona. This provided the stimulus for development of further courses in other disciplines as well as for grappling with the issue of designing and delivering interdisciplinary courses.

Introducing women's studies courses involved scaling a number of hurdles. First, there were no staff members designated to undertake the task. It was a purely voluntary exercise. Then there was the process involved in getting a course approved, a "difficult, tedious and hazardous" process, to use the words of Rowland, which could take an inordinately long time. Third was the issue of resources. There was no funding, no physical space, no administrative/secretarial support. The groups were therefore forced to rely on sensitive deans, departmental heads and administrative assistants for the most basic help. And throughout, there was the constant criticism, even ridicule, from insensitive colleagues. As Marjorie Thorpe, the first coordinator of the St Augustine group, put it: "I don't think that they took the group seriously. They may have taken individual members seriously but not as they were performing women's studies tasks" (quoted in Kaminjolo 1993).

Nonetheless, the groups persevered. They were never strident, never confrontational, never hostile or difficult. They simply continued their efforts to create and deliver teaching courses, undertake research and engage in outreach activities.

Teaching

A major decision of the March 1982 meeting was that the proposed programme should be integrated and interdisciplinary, consisting of teaching, research and outreach. As the WDSGs began to address this recommendation, they discovered that the twin issues of integration and interdisciplinarity went well beyond the disciplinary paradigm of designing appropriate courses, designing and undertaking research, and ensuring the relevance of the work. Also to be considered were the practical issues, such as how best to gain acceptance within the university; where in the structure should the programme be placed; how best to protect those staff members who wished to become involved but who were already carrying a full teaching load along with administrative duties; and what infrastructure and support systems were necessary to make the programme viable.

The issues were many and complex, but it was agreed that the primary focus of the twin concerns of integration and interdisciplinarity should be on teaching. Accordingly, in the late 1980s, the WDSGs took steps to develop and introduce the first undergraduate course, Women's Studies: An Introductory Course. This was an interdisciplinary and modular course introduced at St Augustine in 1986, at Cave Hill in 1987 and at Mona in 1989. In each case, the course was located in the then Faculty of Arts and General Studies. This course marked the first major milestone in the progress towards the establishment of a full-fledged programme. It was an undergraduate course: developed and team-taught, without compensation, by members of the groups, interested academics from a variety of disciplines and interested persons, with the relevant expertise, from outside the academy. It was managed and administered by the coordinators of the groups.

> I was also part of the team that taught the very first course – introduced by Marjorie Thorpe at St Augustine in the then Faculty of Arts and General Studies – AR301 – Introduction to Women's Studies with Special Reference to the Caribbean, team taught by – Marjorie Thorpe, Jeanette Morris, Maureen Cain, Gwendoline Williams and myself. I can still recall students performing an extract from *For Colored Girls* . . . as part of their course activity. Today there are at least twenty gender-based courses on the books at St Augustine. (Rhoda Reddock, testimonial)

Those who shared in the teaching of this course recognized the validity and significance of feminist scholarship and brought their diverse theoretical frameworks, disciplinary understandings and methodological approaches to knowledge-generation and knowledge-sharing to the women's studies classrooms. Although this was valuable and provided a welcome introduction to gender through a consideration of many themes – in literature, education, history, law, religion and science – integration was difficult, and the pedagogy utilized varied with each presenter. Group members, however, were inspired by a common purpose, and the cohesion and strength of the groups were facilitated by the spirit of collaboration generated through regular campus and regional meetings and seminars.

Apart from that collaboratively taught course, several lecturers, both within and outside the groups, were individually teaching courses or segments of courses in all faculties except natural sciences, medical sciences, agriculture and engineering. Of interest was the involvement of some men, especially at Mona, in the teaching. New courses began to be introduced, each campus group choosing titles and content in which they had the greater comparative advantage.

The process of course development and introduction was not seamless; rather, a number of administrative and bureaucratic hurdles had to be crossed. First was the question of release time for the group coordinators, all of whom were full-time lecturers who were giving of their spare time voluntarily in an effort to coordinate the activities of the groups, including the teaching of courses. It took much negotiating on the part of the then regional coordinator to garner agreement to 30 per cent release time from substantive duties in order to execute this coordination. Barbara Bailey, professor emerita and retired university director, IGDS, points out, however, that "in reality, this was never the case, since that person often continued to carry a full teaching load in their department of origin". She continues: This person therefore had little "legitimate power in terms of positioning within the institutional hierarchy and was very much dependent on the goodwill of persons with legitimate power to act as 'patrons' of the programme, particularly for approval and mounting of undergraduate interdisciplinary programmes" (Bailey 2003, 7).

Speaking of the Mona experience, Hermione McKenzie goes further. She notes in her testimonial: "Course proposals experienced much delay and hesitancy in the university's approval process and in addition there was much genuine difficulty among members of the group as to who should voluntarily undertake additional teaching over and above their teaching loads. There was a belief that we as women should not exploit ourselves further within the conventional stereotypes of unpaid and sacrificial labour."

This was also a concern in St Augustine, where, according to Rhoda Reddock, "the early experiments with teaching took place, in virtually all instances, with the voluntary labour of faculty members already overburdened with teaching and administrative duties common to Third World universities" (Reddock 1994, 108).

Another hurdle was that of the absence of logistical support for the coordinators, which created additional difficulties for those individuals. Without provision for any kind of support, it became necessary to rely on the goodwill of the department in which the coordinator was located; for example, Kathleen Drayton draws attention to the women in the Faculty of Education at Cave Hill who "typed, photocopied, telephoned and took messages and filed, all for no material reward . . . [and] the director of in-service who turned a blind eye to our use of departmental supplies and equipment. We could not have functioned otherwise" (Drayton 1993, 8). Yet another issue was the absence of physical space as well as basic office equipment for the groups. Each campus tried to assist. At Cave Hill, the in-service section of the Faculty of Education, and, in St Augustine and Mona, the ISER, generously provided some limited but welcome office space. In an attempt to address these problems, the RSC approached the Ford Foundation, which agreed to provide support to facilitate the work of the committee, to offset the salary of a full-time regional coordinator, who was appointed in 1986, and to prepare a proposal for the formal introduction of a WDS programme within the UWI.

Research

Research efforts were not as well coordinated as in the case of teaching and were mostly individual initiatives scattered across the departments and across campuses. These tended towards research which supported teaching and provided an analysis of theoretical issues. In addition, supervised research papers produced by students provided useful information on which some of the outreach activities were centred. For example, data on sexual harassment in Barbados produced by students at Cave Hill were presented by the Cave Hill group to the National Advisory Council on Women and were used subsequently by the Barbados Workers Union (Drayton 1993, 14). Through the Internationaal Onderwijs Programma (International Education Programme)/UWI/ISS phase 1 project, a small research fund for WDSG members was established, which assisted successful applicants with small sums of money for ongoing projects.

In an effort to devise a research strategy which could involve members of all three campus groups, a proposal was developed for a four-part project entitled "Caribbean Women in Transition: A Research Programme on Women, Gender and Caribbean Development". The proposal envisaged a number of activities, each with its own set of requirements, all connected. Among the activities were included

- two cross-campus collaborative projects under the themes "Gender Ideology and Its Impact in the Caribbean", and "Gender Perspectives in Science, Development and Technological Change in the Caribbean";
- four annual research awards in the name of a prominent Caribbean woman and based on the specified thematic areas;
- small research grants to support independent initiatives which fall under the designated thematic areas;
- seminars to share research findings;
- training in research methodologies at home and/or abroad;
- publications support; and
- administrative support.

It was a highly ambitious and creative proposal, which, regrettably, never materialized, signalling the difficulty of raising funds for research in the new discipline (WDS St Augustine, n.d.). The proposal, described as "very comprehensive" was later modified and redesigned into a new initiative entitled "Gender in Caribbean Thought: Breaching Frontiers and Understanding Differences" and intended "to stimulate individual research and lead to publications for teaching purposes" (UWI CGDS 1996, 36–37).

Outreach

The groups excelled in terms of the number and variety of outreach activities, the number of group members involved, the range of participants reached and the impact on the groups with which they worked and the wider society. The Cave Hill group, with the smallest membership of about thirty-five (circa 1990), maintained links with the Bureau of Women's Affairs and a wide variety of women's NGOs on which they depended for support of their many outreach activities. In the first three years, for example, the group organized a theatre production called *Lights*, a forum on Women and the Law, a public seminar on Sex and Gender, another on Women in the Sugar Industry, a showing of the Cuban film *Retraito de Teresa*, a public tribute to Dame Nita Barrow on her appointment to the Eminent Persons Group visiting South Africa and, in collaboration with WAND, a public lecture by Angela Davis, the celebrated American activist. This schedule was a remarkable achievement for the smallest of the three groups, whose members, like their colleagues in the other two groups, had to carry out these activities in addition to their regular teaching, research and administrative duties in their respective departments.

The Mona group was no less active. With a membership of about sixty-five, the group maintained links with the Sistren Theatre Collective, the Bureau of Women's Affairs and a number of women's organizations. They introduced a newsletter, managed by one of their members, Tereza Richards, librarian of the Mona campus.

> One of the objectives of the Women's Studies Working Group (UWI, Mona) when it was established was to generate and disseminate information on the position of women in society. From this objective came a newsletter which served as a networking tool for the WDSG. The *UWI Women and Development Studies (Mona Group) Newsletter* was published between 1988 and 1997. . . .
>
> The newsletter served to document the various activities organized by the group (such as seminars, symposia, conferences, special lectures); preview upcoming events; highlight personal reflections by group members; report on events in which group members had participated; provide information on published and other resources; and present to the wider community the achievements of the WDSG. (Thereza Richards, testimonial)

They held lunchtime meetings every other week, which were addressed by an array of local and visiting speakers – for example, Filomena Steady of the United Nations; Gloria Hull, an African American writer; Barbara Smith, publisher of the Kitchen Table Press; and the Reverend Barbel von Wartenberg (McKenzie 2004, 404). Starting in 1983, the Mona group began to sponsor an annual one-day symposium to mark International Women's Day. These provided an avenue for access to international personnel working with women's issues and also an opportunity to broadcast ongoing research beyond the group itself. The themes of the symposium carried such titles as "A Review of Women's Research and Action Projects" and "The United Nations for Women: A Jamaican Perspective". The Mona group also organized a function for the wife and daughter of Archbishop Tutu during their visit to Jamaica. The Mona group met with Federico Mayor, then director of UNESCO, who was visiting Jamaica and wanted to meet a gender group.

A key interest of the Mona group was the issue of gender-based violence (GBV) – in particular, violence against women and children. Veronica Salter describes their concern and response to this scourge in her testimonial:

> When violence was at what we thought was an unprecedented peak, we held an Ecumenical Memorial Service for the over nine hundred victims. Persons came from affected communities with children of victims when they heard of it. As each name was called out, a flower was placed in front of the altar. There was a huge pile at the end of the ceremony. We had representation from all the religious groups in Jamaica – Buddhist, Christian, Hindu, Jewish and Rastafarian.

The Mona group's biggest milestone, however, was their involvement in the 1992 launch of the umbrella organization Association of Women's Organisations of Jamaica, the creation of which was the idea of the then group coordinator, Alafia Samuels. She and Hermione McKenzie, a member of the group, were founding members of the association, which, in time, came to embrace a large number of women's organizations as well as individual women:

> The vision was to be the umbrella organization for all women's organizations who chose to participate, to collectively address those issues that all women agreed on – so domestic abuse, rape, violence against women, violence against children, social status of women, etc. We would have open meetings to which all persons could come, and a coordinator would lead. I was privileged to be elected the coordinator from its inception in 1989 to 1991, when I demitted office to become a mother. (Alafia Samuels, testimonial)

At St Augustine, where membership reached about seventy by 1990, the group maintained close links with the Ministry of Social Development and Family Services (in which the Women's Bureau was located), with the Ministry of Food Production and Marine Exploitation, with World Health Organization and Pan American Health Organization, and with a wide range of NGOs, including CAFRA. However, special emphasis was placed on working with secondary schools by organizing lectures and panel discussions, in which the students were involved. The WDSG delivered lectures, organized seminars and conferences, hosted visiting scholars and engaged in a host of activities which served to increase the ever widening impact of its presence. Information provided by Kaminjolo (1993) indicates the volume and variety of these activities, through which the group reached a wide spectrum of the society, including senior lecturers and professors of the university, government personnel, members of the clergy, representatives of national and regional NGOs, and international agencies.

Apart from these group-centred efforts, there were also a number of nationally based initiatives – for example, assistance in the training of government personnel – in which individual members were often invited to participate. WDSG members across the three campuses were also constantly being invited to provide advice or assistance to regional entities such as the CARICOM Secretariat and CAFRA. In effect, the campus groups were gradually being recognized and accepted as experts in a specialized area of knowledge which had relevance to the activities and operations of the requesting entities.

Outreach, however, was not limited to national and regional activities. It also involved accessing knowledge from and upgrading skills using as many external sources as possible. According to Kathleen Drayton, WDSG members at Cave Hill were involved in virtually every major international conference of the day and attended meetings on every continent of the world. She recalls that members went to Mexico and Latin America; to Copenhagen, Moscow, Crete and elsewhere in Europe; to Singapore, Tokyo, Thailand, Australia and Papua New Guinea; to North, West, East and South Africa; and throughout the Caribbean (Drayton 1993, 14). The groups at Mona and St Augustine were no less peripatetic. These were not joyrides; members wrote and presented papers, sat on panels, delivered addresses and generally worked hard to ensure that the presence of the Caribbean was felt. They also strove to learn from the experience of others and to extract those lessons which could be of benefit to the Caribbean initiative. In effect, these meetings and conferences allowed important contacts to be made and recognition to be gained for both the WDSGs and UWI.

Extending the Programme: Diffusion

The IOP/UWI/ISS Programme Phase 1, 1985–1990

As the WDSGs became better known through their teaching and outreach activities, the demands on them grew, and so did the limitations of the circumstances under which they were functioning. The time had now come for the RSC to review the recommendations of the March 1982 meeting. By 1985, the RSC had fulfilled the first of its operational objectives, which revolved around the functioning of a women's studies network across the three campuses; agreement had been reached on the possible shape of a comprehensive programme of WDS; and the campus groups had embarked on an intensive programme of teaching and were engaged in a variety of outreach activities. However, according to the 1982 recommendations, the ultimate aims of the RSC were to develop

- general objectives for a formal programme of WDS in the UWI;
- structure and content of an integrated programme of teaching, research and outreach; and,
- a three-year strategy leading to the introduction of the proposed formal programme.

In effect, while the groundwork had been laid, the ultimate objectives had not yet been met. To meet these objectives, the RSC, in collaboration with the three campus groups, began the process of developing a formal proposal. The proposed strategy, the main objective of which was staff development, included

- a series of disciplinary and interdisciplinary seminars across the three campuses designed essentially for staff-training purposes;
- three MA/PhD fellowships to study WAD at the ISS in order to prepare staff to undertake full responsibility for the academic and technical aspects of teaching, including at the graduate level;
- three-month seminar fellowships for staff;
- support to small research projects on gender issues to support teaching and linked to the production of relevant texts on Caribbean women;
- support of staff and personnel in the RCU; and
- equipment for offices and teaching material such as journals.

The UWI was expected to provide physical facilities for offices and classrooms.

The proposal, with the support of Vice-Chancellor Preston was submitted to the Netherlands government through the ISS in 1985 and was approved and funded for the period 1985–90. This was no small achievement for a group which had been in existence for just two years. Not only was this first effort at major fundraising by the WDSGs successful, but it also served to reinforce a relationship between the UWI and the Netherlands government, through the ISS, which had also been instrumental in providing significant funding to the WICP.

Just before the WDSG funds were received, a panel of donors consisting of the Commonwealth Fund for Technical Cooperation, the Global Ministries of the United Methodist Church, the Ford Foundation and UNIFEM provided funding for a two-week, inaugural, interdisciplinary seminar. Held in Trinidad and Tobago in September of 1986, that seminar marked the first intercampus activity of the fledgling WDSG. It provided an opportunity for "lecturers, researchers, activists, planners and policy makers involved in the area of women and development to come together as both participants and resource persons to examine some of the fundamental questions which needed to be addressed . . . in preparation for . . . [the] launch of an official programme of Women's Studies on the three campuses of the UWI" (Mohammed and Shepherd 1988, xiii).

It was a two-week seminar fashioned after a similar one designed by the Institute of Development Studies, Sussex, and, indeed, Dr Kate Young of that institute attended. The twenty-two papers from this inaugural seminar were presented in a publication edited by Patricia Mohammed and Catherine Shepherd, which is now in its second edition. The volume was a basic text for the first course provided by the WDSGs, Introduction to Women's Studies, which was mentioned earlier. According to the editors, "the papers provide the inspirational backdrop against which academic inquiry in Women's Studies must be conducted. . . . They provide a source book which can be used to introduce both students and novices to the complexity which is Women's Studies" (ibid., xvii).

This inaugural seminar was immediately followed by the receipt of funds from the IOP/UWI/ISS in October 1986 and the introduction of a series of seminars which comprised the first major component of the project. The series consisted of three interdisciplinary and eight disciplinary seminars spread across the three campuses and spanning the period 1986–94 (see appendix 4). Once again, the collaborative nature of the WDSGs came to the fore. The three interdisciplinary seminars were planned, organized and conducted, one per campus. While there were five general aims of the three seminars, each campus group devised its own theme, objectives specific to its particular circumstances, and its own planning and operational strategy. The three campus groups were coordinated by a regional course director, Patricia Mohammed. By the end of the three seminars, there had emerged a clearer understanding of "the critical importance and relevance of women's studies" (UWI WDS 1987, 25).

The eight disciplinary seminars were shared between the campuses – three at Mona (conducted by the departments of Education, History, and Natural Sciences – the latter two staged after institutionalization); two at St Augustine (by Arts and General Studies, and Agriculture); and three at Cave Hill (by Social Sciences, Law, and Medical Science) (see appendix 4). In each case, the seminar was planned by the WDSGs in collaboration with the relevant faculty. These seminars were created by the programme as a mechanism through which faculty members and other interested persons could be brought into discussions with the WDS groups on issues to which they may not previously have deemed women and gender issues to be relevant. By the end of the series, every faculty, except Engineering, had participated. Other participants were drawn from across the region and included personnel from the three UWI campuses, the University of Guyana, secondary school teachers and students, activists, policymakers from national, regional and international agencies and the general public.

Well over 120 papers covering a wide range of topics and using a variety of methodologies were produced and presented (see Leo-Rhynie, Bailey, and Barrow [1997] for a selection). These papers, as well as those not published, produced a wealth of information on a wide range of topics, offered insights into an array of methodologies and generated considerable interest in the options available for the introduction of a programme of WDS. Many of them were used in both teaching and research. In addition, there were selections printed in two publications (see Mohammed and Shepherd 1988; Leo-Rhynie, Bailey, and Barrow 1997) which served to provide not only an outlet for the research findings of a wide range of UWI staff but, perhaps more importantly, also a method of diffusion of information about WAD issues to a wide variety of stakeholders. In addition, they served to publicize the work which was being done on these issues by staff of the UWI. They thus provided an important avenue through which the UWI reflected its institutional acceptance of WDS as a valid input into its academic programme.

> The period of the interdisciplinary and disciplinary courses was really a critical period, and I think that that format was an excellent basis on which to build an academic programme. This allowed for the creation of regional knowledge, the collective exploration of the existing international scholarship as well as the inclusion of other scholars from all the existing faculties. It also established the academic credentials of the field and allowed for a number of the early edited collections. Patricia Mohammed was important in this area both for her leadership of the inaugural course, which was the first regional academic conference on women's studies, and, later, in her work as workshop coordinator. I cannot forget Catherine "Cathy" Shepherd, the documentalist who provided an important support to persons who had to prepare for these training seminars (she developed bibliography, reading lists, etc.), a contribution which was extremely critical in those pre-Internet days, and I would think the inclusion of a documentalist at this phase of the process could be seen as a best practice. (Rhoda Reddock, testimonial)

During phase 1, graduate fellowships to the ISS were won by applicants from Mona and St Augustine, while staff from the three campus groups benefited from short-term fellowships. Project support to the Regional Coordinating Unit (RCU) and the campus groups also took the form of provision for administrative assistance to the coordinators. This was a significant help to the coordinators, who had been working under considerable strain trying to deal with both the academic and administrative matters on their own initiative. The campus groups were fortunate to find women with excellent organizational skills who, even today, still have fond recollections and a vibrant institutional memory of those early days.

Other Donors

As for most activities of the university, fundraising was critical. For the WDS groups, this was even more critical, given the reluctance of some sources within the administration to support the idea of women/gender studies being incorporated into the academic programme. Fundraising therefore became one of the foremost, and certainly most time-consuming, activities of those interested in promoting the WDS programme. While the IOP/UWI/ISS project funds were critical to the programme, they did not cover all that needed to be done. Therefore, it was important to seek out and negotiate with as many potential donors as possible to enable the programme to achieve its funding requirements and stated programme goals.

Given the international sensitivity to the idea of researching and teaching about women's issues, a number of donor agencies, besides the Government of the Netherlands and the Ford Foundation, became extremely interested in the campus groups' activities and became generous supporters. These additional donor funds, together with the ISS project funds, indicated that the WDSGs had brought significant funding into the UWI in just three years. To these donors the WDSGs will be ever grateful.

Strategies for Institutionalization

One of the stipulations by the Government of the Netherlands during the negotiations for the UWI/ISS phase 1 proposal was that, once their funding ceased, UWI would assume full responsibility for the programme. According to the project proposal:

> The impetus for teaching and research in Women and Development emerged within the University of the West Indies prior to the beginning of this project and

> will continue after the project. It is understood that, as the project continues, the University of the West Indies will assume greater responsibility for Women and Development Studies. . . . It is for this reason that the programme, as envisaged, is to be integrated into the existing structure of the University at all levels. (IOP/UWI/ISS 1985, 31–32)

This seems to have triggered some alarm among some UWI administrators. In January 1985, the RSC was summoned to appear before a subcommittee of UPEC despatched to Cave Hill to respond to queries about the proposal to introduce a formal programme of WDS. This was the subcommittee which would advise the vice-chancellor on whether or not to sign the statement of intent of collaboration with the ISS.

The meeting was an interesting example of implied intimidation and manipulation. The first stage was to arrange the seating to suit the chair of the subcommittee. Everyone sat at a long, refectory-type table, the four members of the subcommittee on one side, five members of the RSC on the other; but, whereas the subcommittee members sat with their chair in the centre of their group, the RSC members simply sat anywhere. This did not meet the approval of the subcommittee chair. He insisted that the RSC chair should sit directly in front of him – a move the RSC group interpreted as an effort to stare her down into submission. Next was a complaint about these women securing funding which would otherwise have been available to mainstream university programmes, and WAND was identified as the main culprit. There was also a comparison with the black studies programme of the 1960s in the United States, which had since been disbanded, the implication being that the WDS proposal would suffer a similar fate.

Perhaps the greatest bone of contention was the insistence that the WSGs were proposing a *project*, not a *programme*, the former being of a short, limited, finite duration; the latter having long-term implications for the university.

As Kathleen Drayton records:

> None of the members of the subcommittee were [sic] sympathetic to WDS or to the proposed programme. Indeed, they asked for assurances that it was a "project" and not a "programme". It was a stormy meeting, but WDS held its own. Of course, we had a very effective weapon at our command. We were bringing substantial sums of money into the UWI, and the work of the group was bringing international recognition to the University. (Drayton 1993, 10)

The arguments on this project/programme point were long and harried, but the RSC was disciplined, unified and determined that, whatever the subcommittee chose to call it, the vision and the reality of the proposed programme were clear and would not be diluted. The WDSGs had designed a proposal to implement an integrated programme of teaching, research and outreach for incorporation into the UWI curricula and institutional structure. The proposal, for which they had already received assurances of funding, related to the first phase of that programme. The RSC knew that it needed to have the support of the administration in order to ensure that its request to the Government of the Netherlands would be supported by a formal request from the university authorities. The RSC also knew that securing that support required assuaging the concerns of members of the subcommittee and that is precisely what was attempted. Eventually, the discussion moved from the project/programme issue to clarification of details of the proposal and working out the next steps in the process. The important thing, as Peggy Antrobus has stated in her testimonial, was that "the discipline and unity of the group helped to produce the agreeable outcome . . . we succeeded in securing the decision which we needed to go forward, despite the resistance of some in the administration".

Following this meeting, the subcommittee reported to UPEC, which, at its meeting of 29 April 1985, noted its concerns, including a strong reservation about introducing teaching of women's studies at undergraduate level. Of the minutes in paper 27 of that UPEC meeting which relate to WDS, two read as follows:

> 151. UPEC noted that there was a strong reservation in the University about undergraduate teaching in Women's Studies and that it was necessary to clarify whether acceptance of the ISS funding would entail a commitment to introduce such courses.
> 152. UPEC noted that there was no reservation about research activities and that the reservation did not apply to adjusting the balance in existing undergraduate courses, only to the introduction of special courses. (UWI/UPEC 1985)

Interestingly, similar statements seem to have been made over ten years earlier, when a group of women at Mona had just completed a survey, in Jamaica, of five hundred domestic workers and five hundred employers. According to Rosina Wiltshire, former WDSG coordinator (St Augustine):

> The study sparked a national debate and assisted in building a framework for evidence-based policymaking in the critical sphere of Gender and Development. This was an important catalyst for justifying the need for a Women's Studies Programme at UWI.

> Some of us approached the UWI Mona administration to make the case for a women's studies programme or, at a minimum, some courses in the arts and social sciences. We were advised that we could encourage students to do further research in the area, but the administration did not feel that there was enough evidence that there was an academic foundation for courses, or that there was demand for such courses or a programme. We sought out interested students. All students in the Social Sciences were required to do a Caribbean Studies course, and Rhoda Reddock was one of the first students who focused her Caribbean Studies project on gender with research on men in the prison system. (Rosina Wiltshire, testimonial)

Thirteen years later, the administration argument was still the same. Also of concern was that the university would not commit to action which may not have been endorsed by the various academic bodies. These concerns were subsequently relayed to the RSC, along with a lengthy list of suggestions for amending the project document which had already been discussed and agreed on during a visit to the ISS by Joycelin Massiah, which was made at the request of the ISS. The project document, however, was revised by the RSC, taking into account some of the UPEC suggestions; the programme was accepted; and, in June of that year, the then vice-chancellor of UWI, A.Z. Preston, and the rector of ISS signed a statement of intent of collaboration between the UWI and the ISS (IOP/UWI/ISS 1985, appendix 2).

Among the articles of the agreement was one requiring joint effort to allow the activities described in the proposal to "continue independently of the Institute of Social Studies at the end of the period of the Agreement". The WDSG was thus strengthened to begin lobbying for a number of concessions intended not only to satisfy the ISS requirements but also to strengthen moves towards institutionalization of the programme. On the academic side, the campaign was for independence from the faculties and location in the University Centre. It was argued that this was the position of other units which were responsible for multi- and/or interdisciplinary programmes, as was the WDS programme. The RSC held out for a tiered structure in which there were three campus groups responsible for their own programmes and a RCU responsible for oversight of the three, but also with the capability to develop its own teaching courses and research. The RSC campaigned for the appointment of urgently needed staff, including a professor/regional coordinator based at the RCU, a senior lecturer to head each of the campus units, and support staff for both the RCU and the campus units. The need for equipment, physical space and communication facilities was also emphasized.

None of this came immediately, but eventually, over a period of time, it could be claimed that the WDS got what it wanted, primarily through yet another strategic move. In 1986, the RSC successfully negotiated for the appointment of Lucille Mathurin Mair, renowned Jamaican historian, national and international diplomat, feminist and former staff member of UWI, as the first regional coordinator. Following her resignation in 1989, the RCU invited another Jamaican woman, formerly of the Commonwealth Secretariat, Dorienne Wilson-Smillie, to function as temporary regional coordinator. In large measure, the success of WDS in achieving its requirements was thanks to the considerable diplomatic and negotiating skills of these two remarkable women.

The steps towards institutionalization also took the form of finding a place within the administrative structures of each individual campus. Representation on academic boards would provide space in which to bring the academic work of the groups to the attention of the wider academic community. Representation on planning and estimates committees would allow inputs into decisions about allocation of resources. Cave Hill took the initiative in capturing these spaces. They had been invited to sit on the academic board, which invitation they accepted with alacrity. However, they had to lobby hard for a seat on the Cave Hill Planning and Estimates Committee, which they were given in 1988/89 and have retained ever since. The other two campus groups encountered greater resistance to their grasping such opportunities, but, eventually, they too became members of these committees on their respective campuses. These gains were not always recognized, however. For example, both the UWI Overview Development Plan (1990–2000) and the UWI Centre Development Plan (1990–2000) carry sections on WDS, with the commitments of the university clearly spelled out. The centre development plan envisaged four major objectives of the programme:

1. To institutionalize gender studies in the university
2. To sustain and administer a long-term research programme on gender issues in Caribbean development
3. To expand the programme of course offerings in gender studies
4. To expand and enhance the outreach activities in the field of gender studies and gender policy

The plan further states: "The Development Plan proposed that the University provides a complement of professional and support staff at each campus and provides adequate infrastructural support in the form of office space, capital equipment and communication facilities" (UWI Office of Administration 1990, 5–6). These objectives and required provisions were crystal clear and were made by the highest authorities in the university. Yet, according to Kathleen Drayton, it appears that the Cave Hill campus authorities were taken by surprise by the provisions it was expected to make. Despite the fact that the same papers which formed the basis of what appeared in the UWI documents cited above were presented to the Cave Hill Planning and Estimates Committee, none of it appears in the Cave Hill submission. It was claimed to be an oversight (Drayton 1993, 16–17).

This entire experience of trying to obtain administrative support for the proposed programme strikes at the heart of the issue of women operating in a patriarchal setting and trying to draw attention to the situation of women. In this case, a university setting, a women's studies programme can be seen as an evolutionary or even revolutionary attempt to change the status quo – that is, the existing power structure. Some pushback against such efforts is virtually inevitable. The trick is to be able to find a way to counter that resistance. Rowland (1982) has identified the issues of status, concrete resources, expertise and self-confidence as factors determining how much power can be exercised, particularly by women trying to introduce women's studies courses or programmes. For her, each of these factors favours men, but the one factor which is not in the list is that which operates among women and that is the concept of "sisterhood", which relies on numbers and pressure. In the effort to obtain the support of the UWI administration, the women involved were certainly performing as a united group, even though attempts were made to suggest that there were "disagreements among the groups". They certainly applied, if not pressure, at least a range of strategies, devised at various levels, to accomplish their goals. Not least among those strategies was identifying allies and seeking out the assistance of sympathetic men and women in the system for advice and information. The example of Zaffar Ali cited earlier is a case in point. Marlene Hamilton is another. But regardless of the source and kind of assistance, attempts to belittle the WDS effort continued.

Having achieved some measure of administrative recognition, the WDSGs faced the next hurdle of the appointment of a full-time professor, as stipulated in the project agreement. This occurred under phase 2 of the IOS/UWI/ISS project proposal, where the concern centred on institutionalization.

IOP/UWI/ISS Project Phase 2, 1990–1993

The year 1990 was critical in the life of the WDSGs. Management audits were conducted on each of the campus groups (see Chaderton and McClean 1990, for Cave Hill; Addae and Williams 1990, for St Augustine; Crick 1990, for Mona) as was a major evaluation of the IOP/UWI/ISS project (Biervliet and McPherson-Russell 1990). There were strong similarities in a number of the recommendations offered in these documents. For example, both the Cave Hill and St Augustine audits made recommendations around the need for increased membership of the groups; improving communication between members and between the membership and the groups beyond the campus; strengthening the organizational structure; and designing, implementing and monitoring a strategic plan. The St Augustine audit recommended the creation of an autonomous entity within the UWI, to be called the CGDS, suggesting the structure, roles and relationships among group members and between the groups and a proposed central coordinating unit (Addae and Williams 1990, 38–40). The Mona audit drew attention to the need for better communication between the group and the project office and also within the group itself. This audit pinpointed the general lack of understanding by group members of the process as well as of the implications of institutionalization. Also recommended was a more formalized structure for the group as its role changed with institutionalization. A phased approach towards an agreed ideal structure was recommended. The mid-term evaluation of the IOP/UWI/ISS project, while not focused directly on the operation of the groups, did include a recommendation about the need to maintain the momentum towards institutionalization of the WDS programme within the UWI (McPherson-Russell and Peters 1988). The 1990 evaluation report endorsed these and other recommendations and offered some others, mainly in respect of an extension of the existing phase of the project of cooperation between UWI and ISS (Biervliet and McPherson-Russell 1990).

Taking these recommendations into consideration, a proposal for follow-up to the earlier phase was submitted to the ISS and accepted by the Netherlands Ministry of Development Cooperation, International Education Department. During this phase, the overall objective was to assist the UWI to become self-sufficient in the field of WDS. To this end, the proposal set out to

- generate an integrated body of theoretical knowledge and methodological approaches;

- contribute to assisting women and men to realize their full potential; and
- institutionalize WDS, supported by the UWI, as an integral part of teaching and research in various disciplines, enhancing a multidisciplinary approach. (IOP/UWI/ISS 1990, 12)

To achieve this, the proposal included in its provisions

- assistance to the coordinators;
- project administrator in the RCU;
- operational costs for all units;
- incidentals, especially in the area of communications;
- continuation of the small-research funds to staff;
- three short-term staff fellowships to the ISS; and
- support for expansion of the teaching, research and outreach components of the programme.

While these provisions were all essential to the process of consolidating the achievements of phase 1, the ultimate objective of the phase 2 proposal was the institutionalization of the programme through the establishment of an operational structure which could be integrated into that of the UWI at large. Thus, while phase 1 had already achieved agreement on a structure consisting of three independent campus units located in those departments/faculties which best suited their individual needs, coordinated by a regional unit located within the University Centre, there was still no representation on the key bodies in the university structure. Penetration of academia was the objective, and the work of the WDS groups was geared towards this goal. The enthusiastic response within sections of the academy was indicative of the attractiveness of this new area of scholarship. The administration of the UWI was not as enthusiastic, however. When phase 1 of the project was coming to an end, there was some reluctance on the part of the UWI administration to honour this agreement, since questions were still being raised as to the legitimacy of WDS as an area of scholarship and the necessity to establish a centre for it. The vice-chancellor, Sir Alister McIntyre, insisted that the agreement made by the former vice-chancellor (Preston, who was then deceased) should be honoured.

Acquiring the rights to sit on those bodies therefore became one of the important tasks during phase 2. However, as Barbara Bailey (2003) points out, by agreeing to the terms and conditions of the phase 1 proposal, as quoted earlier, tacit commitment had already been given to institutionalization of the programme. In his letter of 9 February 1990 to Els Mulder, senior project officer and head of the project unit of the ISS, Vice-Chancellor McIntyre specifically gave the assurance that the UWI was seeking the most appropriate strategy for integrating WDS into its administrative and academic structures while at the same time preserving some measure of autonomy and flexibility for the individual campuses. Following representations from the WDS groups, McIntyre advised that he had invited the regional coordinator to sit on the University Academic Committee (UAC) and UPEC. These decisions were not made without arguments from those who disagreed. However, since the terms of the agreement with ISS had so required, the opposition did not prevail.

To further strengthen the process and fulfil the requirements of the IOP/UWI/ISS project agreement, procedures were put in place for the appointment of a suitable candidate at professorial level to assume the position of regional coordinator. This was achieved in March 1992 with the appointment of Elsa Leo-Rhynie as the first professor and regional coordinator of WDS, exactly ten years after the WAND meeting of March 1982. This represented a major milestone in the journey towards institutionalization. Of note is the fact that, two years earlier, Marlene Hamilton had been appointed as the first female deputy principal, Mona, and pro vice-chancellor at UWI. She had been the Mona representative at the meeting in March 1982 at which the proposal to introduce a programme of WDS at UWI was considered. With no funding, she was given responsibility for Gender and Science Education and for the WDS programme as part of her PVC portfolio. She identified institutionalization of WDS within the university structure as her first priority, with the appointment of the professor of women's studies and the need for representation of WDS at decision-making levels within the university as her other priority concerns.

An interesting aspect of these two appointments relates to how they were received by the academic community, especially at Mona. In the case of Marlene Hamilton, her appointment was welcomed by both women and men as an important milestone in the university. In the case of Elsa Leo-Rhynie, although there was general support by both women and men, there was an undertone of dissatisfaction, even resentment, coming from some women, which was undeserved, intimidating and apparently intended to undermine any of her initiatives. Once again, the choice of disregarding or confronting negativity loomed large. Fortunately for the WDSGs, both of these women chose to disregard these murmurings and simply got on with the work entrusted to them.

Immediately, they began to work together to accelerate the move towards yet another milestone on the institutionalization journey. The first goal was the desirability of changing the focus of the programme from women to gender and therefore changing the name of the programme from WDS to GDS. In Elsa Leo-Rhynie's (1992, 8) words:

> If . . . [the] objective [of WDS] . . . is to establish curricula to address issues of and analyses based on gender, if these issues are discrimination, domination, subordination, exploitation, oppression of one gender by another, if these situations could have come about because of the nature of roles assumed and interactions between the genders in specific cultures, races and classes, then the study of one group, with the objective of changing these relationships and situations, seems impossible without reference to and comparisons with the other.

Once again, there was spirited discussion across the campuses. Linnette Vassell (2004, 695–96) describes the arguments as expressed at Mona:

> Proponents for naming it "gender studies" were of the view that this was in keeping with the increasing acceptance of women's studies within the academy . . . [and] was therefore politically correct and would . . . propel academic studies to be more questioning of structures, of roles and relationships of men and women in society, including, it was hoped, structures within the university itself.
>
> Those who called for the retention of "women's studies" expressed fears that, in the context of the male backlash and the discourse around male marginalization, the word "gender" would distort the focus on women's oppression in society and would obscure the reality that needs to be eradicated, that gender relations denote unequal power relations between men and women.

Comments from St Augustine ran along similar lines, as the earlier quotation from Rhoda Reddock indicates. Eventually, after all views were aired, the arguments finally ended with amicable agreement on the name change.

The next step was to create an entity which would reflect the objectives of WDS while at the same time demonstrating the new thrust. By May 1992, Elsa Leo-Rhynie produced a formal proposal for the establishment of a centre for gender studies at the UWI.

Notes

1. In July 1990, representatives of the three campus groups attended an Association of Atlantic Universities/CIDA management training workshop in Jamaica. On their return home, three members of the St Augustine group decided to initiate a series of similar workshops for the benefit of staff on their campus. With no physical space of their own, the group met periodically under a Samaan tree, a large flowering tree on the campus – hence the name "group under the tree". Between 1991 and 1992, the group organized three workshops and were hoping to organize two more in 1993 and 1994 (Kaminjolo 1993, 48).
2. Others attending the Halifax conference included Edris Bird of the UWI Extra-Mural Department, Antigua; Norma Forde of Cave Hill and Sybil Patterson of the University of Guyana.
3. As part of this initiative, Lucille Mathurin Mair delivered a lecture entitled "Brown was Beautiful" at the Cave Hill campus in February 1985 and on the Mona campus on International Women's Day, 8 March 1985.

Section 3

INSTITUTIONALIZATION
THE TRIANGLE OF EMPOWERMENT, 1992–1996

ELSA LEO-RHYNIE

CHAPTER 5

THE FIRST ANGLE

Purpose and Direction

> This centre (CGDS) is the culmination of the work of many persons of different capabilities over many years, and despite the vagaries of personality types, the different agendas which have surfaced from time to time, and the pain that has sometimes resulted, I think that we can and should all feel proud of having attained this place.[1]
> —*Louraine Emmanuel*

THE PATH WHICH LED TO THE INSTITUTIONALIZATION OF GDS in the UWI was not an easy one. The WDSGs were highly motivated towards this goal and it was pursued aggressively in the face of considerable resistance and reservations concerning the academic "respectability" of this new area of scholarship. Group members were not deterred; the collaboration and activities of the groups reinforced their sense of purpose, as did the support which had grown among several enthusiastic academics who considered the issues of gender exciting, with significant potential for research.

The Triangle of Empowerment

On assuming office, the professor/regional coordinator of WDS found herself in the centre of what Virginia Vargas and Saskia Wieringa (1998) have described as a triangle of empowerment. Vargas and Wieringa emphasize that the angles of this "triangle" are not fixed and separate but have a certain fluidity. In this instance, one of the angles represented the purpose and direction in which the institutionalized entity would go and the structure which would allow for this. Another angle was the institutional demand – the expectations and support – from the WDSGs as well as from the university's leadership and management and how these would be met; and the third angle was the strategy to be employed to attain the stated goals and satisfy the demands from the various stakeholders. The interests and issues associated with the three angles converged in some regards, and were at conflict in others.

The First Angle: Defining Direction and Establishing a Framework

The second phase of the IOP/UWI/ISS project sponsored by the Government of the Netherlands (1990–95) was geared towards strengthening the presence of women's studies and gender studies at the UWI and continued the capacity-building work started in phase 1 (1986–90), but also initiated and implemented action for the institutionalization of gender studies within the academy. The regional nature of the project and the scope of its programmes, as well as its link with the ISS in The Hague, located it in the regional University Centre, where it was managed by a consultative committee and an advisory committee, both chaired by the vice-chancellor's representative, PVC and deputy principal of the Mona campus, Marlene Hamilton. Hamilton was well acquainted with the work of the WDSGs, as she had been in attendance at the very first meeting of university women in 1982 and had not only been involved in several of their activities but had also introduced, in the then Faculty of Education, the first graduate course in gender and education. Marlene Hamilton, professor emerita, retired PVC, recalls in her testimonial:

> The interest which developed . . . led Elsa and me to design the first postgraduate course on gender and education, this, offered in the then Faculty of Education, taught by us both. The response was *very* positive, partly because this was initially viewed as a "soft" option. This perspective was to change, and more and more graduate students began to infuse their research undertakings with gender considerations. This also began to be reflected in my own research and writing during the period.

Phase 1 of the IOP/UWI/ISS project (1986–90) was evaluated twice by the Centre for the Study of Education in Developing Countries in The Hague, Netherlands. The first evaluation in 1988 was formative; it set out to assess the progress and achievements of phase 1 midway through the project term, while the end-of-project evaluation in 1990 was summative and was designed to determine the significance, effectiveness and efficiency of the project activities. Effectiveness was assessed in terms of the satisfaction of short-term objectives such as preparation for teaching, documentation, research activities and the establishment and strengthening of links with national and regional organizations and institutions. Efficiency considerations included allocation and use of project funds in the areas of personnel provision, material inputs and activities undertaken. Many achievements related to the project objectives and activities were noted, and the overall assessment was very positive; the evaluation team expressed its satisfaction with the significance of the project in the UWI, noting that "both at national policymaking level and at top-level decision-making in the university, the evaluation team came across hard evidence indicating the significance of the project" (Biervliet and McPherson-Russell 1990, 73). A number of areas for improvement were identified by the evaluation team, including

1. the need for institutionalization of WDS into the UWI academic structure;
2. the continuing need for staff development;
3. the importance of ongoing research in support of teaching; and
4. the need to retain and strengthen links with national and regional organizations and institutions.

Marlene Hamilton played a pivotal role in addressing these issues and in the establishment of the CGDS. In her role as PVC with responsibility for WDS, she kept the UWI administration informed as to the progress of the project and its impact on the university and on society in general, thus providing the vice-chancellor with strong justification for institutionalization, when that was threatened, in the face of the scepticism noted in chapter 4 as well as the UWI's financial problems. As the only PVC ever to have WDS as part of her portfolio, she chaired the IOP/UWI/ISS Project Advisory Committee and was the critical link between the WDSGs, on the periphery, and the mainstream of the UWI. She was instrumental in ensuring that the project activities and reporting met scheduled timelines and that the several activities taking place on the fringes were reported on and represented in the mainstream. Despite her claims to the contrary, Marlene Hamilton's interest in and oversight of the project was significant and continued even after the establishment of the CGDS.

In response to the evaluation of the Netherlands government project and to the expressed need for institutionalization of WDS in the UWI academic structure, the post of regional coordinator and professor of WDS was advertised and applications invited. The first appointee was Elsa Leo-Rhynie, a former senior lecturer in the UWI School of Education, Mona campus, who had been an active member of the WDSGs and who had a number of publications in the area of gender and education. She had collaborated with Marlene Hamilton in the development and teaching of sex roles in education, the first graduate course in gender at UWI. Assuming duties in March 1992, Elsa Leo-Rhynie returned to the UWI from a post as executive director of a private management training institution in Jamaica. Her appointment was not enthusiastically received; reservations as to her commitment and competence were both explicitly and subtly communicated, despite the fact that, in the nearly five years of her official absence from the Mona campus, she had maintained contact with the WDSGs, had participated in the disciplinary seminar in education, had supervised a number of graduate students, and had been involved in research and several public events relating to women in education as well as in business.

> On becoming deputy principal of Mona in 1990, I was given the title of PVC, with responsibilities for gender and science education. I was, regrettably, provided with *no funding*, so I really do not know how this was expected to fly. For the four years I held this post, I was singularly unsuccessful in making any meaningful contribution . . . except for overseeing the advertisement and appointment of the first professor and head of the unit, Professor Elsa Leo-Rhynie, meeting and greeting a few ISS representatives, and showing up at some meetings to say a few words on behalf of UWI. It is a testimony to the quality of the first professorial appointment, that the programme became institutionalized in due course (a commitment which the vice-chancellor had made to the ISS) despite a lack of support from either the campus administration or, indeed, of some academics who questioned the viability of a gender-based programme and were seemingly blinkered to the potential of such programmes in an academic setting. (Marlene Hamilton, testimonial)

The first task of the professor/regional coordinator was to establish the framework for an academic centre through which the work started by the WDSGs would be expanded and incorporated into the academy. Leo-Rhynie's (1992) agenda was made clear in her inaugural professorial lecture entitled "Women and Development Studies: Moving from the Periphery" and delivered in December 1992 as part of the symposium celebrating the tenth anniversary of the WDSGs. Acknowledging that several controversial issues surrounded this movement of women's studies into the mainstream of the academy, and wishing to both inform and engage support for the initiative, she highlighted three of these issues:

1. The multifaceted nature of WDS and the assumptions governing scholarship in this area;
2. The role of men in women's studies and the need for inclusiveness; and,
3. The justification for gender studies versus women's studies.

Discussion and resolution of these issues were pivotal in preparing the proposal for institutionalization, and determining the mission and objectives of the entity to be formed.

Obtaining Acceptance and Approval

It was important that the establishment of the centre be informed by a consensus of those who had worked to ensure its coming into being. A regional meeting of the coordinators of the WDSGs was held in April 1992 at the UWI Cave Hill campus in Barbados to consider and determine the structure and organization of the proposed new entity. The views of stakeholders differed markedly in terms of how to proceed, with some representatives arguing that a survey needed to be made of other women's studies programmes in universities overseas, as well as of the ISS, and use made of that experience to design the programme for UWI. Others felt that the WDSGs and the organizational arrangements made for the administration of the IOP/UWI/ISS project already provided the groups with a workable blueprint from which to design the centre. Also, any delay in establishing the centre could close the window of opportunity and reduce the limited support the initiative was already experiencing within the academy. There was much discussion and even heated disagreement in some instances, but eventually consensus was reached on the most important issues. A proposal was prepared and submitted to the UAC at its meeting on 27 November 1992. Unfortunately, the regional coordinator's lack of understanding of the hierarchy inherent in the university's committee structure resulted in the first rebuff from the administration and delayed consideration and approval of the proposal. The UAC's minute 84 from that November meeting stated: "UAC noted the proposal for a Centre for Gender Studies at the UWI and agreed to advise the regional coordinator that this was a matter which should be referred to the University Planning and Estimates Committee in the first instance." The value of having networks within the administration was clearly demonstrated when the senior assistant registrar, the late Hugh Moss-Solomon, who had prepared the UAC minutes and who was a friend of the WDSG administrative officer, Louraine Emmanuel, contacted her and offered to assist in framing the proposal in such a way as to make it acceptable for the UPEC and, subsequently, UAC. Moss-Solomon's advice and guidance were extremely valuable in this regard and enabled the initiative to successfully counter any pushback from the administration. He became an indispensable sounding board for most submissions from the WDSGs and CGDS to the administration, and a guide on the intricacies of the committee system which governed the university. He also coached the WDS representatives on the use of networks and lobbying within the committees to increase the possibility of having one's proposals accepted. Successfully moving from the periphery into the mainstream clearly required adoption and use of the tools of the mainstream to effectively manoeuvre within this environment.

Rowland (1982, 489) confirms that this experience is not unique to UWI. She points out that

> there is a political power structure which is different to that of the *official* political structure. To be able to work that system, you need to know how the structure of the institution works, who is on which committee, and which people are opponents and allies. It is the need to have a voice on important committees and to have access to information quickly which makes it mandatory for us to know the more subtle points of decision-making in the institution.

UPEC and UAC received, considered and agreed to recommend that the proposal be accepted. Minute 111 of the University Finance and General Purposes Committee meeting held on 6 May 1993 reports: "F&GPC received and noted F&GP P. 59 containing the recommendation to UAC and F&GPC for the establishment of the Centre for Gender Studies". Minute 112 reads: "F&GPC on the recommendation of UPEC and UAC agreed that the Centre for Gender Studies be established on the understanding that: (i) Financial details of the estimates for the Centre would be determined when the Triennial Estimates exercise was completed; (ii) The University would continue to seek grant funding for the Centre; and, (iii) The University would seek to determine how the shortfall in financial provision could be met."

The financial situation at the university was particularly precarious at this time, and the only expressed conditionalities were related to the financial support which the CGDS would require from the UWI. Initially, UWI's financial commitment to the centre's establishment was limited to salary and emoluments for the professor/regional coordinator. Minutes of a meeting of the

IOP/UWI/ISS Project Advisory Committee on 5 May 1992 at Cave Hill had indicated the necessity to have discussions with the vice-chancellor on this matter. Funding for the proposed centre was an urgent and ongoing concern: at a later meeting of the Project Advisory Committee on 10 December 1992, the regional coordinator reported that the Netherlands Government Ministry of Development Cooperation had agreed to extend phase 2 of the project to December 1995 to allow for the project activities to be completed, but the ministry indicated that financial support for staff and operating expenses for the RCU would not extend beyond September 1993, the date set for institutionalization.

Establishment of the centre had several implications for the WDSGs. Minute 82 of the Project Advisory Committee meeting on 28 June 1993 noted that these implications needed to be determined. They related particularly to the setting up of boards of studies on the three campuses, the relationship between full-time staff members and the WDSG campus coordinators, definition of terms of reference, and a mission statement, as well as a work plan of activities for the 1993/94 academic year. Minute 59 also noted that the effects of the change on the WDSGs' operations, particularly on staffing, budget and structure, needed to be examined prior to the implementation date for the centre.

One important area of change was the availability of WDSG members for teaching the courses already developed, approved and offered to students. The 30 per cent release time negotiated for WDSG coordinators and for lecturers who were assisting with the teaching of courses developed by the WDSGs was not always allowed, and, in instances where some release time was granted, institutionalization marked the end of such arrangements. A letter dated 28 September 1993 to the regional coordinator from the dean of the Faculty of Education at St Augustine underscores the nature of the problem. As the then university dean, the span of his responsibility and his statements pertained to all three campuses. The letter reads:

> We are pleased to cooperate with this field of study by recognizing the already established teaching activities of our current staff as part of their normal teaching load. However, you will appreciate that when we recruit staff, we do so for purposes which relate to the course offerings approved for our Faculty. Consequently, additional unregulated teaching commitments would not be in the best interests of our Faculty. We would therefore prefer that any involvement of our faculty members in teaching within the framework of GDS should be the subject of prior discussion with the heads of their departments and should have prior approval of the Faculty.

The view expressed here was a generally held one – in the few cases where the faculties had reduced the teaching load of lecturers who were associated with the WDSGs as coordinators or lecturers in gender courses, institutionalization meant that this teaching had to be regularized within the lecturer's workload and the framework of the university's administration. In light of institutionalization, consent for such involvement was not usually forthcoming. To their credit, a number of lecturers contributed voluntary "overtime" to keep the courses serviced.

Resource Constraints

In all instances, the physical location of the units was inadequate and makeshift. Establishment of the CGDS came at a time of financial stringency in the countries of the Caribbean, particularly Jamaica, where the RCU and Mona unit were located. Allocation of funds to this new area of scholarship was difficult, and the centre, from the outset, had to seek funding to supplement the limited provisions from the UWI budget. Housing the units was particularly problematic, as space had to be "donated" by faculties, often reluctantly, to accommodate the staff. The concept of "patronage" is used by Rowland (1982) to explain that women in academia rarely have direct access to resources and have to gain such access through "patrons". This patronage was extended to the various units of the CGDS by different entities; the Cave Hill and St Augustine units were provided with space by the then Faculty of Education and Faculty of Natural Sciences respectively, while, at Mona, the RCU was housed in offices assigned to the then ISER and the Faculty of Social Sciences. Two small offices adjacent to each other along a corridor in ISER housed the regional coordinator and the administrative officer. A cubicle in another section of the Faculty of Social Sciences provided the clerical assistant with a workspace. The Mona unit was allocated a small room in the Faculty of Arts and General Studies to house both the lecturer and the administrative assistant, Hilary Nicholson. On all three campuses, the allocated space also functioned as the secretariat for the WDSGs.

At Cave Hill, the CGDS occupied a room, which served as the lecturer's office, in the School of Education, Black Rock, some distance from the main campus, for one year, 1993–94. They were relocated to the main campus and occupied the top floor of the residence of the first campus principal, Hill House, from 1994 to 2003. There, the space provided consisted of three rooms, two upstairs and one downstairs, with a conference room downstairs shared with the maintenance department. Eudine Barriteau, professor, first head of CGDS Nita Barrow Unit (NBU) and now principal of the Cave Hill campus, recalls in her testimonial:

> The next issue was space. We first occupied an office in the School of Education at the Lazaretto site. I asked for basic supplies and office space. I remember the bursary sending someone to see if we had a kettle, desk and chairs, all resources that belonged to the School of Education. By 1994, there was a new secretary, Sharon Taylor, after Margaret Warner resigned, and an office space had been identified in the old principal's residence on the main campus. The CGDS was located there, 1994 to mid-2003. Even the initial occupancy was a challenge. Although the space had been promised, the actual move was not happening. One day, I got a call stating administration had planned to move a senior staff member from the School of Education into the assigned offices the following week and I should move fast. I remember the secretary and me loading files, boxes, plants into my car and occupying the two offices. I explained this to the less-than-welcoming response as assisting administration in making the move. The tip-off had come from a supervisor in Maintenance.

Space issues also plagued the St Augustine unit: "The WDSG/CGDS St Augustine was initially housed at the ISER. . . . Just around 1993/94, we identified space in the Department of Chemistry and were able to negotiate use of some space. I became head [of CGDS St Augustine unit] in 1993, and, after about three–four years, we managed to get an additional 12 feet of space from the Chemistry Department, then headed by Professor Dyer Narinesingh" (Rhoda Reddock, testimonial). The inadequate space and lack of up-to-date equipment such as computers made it difficult to function, underlining the marginal place the centre occupied in the university's priorities. Much time was spent trying to identify space on the campuses which could accommodate the offices of the CGDS. Despite the challenges and expressed scepticism of others in the university as to the value of the centre's work, however, staff members were motivated by their involvement in an initiative they were convinced was an important area of scholarship. This motivation was sustained by the building of networks and involvement of women from all three campuses in activities such as the two-week workshop "Management Training for University Women" held in Runaway Bay, Jamaica, in 1990. Grace Sirju-Charran (2013) recalls this memorable event (in conversations recorded at the IGDS twentieth-anniversary conference):

> We had to bond together, it was very intimate; we got to know each other very well over that two-week period, but it was very enriching as we found out about each other, supported each other; and it was such a wonderful experience that, when we came back, we decided to maintain that connection which we built during those two weeks, and we founded the Group under the Tree, and we would have weekly/monthly meetings where we kept abreast of each other and how we were coping within the university.

Non-financial but useful support for the establishment and work of the centre came in 1994, when the Frank Rampersad Report[2] commented on the WDS project which fell under the auspices of the vice chancellery. The report confirmed that the establishment, within the university, of units committed to WDS was consonant with the heightened international concern that women's status in society should be examined and the full mobilization of their creative abilities should be facilitated.

Visibility and promotion of women through initiatives to be undertaken by the UWI were recommended by the report, as follows:

- The acceleration of the institutionalization of WDS in the university
- The promotion of long-term research on gender issues in Caribbean development
- The expansion of course offerings in gender studies, including courses not designed for degree credit
- The enhancement of outreach activities in the field of gender studies and gender policy

These recommendations were all consistent with the mission of the CGDS, but the report did not identify any sources of funding which could hasten achievement of these goals.

Adoption/Institutionalization

The CGDS came into being in September 1993, at the start of the 1993/94 academic year. It was established as a teaching and research centre, operating at both undergraduate and graduate levels, and it also had a very strong outreach objective, which included working with the countries where there was no UWI campus and providing training through specialized courses. The centre consisted of four units: an RCU and three campus units. The RCU was staffed

Plate 5.1. Proudly displaying the CGDS banner for the first time: Louraine Emmanuel and Elsa Leo-Rhynie at a secondary school college fair in January 1994

by the professor/regional coordinator; an administrative officer, Louraine Emmanuel; and a clerical assistant, Pauline Thomas. Louraine Emmanuel had been assigned to work with Lucille Mathurin Mair as senior administrative assistant when Mathurin Mair became director of the IOP/UWI/ISS project in 1986, and she worked with Mathurin Mair's successors, Dorienne Wilson-Smillie and Hermione McKenzie.

In September 1993, Rhoda Reddock was appointed a senior lecturer in charge of the St Augustine unit, while Eudine Barriteau-Foster was the lecturer in charge of the Cave Hill unit. Patricia Mohammed assumed duties as lecturer in charge of the Mona unit in January 1994. These academic staff members served as head and sole academic of their units, with administrative and secretarial assistance being provided for each entity. Funds for the support of the campus units were the responsibility of the respective campuses and varied, depending on the resources available to each campus. Concern was expressed that, in some instances, the posts provided by the UWI resulted in "downgrading" of the status of existing posts; for example, Kathleen Drayton (1993) noted the "excellent organization and management skills" of her assistant, Margaret Warner, and her valuable contribution to the success of the disciplinary seminars held at Cave Hill between 1987 and 1993. She commented: "It is a crying shame that now that the ISS project has ended, the UWI should refuse to give her a contract with adequate job security and that it should plan to downgrade her post for 1994."

From the outset, each campus unit functioned differently from the others, and the regional coordinating unit had a specific role, particularly in relation to the implementation and management of the IOP/UWI/ISS project. The uniqueness of each unit enriched the work of the centre, while the cross-campus cooperation and collaboration, which began with the WDSGs, continued and ensured that all were working to satisfy the centre's mission and objectives.

Operationalizing the Decisions

The proposal for the establishment of the CGDS reflected a consensus of the views of the various stakeholder groups. There was considerable discussion and some disagreement over some of the issues. Minutes of the WDS Project Advisory Committee meeting on 28 June 1993, chaired by Marlene Hamilton, record that the regional coordinator communicated the decision of UPEC at its 6 May 1993 meeting to accept, in principle, the establishment of a centre for gender studies and that the steering committee had agreed that the centre should be named "The Centre for Gender and Development Studies" and that the name for the centre should be used with effect from 1 September 1993 (minute 58).

The contentious issue of the naming of the centre, described previously, persisted. There was strong feeling that the activist work that had led to recognition and acceptance of women's studies within the academy was focused on women, and that the radical feminist view of male exclusion should prevail. Gender was seen as more neutral, non-controversial and socially acceptable, hence not adequately capturing the political nature of studying the inequity in the power relationships between men and women in society, which was also blatantly reflected in the UWI governance structure. This view was countered by the argument that gender was a more complex and comprehensive concept, incorporating issues such as the relationships between and among women and men, in various private and public aspects of their lives. The intersection of these relationships with race and social class would also be an important element of the analysis.

The issue was addressed by Elsa Leo-Rhynie (1992) in her inaugural professorial lecture when she stated: "Our gender identities have been built through our membership and participation in domestic, educational, economic, cultural and community groups and/or institutions. . . . The ways in which differences based on power have evolved and been perpetuated in society must be considered, by examining the interrelationships of both groups as well as those factors which significantly affect these relationships" (Mohammed 2002, 157).

The use of "gender" rather than "women" also acknowledged and represented a conceptual shift in the international discourse away from the terms "women in development" and "women and development" to "gender and development" (Rathgeber 1990), as was being debated in the literature on development research and practice. Other writers also increasingly acknowledged the importance of adding men and men's issues to the debate; feminist author bell hooks (1989, 127), for example, noted that "reconstruction and transformation [of] behaviours of masculinity is a necessary and essential part of feminist revolution". Opposition to the use of "gender" came from other sources and for other reasons; Marlene Hamilton (testimonial) notes that "there was *great* reluctance from the then vice-chancellor (Sir Alister McIntyre) re the proposed name change – he felt he could garner funds for WAD but not for 'gender'. I think he was proved wrong." Differing views on this issue persist to the present.

The RCU was the original entity established by the RSC of the WDSGs to implement the IOP/UWI/ISS project and was headed by Elsa Leo-Rhynie, who, as regional coordinator, provided leadership in the transition from WDSGs operating on the periphery of the UWI to the institutionalized CGDS. The unit had regional management responsibilities and was attached administratively to the University Centre, with the regional coordinator reporting to the vice-chancellor and the university-wide administration. This arrangement has continued with both successive regional coordinators; the post is now designated university director.

The campus units came into being in September of 1993, and, although they worked closely with the RCU, they reported to their respective campus principals and administrations. CGDS was fortunate to have excellent faculty to take charge of what were single-person units; Eudine Barriteau-Foster at Cave Hill, Patricia Mohammed at Mona (who assumed duties in January 1994) and Rhoda Reddock at St Augustine. All three provided exceptional leadership: facilitating the teaching, research and outreach of the centre and building its reputation and acceptability within the academy. All three functioned under trying and frustrating working conditions; they faced challenges of proving the "academic respectability" of gender studies, of securing the physical and human resources needed to function effectively, of negotiating linkages with faculties and their colleagues to facilitate the infusion of gender studies into existing courses and programmes. All three have demonstrated their significant commitment and contribution to the work of GDS by earning promotion to the rank of professor. Barriteau and Reddock have served as deputy principals on the Cave Hill and St Augustine campuses respectively and, therefore, have been in positions to influence policy relating to the governance of the institution. The appointments, in 2014 and 2015, of Eudine Barriteau as PVC and principal of the Open Campus and Cave Hill campus, respectively, are hailed as major achievements and opportunities.

The mission and objectives would be as follows: the CGDS, UWI, is committed to a programme of teaching, research and outreach which questions historically accepted theories and explanations about society and human behaviour; seeks an understanding of the world which takes women, their lives and achievements into account; and critically examines origins of power differences between and among men and women, and the range of factors which perpetuate these differences. Gender and other related factors are used as tools of analysis in the generation and reconstruction of knowledge, which will inform the programme and act as a catalyst for change.

The specific objectives of the centre are as follows:

1. Develop an integrated, interdisciplinary programme of gender studies within the university, at both undergraduate and graduate levels. This includes facilitating the incorporation of gender analysis in all disciplines.
2. Produce and disseminate knowledge, based on the generation and analysis of research data on women, men and gender-related issues in the Caribbean.
3. Establish and maintain linkages with national, regional and international institutions concerned with gender and development, provide advisory services, influence policy directions and assist with capacity-building in these institutions.

The mission statement and objectives clearly identified the teaching, research and outreach intent of the centre. Although the original statement has been slightly modified over the years, the essential elements remain unchanged.

Autonomy as an interdisciplinary centre was a major priority in the establishment of the CGDS, and this was a hard-fought battle, as a successful outcome would make CGDS unique within the UWI. This autonomy, however, was considered vital in order to emphasize the relevance of gender to all disciplines and facilitate collaboration with all faculties. Bailey (2012, 8) comments:

> The politics of the integration process was subtle. The granting of "legitimate" power and access to high-status institutional mechanisms was not readily yielded. The then Faculty of Arts and General Studies, with its focus on "general studies", was seen by the power brokers as the logical space to locate the programme. This notion, however, was resisted as it was felt that situating the programme in any existing faculty, which, for the most part, was discipline-based, would prove to be constraining in terms of eventually developing full, interdisciplinary, undergraduate- and graduate-level offerings.
>
> The unwavering political stance of the innovators, however, paid off, and, in the final analysis, an autonomous Centre was established in 1993 outside of the existing University faculty structure.

The centre's autonomy has been frequently challenged, and, in 2003, ten years after its establishment, Leo-Rhynie (2003b, 15) noted:

> Attempts are made to include the Centre as part of one or other disciplinary area; the Centre is often omitted from mailing lists which contain information sent to faculties but also relevant to its activities; problems even arise in providing computer codes for courses offered by the Centre and which are not faculty-based. Although the UWI Strategic Plan 2002–2007 lists one of the core values of the institution as "cultivating multidisciplinary and interdisciplinary collaboration", none of the stated strategies addresses how this is to be achieved, and the difficulties involved in sustaining an independent interdisciplinary Centre within the UWI persist.

Integrating the IOP/UWI/ISS Project

An important element in the institutionalization was the inclusion of the IOP/UWI/ISS project and its administration within the ambit of the newly formed centre. Establishment of the CGDS took place midway through phase 2 of the project, which was scheduled to run from 1990 to 1994. The UWI and the WDSGs had set up an administrative structure which ensured that the required reporting on programme/project implementation and use of funds was effectively carried out. With institutionalization, a shift was made to recognize the new centre's involvement in and responsibility for the project, particularly as the post of administrative officer (serving both centre and project) and almost all of the activities of the CGDS were funded by the project.

The RCU of the CGDS, therefore, replaced the WDSGs as the implementation agent of the UWI for the project. Project activities continued to be monitored, with the project advisory committee being replaced by a regional advisory committee, which was responsible for policy and was chaired by the vice-chancellor's representative. Prior to institutionalization, Marlene Hamilton was the chair of the project advisory committee, and she continued to serve in that capacity for the regional advisory committee. The professor/regional coordinator became a member of this regional committee which met twice yearly using the facilities of the UWI Distance Education Centre, which allowed for cross-campus satellite linkup. Other members of the regional advisory committee were the heads of the campus units, three deans, a representative from the University of Guyana, and the tutor/coordinator of WAND. Joycelin Massiah was also a member prior to her resignation from the UWI in 1992 to head the UNIFEM (Caribbean) office in Barbados.

The functions of the regional advisory committee were to

- receive reports from the consultative committee;
- advise on matters relating to teaching, research and outreach;
- advise on administrative and institutional matters; and
- advise, for the life of the project, on implementation activities.

In addition to the regional advisory committee, there was a steering committee that met twice per year and was responsible for guiding the progress of the project; and a joint coordinating/consultative committee on which the ISS was represented and which met once per year. Rhoda Reddock, who had served as the ISS liaison since the project's inception, played a dual role on this committee and, by her own admission, found this to be challenging but very satisfying (Kaminjolo 1993).

Els Mulder (2003, 11) also commented on Reddock's contribution in this regard:

> We should also recognize the very important role Dr Rhoda Reddock played during the first project phase and part of the second project phase as ISS resident representative on the UWI campus, while being employed by UWI as a member of its staff, but with her salary etc. being paid for by the project. It was not easy at all, and sometimes even conflicting to have to function with two different hats and represent both project partners in an equal manner.

Much of the work of the newly established centre was focused on the activities scheduled for the project. The overall objective of the project was "To contribute to the process of improving the quality of life in Caribbean societies through the development of the human resource potential of the region in terms of education and training in the area of GDS." The objectives and activities were grouped into five areas:

1. Institutionalization: specifically, the establishment of the CGDS
2. Teaching activities: including curriculum development for new courses and programmes; coordination of teaching visits from the ISS and cross-campus exchanges; as well as promoting and making arrangements for the fellowship programme for faculty and students
3. Research: development of and fundraising for a regional research programme; arrangement and coordination of local and regional seminars; publication and dissemination of material from the phase 1 seminars; and administration of the small research grants
4. Outreach: development, offering, coordination and delivery of courses and preparation of distance-teaching materials for use in the non-campus territories; provision of consultancy services for WAND for the development of materials; and consultation with members of the West Indian Commission to ensure the consideration and inclusion of gender issues in its report
5. Consultancy: soliciting other projects and activities which would be self-supporting and so would provide resources for the use of the centre

These objectives and activities were scheduled for completion in 1995; the Government of the Netherlands approved a time extension from 1994 to facilitate this, but the activities actually extended into 1996.

The project benefited greatly from the close relationship with and administrative and technical support provided by the ISS. Elisabeth "Els" Mulder, senior project officer and head of the Project Management Unit of the ISS, visited in 1992, 1994 and 1995 to assess the progress of the project and to advise on financial reporting. Frank Suurs and Martin van Bunningen of the Netherlands Ministry of Development Cooperation also visited, in 1994 and 1995 respectively, and held evaluative discussions to gauge the extent to which the project was meeting its objectives.

An important aspect of the project was the financial reporting. The CGDS maintained its own accounts, but preparation of the official accounts and reporting to the Government of the Netherlands were handled by the Special Projects Office of the university. Jelf Williamson from this office in the UWI bursary worked closely with Louraine Emmanuel to ensure the timely preparation of these financial reports. This was a major challenge, given the UWI

Plate 5.2. Project reporting: (*left to right*) Barbara Bailey, Elsa Leo-Rhynie, the ambassador of the Government of the Netherlands, Marlene Hamilton

bureaucracy; the physical separation of the three campuses and the activities undertaken, and the need for integration of the financial reports from three bursaries, often resulted in tardiness in the financial reporting process. Both Louraine Emmanuel and Jelf Williamson benefited tremendously from the guidance of Els Mulder of the ISS, whose experience in the reporting required by the Government of the Netherlands informed the accounting documentation sent to the Netherlands from the project.

Without the project, and the financial and other support it provided, institutionalization could not have been realized. As Kathleen Drayton commented in a handwritten note in 1993: "The ISS Project . . . made a substantial contribution to UWI and to WDS through its support for staffing, infrastructure, activities and staff development over eight years". Barbara Bailey (quoted in UWI CGDS 1996, 59) was more explicit in her acknowledgement of the value of the project in sustaining the initiative:

> If we did not have the Project of Cooperation funded by the Dutch, we would have been nowhere near achieving what we have achieved at this point . . . there was very broad based support for Gender Studies within the university, but there was resistance within the hierarchy. We fought against this, and with the funding avail-

> able we were able to keep the programme alive . . . a lot of people feel threatened by the growth of Gender Studies as they perceive us as having a political agenda.

Determining the purpose and direction of the CGDS not only set the stage for the institutionalization of an already vibrant initiative, but also provided a workable framework for its incorporation as part of the mainstream of the UWI. Securing the autonomy of the centre satisfied one major criterion of the WDSGs, and the next chapter relates the methods used to meet other demands and expectations.

Notes

1. The late Louraine Emmanuel, in a letter to Barbara Bailey and Elsa Leo-Rhynie dated 13 September 2003, following the tenth-anniversary conference.
2. Frank Rampersad led a group commissioned by the UWI to explore, inter alia, the efficiency of the offices of the pro vice-chancellors in terms of their contribution to the achievement of the university's mandate. The report was submitted to the university council in 1994.

CHAPTER 6

THE SECOND ANGLE

Expectations and Support

> Pioneers like Peggy Antrobus, Joycelin Massiah . . . have been at the front line of a movement at a time when others were not necessarily there nor prepared to go there. And the sensitization process has resulted in the needed policy framework, which for the most part reflects the objectives of where we need to be. But there is a bridge that must still be built between that needed policy framework and the realities of the limp existence of many of our people in our societies. . . . Too often the stories abound of women who continue to have no options and no choices. Too often the question of gender is perceived simply as a new name for a woman's programme that includes men's problems, without understanding that the structural imbalance that continues to exist in our society takes us away from the goal of social justice that we have set ourselves.
>
> —*Mia Mottley, former deputy prime minister, Barbados, keynote address, CGDS Tenth Anniversary Conference, 2003*

FROM THE OUTSET, THE DEMANDS AND EXPECTATIONS TO satisfy the mission of the newly created CGDS and to achieve the goal of social justice came from a variety of sources and addressed a range of issues.

Establishing an Effective Working Relationship between the WDSGs, WAND and the CGDS

Management of the IOS/UWI/ISS project was only one of the functions of the WDSGs, and a major issue which arose at institutionalization was the role these groups would be expected to assume once the CGDS was established. The chair of the Mona WDSG in 1994, Barbara Bailey, noted in the report presented at the annual general meeting on 23 June 1994 that "the new structure had implications for the Group which needed to be further explored, such as how the group would relate to the formal structure [of the CGDS and the UWI] and keep alive its activist agenda". There was much discussion about the likelihood of abandonment, by the WDSGs, of their roots in women's struggles, given their acceptance, as CGDS, into academia. This generated some tension between the CGDS, which was now expected to contribute to the scholarship of the academy, and the WDSGs, which saw themselves as supporting the activism of the women's movement. The WDSGs pointed out that gender studies had its origins in the social and political ferment of the 1960s and 1970s, particularly the political activism of feminists, in which the concerns were with power and influence in the lives of women and their relationships with men, the family, the community, the workplace and the state. Loss of the sense of activism, once the CGDS was established, was considered to be a very real threat. The groups felt that they had accomplished their goal but had lost their cause.

Following institutionalization, however, the structure of the WDSGs remained intact, with each group headed by a campus coordinator. The focus was to keep alive the activist agenda of the original groups by continuing the organization and development of outreach programmes to promote gender equity in the university and the region. The campus coordinator for the Mona group, appointed in 1992, was Barbara Bailey of the Faculty of Education. Her counterparts were Maxine McClean of the Faculty of Social Sciences, Cave Hill, and Jeannette Morris of the Faculty of Education, St Augustine.

The groups debated their role in the new CGDS, and, at a meeting of CGDS staff in 1994 (30–31 May 1994), Trinidad group coordinator Jeannette Morris reported that the group had held a retreat and taken some decisions as to their direction following institutionalization. These included the following:

- The group has NGO status and had started up its own bank account for fund-raising.
- They had decided to keep the name Women and Development Studies Group.
- Their focus was outreach and advocacy within and outside of the university community. (Minute 2.2)

The group noted in that meeting that the coordinator of the groups should be voted from within the UWI community and that mission statements and constitutions being prepared for the groups should reflect commonalities but be flexible enough to accommodate the uniqueness of each group (minute 2.3).

At Mona, a meeting on 23 June 1994 to discuss future directions of the group yielded a number of proposals. Development of guidelines from this forum was the business of an extraordinary general meeting held on 22 September 1994. The outcome was as follows:

- The group's name was changed to University Women's Group.
- A nominal membership fee was introduced.
- Membership was extended to both on-campus and off-campus individuals.
- The constitution had been revised but was still in draft form. (University Women's Group Mona 1994)

At Cave Hill, the centre and the groups worked together, led by Eudine Barriteau, who had been recruited by the campus coordinator of the WDSG, Maxine McClean. A statement issued by the Cave Hill unit (quoted in UWI CGDS 1996, appendix 3, 1) reads as follows: "The Women and Development Studies Group remains an integral aspect of the Centre for Gender and Development Studies at the Cave Hill campus of the University of the West Indies. Given the historic precedence and continuing relationship of mutual support and cooperation, the Centre for Gender and Development Studies will continue to provide accommodation, administrative and financial support to facilitate the programme of activities of the WDS group."

Eudine Barriteau recalls in her testimonial:

> I could not believe my luck, on returning to Barbados in 1992, to learn from Maxine McClean [then campus coordinator of the WDS group] that the UWI had active plans to establish a centre for gender and development studies. As campus coordinator, Maxine had offered me the part-time temporary lecturer post of teaching two women studies courses. . . . However, I was more excited by the prospect of this new entity.
>
> I was first appointed a temporary lecturer in CGDS in August 1993. Two things struck me as urgent; the importance of establishing the presence of this new part of the university, and the negative feelings about gender studies on the campus. I was enthusiastic and overjoyed to be there. I felt the gods loved me to have aligned the stars to produce a job in a field that I was really very passionate about. My previous UWI Cave Hill experience stood me in good stead, since the wider atmosphere was less than welcoming. Members of the WDS group were very supportive, but

there was palpable restraint in senior administration, and I would say, while this dissipated after about five years, that guarded, careful interaction lasted for the first ten years of the CGDS's life.

Immediately, I set about creating visibility for the unit by writing to key persons internally and externally and introducing myself and the CGDS to that community. I also tried to get basic procedures integrated into UWI operations. I remember having a little tussle with Margaret Warner to get her to stop going to the post office to buy stamps, post correspondence and collect mail, by insisting that CGDS was now part of UWI, they created it, and, whether they liked it or not, they were going to get it. That meant the mail vans had to collect and drop off our mail like any other department. She was a key staff member on the WDS/ISS project. I think she [was concerned by] my insistence on the need to make the transition to full UWI status and recognition . . .

I set about splitting the existing course into two, and, with persistent lobbying by the 1992/93 classes of students, successfully got the campus (with excellent support from the women and men who were stalwarts of the WDS) to offer the courses for credits. The courses could then be taken as university courses – that is, not for credit or as Faculty of Arts and General Studies courses, but for credit.

The groups have remained somewhat active over the years and, in the period immediately following institutionalization, led several initiatives, working collaboratively with the CGDS units to sustain the activist programme of the WDSGs. Some members of the WDSGs, including Carolyn Cooper (professor and former WDSG coordinator, UWI Mona), contend that the activist thrust of the groups was lost in the institutionalization process and that women, especially women within the UWI, have not benefited from the existence of the centre (now institute):

After three decades, women at UWI are no closer to gender equity than we were before we established the women's studies working groups in the 1980s. Men still "run tings" at UWI. All of our postures of empowerment and all of the rhetoric of transformation mean absolutely nothing. We are impotent. As textbook feminists, we have failed to mobilize in any effective way to ensure that women are trained to assume positions of leadership at UWI. At other institutions, women with leadership potential are identified and groomed. They are given opportunities to develop high-level skills through specialist courses, for example. At UWI, female "power" is highly individualistic and circulates within a very narrow ambit of influence. Our modus operandi is not collectivist. As I've long contended, the institutionalization of the Gender and Development Studies academic programme ought to have

> enabled the sustaining of an activist agenda focused on empowering women as a group. This did not happen. (Carolyn Cooper, testimonial)

The St Augustine campus unit, acknowledging the importance of activism and outreach in gender and development, was able, eventually, to have a post of outreach officer institutionalized to ensure that the unit's activist work in the community was part of the official programme of the centre.

Establishing Acceptable Administration and Governance Procedures

Institutionalization of the interdisciplinary programme of GDS required conformity to the disciplinary demand of structure, organization and administration. It also required acknowledgement and acceptance of the importance of integration of concepts across disciplinary boundaries, which require teaching, research collaboration and partnership. Since the CGDS was not to be attached to any faculty, it was important that an appropriate model be designed for the CGDS and its management to allow for the approval, offering and administration of courses and programmes. The model in use by faculties was inappropriate for meeting the centre's objectives, but its essential ingredients had to be considered and included in whatever arrangements were proposed. The flow chart titled "Consultative Process for Academic Approval of Gender Studies Undergraduate and Graduate Courses and Programmes" (see appendix 5) was developed and approved by the UAC at its meeting in May 1993 for the routing of new courses developed in a faculty and for new interdisciplinary courses and programmes developed in the centre.

Regular reporting on academic and non-academic activities of CGDS faculty members was achieved through the formation of boards of studies on each campus: these are equivalent to faculty boards and are chaired by the heads of the campus units. The boards address academic matters related to undergraduate and graduate students and programmes and direct their opinions and recommendations to the appropriate campus committees. Membership of the boards of studies included the staff of the unit(s) as well as representatives from all faculties, the library, the student body and the women's studies/university women's groups. Representation on the boards reflects the centre's concerns with multidisciplinary knowledge in its broadest sense. The boards of studies were, and continue to be, responsible for

- receiving, reviewing and making recommendations for approval of new courses and programmes;
- receiving, noting and making recommendations on reports from faculties, campus and university committees, as well as identifying implications for CGDS in these reports; and
- disseminating reports on the activities of CGDS to faculties, campus and university committees.

On each campus, the senior lecturer, or lecturer heading the campus unit, was expected to represent the CGDS on the campus academic board and the Campus Planning and Estimates Committee (now F&GPC), as well as faculty and other campus-based boards and committees. The regional coordinator/university director was, and remains, an ex officio member of the CGDS's three boards of studies, of the Mona academic board and of the board of the Faculty of Humanities and Education at Mona. Operating outside the established faculty structure, however, allowed the CGDS units to be overlooked when notices of meetings were distributed. The campus representatives had to be vigilant in monitoring meeting dates and calling the registry offices to ensure receipt of invitations and papers in a timely manner. Omissions were not noted and corrected after one or two occurrences but continued over a period of years, and it was difficult not to draw the conclusion that the "oversight" was deliberate.

The CGDS was challenged at every step. Difficulty in setting up boards of studies was reported; in the minutes of a CGDS meeting held on 13 November 1993 (via the university's distance teaching arm, UWIDITE), it was noted that the campus registrar at Mona, for example, was written to, asking that he schedule and service the meetings. He appeared to have little knowledge of the CGDS and the arrangement for boards of studies, despite the fact that this had been approved at all levels of the university bureaucracy.

There was no precedent for this new board, and the suggestion was made by the campus registrar at Cave Hill that the administrative assistants could service the boards. This suggestion was neither acceptable nor accepted. Campus unit heads were advised that the CGDS needed to ensure that all procedures started off on the proper footing; as institutionalized units, it was the responsibility of the registry to schedule and provide the secretarial support for the boards, as it did for all faculty boards.

> Elsa was also instrumental in getting the campus to recognize and stage the first Board of Studies meeting. After many attempts to do so on my part, with admin-

> istration being less than facilitating, Elsa wrote the then principal and registrar and informed them she would be on the campus at a certain date, and, while there, would chair the inaugural board meeting. This was done, and, after that, they happened routinely. (Eudine Barriteau, testimonial)

Inaugural boards of studies meetings took place in early 1994, and the minutes of those meetings were expected to be tabled at the respective campus academic boards. This arrangement should have established a clear communication channel for issues from CGDS to the established university governance structure. This did not happen for several years after the establishment of the CGDS, despite reminders, protests and appeals. Courses were approved through the "patronage" of the faculties of social sciences, humanities and education until 2009, when the centre was given degree-granting status. The boards of studies persist.

Academic Programming and Delivery

Course Development

There was a growing demand for courses in gender and development, but the limited resources of the departments through which they were offered placed a ceiling on the number of persons registered in the offerings of the CGDS, and existing resources did not permit additional offerings. The CGDS did, however, collaborate with faculties and departments of the university in the development and teaching of other courses.

The report of the professor/regional coordinator for January to June 1993 includes the following comments on teaching/curriculum development:

> At Mona and Cave Hill, interdisciplinary teaching has continued, mainly of students in Years 2 and 3. Two new courses were developed at St Augustine, whose curriculum subcommittee continues to meet to discuss the development of additional teaching material for the coming academic year.
>
> However, no teaching was done this year at St Augustine, and staff at Mona have been finding it increasingly difficult to continue teaching with the resources available to them. WDS has submitted a number of courses which have been approved by the academic board but which cannot be taught because of staffing and coordinating difficulties.

Hermione McKenzie (2004, 409–11) recalls that individuals developed and offered courses in their respective disciplines:

Many of the first courses introduced were postgraduate courses such as The Image of the Female in Literature, in the (then) Department of English; French Caribbean Women Writers and the Novel Form, in the (then) Department of French; and perhaps the first gender course, Gender Roles in Education, introduced by Professor Marlene Hamilton in the School of Education.

But undergraduate courses also took hold. Pioneers like Dr Elizabeth "Betty" Wilson in what was then the Department of French – developed her own course, Francophone Women Writers: Perspectives on Women's Issues in Literature; Dr Claudette Williams in the then Department of Spanish – presented Women Writers of the Spanish Caribbean and later added another course, Spanish American Women's Narrative; Professor Carolyn Cooper – developed African/Diaspora Women's Narrative and later added African American Women's Writing . . .

My own long-standing commitment to the issues of development, the need to situate gender issues within the context of development and underdevelopment, led me to design a two-semester course, Gender and Development in Caribbean Society . . .

In addition to all the above-named gender courses, many lecturers also introduced gender modules or components into other existing courses. Later, the Centre

Plate 6.1. Hermione McKenzie being honoured for her involvement in the UWI gender journey as a senior researcher in the WICP, as group coordinator and active member of the WDSG, Mona, and as acting regional coordinator, IOP/UWI/ISS project, 1991–1992 (Barbara Bailey makes the presentation)

for Gender and Development Studies further added a course entitled Sex, Gender and Society to the Social Sciences curriculum.

Several courses explicitly addressing gender were being taught across the campuses, and, in addition, courses in several disciplines included modules on gender, or they integrated gender in teaching throughout their courses.

Achieving Interdisciplinary Learning

Academic challenges also arose in relation to the recognition of the importance of team-teaching, cross-listing of courses, cross-campus teaching, seeking and obtaining agreement for joint appointments to the CGDS as well as to a disciplinary area, and the designation and listing of lecturers who work in gender, from a disciplinary perspective, as "associate lecturers". These strategies were aggressively pursued in order to ensure both the interdisciplinary thrust and the maintenance of the centre's autonomy, but without much success. A long battle was fought to finally get the only joint cross-faculty appointment approved in the CGDS and the Faculty of Humanities and Education for Paula Morgan at St Augustine.

One of the exciting elements of the gender journey was the opportunity for synergy among academics and across disciplines. Among the members of the WDS groups were sociologists, educators, linguists, historians, psychologists, scientists, doctors, lawyers and economists. All brought their particular knowledge and learning styles to an interpretation and understanding of the knowledge generated in feminist literature. Bridget Brereton notes (in conversations recorded at the IGDS twentieth-anniversary conference), that the "tiny group" created on the St Augustine campus by pioneer Marjorie Thorpe set about educating themselves, by way of seminars and discussions about gender, before attempting to educate anyone else on the campus. She recalls:

> What I came to recognize was that my early fascination with class and race and how they intersected had been missing a crucial analytical component and so I recognized that gender – not always as obviously critical as ethnicity and class, but sometimes – was the third leg of the trinity of analytical tools that we have to use when we are trying to understand social history. So I would like to hope that my work since the early 1990s has had a clear gender perspective.

As Leo-Rhynie (2003b, 5) commented in the Tenth Anniversary Lecture of CGDS delivered at St Augustine:

> All became interdisciplinary learners. This was essential so that they could grasp concepts, and be properly analytical and, where necessary, critical about the material which was now part of their area of scholarship. This learning forced scholars to question certain disciplinary concepts and boundaries, to redefine traditional categories of analysis and also rethink existing paradigms which had strong disciplinary bases. Given the broad concerns of persons working in the area, the limitations of existing methods of enquiry became evident, as did the need for new research methodologies to fully explore dimensions of power and influence which cross gender, race and social class lines.

Gender is only one area of interdisciplinary study requiring integration of knowledge and concepts across the compartments in which they have traditionally resided as disciplines, but it is unique in that it challenges power relationships and hierarchies, including those within the academy. This challenge has resulted in it being treated with suspicion.

> It has always been my regret that, with the introduction of the IGDS, the continued work with the faculties in the development of disciplinary and interdisciplinary knowledge in collaboration with the CGDS/IGDS did not continue in the same way on all campuses. At St Augustine, in the first ten years, when there was only one full-time senior lecturer and even after that, I depended heavily on the IGDS members. They were affiliates of the IGDS, they taught gender-related courses in their various faculties/departments and were invited members of the Board of Studies. This contributed greatly to the multidisciplinary offerings that became available at St Augustine; I am not sure whether this commitment and collaboration has continued in the same way. As a result, St Augustine introduced courses in Agriculture and Science and also carried out important research and publications in the area of environment and natural resource use. (Rhoda Reddock, testimonial)

Interdisciplinarity made imperative a curriculum design and development process which would ensure that the necessary integration took place, and curriculum development committees developed and reviewed courses across campus units. The intent was to achieve interaction and integration of knowledge across as well as within disciplines and also to involve students in a process of relating their learning experiences to their lives and coming to grips with the interrelatedness of their disciplinary learning. Expertise in this regard was provided through seminars led by visiting lecturers from the ISS and ongoing attention to this requirement achieved through teaching exchanges from lecturers versed in interdisciplinary teaching on the three campuses. Inter-campus teaching was facilitated by the IOP/UWI/ISS project and allowed for university-wide sharing of expertise. Inter-campus and interdepartmental teaching also served to increase awareness of the new programme, and, fortunately, the IOP/UWI/ISS project allowed for frequent faculty exchanges across campuses and departments.

Opportunities for integrating gender into new and existing courses were seized upon. One opportunity which was used by faculty of the CGDS as well as WDSG members to encourage and support interest in learning about gender was through supervision of Caribbean studies among final-year students in the then Faculty of Arts and General Studies. Successful completion of these research studies was a requirement for graduation, and several students opted to examine issues directly focused on gender, while others enriched their studies by incorporating gender in their research design and investigations.

Pedagogy

Traditional teacher-centred pedagogy had to be critically examined and changed. The objectives set, the teaching methods employed and the methods of assessment used had to reflect a feminist pedagogy, with students' opinions, their criticisms and their questioning of the teachers' views taken into account. This facilitated development of the cognitive skills of analysis and evaluation which would allow students to interrogate traditional practices and inequities and seek new methods of approaching issues and finding solutions to problems.

Of particular importance was the use of personal experience to enhance teaching and learning, allowing students to appreciate the collective nature of the learning process and the different perspectives from which a problem or an issue can be viewed and approached. The reflexive process, the change from an authoritarian teaching style and the practice of sharing their experiences and arguments were intimidating at first for some learners, but eventually proved to be both stimulating and liberating.

New courses developed, reviewed and taught by faculty associated with the CGDS consciously sought to address both the interdisciplinary and the pedagogical demands and attracted students from most faculties. At the same time, traditional disciplines gradually adapted to accommodate progressive thinking and educational practices. Many have had to become more interdisciplinary in their approach, and gender has become a component of many courses and is even completely integrated, in some instances, as in the case of the humanities and the social sciences. Pedagogical practices, generally, have changed from the traditional, teacher-centred approach to a more learner-centred focus, which is strongly promoted by the Centre of Excellence in Teaching and Learning (formerly Instructional Development Unit) operating on each campus. Thus, the work of gender studies has exerted a significant impact on the rethinking and transformation of disciplinary discourse, its pedagogy, as well as its research methodology. Grace Sirju-Charran explains the pedagogical shift (in conversations recorded at the IGDS twentieth-anniversary conference):

> Gender and Science was path-breaking; it wasn't easy, was not appreciated by my male colleagues – not sure if they understood what it was all about – but it got passed by the academic board, and I began teaching it. . . . I got really good feedback from students, it allowed me to change my pedagogy; I could now open up with students and teach them more than what was in the book. We had discussions, debates, journal writing. The students really appreciated it; they had a voice in the classroom, which they tend not to have in science. So for me, it was a to-ing and fro-ing teaching science and gender.

Research and Publications

The impetus for the establishment of the WDS groups was the WICP and the substantial data produced from innovative research methodology. From the outset, therefore, research was critical in ensuring that material generated from up-to-date, rigorous enquiry and investigation was available to inform teaching in the courses being developed in the centre as well as in the different faculties. The seminars, made possible through the IOP/UWI/ISS project between 1986 and 1994, and described in chapter 4, yielded papers covering a range of topics and using a variety of research methodologies. This evidence of interest in the initiative to explore the historical and contemporary status of women and to contemplate the societal gender systems which governed the status of women and men was gratifying, as it provided validation of the work being undertaken.

The seminars, which were an integral part of the IOP/UWI/ISS project and which were a strategy used to inform academics from all faculties of the importance of gender in every area of scholarship and to involve them as much as possible, achieved this goal admirably. Two final seminars were held following institutionalization and were sponsored by the centre, in association with disciplinary entities. The seminar with the theme "Engendering History: Current Directions in the Study of Women and Gender in Caribbean History", held in November 1993, was co-sponsored by the Mona WDSG and the Department of History. This collaboration extended to a publication edited by Verene Shepherd, Bridget Brereton and Barbara Bailey. Collaboration with the Faculty of Natural Sciences resulted in the Gender, Science and Technology seminar held in February 1994. A preliminary workshop on gender and science was organized by Grace Sirju-Charran from St Augustine, and this set the stage for the seminar. Publication of the papers of this seminar in a volume entitled *Readings in Gender, Science and Technology* and edited by WDSG members Barbara Carby and Vilma McClenan was made possible through funding support from the Canadian High Commission and the Commonwealth Fund for Technical Cooperation. In January 1996, a conference with the theme "The Construction of Caribbean Masculinity: Towards a Research Agenda" was staged at St Augustine and was partially funded by the project.

The research reported at these seminars was fresh and new, and the sharing and collaboration involved in the development and staging of the seminars, and the networks which developed as a result, enhanced the work of each participant and, in turn, the work of the various disciplines. Academics who hitherto had not thought of gender as a field of enquiry now found it a fertile source of new information and research prospects.

> I recall the way in which I was drafted into the work of WAND and the WDS from the moment I joined the staff of the Department of History (as it was then). I recall my admiration for the work of Linnette Vassell, an early advocate for gender mainstreaming in the history curriculum, and the struggles we encountered in the department as we tried to support the WDSG in its mission and vision, project our own academic interest and infuse courses in the department with gender analysis. One senior academic even warned us that we should not become too involved in "this gender thing" because it was "like a ghetto area" that would not take us far in the academy. I have often wondered what he thinks now! Now, there are few departments at the UWI which have no consciousness of gender in their teaching and courses. Of course, without a "Gender 101"–type foundation course that introduces the entire population to the fundamentals of gender analysis, gender equity, equality and justice, the "gender project" will remain unfinished, and the UWI will continue to graduate students who have no awareness or understanding of the roots of gender-based violence and sexism. (Verene Shepherd, testimonial)

Following the concluding seminar of the project in 1994, a volume entitled *Gender: A Caribbean Multidisciplinary Perspective* was edited by Elsa Leo-Rhynie, Barbara Bailey and Christine Barrow. Published in 1997, it comprised a selection of papers from the interdisciplinary and disciplinary seminars and so joined *Gender in Caribbean Development*, edited by Pat Mohammed and Catherine Shepherd, as an additional source of material on theory and methodology as well as reports on innovative and interesting research from a range of disciplines. Partial funding for the publication of this volume was provided by the Commonwealth of Learning.

A fairly comprehensive research programme, drafted and designed with the overall theme "Gender in Caribbean Thought: Breaching Frontiers and Understanding Difference", was expected to serve as a framework for the research work of the new CGDS. It was reviewed at the 30–31 May 1994 meeting of CGDS staff and accepted with the understanding that funds would have to be sought to ensure that the research activities and outputs were realized. Six themes were identified, as follows (minute 7. 3):

Theme 1: A historical sociology of gender relations in Caribbean society

Theme 2: Gender and popular culture in the Caribbean

Theme 3: The construction of Caribbean masculinity

Theme 4: Feminist instincts of a new generation: Gender relations among the young people of the Caribbean

Theme 5: Gender, science and technology: The collaboration of nature and culture in the development of the Caribbean

Theme 6: Rethinking Caribbean economy

These themes were to serve as a guide to priority areas for research, and different units assumed responsibility for particular themes. The St Augustine unit, for example, has pursued theme 3 with great success. The 1996 conference on that campus – The Construction of Caribbean Masculinity: Towards a Research Agenda – yielded papers which have informed both the course Men and Masculinities in the Caribbean, taught on that campus, and the UWI Press publication in 2004 edited by Rhoda Reddock and entitled *Interrogating Caribbean Masculinities: Theoretical and Empirical Analyses.*

The RCU received some funding from the Ford Foundation, but this only allowed for some preliminary work to be done on theme 4. The lack of funding was a major limiting factor in the pursuit of the research programme, and, in some instances, individual interest resulted in research being undertaken in other directions.

The Cave Hill campus unit (later renamed the NBU) has focused on researching the lives of Caribbean women who, like Dame Nita Barrow, have been catalysts for change in the Caribbean. The project Caribbean Women: Catalysts for Change was partially funded by UNIFEM Caribbean. Eudine Barriteau has concentrated several of her research initiatives in this area as well as in examining women and economics.

On the Mona campus, significant work on gender and educational participation and achievement was initiated by Barbara Bailey, and this has yielded several publications. Gender and family was the central focus of researcher Patricia Anderson, while Wilma Bailey concentrated mainly on women and health. An interesting gender initiative spearheaded by the late Barry Chevannes (a member of the Mona WDSG) was the formation of a group, Fathers Inc., which involved public education among inner-city fathers to increase their sense of parental responsibility and involvement in the caring and rearing of their children.

The IOP/UWI/ISS project also provided opportunities for researchers who wanted to work with WAND on its community-oriented research. WAND produced and circulated regular research reports on Issues Concerning Women and Development, which covered a range of topics in education, health and social concerns. Following the retirement of Peggy Antrobus in 1995, collaboration between CGDS and WAND continued, but along slightly different lines, and the revised WAND agenda, coupled with a reduction in funding, gradually resulted in a loosening of the CGDS/WAND link.

Senior staff fellowships were another feature of the project, and these permitted scholars from UWI to spend time at the ISS consulting with colleagues and conducting research using the resources of the ISS. While there, they also led seminars attended by students and staff members at the ISS. A number of students also benefited from the student fellowships offered by the project, which allowed them to visit the ISS, attend lectures and interact with other students and lecturers, and also make use of the library resources for their research. Research grants from phase 2 of the IOP/UWI/ISS project also facilitated the small-scale research activity of scholars.

In 1995, CGDS was strongly represented at the annual Caribbean Studies Association conference in Curaçao, where the centre was responsible for two panels: Gender and Socialization (panellists: Elsa Leo-Rhynie, Barbara

Bailey and Odette Parry), and New Frontiers in Feminist/Gender Theory: A Caribbean Proposal (panellists: Eudine Barriteau-Foster, Rhoda Reddock and Pat Mohammed).

One output from the IOP/UWI/ISS project which proved to be extremely valuable was bibliographies compiled by librarians on the three campuses. These included *Women in Agriculture in Developing Countries, 1985–1990* by Lutishoor Salisbury and Sharon Soodeen-Karamath in 1990; *Women in Science and Technology* by Lutishoor Salisbury in 1993 (updated in 1996); *Women and the Law: An International Bibliographical Survey of Legal and Quasi Legal Materials with Special Reference to the Caribbean Area and Including Relevant Commonwealth Caribbean Legislation* by Joan Brathwaite in 1993; and *Women and Health* by Tereza Richards in 1992. Another bibliography developed for WAND, entitled *Towards Total Wellness: Women in the Caribbean: A Selected Bibliography of Periodical Articles in WAND's Documentation Centre* was compiled and edited by Sue Adams in 1994. These bibliographies were not only valuable resources for researchers; they also resulted in an increased awareness, in librarians, of the gender literature and improved their ability to advise students and faculty seeking assistance with their reading and research.

Findings from the significant research activity fed, naturally, into the teaching carried out by each of the campus units and into the curriculum design and development process involved in the preparation of new undergraduate and graduate courses.

Fundraising for research activities constituted a major portion of the work of the centre, and the four units have raised between them a considerable amount of money for research and outreach activities. Major financial support came from the IOP/UWI/ISS project, but other partners, such as UNIFEM (New York and Caribbean) and the Ford Foundation, also contributed significantly to the work of the centre.

Outreach

It was in the area of outreach that the interaction between the activities of the CGDS and the WDSGs was the greatest. The CGDS was committed to reaching beyond the boundaries of the academy to the various stakeholders, in spreading the theoretical and interdisciplinary message of gender to agencies and organizations regionally. The offering of the summer certificate in GDS, organized by a steering committee of the Mona WDSG and funded by the IOP/UWI/ISS,

Plate 6.2. Participants in the Summer Certificate programme at Cave Hill: with Patricia Mohammed (*extreme left, front row*) and Eudine Barriteau (*second from right, front row*)

was initially included among the list of summer courses of the UWI School of Continuing Studies in 1992. In 1994, the programme benefited from funding provided by the British Development Division, the Commonwealth Fund for Technical Cooperation and UNIFEM (Caribbean). Thirty-three participants from the anglophone Caribbean were registered for the specially designed twelve-week programme, which included residence on the Cave Hill campus and fieldwork in their home countries.

Several participants have testified to the very positive impact of this programme on their lives – both personal and professional. Rose Ann Richards, now an attorney-at-law, recalls:

> In 1994, I was awarded a scholarship to pursue the GDS course at the CGDS at the UWI Cave Hill campus . . .
>
> My interest in gender as a discipline grew and continues to grow. . . . I have been able to apply some of the knowledge which I acquired to several programmes that I have been involved in. . . . I also became a member of CAFRA and was involved in the facilitation of the programmes which provided training in domestic violence for police officers, social workers, etc. Not only was I a facilitator of such training

> in Barbados, but also in the British Virgin Islands, where I lived and worked for five years. . . . I returned to Barbados from the British Virgin Islands in 2005 to pursue a degree in law. As part of my degree programme, I took the Gender and Law course, which I found to be a further inspiration to my gender journey. . . . I have also taught on the now summer certificate course in GDS at the NBU in 2009 and 2011.
>
> I am now a practising attorney, and I have continued to use all my knowledge and expertise in gender to the benefit of my clients. Having been exposed to gender as an academic course, I feel more empowered to advocate for the rights of the oppressed and voiceless. This empowerment has been influential in my membership of a group called Conscious Exchanges, which has coordinated and facilitated two seminars/workshops for women. The founding members of this group are Diane Cummins, Margaret Gill, Juliette Maughan, Sandra Richards, Joy Workman and me.
>
> I endeavour to continue to use this discipline in my personal life, and my professional and voluntaristic service. I hope not only to change but influence law and policy to the benefit of society. (Ann Richards, testimonial)

The impact of these courses has been different for each participant, but all consider the experience of being involved to have been positive and influential.

A similar impact was noted for the Gender in Policy and Planning course, which also involved curriculum design and development carried out within the centre by Gwendoline Williams and Sonja Harris. The programme was offered on both the Mona and St Augustine campuses and has been of benefit to many policymakers. The offering at St Augustine in 1995 attracted twenty-five government policymakers and planners, as well as staff of private sector companies and NGOs from Trinidad and Tobago, Barbados, Suriname, St Vincent and the Grenadines, and Belize. The second course was held in Jamaica in 1996, when supplementary funding was provided by the Commonwealth Secretariat.

The WDSGs, in their drive to disseminate information, prepared and distributed working papers, occasional papers, monographs and a quarterly newsletter. The newsletter was produced on the Mona campus, edited by a WDSG member, Tereza Richards, and, supported by the IOP/UWI/ISS project funds, had a distribution of approximately five hundred copies per edition. It served as a useful networking tool for the Mona WDSG.

> The *UWI Women and Development Studies (Mona Group) Newsletter* was published between 1988 and 1997. The first coordinator was Leona Bobb-Semple of the UWI library, and she was later joined by Tereza Richards, also of the UWI library, as a joint coordinator, who later became sole coordinator until the production of the newsletter became a function of the then administrator of the WDSG office, Hilary

> Nicholson. Tereza continued contributing to the newsletter by submission of reports on events attended and through two regular sections in the newsletter – Booknotes (reviews of select books) and Resources (highlighting books and journals on gender issues in the library's collection) . . .
>
> The newsletter, for the duration of its existence, therefore, utilized a participatory model, as all members were invited and encouraged to submit articles for publication. (Tereza Richards, testimonial)

The WDSGs acted as a catalyst and actively promoted a number of initiatives designed to improve women's lives. On the Mona campus, for example, a homework centre to benefit the children of staff on the campus was established.

Alafia Samuels and Hermione McKenzie, who had both served as coordinators of the WDSG on the Mona campus, were the pioneers in the establishment, in 1992, of the AWOJA, an umbrella group, which, by 1999 boasted a membership of thirty women's groups and an equal number of individual members.

One outreach project which has survived for almost all twenty years of the University Women's Group, Mona, is the homework centre. The presence of schoolchildren on the UWI Mona campus, who were waiting for their parents – mostly mothers – to transport them home after work, and the disruption sometimes caused by their presence in offices and on the grounds led to the development, by the WDS group, of a homework centre, where volunteers supervised their homework and otherwise engaged the children. The homework centre was established on 27 February 1995 with seed money from the UWI, in the Chancellor Hall Dining Room, with thirty children under the management of Pauline Taylor. This venue proved to be inconvenient, and an alternative location was offered by the Student Services Manager of the Hall. Eventually a building, Bungalow W, situated between Mary Seacole Hall and the Health Centre and which had housed the caretaker for Mary Seacole Hall, was converted for use as the homework centre. A small fee is charged so that the children can get a snack and so that some resources can be provided for them to engage in art or craft once homework is completed. The university makes a small annual contribution to the centre. Eulalee Singh served as manager of the homework centre for several years.

Alafia Samuels, medical practitioner and former WDSG coordinator, recalls in her testimonial:

> I was seconded from the Ministry of Health to the Faculty of Medical Sciences, 1984–88, and joined the WDS group, which included Joycelin Massiah, Carolyn Cooper, Rhoda Reddock, Elsa Leo-Rhynie, Hermione McKenzie, Barbara Bailey and many others. In our discussions, we decided that we should involve a wider cross section of women and decided to sponsor the formation of an umbrella women's organization for Jamaica.
>
> The inaugural meeting was held at the Philip Sherlock Centre for the Creative Arts and the room was full. We collectively agreed on the membership, vision, methods of work and name. Full voting membership was reserved for organizations only. Individuals could be members but did not have a vote.
>
> Several names were suggested, including Combined Organizations of Women, which name was soundly rejected. We settled on Association of Women's Organisations; then came the suggestion to add Jamaica (JA), so we all agreed – AWOJA.
>
> We were very successful. A vast array of women's organizations from all levels of society joined and participated – for example, Sistren Theatre Collective, Jamaica Household Workers Association, Woman Inc., Jamaica Labour Party women, People's National Party women, Women's Resource and Outreach Centre, Soroptomists, Women's Construction Collective, Nurses Association of Jamaica and many others. We had high visibility in the media and in society. The highlight of my tenure was leading a delegation to Jamaica House for an audience with the then prime minister Michael Manley.
>
> One notable episode was when the leader of one of the two main political parties, at a public meeting, made some very derogatory comments about women, comparing some event to "women lying down open . . .". The next morning, the first person to call was the leader of that party's women's movement to complain about her leader's statement and to ask AWOJA to respond, since she did not feel able to directly criticize her own leader. Others also complained and we issued a press release; we went on talk shows and, on behalf of all women, criticized the language used.
>
> Noted radio commentator the late Wilmot "Mutty" Perkins called us several times, challenging the unity we portrayed. "How can you speak for all the women? Have you asked them all their opinion?" My response: "I confidently speak for all women in rejecting violence against women and children, domestic abuse and rape."
>
> There were disputes within the organization. For example, should we only focus on woman as "victim" or should we also be self-critical. I felt that, to be honest

> and credible, we had to address women's strengths and their weaknesses, and, in one statement, the final paragraph criticized women who knowingly give a man a "jacket" (allowing him to claim and support a child which is not his). A few women thought that the leader of the women's movement has no business criticizing women and that we should only concentrate on building women up, not on addressing their failings. So we agreed to disagree on that point, but, since the organization operated on consensus, those issues were not raised again.
>
> I believe that my biggest contribution was that the organization continued long after I demitted office, and, up to the present, Hermione McKenzie is president. I believe that the continued success was due in part to the vision that we created and our open methods of work, which allowed the member organizations to continue to support and participate.

The Jamaica Women's Political Caucus was launched to mark International Women's Day 1992 and was a prelude to the All-Island Women's Conference in Jamaica held from 10 to 12 April of that year. Hermione McKenzie, one of the founding members of the caucus, represented the WDSGs at that launch. At the all-island conference, the WDSG, led by Hermione McKenzie, Barbara Bailey and Linnette Vassell, chaired plenary as well as panel sessions and assisted in the preparation of reports and resolutions. The Women's Political Caucus is a member of AWOJA.

The CGDS was also called upon to provide leadership for national projects. In late 1993, Elsa Leo-Rhynie was invited by the minister with responsibility for women's affairs, Portia Simpson, to chair the National Preparatory Commission which was charged with the task of developing Jamaica's submission to the UN WCW in Beijing, China, in 1995. The CGDS was seen as a non-political, non-partisan entity which could report objectively on the status of women in Jamaica. The commission was co-chaired by Elsa Leo-Rhynie and Barbara Bailey (coordinator of the WDSG at that time). Several WDSG members were active on the commission: heading subcommittees, researching background information and facilitating workshops. The commission included representatives of the Bureau of Women's Affairs, women's organizations, NGOs and religious institutions. The national report was submitted in time for it to be sent to the Economic Commission for Latin America and the Caribbean by February 1994 so that it could form part of the regional report for Latin America and the Caribbean. Barbara Bailey actually attended the conference as part of the Jamaican delegation.

Eudine Barriteau, head of the Cave Hill campus, was invited to be involved in a similar process for Barbados and was on that country's National Preparatory Commission for the UN Fourth WCW in Beijing. She also attended the NGO forum associated with that conference as a representative of DAWN, at the invitation of the World Council of Churches.

Rhoda Reddock was involved in preparing for the Beijing conference both as head of CGDS and as a member of CAFRA, which was the regional NGO delegation coordinator. She was an advisor for the preparation of the Caribbean report and was involved with CGDS panel discussions and participation in national-level activities. She attended the NGO forum, where CAFRA organized two sessions, occupied a section of the Latin American and Caribbean tent and delivered a paper at a session arranged by the Association of Feminist Economists. Peggy Antrobus represented WAND and DAWN at the official conference, while Jeanette Morris represented the St Augustine WDS group. Other WDSG members attended either the conference or the NGO forum, and the gathering of women from all over the world proved to be an effective mobilizing force: "Beijing was in many ways the highpoint of feminist organizing in the region. There was collaboration at *all* levels – CARICOM, the Economic Commission for Latin America and the Caribbean, UNIFEM with Joycelin, governments, women's organizations, and so on" (Rhoda Reddock, testimonial).

> At the conference, CARICOM worked as a group, and I recall that I was assigned to participate in the working group that drafted the declaration and to ensure inclusion of Caribbean women's concerns. As a spinoff, I served as a resource person and presented a paper at the Caribbean Subregional Ministerial Conference, in preparation for the seventh session of the Regional Conference on the Integration of Women into the Economic and Social Development of Latin America and the Caribbean, Guyana, September 1997. (Barbara Bailey, testimonial)

Barbara Bailey, in 1993, also represented the UWI vice-chancellor at the Sixth Meeting of Ministers Responsible for the Integration of Women and Development, CARICOM, in Trinidad and Tobago. In that year also, Elsa Leo-Rhynie was invited to be a member of the national task force on crime chaired by high court justice Lensley Wolfe (later, chief justice of Jamaica). The involvement of a representative of CGDS allowed for the inclusion of a focus on women in prisons in Jamaica and highlighted the very different contributing factors in the commission of criminal offences by men and women, respectively.

In keeping with preparations in many countries for the UN designation and celebration of 1994 as the International Year of the Family, the CGDS was asked to prepare a document on the Caribbean family for CARICOM. Elsa Leo-Rhynie was also invited to deliver the 1993 Grace Kennedy Foundation lecture, which was entitled "The Jamaican Family: Continuity and Change".

National and regional planning activities have also been informed through the significant consultancy work of the CGDS, undertaken internationally with the UN and other agencies, regionally with CARICOM and Caribbean women's groups, and locally with bureaux of women's affairs and other government agencies. Some of these projects have not only involved the centre in interesting and valuable research but have also supported the outreach, which is a major component of the mission of the centre, and extended the theoretical analysis to the work of activists.

Examples can be drawn from the campus units, whose faculty members were instrumental in developing national gender policy documents for regional governments, as follows:

- The Government of the Cayman Islands: Patricia Mohammed, during her tenure as head of the Mona campus unit
- The Government of Trinidad and Tobago: Rhoda Reddock (St Augustine) in collaboration with Patricia Mohammed (Mona) and Michelle Rowley (Cave Hill)

Involvement in the development of such policy documents continued over the years and is highlighted in chapter 10.

The IOP/UWI/ISS project as well as other funding sources facilitated exchanges among academics within the Caribbean as well as internationally, and these built capacity and enhanced the work of the CGDS. Inter-campus teaching allowed for lecturers from the three campuses to share their knowledge and expertise – interdisciplinary and disciplinary – with their colleagues and students on the other campuses. The seminars, lectures and workshops led by the visiting inter-campus teachers were very well attended and were significant contributors to capacity-building in gender. International travel for scholarly activity was also made possible through the project as well as other sources.

Through its outreach activities, CGDS has established its visibility, by interacting with institutions and organizations at all levels throughout the region, sensitizing educators, policymakers and the general population to issues of gender and development, and providing strategies to enhance awareness of the critical role played by the study of gender in national and regional development as well as in personal life. This aspect of the role of CGDS was strongly supported by visiting academics and public figures, who made presentations to students pursuing gender courses and also gave public lectures. In many instances, and especially when academics from the ISS came to the region, they visited all three campuses. Visitors were expected from the ISS as part of the project, and the CGDS welcomed Dr Saskia Wieringa on several occasions. She shared theoretical perspectives and research on women and gender and was a valuable contributor to the development and growth of feminist scholarship in the region.

In March 1993, a special lecture celebrating the tenth anniversary of the WDSGs was staged by the St Augustine group. It was given by Marjorie Thorpe, first WDSG coordinator, who spoke on Women's Rights as Human Rights. The group also published a booklet titled *A Decade of Development* (Kaminjolo 1993). At Cave Hill, the Arts Lecture Theatre was the venue, in November 1993, for a symposium celebrating this significant milestone of the WDSGs. Joycelin Massiah gave that lecture. Barriteau recalls in her testimonial: "In September/November 1993, Joycelin Massiah, then at UNIFEM, telephoned to say that the WDS Group would be ten years old in December and the CGDS should celebrate it, and UNIFEM provided some funding to do so. I worked with WAND and WDS colleagues and friends of CGDS to mount a celebratory event in the Arts Lecture Theatre on the campus." At Mona, Elsa Leo-Rhynie's professorial lecture in December 1992 was part of the tenth-anniversary symposium, which had the theme "From Women's Studies to Gender Studies – Transforming Ideology in the UWI and Beyond".

Honouring Women

Another form of outreach and networking was the initiative taken to recognize and honour women selected from the academic, administrative and support staff as persons who had contributed significantly to the work and progress of the UWI. Ten such women were honoured at the Mona campus on International Women's Day, 1993, and four were recognized on that day in 1994.

At St Augustine, anniversary celebrations of the WDSG have been used to honour various women from the university as well as the wider community.

Dr Dorian Powell, one of the WICP senior researchers, was one of the pioneers in women's studies at the UWI; her published articles, reports and papers

Plate 6.3. UWI Mona campus: WDSG honourees, 1993
Back row, left to right: Barbara Bailey, Elsa Leo-Rhynie, Phyllis McPherson-Russell, Nora Mailer, Nina Ballen, Hermione McKenzie, Mary Morgan, Marlene Hamilton
Front row, left to right: Gloria Thompson, Pauline Morrison, Joyce Glasgow, name not recorded, Joyce Byles

researched issues of fertility, reproduction, nutrition and gender. The CGDS Mona unit decided that it would be a fitting tribute to her contribution to name a prize in her honour. This has been awarded annually since the 1995/96 academic year to an undergraduate student and recognizes and rewards excellence, while celebrating the work of a former academic colleague.

A lecture series was also initiated to honour women who were Caribbean trailblazers. At the Cave Hill campus, the Caribbean Women: Catalysts for Change lecture series was launched in 1995 in honour of Dame Nita Barrow, renowned health professional, diplomat and first female governor general of Barbados. This lecture was delivered by Dame Eugenia Charles of Dominica, the first female prime minister in the Caribbean. The Dame Nita Barrow lecture series continues, and publication of the first fifteen of these lectures and other material is pending. The Cave Hill unit of the CGDS has also been named the CGDS (now IGDS) NBU.

The CGDS continued to claim its space in the university by addressing the demands and expectations of the WDSGs as well as of various sources in the mainstream and by seeking the support necessary to meet these expectations from within as well as outside the academy. Success in this regard allowed the CGDS to become a viable and visible academic centre on all three campuses, carrying out teaching and research of a very high standard as well as respecting its mandate for outreach and activism. In the next chapter, the strategies employed to meet the expectations and stated goals needed to satisfy the third angle of empowerment will be explored.

CHAPTER 7

THE THIRD ANGLE

Strategies and Plans

> She told me someone senior had told her the CGDS would not last and that she should try to find a new job as soon as possible and that "Barriteau would regret wasting her good social-science brain on that women's studies foolishness". In the meantime, I was truly enjoying the journey and feeling really blessed to be there. . . . Building, maintaining and respecting networks and relationships were key.
> —*Eudine Barriteau, testimonial*

THE CGDS, ESTABLISHED IN SEPTEMBER 1993, LAID CLAIM to institutionalized space within the academy. The mission and objectives agreed on for the CGDS, the structure to allow for their achievement as well as the expectations and challenges of institutionalization were examined in the previous chapters. These address the first two angles of the triangle of empowerment (Vargas and Wieringa 1998). The third angle focuses on the strategies to be employed in developing the space, to attain the stated goals and satisfy the demands from the various stakeholders.

The Third Angle: Strategies to Be Employed

The CGDS quickly realized that achieving its mission would require extending its reach, to engage in linkages, collaboration and partnerships. This was logical because of

- the need to increase awareness about gender and gender issues within the academy and in the society at large;
- the importance of educating individuals about the tools of gender analysis and their use in planning and policy;
- the expectation in the IOP/UWI/ISS project that other partners would be involved in achieving the objectives;
- the financial situation of the UWI and the absence of meaningful funding from that source.

The major partnership with ISS through the IOP/UWI/ISS project was the foundation upon which the work of the CGDS was built. Els Mulder of the ISS, in a message for the tenth-anniversary conference of the CGDS, noted:

> The institutionalization of Women and Development Studies as an integral part of teaching and research in the various disciplines in UWI, enhancing a multidisciplinary approach, was completed in September 1993 with the establishment of the three Centres for Gender and Development Studies integrated within the structure of UWI. The Directorate General for International Cooperation of the Netherlands Ministry of Foreign Affairs contributed [US$1,117,146 and US$1,488,257]. . . . The money was considered as well spent. (Mulder 2003, 11)

Other partnerships were established, however, as linkages and collaborative ventures were actively and deliberately sought. Some of these are described below.

Consortium Graduate School of the Social Sciences

The director of the Consortium Graduate School of the Social Sciences, the late Norman Girvan, was an early and strong supporter of the CGDS. CGSSS had been formed in 1985 to cater to full-time graduate students from across the Caribbean. Girvan and Leo-Rhynie discussed possibilities for collaboration, which resulted in a proposal being drafted and circulated in September 1993 indicating that the CGDS planned to offer, in collaboration with the CGSSS, an eighteen-month programme leading to an MSc with a concentration in GDS. The structure of the programme consisted of a core of courses already approved and being taught by the consortium as part of the MSc in development studies. Consultation on the design and content of the gender and development concentration was sought and obtained from the ISS in The Hague and from CGDS colleagues. Teaching was to be undertaken by UWI lecturers from different faculties. The three objectives, as delineated in the proposal for offering the MSc in GDS, 1993, were as follows:

1. Development and provision of a comprehensive interdisciplinary programme focusing on gender and development, to meet the needs of women's bureaux, development agencies, public and private sector policymaking bodies and the private voluntary sector
2. Stimulation of research in gender and development as well as the documentation of case studies of action programmes which have been undertaken to assist the development of women and men in the Commonwealth Caribbean
3. Facilitation of the inclusion and integration of gender in development policies and planning in government as well as non-governmental agencies and organizations

The six courses (each of thirty hours' duration) developed for the concentration in GDS were offered, from September 1994 onwards, as an elective for candidates pursuing the MSc in development studies. Faith Webster, executive director of Bureau of Women's Affairs, Jamaica, fondly remembers those days in her testimonial:

> I saw an advertisement in the Sunday *Gleaner* newspaper from the Consortium Graduate School soliciting applications for a masters in development studies. Among the details outlined for this postgraduate degree were specializations in gender, environment and economics. I immediately applied to pursue this course of studies, choosing the gender specialization. . . . My application was accepted, and so I began my sojourn in development studies at the Consortium Graduate School and my affiliation with gender studies at the CGDS (now the IGDS). . . .
>
> The following year saw the CGDS introducing the master's programme in gender and development. I was privileged to pursue my second-year gender course modules with the first batch of graduate students who entered the programme.
>
> It was through the teaching of the theories and concepts on gender and the lively, interactive discussions with lecturers and students alike that my knowledge and appreciation for gender was developed and my gender-analytical skills honed. I can say without a doubt that this is what has prepared me and positioned me optimally to attain the position of executive director at the Bureau of Women's Affairs where I am today. I will never forget those lively, interactive and stimulating classes and will always recall with fondness the time spent in these sessions.

The collaborative agreement between the CGDS and the CGSSS at Mona, Jamaica, came to an end when the consortium merged, in 1999, with the ISER to form the Sir Arthur Lewis Institute of Social and Economic Studies, and the MSc in development studies, as offered by the CGSSS, was discontinued.

In 1995, the MSc in GDS was offered by the CGDS for the first time, following its approval by the UAC in 1994–95. Teaching and supervision in this programme were facilitated by the IOP/UWI/ISS project's allowance for visiting lecturers and cross-campus teaching, thereby allowing scholars like Saskia Wieringa, Eudine Barriteau and Rhoda Reddock to lead sessions and give lectures at Mona to the registered students. This inter-campus teaching not only benefited the graduate programme but also enhanced the undergraduate courses and increased public education. Interestingly, a number of persons registered to do just the course Gender in Policy and Planning alone, as this was seen as being advantageous to them in their careers. June A. Castello, former CGDS lecturer, Mona, now programme officer at UWI Open Campus, recalls in her testimonial:

> In September 1995 . . . the CGDS presented the first offering of the MSc, GDS. I was in the first cohort of three students from CGDS; students also came from the CGSSS, doing either the full gender concentration or electives. This was a very exciting period: the curriculum explored new ideas, giving intellectual and political coherence and voice to an awareness of inequality that many of the students felt. There were unpredictable moments of truthful unmasking as both students and faculty reflected on their actions and the assumptions that drove these. Could women really have it all? One student believed that she was in an egalitarian marriage and was devastated to hear her husband identify himself as the head of household. The professor, having mounted a strong defence of gender equality, had to admit that she had no greater claim to primary custody of her children in the event of a divorce. One of the students sadly shook her head and declared, "Prof, we can't have it both ways".

Research carried out by students at the master's level and, later, at doctoral level challenged the resources of the CGDS for thesis supervision, but encouraged the depth of analysis necessary to add new empirical data to the record and also to further challenge and critique existing theory. Public lectures from academics visiting the campuses further broadened the information-sharing and kept the issue of gender prominent within the academy. Barriteau noted in her testimonial that

> happening simultaneously was a growing sense of camaraderie and cohesion among all the units. In the early days of IGDS, some of us travelled to Mona to teach on the Consortium Graduate Programme in Gender and Development, present seminars and offer lectures to undergraduate students. . . . We were also involved with or continued to be involved with an academic support programme with the ISS. This provided visiting lecturers, staff fellowships for us at the ISS and academic material.

British Council

The WDSGs, in collaboration with the Organizational Development Centre, City University, London, and with funding from the British Council, the IOP/UWI/ISS project and some cost recovery from private sector participants, mounted two two-day seminars on the theme of women in management, in January and February of 1993. Professor Angela Coyle and Reena Bhavnani of the Organizational Development Centre conducted the sessions. The target group for the first seminar was female managers in the private sector, while the second seminar, "Women Managers in Higher Education", was geared towards women in senior administrative positions at the UWI. The outcome of the seminars was the creation of a private sector women managers' network. The very positive response to these seminars resulted in their being offered at Cave Hill and St Augustine in November 1994. The seminars, targeted at private sector women, were offered on a cost-recovery basis and were oversubscribed on both campuses.

Commonwealth of Learning

In 1993, through the auspices of the Commonwealth of Learning, the CGDS collaborated with the Summer Institute in Gender and Development offered by universities in Nova Scotia, Canada; the International Women's Tribune Centre; and the International Development Research Centre in the production of a teaching-resource module, mainly for use in Commonwealth countries and particularly for study by distance education. This evolved into a reader entitled *Theoretical Perspectives on Gender and Development*, published by the Commonwealth of Learning in 1996 and containing inputs from several CGDS faculty members. Eudine Barriteau, in her testimonial, recalls: "We also worked collaboratively on a writing/editing project under the auspices of the Commonwealth of Learning with colleagues from St Mary's, Dalhousie and Mount St Vincent universities in Canada. This produced the text co-edited by the Canadian Group and CGDS as Theoretical Perspectives on Gender and Development."

United Nations Development Fund for Women (UNIFEM)[1]

In 1992, the regional coordinator submitted a proposal to UNIFEM on behalf of the WDSGs, which sought their participation in the microenterprise project then underway with the ISER and the Office of the Prime Minister of Jamaica. The proposal was approved, and was administered by ISER and the WDSGs. The gender component, which was shared between ISER (later, Sir Arthur Lewis Institute of Social and Economic Studies) and the WDSGs (with responsibility later shifted to the CGDS), included the following:

1. Gender analysis of macroeconomic policies, which can be used as a basis for dialogue with public- and private-sector decision makers
2. Research studies on
   - women and microenterprise development in Jamaica: a review of existing data
   - gender differences in the use of credit
   - management patterns and network development among female owners/managers in specific industries
   - analysis of the informal commercial importer sector and its potential for growth and transformation
   - potential for microenterprise development among women in community-based or cooperative projects
3. Training for planners and practitioners: Involvement in this aspect of the project allowed the CGDS to acquire additional human resources in the form of a programme coordinator, June Castello, who worked with interns from the Women's Bureau, the Association of Development Agencies and a staff member of AWOJA.
4. Public education programme

The public education programme assisted women in addressing problems identified in the research studies and involved the interns as trainers. A curriculum development specialist worked with the coordinator and the interns to prepare the modules for this programme. The document *Training Modules for Women in Microenterprise*, prepared by Joan Browne and Barbara Bailey, was published in 1997 with additional funding assistance from the Government of Japan. The document is still in print and is a much sought-after resource.

> I came to CGDS in 1994 to work in the capacity of project coordinator and research assistant with the Women in Microenterprise Development Project, which was funded by UNIFEM. The RCU was then a small powerhouse, with only three persons. Recognizing the challenges faced by female micro-entrepreneurs because of their gendered status, the project sought to both close gaps in the literature and develop training materials to assist women who were either micro-entrepreneurs or desired to become micro-entrepreneurs. When I joined, the project was scheduled to deliver four regional workshops in which the training materials were piloted. Participants were introduced to core concepts and the unequal ways in which societies treated women. Attention was focused specifically on the treatment of women in the business sector; strategies were shared to encourage women to see the viability of microenterprise, to organize their lives so that familial and business responsibilities would both be discharged. Many left confident that they could have it all. (June Castello, testimonial)

The microenterprise project was a model of how the academic thrust of the centre (in terms of research and analysis) was combined with the activism/outreach (training and public education intervention) which was an important part of the centre's mission.

The tremendous value of linkages and supportive networks was once again demonstrated following Joycelin Massiah's assumption of the post of director of the UNIFEM Caribbean office. Her leadership of the WICP project and involvement in establishing the WDSGs gave her a vested interest in the CGDS, its growth and progress. This smoothed the way for proposal submission by the CGDS when seeking funding from UNIFEM Caribbean for important projects.

In 1993, UNIFEM (Caribbean) facilitated the formation of a working group comprising representatives from UNIFEM, CARICOM, WAND and CGDS to discuss implementation of a long-term regional gender training programme. Barbara Bailey was the CGDS representative on this working group. The programme targeted women in five Caribbean countries, and the theory module developed in collaboration with the Commonwealth of Learning was field-tested with resident tutors of the UWI School of Continuing Studies. This was followed by a more widespread regional programme.

UNIFEM (Caribbean) sponsored a visit by the regional coordinator to Suriname in 1993 to meet with representatives of women's organizations in that country. Saskia Wieringa was also in Suriname on assignment from the Netherlands government and the ISS, and she participated in these meetings, which involved discussion on the collaboration of the Surinamese women's organizations with women from the University of Suriname. The objective was to explore the possibility of introducing a programme in women's studies at their university. Other possibilities discussed included seeking funding for projects as well as capacity-building through establishing links with the ISS and the CGDS. The possible participation of Surinamese students in the CGSSS master's programme with a gender concentration scheduled to begin in 1994 was also considered.

UNESCO/Caribbean Network of Educational Innovation for Development

UNESCO/Caribbean Network of Educational Innovation for Development sponsored implementation of a recommendation of the 1994 IOP/UWI/ISS Gender, Science and Technology seminar that a research investigation be conducted to explore the status of science and technology education in the English-speaking Caribbean, with particular reference to gender. The research was conducted by Elsa Leo-Rhynie, Barbara Bailey and Peter Whiteley, and the results were presented at a regional conference held in August 1995 in Barbados.

United States Information Service

The United States Information Service awarded Elsa Leo-Rhynie a visiting fellowship to the United States of America in August 1992 as a participant in a programme examining Equal Opportunity and Legal Protection for Women.

International Planned Parenthood Federation

International Planned Parenthood Federation in New York sponsored a research study exploring the "dynamics of decision making among Caribbean women". Pat Mohammed, assisted by Althea Perkins, conducted the research in three Caribbean countries – Barbados, Dominica and St Lucia. It was completed in 1995, and the research findings were published in 1998 by the UWI Press and International Planned Parenthood Federation: *Caribbean Women at the Crossroads: The Dilemma of Decision-Making among Women of Barbados, St Lucia and Dominica.*

Involvement with Other Agencies and Organizations

Training in gender analysis has been a priority for several agencies in the region for over twenty-five years, and they turn to CGDS and WAND to collaborate in the design and implementation of programmes to benefit women's organizations and other interested parties across the region. Collaboration with these agencies over the years has permitted the offering of a number of outreach training programmes which were partially funded by the IOP/UWI/ISS project. The interdisciplinary and outreach activities of the CGDS, combined with WAND's particular expertise in participatory methodology with grassroots organizing, made collaboration attractive to regional NGOs such as CAFRA, Caribbean Network for Integrated Rural Development, Caribbean Policy Development Centre, and Caribbean People's Development Agency, as well as national-level women's organizations. Women's bureaux, non-governmental organizations, teacher training institutions, religious women's organizations, community groups, and other groups whose objectives focus on challenging structures of male power and the improvement of women's lives have all drawn on the expertise of the CGDS/IGDS over the years.

Involvement with UWI Policy

Work with organizations external to the UWI continued alongside initiatives within the institution. On 28 June 1993, draft guidelines on sexual harassment were prepared by the chairperson of the IOP/UWI/ISS Project Advisory Committee, Marlene Hamilton, who was also chair of the UAC subcommittee established to examine this matter. The WDSGs were represented on this subcommittee and the draft document was circulated for comment. Minute 7a of a WDSGs executive meeting at Mona on 6 October 1993 notes that the groups proposed modifications to the document and emphasized the urgency of establishing a reliable mechanism to allow this issue to be handled sensitively and expeditiously.

The meeting also reported on the draft modifications to the legal document entitled "Rights, Freedoms and Responsibilities of Students" to include the issue of sexual harassment. Elsa Leo-Rhynie was a member of the committee which prepared the draft, and the final version benefited from the input of the WDSGs.

> After women's studies took its rightful place in academia, activism continued with the women's group. I was president for five terms, and we fought for day-care and breastfeeding facilities for students and staff (we ended up with a homework centre). We dealt with the issue of sexual harassment at a highly successful forum, one of the few that saw large numbers of administrative and ancillary staff in attendance. The groundwork was laid for the eventual adoption, over a decade later, of the Sexual Harassment Policy. What was alarming to me was that, over the years, the same names (as harassers) were called again and again by women. (Veronica Salter, testimonial)

Establishment of the CGDS coincided with the appointment of a new chancellor for the UWI. The very dynamic Sir Shridath Ramphal, taking note of changes in higher education across the world, instituted a commission on governance of the UWI, which carried out its activities over the 1993/94 academic year. The report of that commission (UWI Office of Administration 1994) made recommendations for a new governance structure for the UWI, which have since been incorporated into the university's charter. Elsa Leo-Rhynie, in her position as regional coordinator of the CGDS, was invited to sit as a member of the implementation committee considering the role and function of the proposed Board for Undergraduate Studies (BUS), to ensure that gender as a factor in quality higher education was considered. The mandate of this board included the major task of establishing a system of quality assurance in the university, in response to the identification of academic quality control as one of the priority initiatives for implementation at the UWI.

The CGDS sought to earn its place as a valid and valued area of scholarship in the academy, not only through its academic offerings, but also through its outreach activites. The WDSGs on all three campuses held seminars regularly and featured local and overseas scholars and professionals as guest speakers and panellists on a wide range of topics. The variety of topics covered was indicative of the relevance of gender to diverse issues and interests and reinforced the multidisciplinary and interdisciplinary approach taken by the CGDS. The seminars also served to strengthen links with government agencies and NGOs, as well as women's bureaux and women's organizations. The annual departmental reports of the campuses list most of these seminars. The activities attracted an increasing number of undergraduate and graduate students and researchers and gradually established the relevance of gender and the significance of a centre which concentrated on this important, interdisciplinary scholarly discourse in understanding development in the Caribbean and elsewhere.

Legitimacy of the centre and its work was also reinforced by the significant external grant funding it was able to attract to support some of its activities. The centre initiated innovative and highly visible scholarship in what was an emerging academic area and was called upon to provide expertise to national and regional governments and agencies needing to incorporate gender into their plans and programmes. Several funding agencies also required that projects include a consideration of gender – the Canadian International Development Agency Institutional Strengthening Project on the Mona campus (1992–96), for example – and the expertise and contribution of faculty in the centre in this regard also helped in reducing the conservatism and scepticism of some sectors in the university.

Strategy for Further Development

The first phase of the IOP/UWI/ISS project (1986–90) focused on training staff for teaching interdisciplinary courses in women and gender studies, outreach activities, pilot teaching and bibliographic and curriculum development. The second phase (1990–94) comprised activities aimed at strengthening the presence of women and gender studies at the UWI and ensuring its institutionalization. This second phase ended officially in 1993–94 when no further funds were made available to the UWI and CGDS. Permission was given by the Government of the Netherlands, however, to use already approved funds to complete unfinished elements pertaining to the project, up to 1996.

The newly established CGDS was anxious to consolidate the benefits accrued from the project and maximize the potential gains by engaging in a new four-year project of education and training designed to stimulate and bring about significant change in the countries of the region. Plans for achieving this included the offering of master's and doctoral programmes in gender and development, as well as the encouraging of not only the use of new and exciting methodologies in the production of interdisciplinary knowledge in the Caribbean setting but also the conduct of research and social action which

Plate 7.1. Strategy Meeting at UWI St Augustine: (*Back row, left to right*) Rhoda Reddock, Barbara Bailey, Pat Mohammed; (*front row, left to right*) Eudine Barriteau, Louraine Emmanuel, Elsa Leo-Rhynie, June-Ann Castello

would address issues such as inequity, exploitation and domination based on gender, race, ethnicity, class and age, among other factors. Interrogating the meaning of gender and development in the Caribbean; assessing what is a gendered approach to sustainable development; formulating a conceptual framework for gender analysis in Caribbean countries; compilation of a comprehensive database on the situation of women vis-à-vis men in education, employment, professions, as household heads, in political and social life; and qualitative analysis of how masculinity and femininity have been and continue to be constructed over time were all considered to be critical in assisting developmental planners, policymakers, educators and others to make interventions promoting gender equality and equity from a more informed perspective. The data would also be used to carefully analyse and challenge the popular thesis that development in the region had emasculated and marginalized men.

CGDS proposed to undertake these activities in a phase 3 IOP/UWI/ISS project, working in close collaboration with WAND. The success of the two phases of the IOP/UWI/ISS project made it possible for the CGDS to propose this phase 3, and discussion of the special initiatives and objectives of this new phase was planned for a meeting in May 1994. Els Mulder of the ISS, who had visited the UWI some weeks before this meeting, had indicated, however, that the new application for project support would differ significantly from that of the previous projects and would not directly involve the ISS. The submission would have to be made, under the Direct Support to Training and Institutions in Developing Countries programme, directly by the UWI/CGDS to the Government of the Netherlands through its embassy in Jamaica. Els Mulder provided the *DSO Checklist for the Formulation of Project Documents* to assist the CGDS in preparing the proposal for direct-support funding from the Government of the Netherlands and indicated that there was every likelihood that the funding would be provided once the formal evaluation of phase 2 of the IOP/UWI/ISS had been completed. The ISS provided valuable assistance, through Els Mulder, in the development of the new proposal, particularly in the area of budget preparation. Given that the ISS would no longer be a partner in this new project, the CGDS was advised to include any involvement of the ISS and its representatives – for teaching or other activities – as part of the project inputs with budgeted line items.

The two-day meeting (30–31 May 1994) involved consultation to identify priority objectives for this new project; outline fully the resources needed to ensure that these objectives could be satisfactorily met; and distribute the work of preparation to enable the proposal to be ready with a first draft by January 1995. A later meeting of CGDS staff held on 19–20 December 1994 discussed preparation of the preliminary draft of the proposal for submission to the Government of the Netherlands with a request for funding. The minutes of the meeting indicate that Elsa Leo-Rhynie shared with the CGDS staff an important implication of the proposal being submitted to the Government of the Netherlands. Jamaica was the only one of the three countries with CGDS units that qualified for support under the DSO programme, and so care had to be taken in the drafting of the proposal; requests which involved the other campuses in regional activities would need to be presented under the aegis of the UWI without specifying the country (minute p. 1).

The project document summarized the outcomes of these consultations in a logical framework matrix which identified project objectives, outputs, activities and inputs.

The project objectives addressed four major areas:

1. Regular teaching programmes at undergraduate and graduate levels, as well as in non-formal settings, and resources to support these

2. Short courses to train personnel within select government and other agencies as well as in the private sector, to plan for the processes of development using a gender perspective and to expand the reach of these programmes through distance mode
3. Seminars/workshops targeted at training middle and senior management women in tertiary-level institutions, and also teacher educators so as to have an impact on the socialization and education of students
4. Capacity-building to strengthen the theoretical and knowledge base of CGDS staff, associate staff of other UWI departments and the staff of WAND

The proposal also identified complementary activities, which were to be funded by other donors. There was great disappointment following submission of the draft proposal to Els Mulder and Saskia Wieringa of the ISS for their review, as a letter dated 14 August 1995 from Els Mulder, copied to Saskia Wieringa, expressed serious doubts as to the DSO funding of the following:

- Development and production of curricula and videos for use at community level
- Community-based activities, such as workshops and training with popular theatre groups
- Consciousness-raising on gender issues
- Developing participatory teaching methodologies; activities and training for youth groups and non-regular (programme/course) training for students in self-development and gender awareness

Mulder also seriously doubted whether DSO funding would be made available for "the Campus Women's Group Newsletter, WAND Occasional Papers . . . and WAND's Monthly mail-outs; funding of public education in the form of public campus-based seminars . . . public lectures and panel discussions".

This prompted a fax message to the CGDS units from the regional coordinator on 19 September 1995, advising that "certain activities, items etc. would not meet the criteria for a project in higher education, which category this proposal would fit. It means that much of the community-based (WAND) and outreach activities have had to be cut."

It was clear that, with institutionalization, the focus of the funding from the Government of the Netherlands was to be support for the academic programme rather than the outreach activities which had been a major part of the work of the WDSGs. This was a major blow to the WDSGs and their well-established

Plate 7.2. UWI and ISS collaborators: The Tenth Anniversary Conference, Mona, 2003
Front row, left to right: Els Mulder, Peggy Antrobus, Saskia Wieringa, Joycelin Massiah, Barbara Bailey, Louraine Emmanuel. *Behind, left to right:* Jennifer Edwards, Gloria Barrett-Sobers, Pat Mohammed.

programmes, as it was anticipated that the funding necessary to support the outreach agenda of the centre would have come from this source, as it had in earlier phases.

Support from the Government of the Netherlands for the ongoing gender initiative was eventually achieved through a DSO/UWI project. The genesis of this project is explained in the next chapter.

Once again, therefore, the CGDS/UWI relied on external funding for the operations of the CGDS, which contributed in a significant way to its status and visibility in the academy. Support from the UWI did not increase substantially – although the institution was committed to maintaining the CGDS, staff of the centre were challenged to develop and offer services, including courses, to the general public on a cost-recovery basis so as to build a fund which could be used in the maintenance of its outreach activities. It is a testament to the staff of the CGDS that these hurdles only motivated them to be more creative and to work harder to achieve the mission and goals which had been set. Eudine Barriteau describes in her testimonial some of the new initiatives undertaken, for example, at Cave Hill at that time:

> By 1996, the CGDS was gaining wider acceptance, the embryonic teaching programme was taking off, and I moved to create new courses, starting with two courses on men and masculinity, which were developed working closely with Linden Lewis, who was then a visiting research fellow at ISER, and Eliseus Joseph, who used to teach the unit on men and masculinity in an existing course. The Caribbean Women Catalyst for Change project had started in 1994. By 1996, we were very involved in researching Dame Nita Barrow as the first subject of that project, but she had passed away in December 1995. We had started the Caribbean Women Catalyst for Change lecture series on 3 November 1995, with the inaugural lecture delivered by Dame Eugenia Charles. On Dame Nita's passing, we sought to honour her legacy and memory by dedicating the lecture series to honouring her memory and holding it every November on the Friday closest to the anniversary of her birth, 15 November.

A major project funded by the CIDA and involving the RCU and St Augustine units of the CGDS was the Island Sustainability, Livelihood and Equity project. It began in 1995 and ended in 2000. It involved seven partners – four Canadian universities, one each from the Philippines and Indonesia, along with UWI. Although gender was not the project's major focus, its integration was mandatory; its inclusion and the involvement and contribution of the CGDS in this regard proved to be significant to the project's success.

First Relocation: Strategy to Improve Working Conditions

The constant lobbying for additional space finally resulted, in 1996, in the relocation of the RCU and the Mona campus unit of the CGDS from its various locations – ISER, faculties of social sciences and arts and general studies – to office space on the Mona campus previously occupied by the campus printery. The space was still inadequate, but no longer was the CGDS the recipient of "patronage" and it could now claim "ownership" of premises. This allowed the staff of both units to share equipment and to communicate more easily than they were previously able to do, given that their offices had been located at different points on the campus. Although still not adequate for its operations and with no allowance for growth, the relocation significantly increased the efficiency of coordination of the range of activities taking place at both national and regional levels, lifted the morale of staff and students and provided a home for the centre. Teleconferencing facilities which were part of the University of the West Indies Distance Teaching Experiment, a network of audio communication among the countries served by the regional university, permitted monthly staff meetings. This network, upgraded to the UWI Distance Education Centre and now an integral part of the UWI Open Campus, has also been used to facilitate and thus increase the offerings of a certificate and ultimately a diploma in GDS to individuals in the campus countries as well as those of the Eastern Caribbean and Belize.

The triangle of empowerment (Vargas and Wieringa 1998), as applied in this case, provided a useful mechanism for examining the various elements associated with the institutionalization of the CGDS. Claiming a space within the academy and determining the purpose, direction and methods of functioning were essential elements in the development of the centre, and, with the valuable support from partners, particularly the Government of the Netherlands and the ISS, the CGDS was well prepared to pursue its mandate.

In 1996, Elsa Leo-Rhynie was appointed deputy principal of the Mona campus, and Barbara Bailey, who had been a very effective WDSG coordinator, assumed the position of regional coordinator and later became the first university director of the IGDS.[2] She was granted leave from the Faculty of Education (now renamed School of Education) initially for a two-year period, but this was extended and converted to an appointment on tenure. Her leadership of the CGDS over the next fourteen years until her retirement included implementation of the DSO/UWI project, which started in 1998. The introduction of a minor and later a major in gender studies were critical achievements during her tenure as was her networking capability. She established important links with national, regional and international entities, thus enabling the CGDS to attract considerable funding to support research projects, academic programmes as well as bursaries for students. She also spearheaded the very important change of status of the centre when it was upgraded to the IGDS.

Notes

1. This section is based on the report of the professor and regional coordinator, January to June 1993, minute 62.
2. The title of regional coordinator was redesignated as university director in 2005.

Section 4

CONSOLIDATION, 1996–2010

BARBARA BAILEY

CHAPTER 8

PURSUING THE MANDATE

Transitions and the Teaching Programmes

> In Hinduism, the ritual of *maticore* is held a few nights before the wedding ceremony to allow older and more experienced women to convey their knowledge of gender and sexuality to the young, generally prepubescent, brides. In this gathering of young and old women, stories are shared, experiences passed on through humour and song, and solidarities built between generations of women.
>
> Although differently constituted, the emergence of women and gender studies, since the last two decades of the twentieth century, in the Caribbean can be likened to the *maticore* ritual. There was need for a dedicated space for women to develop methodologies of research, to debate explanatory theories of gender in the Caribbean, to produce bodies of evidence and to create a new multidisciplinary area that embraces both men and women equally, as its application is relevant to the relations among and between both sexes.
>
> —*Patricia Mohammed*

Introduction: A Period of Transitions

The close of phase 2 of the IOP/UWI/ISS project marked a significant transition from project funding to university-based funding for each of the four units of the CGDS. Between 17 February and 9 March 1997, an external evaluation of this phase of the project was carried out by the ETC Foundation[1] of the Netherlands, and, in the report, it is noted that "on August 1, 1996, UWI's new Governance Structure came into effect. CGDS has in this structure its own place, which implies also its own responsibility for the management of the budget allotted. Also, a new system of accounting was introduced. This means that the Regional Coordinator and the Unit Coordinators have become budget-holders for activities falling under their responsibility" (Kamphuis 1997, 18).

The institution of these new arrangements signalled the fact that, by agreeing to the terms and conditions of the project of cooperation in 1986, Vice-Chancellor Preston had, in fact, given tacit commitment to the institutionalization of a programme of WDS. In fact, in the project document, it was acknowledged that the innovation had originated within the UWI prior to the beginning of the project and would continue after the project had ended. For that reason, it was envisaged that the tripartite programme of teaching, research and outreach would be integrated into the existing structure of the university at all levels; and, by the end of phase 2 of the project, it had done so in regard to providing staffing and physical accommodation for each of the four units of the centre. The ETC evaluation report, however, points to the fact that, at the time of the evaluation in 1997, not only was staffing of the units extremely skeletal but accommodation was also minimal. With regard to staffing, it is noted that

> the Regional Coordinating Unit . . . is temporarily staffed by a Senior Lecturer/ Acting Coordinator . . . and an Administrative Officer. . . . The academic staff of each (campus) unit comprises of one Lecturer (Senior Lecturer for Trinidad) who is head of the Unit at the same time. Support staff in total comprises of Clerical Assistants/Secretaries (3 posts), and Graduate Research Assistant (1 post). All academic and administrative/secretarial staff is assigned on permanent contract, except for the Trinidad Unit. (ibid.)

With regard to accommodation, it is noted in the same evaluation report that "the available space is in all units limited, but office and teaching facilities are in principle present. Library facilities are restricted; each unit has a small documentation centre and study space. . . . The premises are adequately maintained for their purpose" (ibid.).

These limitations clearly pointed to the need for further funding, for continued support of the institutionalization process as well as to address some of the institutional shortfalls, and led to the possibility of soliciting additional support from the Royal Netherlands Embassy under the DSO programme. An explicit purpose of the external phase 2 evaluation, therefore, was to indicate whether a possible extension, or else a phase 3 continuation of the project under the DSO Programme, could be pursued; and, to this end, a proposal prepared in keeping with DSO guidelines, by Elsa Leo-Rhynie in July 1996, was also reviewed. The evaluation team concluded that the proposal for a third phase of activities deserved serious consideration but recommended that the comments provided by that team be taken into account prior to submission.

Between March 1997 and February 1998, taking into account the comments raised by the evaluation team, the proposal developed by CGDS was used as a reference document for the actual proposal prepared by a contracted consultant, Lorraine Blank, appointed by the Royal Netherlands Embassy of Kingston, Jamaica. Funding for the earlier phases of the Government of the Netherlands project of cooperation in teaching, research and outreach originated and was managed from The Hague. In this further phase, funding was tied to the Jamaican Netherlands embassy and was therefore intended to primarily benefit Jamaica-based activities. However, given that the RCU was the executing agency, creative means were found to develop activities that could include the campus units as well as have a wider reach to the non-campus countries, now referred to as the UWI 12.

Els Mulder (2003) explained in a message for the tenth-anniversary conference of the CGDS: "The Ministry decided to continue its support to UWI/CGDS for another few years through the Direct Support Programme. ISS was no longer involved in the actual execution of activities financed by the Direct Support Programme but, of course, the existing strong UWI/ISS network was kept alive and is still very much alive."

The explicit intention of this further funding support from the Government of the Netherlands was to ensure that gains made through funding between 1986 and 1997 could be consolidated. In the phase 3 (DSO/UWI) project document, it was, therefore, acknowledged that, "while UWI is committed to providing the core funds necessary to maintain the current activities of the CGDS, additional funding is required to strengthen UWI initiatives begun under phase 2 of the project; to promote enrolment in CGDS programmes among low-income students; and to ensure a smooth and complete transfer of all responsibilities for teaching, research and outreach and their financial consequences to the UWI" (Blank 1998, 3). In its final form, the centrepiece of this further phase was funding to support the development and implementation of a distance education certificate programme in GDS. There was also support, inter alia, for undergraduate and graduate students in the form of tuition fellowships; research grants, inter-campus teaching exchanges; development of a reader and an annotated bibliography of gender and development sources with particular reference to the Caribbean; and training workshops on gender issues in education for teacher educators as well as gender analysis in policy and planning for public- and private sector policy analysts.

The shift to Jamaica-based funding in the DSO/UWI project of cooperation (June 1998–May 2003), and the delegation of the role of budget-holders to the campus heads, heralded a time for consolidation of gains made in the earlier phases of the IOP/UWI/ISS project, but, more critically, these changes would ultimately have far-reaching implications for the relationship between the RCU and the campus units and between the university's Office of Finance and the campus bursaries.

Under this new project, the agenda of consolidation of the programme of teaching, research and outreach in gender and development over the fourteen-year period between 1996 and 2010 was framed by a number of factors in the UWI academic environment. Chief among these would be the generally limited institutional resources, financial and human, made available to the units, resulting from the economic crisis facing Caribbean governments during the period under review. Significant variation among the campus countries in terms of shrinking financial support to tertiary education resulted in marked differences in support to the units.

Limited institutional financial resources were, to a large extent, compensated for by fairly strong support from external funding sources, fuelled as this was by the success of the UN Fourth WCW held in Beijing in 1995. In the DSO/UWI proposal, it is noted that

> a very persuasive lobby has recently come from the women of the Caribbean who, in the preparation of national and regional plans for the world Conference on Women in 1995, and in the formulation of the Platform for Action, have focused on the central role of education in bringing about any long-term systemic change in society. . . . Achievement of these objectives demands research to provide reliable information to guide policy initiatives in all sectors and a cadre of professionals who have an understanding of gender and development issues. (ibid.)

The importance of producing individuals with the skills and understanding to engage in gender mainstreaming was reflected in the Beijing Plan of Action, and, as a result, beyond the funding secured from the Jamaican Netherlands embassy activities in teaching, research and outreach, funding was also forthcoming from a number of bilateral and multilateral funding agencies.

The end of the DSO/UWI funding in 2003 would eventually lead to a significant shift in the relationship between the RCU and the campus units. In the absence of targeted funding to support activities across all units, the coordinating role of the RCU, such as existed under the IOP/UWI/ISS project of cooperation, diminished significantly, and, although funding was still sought for regional projects, each unit increasingly took on the task of seeking funds to support campus-based initiatives. This significant shift in the function and role of the RCU would eventually lead to the need to review and revise its management structures vis-à-vis its relationship to the campus units as well as other university entities, such as WAND, and external entities, such as the University of Guyana, where links had existed during the life of the project of cooperation. The CGDS mission statement would also be ultimately revised, although not significantly, to take into account conceptual shifts in the feminist and development discourses from WAD to gender and development. The flow chart for programme/course approval was also modified to take into account the new governance structure introduced in 1996 (see appendix 6). In this instance, undergraduate courses had to be routed through the Academic Quality Assurance Committee established at Mona in 1996, while undergraduate programmes were submitted to the BUS, and graduate courses/programmes to the Board for Graduate Studies and Research.

Pursuing the Mandate: The Teaching Programmes

Establishment of the CGDS within the structures of the academy brought with it the challenge of proving to the sceptics that women/gender studies was a legitimate academic field of study that comprised its own unique body of concepts and tools for interrogating related issues and, therefore, could be pursued with the same rigour and respect as all other academic disciplines available to the clientele of the university. This called for a transition from the discrete courses developed and offered through the agency of the WDSGs on each campus, mainly through the Faculty of Arts and General Studies, to the development of programmes that students could opt to pursue at all academic levels. This is eloquently summed up in Ronnie Salter's testimonial, which points out that, with institutionalization, "the pressure started to build for our way forward – namely, a recognition of women's studies as a legitimate area for teaching and research within the university. WDS was very active in other areas also, and, after women's studies took its rightful place in academia, activism continued, with the women's group". Although this transition would prove to be an uphill task, given that, at that time, staffing in all the units was minimal, the earlier disciplinary and interdisciplinary seminars that had occurred under the IOP/UWI/ISS project of cooperation created a space for the emergence of an indigenous theorizing on the situation of women and the relations of gender in the Caribbean and for the cultivation of an epistemological approach which incorporated women's voices and inserted women's ways of knowing into knowledge production. Although, initially, the inclusion of a gender analysis in teaching and research was somewhat tentative, over time it became a refined and widely accepted practice in the development of courses and the crafting of individual and institutional research projects, not only in the CGDS but across many disciplines.

The success of the teaching and, by extension, the research agenda of the centre was undergirded by the fact that, beyond the academy, gender analysis had been widely accepted as necessary for informing equitable and sustainable development processes. The gender and development paradigm is now universally promoted as the means of integrating gender equality concerns in national, regional and international projects, programmes and policies. In the region, the CGDS not only led the vanguard in this regard but, through its gender and development academic programmes, has produced a small but significant cadre of persons throughout the region with the requisite skills to engage in this critical work in their respective societies.

The Certificate/Diploma GDS Programme

An immediate and major objective of the DSO/UWI project was to "expand the reach of CGDS teaching programmes to groups socially, economically and geographically distanced from the normal teaching of the UWI" (Blank 1998, 6). This would be achieved, inter alia, through a grant of US$172,000 to "develop and implement a distance education programme in Gender and Development Studies at the certificate level. The programme will be delivered via the University's distance education system. This programme is consistent with the UWI policy to expand course offerings to non-campus territories through distance programmes. The . . . programme will promote study of Gender and Development studies among individuals, especially women, who cannot leave work and family to study on-campus" (ibid., 8).

Development of this three-semester, part-time programme started in the 1997/98 academic year and followed a rigorous curriculum development process, starting with outlines for eight three-credit courses for presentation to the Mona campus Academic Quality Assessment Committee and the academic board as well as the BUS, thereby ensuring that necessary approvals were secured. Subsequently, course writers were identified from within the CGDS, other UWI faculty and individuals beyond the UWI, and quality assurance was guaranteed by establishing a process of external peer review of content and of internal review by curriculum specialists attached to the CGDS. Six of the eight courses were designed at level 1 and two at level 2. The other component of the programme was a six-credit research project carried out on completion of the course requirements.

It was expected that the programme would start by the 2000/1 academic year, but, at that time, although the development of course material was well underway, it became evident that the commitment to deliver the distance-mode programme within timelines stipulated in the project agreement would be severely compromised. The limited capacity of the RCU, which, until that time, had only a single academic staff position on the establishment, was the major drawback. Representations made to the then vice-chancellor, Rex Nettleford, about the obligation of the UWI to deliver outputs under the DSO/UWI project, resulted in the temporary appointment of Yasmeen Yusuf-Khalil, a specialist in instructional design and curriculum development, in January 2002. Her terms of employment were to coordinate the development and implementation of the eighteen-month distance-mode certificate programme in GDS. Start-up was in the second semester of the 2002/3 academic year, with an intake of fourteen students in the pilot cluster, and ten of these students were awarded tuition fellowships under the DSO/UWI project.

The programme was offered through the School of Continuing Studies (formerly the Extra-Mural Department of the UWI), and feedback from students in the programme and resident tutors at the university centres indicated that, because the programme was offered at the certificate level, the financial gain graduates received was not commensurate with the high quality of the programme. Based on these reports, and the fact that the programme already met diploma-level requirements, an application for a change of designation from certificate to diploma in GDS, without any change to the content of the programme, was made to the BUS in May 2005. Official confirmation of the change was granted at the board meeting of 31 May 2005. The diploma was awarded to the second batch of graduates and retroactively, with approval from BUS, to individuals from the first cohort who had met all programme requirements.

The diploma programme was sought after by a number of persons who held senior positions, particularly in public sector entities that required individuals who could provide technical expertise in gender analysis and the integration of gender in planning, programming and policy development. The relevance of the programme was confirmed by an external evaluation team which undertook a review of the programme under the aegis of the Quality Assurance Unit of the BUS in 2006. The team reviewed the curriculum, spoke with the programme coordinator and took full advantage of the opportunity to speak with currently registered students at various stages in the programme, as well as via teleconference with some graduates from Antigua, Barbados, Cayman Islands, St Kitts, Dominica and St Lucia. In the report, the team observed that the fact that they (the graduates) took time out from their busy schedules to speak with us (and then, later, among themselves) provided further tangible evidence of their appreciation of the programme, and of the collegiality they had developed among themselves. "From our discussions with the students and graduates, all of whom expressed deep enthusiasm for what they had learned in their studies, and from our review of the materials provided, we see this as a success story for the RCU. It is a most impressive programme and represents an innovative way to build capacity throughout the region. We recommend its continuation and growth" (BUS 2006).

When the School of Continuing Studies of the UWI transitioned into being a component of the Open Campus in 2008, all distance-mode, online programmes developed and administered by various departments were brought under the purview of the Open Campus. The CGDS diploma in GDS was among programmes taken over to be administered and managed by that campus. Given that the programme had been commissioned under the DSO/UWI project and its development had been fully funded through this project, the CGDS was adamant that an agreement had to be reached, including, at the very least, clarity about ownership of the programme and students, issues of revenue sharing and terms to govern the termination of the programme.

The draft memorandum of understanding produced by the Open Campus, however, did not adequately address the main concerns raised by the CGDS (by then, the IGDS), and, at a further meeting, it was agreed that the IGDS should draft the terms to be included in the memorandum of understanding. This was done, but, unfortunately, the process was not completed before the then university director demitted office in July 2010. The memorandum of understanding is still outstanding, and, in the 2011/12 academic year, the programme was suspended. Suspension raises serious concerns, given the outcome expected by the funders of the DSO/UWI which supported the development and early implementation of the programme.

A concern that surfaced in the DSO/UWI proposal was the fate, subsequent to the development of the eighteen-month certificate/diploma programme, of the eight-week residential summer programme, first offered in 1992, during phase 2 of the IOP/UWI/ISS project. In the project document, it is stated:

> In the past, external funding has been used to subsidize the cost of the summer programme. Funding from Phase III will be used to provide partial scholarships in 1998. Ten (10) scholarships in the amount of US$2 000.00 each will be provided to low-income participants from the region. The last offering of the summer programme will be 1998. The summer programme will be replaced by the distance certificate programme to be developed with project funding. (Blank 1998, 11)

The certificate/diploma programme, which provided lower-level matriculation to UWI, was considered to be a more sustainable approach to reaching those in need of training in GDS throughout the region. It was considered preferable to an externally funded, short-term, non-credit programme, which only offered a certificate of participation provided by the CGDS, through the then School of Continuing Studies. Nonetheless, in the final analysis, responsibility for the summer programme was assumed by the Cave Hill unit, which has raised funds biennially to offset costs incurred in mounting the programme.

Given the nature of the two programmes, one or the other could be perceived as being redundant. The impact of the face-to-face summer programme on the uptake of the distance-mode diploma programme offered through the Open Campus has never been assessed, but, given the potential benefit of the diploma programme, it should be reintroduced and some assessment made of the wisdom of retaining the summer programme at the same time.

The Undergraduate Minors

Information gleaned from departmental reports indicates that, by 1999, all three campus units were involved in the delivery of undergraduate minors. However, residing outside the existing faculty structure meant that, as with the earlier courses offered under the aegis of the WDSGs, the units lacked legitimate status to register students and had to continue to depend on the willingness of existing faculties/departments to act as the conduit through which to offer programmes. This brought with it further challenges, such as the allocation of teaching space for the delivery of such courses.

A report (UWI AB 1997, minute 124) from a 1997 meeting of the St Augustine academic board indicates that an undergraduate minor in gender studies, established in that year, was to be offered through the Faculty of Humanities and Education, while the 2005 BUS report of the external review of the St Augustine unit notes that a minor in GDS, established in 2000/2001, was offered through the Faculty of Social Sciences. The 2012 St Ausgustine self-assessment report indicates that the minors continue to be available to students from these faculties as well as other faculties and departments.

The complement of courses available to students pursuing the minors at St Augustine reveals that the unit has developed a tradition of offering undergraduate gender-related courses developed and taught in other departments and subject areas including, inter alia, history, Spanish, French and agriculture. Lecturers who deliver these courses are regarded as adjunct staff of the CGDS. In the 2005 report of the external evaluation of the unit by the BUS, it was noted, however, that "the courses developed within the CGDS appear to support the aims and objectives of the Centre; but the individual offerings in the 'affiliated' departments are not as explicitly geared towards the learning outcomes of the CGDS. They satisfy their disciplinary objectives and some of the CGDS objectives. But at the very least, they broaden the range of gender and gender-related course offerings" (UWI BUS 2005, 5).

In December 1998, the Mona academic board granted approval of a minor in GDS which has been offered since 1999 by the Mona unit. Students required five level 2 and 3 courses (fifteen credits) to declare the minor, three of which had to be CGDS courses and the other two could be chosen from the gender-related courses offered by other departments on the campus. The minor, therefore, became an increasingly attractive option for many students, especially those from the faculties of humanities and education and the social sciences. The 2012 self-assessment report of the Mona unit indicates that, in the 2008/9 academic year, the minor was updated, and the range of courses from which students could make choices was expanded by the development and approval of new level 2 and 3 courses.

In 1999, the Cave Hill unit reported that fourteen gender courses were offered by the centre through the faculties of humanities, social sciences and law. On that campus, an approved minor was made available through the Faculty of Humanities in 1999 and through the Faculty of Social Sciences in 2003. The more recent, 2012 self-assessment report indicates that these minors continue to be available but that, "while there has been increased interest in gender courses", the unit has been unable to ascertain if there has been a significant impact on students' decision to choose a minor and that "the Institute has to devise a more systematic strategy to encourage more students to take Minors" (UWI IGDS 2012b, 11).

The same report also indicates that

> in March 2008, the staff at IGDS, Cave Hill, began the process of critically assessing all courses offered – an initiative spearheaded by the Regional Coordinating Unit of the Institute for Gender and Development Studies. This resulted in the revision of the Minors in Gender and Development Studies for students in the Faculty of Humanities and Education, and the Faculty of Social Sciences. This reassessment exercise was useful in identifying Gender courses that best complemented programme requirements in the respective Faculties and also served to update new course offerings for the Minor. (Ibid., 17)

Graduate Programmes

The thirty-credit MSc in GDS, developed by the RCU, was approved in 1994 by the then UAC on a self-financing basis, with no support from the university or campus grants committees, and was first offered in September 1995. Initially, teaching of courses was partly facilitated by the regional coordinator and through inter-campus teaching exchanges of CGDS faculty, funded by the IOP/UWI/ISS project. The DSO/UWI project continued funding support in the form of tuition fellowships over the period 1999 to 2003. Delivery of courses and supervision of students was strongly supported by staff of the Mona unit, and off-campus individuals with the requisite knowledge base and competencies were also approved to teach specific courses within their area of expertise.

In 2004, further funds were made available for support of the sixth cohort of students through a project funded by the Government of Japan through the Japan WID Fund administered by the UNDP, Jamaica.

Increasingly, students applied to read for this MSc degree, accepted the offer of a place and subsequently left the programme because, even with the financial support provided by the fellowships, they faced other barriers which constrained full-time study. Additionally, some students who were offered a place but not a fellowship were unable to accept because of inability to finance the programme and/or not securing leave from their jobs to facilitate full-time registration. In 2001/2, the attrition rate had serious financial implications for the centre since the cost of part-time lecturers was offset by intake from tuition fees. As a result, in that year, with the permission of the Board for Graduate Studies and Research, semester II courses were offered as reading courses. In the 2003/4 academic year, a submission was therefore made to the chairman of the Mona campus Committee for Graduate Studies and Research for a change of enrolment status from full-time to part-time, to be introduced for the 2004/5 academic year.

Although the St Augustine Unit developed a taught MSc in GDS during the 2004/5 academic year, a revised version of this programme was not approved until the 2007/8 academic year. A taught MSc programme has never been offered by the Cave Hill unit.

MPhil/PhD programmes are offered on two of the three UWI campuses. At St Augustine, this offering was established in the 1997/98 academic year. Students were accepted into this programme every three years, and, by 2003/4, the unit had accepted the third cohort of MPhil/PhD candidates. In the 2005 report of the BUS external review, it is noted, presumably in relation to this programme, that

> some Graduate students felt that the taught aspect of research programmes was too long, but the CGDS believes that, for those with no prior exposure to gender courses, a year-long course was the minimum that would be considered adequate preparation. The students' concerns may have been driven by anxiety over completion schedules of the degree programme (the taught course component was a source of delay), though they accepted the importance of such courses, especially those that focused on theory and methods, for students who had returned to the academic environment after a long absence. (UWI BUS 2005, 5)

The first graduates of the programme were Gabrielle Hosein and Donna Drayton of the 1997 and 2000 cohorts, respectively, both graduating in 2004 and both subsequently joining the staff of the St Augustine unit of the CGDS.

At Mona, MPhil/PhD candidates in GDS were accepted for the first time in the 1998/99 academic year as part of the graduate offerings of the RCU. Applicants with no background in gender studies were provisionally accepted and required to do three qualifying courses drawn from the taught MSc programme. Candidates with an MPhil degree could be accepted directly at the PhD level.

In the 2006 report of the external team that undertook a review of the CGDS Cave Hill unit, it is noted that the team concurred with an external review report that the "CGDS cannot offer the [postgraduate] programme without the appointment of another academic staff member" (20). Staff of the unit and, particularly, the head of the unit, Eudine Barriteau, however, supervised a number of graduate students from the CGDS and the faculties of agriculture and natural sciences and social sciences at St Augustine, as well as those from social sciences at Cave Hill.

At the start of academic year 2007/8, with the addition of a temporary lecturer, the Cave Hill unit introduced the MPhil/PhD programme in GDS. A distinguishing mark of the programme at Cave Hill was that it served candidates from outside Barbados. The first cohort of eight students included one each from Martinique, Trinidad and Tobago, and the United States, and five from Barbados, while, in 2009/10, an additional eight students were admitted to the programme (UWI IGDS 2012, 12).

Impediments to Pursuing the Teaching Mandate

The UWI, having formally established the CGDS as an integral part of its academic programme, failed to provide the necessary financial resources to adequately support the development and delivery of programmes in GDS to all UWI constituents, a critical dimension of the mission of the CGDS. This failure points to the major constraint which all units of the centre faced once major external funding through the Netherlands projects came to an end in 2003. At St Augustine, the external review team noted that "two full-time staff was inadequate to service the needs of the CGDS and to carry out all of its objectives – which it has set itself" (UWI BUS 2005, 12); while at Mona, the review team's initial observations were summarized as a question: "How could two Centres [Mona and RCU] so under-resourced in every way produce so much?" (UWI BUS 2006b, 4).

The lack of adequate financial resources spawned a number of other obstacles, catalogued in the self-assessment studies conducted by all four CGDS units in preparation for the first round of quality assurance reviews carried out by BUS between 2005 and 2006. The major impediments identified in the report submitted by the external review team at the St Augustine unit in 2005 are reflective of those faced by all the CGDS units at that time. The following are highlighted in the report:

1. Physical infrastructure: A tour of the facilities revealed that the centre is, indeed, challenged in terms of space and that, as pointed out in the [self-assessment report] – "accommodation is inadequate for the existing and expanding needs of the Centre and certainly for the range of teaching methodologies it employs" (UWI BUS 2005, 10).
2. Human resources: From a look at the CVs of the full-time staff at the CGDS, from our knowledge of the qualifications of some of the affiliates and from our perusal of the organogram, it is quite obvious to us that all categories of staff are very qualified – full-time, part-time, affiliates – and this enhances the teaching. . . .
3. Appropriateness of location: The CGDS appears to be isolated – as far as the students are concerned. . . . Students also feel that "the CGDS would have greater visibility among the student population if its sign were seen as an everyday occurrence" (11).
4. Classroom space/lecture theatres: "The CGDS is also challenged in this area at the moment, especially because of the current UWI culture of faculty and department establishment of 'ownership' of buildings and class/lecture rooms" (11). Added to this, "the timetabling of other majors/minors proved to be prohibitive, by not leaving students enough space to take additional programme courses" (9).
5. Information technology (IT) resources: "The CGDS obviously needs more computers as staff now must share access/use; and a new photocopying machine to facilitate the work of staff, affiliated members of the centre and students (who appreciate and have come to rely on the paid photocopying services, especially for hard-to-come-by articles on the required reading lists)" (11).
6. Negative perception/invisibility of Gender Studies: Dissuasion from faculty and advisors for students registered in their faculty to enrol in the Minor in Gender Studies based on a negative and stigmatized perception of Gender Studies that permeated the campus and devalues it as a discipline and reduces it to something that is only for and about women (9).

In the last instance, a similar observation is made with respect to gender courses at the Cave Hill campus by that external review team:

> A popular, yet uninformed, opinion about the content and subject matter undertaken in gender courses continues to circulate. Even some students interviewed

> who explained how they had benefited from gender studies courses nonetheless indicated that they had to surmount negative cultural expectations about course content. Combined with a distinctively negative attitude among some non-CGDS staff members and students in the wider campus that the CGDS is feminist, highly political and anti-male, this uninformed opinion is a factor limiting CGDS achievements. From year to year, more students are not encouraged by other staff to take gender courses taught by the CGDS and, in fact, may be actively discouraged from doing so. (UWI BUS 2006a, 16)

The persistence of these challenges even after formal establishment of the centre clearly confirms observations made by Rowland (1982) in relation to hurdles that are encountered in efforts to establish women's studies courses in institutions of higher education. The lack of adequate support and the resistance to innovative ideas are not unique to the CGDS experience of introducing a programme of gender studies to the academic landscape of the UWI.

Bailey (2003) highlights some of the issues identified by Rowland that are encountered in establishing women's studies courses within institutions of education. Most relate to traditional power structures designed to obstruct movement; for example, she identifies concerns associated with the status of persons involved in the process in relation to the institutional hierarchy and the extent to which they have "legitimate" power. This, in turn, determines ready access to concrete resources to support the programme. This proved to be the case at the UWI, where, even though there was approval for the establishment of the centre at the highest administrative level, those on the ground charged with responsibility for implementation lacked "legitimate" power in terms of positioning within the institutional hierarchy. They were, therefore, dependent on the goodwill of persons to act as "patrons" of the programme, not only for approval and mounting of undergraduate interdisciplinary courses, but also for providing a physical space for teaching and for staff offices. This accommodation, however, was not altogether altruistic since, in the final analysis, the benefits of such programmes accrued to the departments through which they were offered, with enrolment in these courses increasing full-time equivalent enrolment and resulting in greater income from tuition fees. Rowland also raises concerns about ways in which the expertise associated with women's studies programmes is undervalued because of the paranoia associated with interdisciplinarity, as well as issues of the self-confidence of those involved, which again relates to positioning within the hierarchy and, therefore, to status.

Despite the institutional resistance to establishing gender studies programmes at both undergraduate and graduate levels, students testified to the "overwhelming impact that gender courses had on their ability to question and critique established ways of thinking" (UWI BUS 2005, 6), an explicit dimension of the mission of the CGDS. This was particularly the case at St Augustine, where the review team noted that

> for many of the women, this course was a first chance to learn about gender and feminist critiques of knowledge, society, media, work and sexuality. Young women in the class soon began to question the relative absence of gendered teaching in disciplines such as politics and government, economics, sociology and the sciences. . . . These ideological transformations have been experienced on multiple levels, for example, personal/interpersonal, academic, community, and national. Beyond the classroom, students also reported that they have been greatly impacted by the Centre's Wednesday brown-bag lectures/discussion. The current and recently graduated students additionally referenced the visiting scholars in the Centre as an additional source of intellectual expansion. (UWI BUS 2005, 7)

Students interviewed at the Cave Hill and Mona campuses during the external reviews gave similar testimonies. At Cave Hill, it was noted in the review report that "student learning outcomes, as reported in evaluations and discovered in the Review Team's interviews with students, reveal a consistently high level of student awareness of how gender studies courses enhanced the development of their thinking and analytical skills. In addition, interviewees reported that CGDS courses increased their social awareness and encouraged personal empowerment, which, in turn, fostered the desire for further education" (UWI BUS 2006a, 24). In the evaluation report for the Mona campus, which covered both the RCU and Mona unit, it is noted that the team was "impressed with the diversity and quality of research projects completed by the MSc students. Their contributions to the communities they are engaged with promise to be significant, given the quality of their training and, in the case of those we met, their obvious passion to work on gender inequities in their respective contexts" (UWI BUS 2006b, 5). In relation to the undergraduate programme offered by the Mona unit, the team noted that "the students we met, speaking specifically about AR20B, but also in some cases about other GDS courses, were enthusiastic about the content taught. They found the topics relevant, fascinating, easy to relate to their own experiences and 'eye-opening' in terms of their own development" (ibid., 9).

A comment made by the team that visited the Mona campus, in relation to the teaching programmes available at that time, eloquently attests to the fact that, in spite of the financial, human and physical constraints, the CGDS had managed to overcome these obstacles, and its objectives of "educating students to better understand gender issues critical to the nation and region, and to create capacity for the promotion and fostering of gender analysis and its integration into institutions, programmes and policies, are surely being well realized" (ibid., 6).

Consolidation and Articulation of Undergraduate and Graduate Programmes

In spite of the declared impact of the various teaching programmes on students across all three campuses and even before the BUS reviews, it was evident that a more systematic approach to programme development was necessary to ensure that the centre was meeting its mandate, as mentioned before, to "develop an integrated, interdisciplinary programme of Gender Studies within the university at both the undergraduate and graduate levels".

In the 2006 report of the external review of the Cave Hill unit, it is noted that the lack of integration of the teaching programmes on the three campuses was first identified in the IOP/UWI/ISS May 1996 evaluation report, where it was noted that, inter alia,

1. an integrated approach to curriculum development is not followed;
2. the handling of the elements of curriculum development depended too much on individual approaches;
3. coordination of disciplinary courses does not have a clear structure and is different on each campus; and
4. course offerings are, in the first instance, the result of personal commitment of lecturers from different faculties. (Ibid., 11–12)

These issues persisted, to varying degrees, across the three campuses through the first decade following the establishment of the CGDS. For that reason, a position paper setting out a proposal for articulation of teaching programmes at all levels was developed by the regional coordinator, for tabling at the 2004/5 Regional Planning and Strategy Committee meeting held in May 2005.

For the most part, these programmes had been developed independently of each other, with no explicit attempt to ensure articulation among the different offerings and the possibility, therefore, for a programme at a lower level to be used to satisfy requirements for entry to a higher level. The only case in which an explicit relationship existed was where, at that time, the minor offered by the Mona unit was used as one criterion for selection for admission to the taught master's programme offered by the RCU.

In addition, the external quality assurance reviews pointed to concerns related to academic offerings of specific units of the centre. In the Mona self-assessment report (UWI CGDS 2006), the fact that students were unable to pursue a major in GDS was noted, as well as the fact that this meant that there was no firm base on which to build a strong, graduate-level programme, which possibly accounted for the relatively low interest at that level. This gap was also noted by the external teams that reviewed the CGDS units across all three campuses. In the St Augustine report (UWI BUS 2005, 5), the comment made was that, "while the Minor is much appreciated, some students expressed the need for the development and offer of a Major, a goal also of the CGDS". In the Cave Hill report (UWI BUS 2006a, 12), the evaluators noted that "the CGDS . . . gives priority . . . to the deepening of academic programmes through mounting postgraduate degrees and an undergraduate major, along with the continuing enhancement of the Summer Institute in Gender and Development Studies as a means of achieving this objective".

> By 1997/98, I realized that the campus and Barbados knew about the CGDS, and the thrust at visibility was successful, and it was time to think of strengthening the undergraduate programming and deepening a research profile. By 2003, at the end of ten years, it was time to think of even greater research contributions. I think I wrote down somewhere that the first five years were dedicated to visibility and entrenchment, the next five to programme development, including the Summer Institute, and the third five to strengthening Caribbean feminist scholarship and developing a postgraduate programme. (Eudine Barriteau, testimonial)

Although this was raised in the RCU self-assessment study, no direct reference was made to the need to introduce a major in the 2006 report of the external review of the units at the Mona campus. The reviewers, however, recommended, "as a matter of priority, a thorough review of the existing six courses, with a view to rationalization" (UWI BUS 2006b, 10). They also advised that "the course load for the MSc programme should be reduced from the current eight courses to seven or six, with an adjustment of credits per course from three to four, to reflect the more intensive nature of graduate studies" (ibid., 19).

The major concern expressed by individuals accessing programmes offered by the CGDS at Mona, particularly the non-degree certificate and undergraduate minors, was the absence of explicit arrangements which allowed participants in an undergraduate programme to move incrementally to the next level; that is, the opportunity to move seamlessly through programmes in GDS from the lowest to the highest level. In response, a two-day retreat was mounted by the RCU to discuss these concerns and arrive at strategies for improving a seamless articulation of programmes. Figure 8.1 illustrates these proposals.

In May 2006, a proposal to offer a BSc major in GDS, in collaboration with the departments of sociology, social work and psychology, was developed by the university director, Barbara Bailey, to be offered through the Mona unit. A limiting factor in the configuration of courses for the proposed major was that it drew heavily on level 1 courses offered in the non-degree diploma programme.

Figure 8.1. Proposed links to facilitate articulation of undergraduate and graduate programmes in Gender and Development Studies

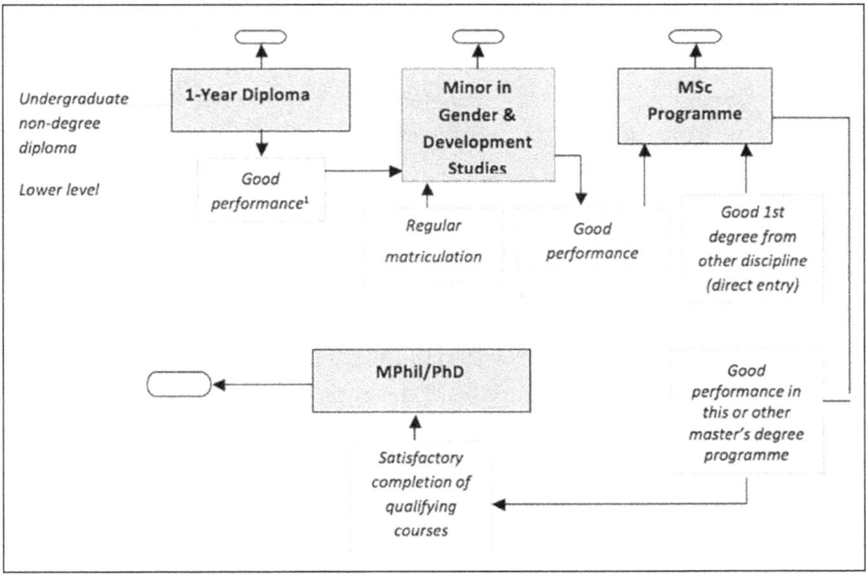

[1]An associate degree programme had been proposed (advanced placement for diploma graduates), but it has not yet materialized. Consequently, the situation, at present, is that diploma graduates with a satisfactory level of performance in that programme could use that qualification for regular matriculation requirements to enter an undergraduate programme.

This, in effect, would militate against students who pursued the diploma, performed creditably and then wanted to apply for entry to the major in GDS. To avoid this, it would be necessary, in the short run, to develop additional level 1 courses and expand the base from which selections for the various programmes could be made. The major was eventually finalized by Leith Dunn, who was appointed head of the Mona unit in 2006, and was approved by the academic board on the recommendation of the Academic Quality Assurance Committee in 2007/8, becoming available for registration in the following academic year. A major has not been developed by either of the Cave Hill and St Augustine units.

Curriculum Review Activities

The external quality assurance reviews of the CGDS units over the period 2005 to 2006 focused on all aspects of teaching and learning, in an effort to ensure the maintenance and enhancement of the quality of learning of students and to guarantee the continuation of appropriate output standards. Recommendations were made to improve programme offerings and to extend the reach of these programmes. In an effort to respond to the proposal to rationalize the graduate programmes and respond to the quality assurance recommendations, both the St Augustine unit and RCU undertook reviews of their graduate offerings in the 2006/7 academic year.

In the case of the St Augustine unit, the details of the review and the outcome are extracted from the 2012 self-assessment report (UWI IGDS 2012a) covering the period 2007 to 2012. There, it is acknowledged that two previous events informed the review: firstly, agreements reached at the May 2004 CGDS regional meeting to work on a revision of the graduate programmes; and, secondly, recommendations ensuing from the 2005 quality assurance review as well as comments made by students at that time. Subsequently, in the 2006/7 academic year, the entire postgraduate programme was substantially revised, and it was envisaged that the new programmes would cater to the range of options that graduate students would wish to pursue. These programmes would contribute to the following overall goals:

1. Improvement of the quality of gender-based analysis in the public, private and not-for-profit sectors
2. Demonstration of the breadth of the field of gender studies, its history of

thought and development, its research methods and its applications to the Caribbean situation
3. Equipping senior professionals with a range of modern techniques and an enhanced capacity to address developmental issues in the workplace
4. Developing a cadre of well-trained gender specialists ready for work in a variety of contexts
5. Facilitating gender-based research and publication in diverse disciplines
6. Exposure of students to the importance of appreciating difference vis-à-vis gender and other social categories of analysis

In the case of the Mona campus, the RCU organized a two-day retreat (5–6 March 2007) and included staff of the Mona unit involved in the delivery of the graduate programmes as well as adjunct, part-time lecturers and supervisors. The meeting was convened to consider and respond to recommendations contained in the February 2006 self-assessment report and to concerns raised by the BUS review team regarding the graduate programmes offered by CGDS.

The focus of the discussions at the retreat was on the existing MSc and MPhil/PhD programmes, but, subsequently, it was determined that the revised programmes should be harmonized with the offerings at St Augustine by the introduction of a one-year postgraduate diploma at Mona. It was anticipated that this diploma would also allow for the possibility of the transfer of students between the Mona and St Augustine campuses and would substantially increase enrolment in the graduate programme at Mona.

A Final Comment

Several challenges had to be overcome to arrive at a clearly articulated package of programmes in GDS available at all levels. In the twenty years under review, the programmes offered by the CGDS/IGDS have moved from a tentative start of stand-alone courses to, eventually, minors offered and conferred through existing faculties. Currently, the IGDS has attained degree-granting status and offers a fully articulated complement of programmes where students can, as long as entry requirements are met, move seamlessly from a lower-level matriculation diploma programme right through to a postgraduate MPhil/PhD degree. Given the human, financial and physical limitations with which all the units have had to contend over these twenty years, this transition is nothing short of miraculous, and all who have made this possible are to be commended.

Note

1. ETC is a Netherlands-based, not-for-profit organization working worldwide to strengthen resilience in support of people-centred development in rural and urban settings. They report that, in all areas, they enhance gender equality.

CHAPTER 9

PURSUING THE MANDATE

Research and Publications

> The issues with which the gender discourse has been involved have been so multifaceted that they can only be satisfactorily addressed through interdisciplinary research and study. Gender is now recognized as an important tool of analysis in the generation and reconstruction of knowledge. Like race and social class, it has become pivotal to the understanding of many historical, social and political issues and is a central consideration in any discourse on development, and its intersection with so many issues has facilitated interdisciplinary approaches to analyses of a variety of issues.
>
> —*Mona Academic Conference 2003 concept paper*

Building Research Capacity

Research was seen as a critical dimension of the tripartite mission of the newly established CGDS from its inception onwards and, in fact, was pivotal to fulfilling all aspects of the mission which called on the centre, through its programmes and activities, to "question historically accepted explanations about society and human behaviour; Seek an understanding of the world which takes women, their lives and achievements into account; and, Critically examine the origins of power differences between and among women and men and the factors which perpetuate these differences" (UWI UAC 1993).

In the ETC Foundation's (Kamphuis 1997) evaluation of phase 2 of the IOP/UWI/ISS project, however, it was acknowledged that resources provided through the two phases of the project had been insufficient to support the research objectives and that the absence of funding for the regional research agenda of the CGDS had resulted in an overemphasis on small research projects funded by the University Research and Publications Grants Committee and by small grants from other donors. In 1998, further direct support was secured through the Royal Netherlands Embassy in Jamaica to fund a third phase of activities, through the DSO/UWI project, aimed at consolidating achievements under the previous phases, and activities to build the research capacity of the CGDS were included. The immediate objectives related to research included, inter alia,

1. enhancing the research capacity of the CGDS through faculty training and research grants;
2. providing graduate student research grants;
3. establishing a small computer laboratory for graduate students; and,
4. funding to reproduce and disseminate research reports produced through the research grants.

The faculty research grants envisaged by the project were intended for training in research methodologies and were especially useful for enhancing the capacity of CGDS faculty and exposing them to new research techniques that were particularly relevant for the gathering of qualitative data and for applying tools that could facilitate an analysis of social, economic and political gendered phenomena.

Patricia Mohammed, the recipient from the Mona unit for the faculty research grant, acquired training in the use of methodologies appropriate for researching gender imagery and using iconography which requires different methods of research and analysis, most of which have been developed by Europeans. Until that time, this area of research in the Caribbean had been limited mainly to the examination of contemporary media images and their effect on men and women. The research grant, taken up in 2000, facilitated visits to the ISS; the University of Belfast, Northern Ireland; University College, London; and several museums in Amsterdam, the Hague and London. During these visits, she met with persons who had been working in this area, who could guide her to research sources that were relevant to the Caribbean region and could advance her effort to develop appropriate methodologies for researching gender through imagery. Through this exposure, Mohammed has developed the art of using iconography to interrogate gendered phenomena and to pursue her interest in studying the evolution of Caribbean identities through this medium. This has resulted in a number of text-based materials and films that have been used to inform the teaching of gender courses offered by the CGDS/IGDS.

Eudine Barriteau, head of the Cave Hill unit, used her grant in July 2000 to do a graduate course in contemporary feminist theory at George Washington University. Her focus was on the research methodology used in the area of policy analysis and the intersections of contemporary feminist concerns with the development and implementation of public policy. Exposure to this course enabled her to gain new insights into feminist theorizing and to establish new contacts at Howard and George Washington universities. This training also enhanced her ability to make the best use of the data and recommendations that resulted from a research project on gender and the economy in which the Cave Hill unit was engaged at that time.

In July 2001, the regional coordinator, Barbara Bailey, attended the fifty-fourth Summer Institute in Survey Research Techniques at the University of Michigan in the United States and benefited from formal exposure over four weeks to two courses: Focus Groups as Qualitative Research, and Ethnography: Introduction and Overview. The information gleaned from these courses not only enhanced her own research capacities but also proved very useful for evaluating the applicability of each perspective for use in interdisciplinary projects of the centre. In addition, the information gleaned was useful for reviewing the research methods course taught as part of the offerings of the MSc in GDS programme.

In 2002, Rhoda Reddock of the St Augustine unit completed a course on ethnographic and qualitative research methods at the University of Essex Summer School. Some of the methods learned were integrated into her graduate teaching programme and also enhanced her ability to supervise graduate students involved in various types of research.

Given the wide range of personal, national and regional research initiatives in which all units of the CGDS subsequently engaged, in retrospect, it is very evident that the opportunity afforded through this project for the senior staff of all units of the CGDS to gain exposure to qualitative research techniques was invaluable and paid rich dividends. This enabled the CGDS to position itself as a source of expertise in feminist research techniques and to attract substantial financial support from bilateral and multilateral funding agencies for research projects employing such approaches; and, through this engagement, to build a reputation which, over the years, has served national governments and regional and international entities.

Dissemination of research was a focus of the DSO/UWI project, and this was facilitated through research grants to faculty and graduate students. Patricia Mohammed's grant was used to assist in conducting research into the life of Eric Williams, a former prime minister of Trinidad and Tobago. This resulted in a paper, "A Very Public Private Man: Sketches in a Biography of Eric Eustace Williams", presented at a conference at Wellesley College in Massachusetts in April 2000, the theme of which was "Eric Williams and the Pan-African Movement", and at the Caribbean Studies Association conference in May 2000. In 2001, the paper was published in a reader, *Caribbean Charisma: Legitimacy and Political Leadership in an Era of Independence*, edited by Anton Allahar and published by Ian Randle. This research ultimately served as a resource for the expansion of work on masculinities.

Eudine Barriteau used her grant to produce a working paper on the male marginalization discourse, titled "Examining the Issues of Men, Male Marginalization and Masculinity in the Caribbean: Policy Implications". Rhoda Reddock received the fourth research grant, which she used to complete writing the biographies of two popular feminist activists from Trinidad and Tobago: Beatrice Greig and Christina Lewis. The publication was geared towards a popular audience and could be used to create awareness, among secondary school students and the Caribbean public in general, of two women who have made significant contributions to national development.

The RCU also received a research grant, which was intended to produce a monograph on student performance titled *Unmasking Gender Stereotypes: Quantitative and Qualitative Dimensions of the School Experience*, based on data that had been collected and analysed with supplementary funding from the Canada/Caribbean Gender Equality Fund (CCGEF). Unfortunately, although assigned an ISBN number, the monograph was not completed because of the illness and death of the co-author who had worked on the collection of data. The DSO/UWI project also supported research grants for graduate students on all three campuses, which resulted in the publication of papers covering a range of topics and geographical areas.

A further output of the DSO/UWI project, related to research and dissemination of findings, was the publication of teaching materials in the form of books and bibliographies prepared by staff and associate staff of the CGDS. Two readers that have, since their publication, supported teaching at both the undergraduate and graduate levels, were supported by this project. *Gendered Realities: Essays in Caribbean Feminist Thought*, edited by Patricia Mohammed, and *Confronting Power, Theorizing Gender: Interdisciplinary Perspectives in the Caribbean*, edited by Eudine Barriteau, were published by the UWI Press in 2002 and 2003, respectively. In addition, a book entitled *Writing Rage: Unmasking Violence through Caribbean Discourse*, by Paula Morgan and Valerie Youssef, associates of the St Augustine unit, was produced under this project and, in keeping with the intention of the project to develop research capacities, applied, as mentioned in its listing on the Google Books website (http://www.abebooks.co.uk/Writing-Rage-Unmasking-Violence-Caribbean-Discourse/16402784076/bd), "strategies of linguistic and literary analysis to a range of real-life and fictional discourses on the theme of violence".

Under the project, the annotated bibliography *Gender and Education in the Commonwealth Caribbean*, compiled by Lynda Quamina-Aiyejina in 2007 and described as "the first-ever comprehensive bibliography of existing research on gender and education in the Commonwealth Caribbean" (http://www.ungei.org/resources/1578.htm), was supported by, and later published in collaboration with, the Institute of Education of the Mona campus. Although support from UNESCO to cover the cost of publication has been acknowledged, there is no similar recognition of the major contributor to the development of the bibliography, the DSO/UWI project.

Ease of access to sources is as, or even more, important than dissemination. Over time, the campus units had collected, through gifts and purchase, a significant number of books, offprints, journals and mimeographed articles and had developed a significant special collection, some through phase 2 of the IOP/UWI/ISS project. The centre also received gifts of collections such as that of Dorian Powell, whose work was on family, and the Dame Nita Barrow collection, which was acquired by the Cave Hill unit. All units benefited from funding to catalogue holdings in their reading rooms, which greatly improved ease of access for students, visiting and local researchers, and staff. Regrettably, because of lack of sustained funding for a documentalist, the collection at Mona was moved to the main library and integrated into the general holdings, a move which significantly reduced ease of access for all categories of users, including CGDS personnel.

A Call for Research from within the Academy: A CGDS/IGDS Flagship Project

It is of note that, even before the close of the DSO/UWI project, the expertise that resided in the CGDS to use gender as an analytical tool to interrogate gendered phenomena and engage in research projects, small and large, had already been recognized both within and beyond the academy. In 1997, the then vice-chancellor, Sir Alister McIntyre, attended a CARICOM Heads of Government meeting where, in the wake of the prevailing discourse on male marginalization led by Professor Errol Miller, a call was made by the heads of government for the necessary research into socialization processes both in the home and the school system. In that same year, this call was taken up at a UWI Council meeting, where members expressed alarm at "the falling level of male participation and underachievement in the education system".

Following this meeting, the vice-chancellor charged the RCU with the responsibility to undertake an investigation of this phenomenon, and, with assistance from the UWI campus principals, bursars and the campus units, the RCU convened a regional meeting in Jamaica in 1997, involving all CGDS units and stakeholders of the CGDS, to explore the parameters of such a study and the requirements for its execution and completion. These stakeholders included the three UWI Schools of Education, the Mona Faculty of Social Sciences, the BUS and other regional and international organizations, including the CARICOM, the Organisation of Eastern Caribbean States, the Caribbean Examinations Council and the UNIFEM Caribbean Office.

The concern raised at the Heads of Government and the UWI Council meetings centred on male underachievement. At the initial meeting convened by the RCU, it was acknowledged that, despite the fact that research initiatives existed and had focused on various issues with regard to the impact of gender on education, no extensive regional research programme had been undertaken, and such a programme could guide policy formation and inform education in ways appropriate to both sexes.

There was consensus, therefore, that the concern should be broadened to incorporate a gender perspective which would allow for an in-depth understanding of points of male/female advantage and disadvantage at the secondary and tertiary levels of Caribbean education systems. The main areas of concern would be enrolment and attrition, participation and achievement, and the personal, social, cultural and economic factors determining observed patterns in these areas. The aim of the proposed project, therefore, was to understand the socialization influences that contribute to the nature and extent of gender imbalances that exist between male and female students in the education systems in the CARICOM region and to obtain empirical data from which conclusions could be drawn to inform the development of relevant policies and interventions in CARICOM member states.

The report of this meeting was shared with the Caribbean Development Bank and, in November 1997, the CGDS requested technical assistance from the bank to retain a consultant to prepare and cost a research proposal to study gender imbalance at the secondary and tertiary levels in education systems in the nineteen borrowing member countries of the CDB. The bank agreed to provide a grant to recruit a consultant to undertake a review of the available literature on gender imbalance at the secondary and tertiary levels in education systems in CDB's borrowing member countries and to prepare and cost a proposal for substantive research. Dr Anthony Layne of the School of Education, Cave Hill, was contracted to undertake these tasks. The draft proposal was discussed at a regional workshop and with the CDB in February 2000 and feedback for modifications passed to Dr Layne. The final product was submitted to the bank in April 2000.

Given the scope of the study that was envisaged, securing funding for this project proved to be a major challenge, and, even while the CGDS awaited a response from the CDB, several other funding sources were approached for support. This proved to be highly labour-intensive, given that the overall proposal had to be broken down and proposals for each segment adapted to meet the focus of the various agencies to which submissions were being made.

In the final analysis, the project was divided into three phases, consisting of different activities, and funding secured from agencies with complementary objectives. Given funding constraints, the main run of data collection was carried out in Belize, Jamaica, Guyana, and Trinidad and Tobago, with a pilot study in St Kitts and Nevis. Data were collected from a wide range of informants, including students, teachers, principals, guidance counsellors, education officers, parents, labour-market recruiters and dropouts from the formal system.

Research activities were eventually implemented in three phases corresponding to availability of funding.

Phase 1: Establishment of a Database

Funding received from the CCGEF, Barbados, and the OECS supported the development of the database on enrolment, participation and performance indicators at the secondary and tertiary levels of education systems in CARICOM member states. The database identified and analysed significant gender differences in enrolment and participation as well as points of difference based on calculation of gender parity indices and gender achievement gaps.

Phase 2: The Specialist Studies

The four studies focused on gender differentials in education at the secondary and tertiary levels of the education systems of the region, with particular reference to the anglophone Caribbean. Three of the following studies were funded by the CCGEF, Barbados, and the OECS and the fourth by UNESCO:

1. Sex differentials in educational outputs and the relationship of these outputs to social outcomes for either sex, carried out by an independent consultant, Sybil Ricketts

Plate 9.1. Gender Differentials project: Barbara Bailey observes a single-sex classroom in Trinidad

2. Alternative pathways for tertiary education, undertaken by Eudine Barriteau, head of the Cave Hill unit
3. Demographics of the school population in Caribbean education systems, with a focus on race, class and sex differences, by Wilma Bailey of the Department of Geography, Faculty of Pure and Applied Sciences, Mona
4. Attrition/dropout in selected Caribbean countries, with particular reference to the secondary level, carried out in Belize, Guyana and Trinidad and Tobago by Monica Brown of the Institute of Education, Mona

Phase 3: The Major, In-Depth Study

This phase consisted of a major, in-depth study of the social, economic and cultural factors impinging on educational enrolment and performance, particularly at the secondary level of Caribbean education systems. Funding was received from the CDB in November 2002.

In addition, support was secured to

1. appoint a project coordinator, Suzanne Charles, attached to the RCU, with funding from the Office of the Principal of the Mona campus for a two-year period, August 2003 to July 2005;
2. undertake a pilot study, conducted by Wilma Bailey, of the demographics of the school population in Jamaica, with funding from the Mona campus Research and Publications Committee,
3. develop an annotated bibliography of regional and international sources on gender issues in education, supported by a research grant from the DSO/UWI project.

Once funding was obtained from the CDB in November 2002, three further workshops were held between that time and December 2003 to further delineate the scope of phase 3 activities. The first was held in Trinidad and Tobago to discuss the research proposal and further detail the scope and sequence of activities related to this phase. The second was held in Jamaica in November 2003 and involved input from a representative group of academics and education officials (UWI, MOE, a representative from Belize, OECS Education Reform Unit, UNIFEM Caribbean, CARICOM) with a knowledge and interest in the research theme, to fine-tune the phase 3 design. The third meeting was held in December 2003 in Barbados to further develop instruments for the collection of both quantitative and qualitative data, but, prior to this meeting, a small, multidisciplinary, Jamaica-based group met to prepare a first draft of the research instrument.

Some twelve years elapsed between the call for the research and completion of the project, and although, over that time, many persons were pessimistic that the funds would ever be realized, the regional coordinator was adamant that the research was critical for testing the claim of the male marginalization thesis in Caribbean education systems. By the end of the 2002/3 academic year, the project had realized adequate funding from a number of agencies, as well as a Mona campus research fellowship, to offset the remuneration of a project coordinator for a two-year period.

The approach to securing funding which, in fact, only covered fieldwork, coding of the data and the recruitment of short-term consultants to analyse and develop reports for small segments of the data, allowed the CGDS to establish collaborative synergies among multiple funding sources. In addition, the CGDS succeeded in drawing on the expertise residing in a multidisciplinary team of academics and professionals and on the advice of professionals in the region, a strategy that later extended to other projects, albeit less elaborate than the Gender Differentials project. Ultimately, however, most of the data gathered was analysed and reports compiled in-house by the project coordinator, Suzanne Charles, and the university director. Some of these findings were published in a special issue of the *Caribbean Journal of Education* edited by Barbara Bailey, with contributions from those who had supported the development of these reports.

Over the life of the project, updates were regularly tabled at meetings of the Council on Human and Social Development of the CARICOM so that ministers and regional organizations in attendance, including the CDB, were always kept abreast of progress on the project.

The findings from this multifaceted research project were presented and discussed at a regional policy forum organized in Barbados in April 2010 by the CDB in collaboration with the RCU. Outcomes were shared with chief education officers, a permanent secretary from a CDB borrowing member country and other stakeholders, including representatives of the OECS, UNICEF, CARICOM and the Caribbean Examinations Council. Informed by the findings, a four-pillar policy framework for addressing gender differentials in education was also discussed. The framework consisted of four interactive elements which impact schooling and the educational process – the state, the school, the home and the community. There was agreement that the formulation of educational policies and/or educational reforms and/or interventions to address gender disparities and promote greater gender equality and equity in Caribbean education systems would be futile unless the impact of these four interactive pillars were simultaneously considered and solutions found to mitigate impacts on educational outputs and outcomes. Based on participant feedback, the framework was modified and finalized.

The culminating activity of the Gender Differentials project was the presentation of the final policy framework to ministers of education of CARICOM member states in attendance at the twentieth meeting of the Council for Human and Social Development held in Guyana, Georgetown, in October 2010. The framework was adopted by the council, and there was an indication from the CDB that further funds might be found to support implementation of the policy in selected Caribbean countries. It is apparent, however, that this has not been the case. Despite the investment of significant time, effort, human and financial resources, as always, the weak link in the chain remains intact: lack of political will and low implementation of evidence-based policy decisions adopted at high-level meetings such as the Council for Human and Social Development.

Nonetheless, this can be regarded as a flagship project carried out by the CGDS/IGDS, involving all units of the CGDS and a prototype that, in the future, could be adapted to the specific needs of large-scale, multidisciplinary, cross-campus, multi-agency, multiphase research projects, in collaboration with regional entities, such as the CARICOM, and regional stakeholder groups relevant to the issue under consideration.

Influences beyond the Academy on the CGDS Research Agenda

A spinoff from the Gender Differentials project was heightened interest in gender issues as well as agencies turning to the CGDS for expertise. One such initiative was a collaborative project between the RCU and CARICOM to develop a training module for teacher educators on gender issues in education. The content of the module was informed by an investigation into teacher educators' perceptions and understandings of gender issues in education, carried out during the 1998/99 academic year and funded by CARICOM. Following this, CARICOM commissioned the development of the module *Gender Issues in Caribbean Education*, which was authored by Barbara Bailey and Yasmeen Yusuf-Khalil of the RCU, CGDS, and Monica Brown of the Institute of Education, Mona.

To ensure buy-in, input was sought from teacher educators from teacher training institutions in selected CARICOM member states, in terms of issues to be included as well as how such a module could be accommodated in the existing college curriculum. The intention was that the module would be integrated in the curriculum of all regional teacher training institutions as a mandatory component of the training programme for teachers of all levels of education. To this end, two subregional training workshops were held for teacher educators to build familiarity with the content of the module as well as to discuss various strategies that could be used to facilitate inclusion of the module in the range of contextual settings in teacher training institutions across the region. It is very disappointing, therefore, that, from all reports, implementation has been minimal.

The mounting of the UN Fourth WCW in Beijing in 1995 also heightened interest in critical issues affecting women globally and the need for research on their impact as well as for the training of a cadre of persons who could implement the actions related to the twelve critical issues identified in the platform for action emanating from that conference. In response, funding sources were soon mobilized to support initiatives that would facilitate implementation of the platform for action, including work within academic institutions such as research and training initiatives. Two funding sources would prove beneficial to the CGDS. The CIDA established sizeable national and regional funding mechanisms, the CCGEF, to serve Jamaica, Barbados and the OECS countries. The Japan WID Fund also made funds available to the Government of Jamaica, which were administered by the UNDP.

In 1995, leading up to the fourth WCW, the CARICOM Secretariat had developed the *Regional Report on the Status of Caribbean Women*, authored by Alicia Mondesire and Leith Dunn (1995, 85), which identified and ranked, in order of priority, the major issues affecting these women, as follows: violence against women; poverty; insufficient mechanisms to promote women's advancement; inequality in the sharing of power; access to health, education and employment; and migration.

Bailey (2004, 641) notes that, by the time of the Beijing +5 meeting in 2000, language in the outcome document related to actions required in respect of violence against women was stronger, calling for the creation of an environment that does not tolerate any violation of the rights of women and girls. Further, she notes that, in the document, it was acknowledged that there was a need to "continue to undertake research to develop a better understanding of the root causes of all forms of violence against women in order to design programmes and take measures towards eliminating these forms of violence".

The RCU immediately submitted proposals to both the CCGEF and the Japan WID funds to undertake national and regional research projects on the root causes of violence against women in Jamaica and the wider Caribbean.

The first research project on GBV funded by the Jamaican branch of CCGEF was initiated in the 2001/2 academic year. The intention was to develop a research activity aimed at identifying indicators of the "culture of violence" evident in Jamaican society and, thereby, to contribute to an understanding of the phenomenon, with a view to informing interventions which could reduce the incidence of such violence. It was expected that, in the long term, findings would be used to inform national policy positions, public education programmes and strategies aimed at significantly reducing the occurrence of all forms of GBV, especially those targeting women and girls. Based on a suggestion by the funding agency, the RCU, in collaboration with the Mona unit, hosted a round table in March 2002 with other groups and organizations which were involved in similar activities. The wide-ranging discussion clarified several issues and also brought others to light, all of which pointed to the depth and complexity of the problem and the need for a more nuanced research design. Using some of the matters raised at that forum, the proposal was reformulated and submitted to the fund for further consideration.

The final research design was multifaceted and based on data collected in two phases, derived from both primary and secondary sources, as follows. Activities were coordinated by Althea Perkins, attached to the Mona unit.

Phase 1: Development of an Annotated Bibliography

The first consisted of a documentary review and compilation of an annotated bibliography on GBV in the Commonwealth Caribbean. The starting point for this exercise was information that had been supplied by individuals attending the round table held in March 2002. Follow-up visits were made to these agencies, and existing material that addressed GBV was identified. The material was not only catalogued to facilitate ease of reference in the future but was also analysed to identify existing information on root causes of GBV. This informa-

Plate 9.2. Barbara Bailey presenting a copy of the *Annotated Bibliography on Gender-Based Violence in the English-Speaking Caribbean* (funded by the Japan WID Fund) to the Japanese ambassador to Jamaica

tion was used to shape phase 2 in terms of gaps in existing research; possible informants and data sources; and, strategies that could be used for studying the problem.

Phase 2: Data Collection and Analysis

The aim of this phase was to determine how socialization practices contributed to the acquisition of violent and aggressive behaviours and the impact of social and economic factors in this regard. Primary data were collected from students at all levels of the education system, children in places of safety, church, community and civic groups in such a way as to ensure inclusion across age groups, socio-economic status and location. Secondary data on root causes of GBV were also gathered from cases related to GBV recorded by attorneys, counsellors, psychologists, social workers, psychiatrists and general practitioners. Individuals selected in these categories were known to have clients who had been victims of domestic violence. Finally, data were also derived from a review of newspaper accounts relating to GBV, including that associated with forced prostitution and drug trafficking; statistics from the Women's Crisis Centre for 2002–4; and data on domestic violence from reports of workshops that had already taken place.

Major findings were disseminated through a stakeholders' workshop held in September 2005 and attended by representatives of governmental and non-governmental organizations, educators, faith-based organizations and other relevant groups. The discussion was aimed at arriving at consensus on factors identified in the study that could be regarded as producing and reproducing a culture of violence and, therefore, could be considered as root causes, on possible strategies to address and/or eliminate these causes, and on concerns that were central to all components of the research project. Participants were urged to use the findings and recommended solutions to inform policies, programmes and interventions in their respective spheres of operation.

Following the fourth WCW, attention was also focused on women's economic empowerment and the call in Strategic Objective F3 of the Beijing Declaration and Platform for Action (http://www.un.org/womenwatch/daw/beijing/pdf/BDPfA%20E.pdf) was for governments to provide business services, training and access to markets, information and technology, particularly to low-income women, and, more specifically, to "develop programmes that provide training and retraining, particularly in new technologies, and affordable services to women in business management, product development, financing, production and quality control, marketing and the legal aspects of business" (#173b, 73).

This fitted directly into activities already initiated by the Office of the Prime Minister (Jamaica), which had established a microenterprise project in 1992 in collaboration with the then ISER of the UWI, in which the WDSG at Mona and, subsequently, the newly established CGDS participated. One activity under the first phase of the Women in Microenterprise project, undertaken by the CGDS, was the preparation of a draft of a training module for women in microenterprise. Beyond this initial phase, funds were raised by the CGDS from UNIFEM, New York, and the Government of Japan WID Fund for two further phases of ground-breaking activities with women engaged in small-business development in Jamaica.

Phase 2 covered the period January 1997 to December 1999 and was funded by the Government of Japan through its WID Fund. The report of this phase, prepared in 1999 by Joan Browne for the RCU of the CGDS, indicates that it involved four distinct activities:

1. The final study in the series of studies carried out under phase 1 was entitled *A Gender Analysis of the Impact of Macro-economic Policies on Microenterprise Development in Jamaica*. The study was conducted by Sonja Harris and Associates, and the findings suggested that, at that time, the prevailing macro-economic policies separated social development from economic growth, and the microenterprise sector from the rest of the economy, failing to identify true micro-entrepreneurs as resourceful segments of the labour force.
2. A needs-assessment workshop carried out under phase 1 with eighty women involved in entrepreneurial activities pointed to the need for training in four specific areas: business management, gender relations, confidence building and balancing the multiple, competing roles of women. Under this phase, existing materials were reviewed, but none addressed the specific challenges identified in the needs-assessment workshop. A training manual consisting of five modules was developed, specifically geared to the issues raised by the women.
3. Five regional training workshops were held, with the first event aimed at training ten trainers. These trainers then assisted with the delivery of subsequent workshops to seventy-nine women in four regions of the island – Montego Bay (western region), Mandeville (central region), Ocho Rios (northern region) and Kingston (for St Thomas, the Greater Metropolitan Area and St Catherine).
4. This training manual was piloted and tested in the "training of trainers" workshop as well as in a series of workshops held across the island. After each round of training the material was revised based on feedback received from participants. Based on the collective feedback the modules were restructured and the language and exercises modified to match the competence levels of the trainees. The revised manual was eventually published by the RCU of the CGDS who had responsibility for the project.

The following are some of the workshop participants' testimonials (UWI CGDS 1999):

- "I was able to learn because the trainers stopped to explain whatever was not clear to me. A lot of words I had heard in business and not understood were simply explained." (Montego Bay)
- "The workshop has made me feel like a different person. I no longer feel like a freak." (Montego Bay)

- "I was afraid to come here because I didn't think I could learn all these things, but you made it so easy to learn." (Mandeville)
- "More business people should have the chance to get this training." (Mandeville)
- "I hope more women will have the chance to be part of this programme." (Ocho Rios)
- "In my community, it is vital for women to develop some self-esteem and turn to depending on themselves, so this will be vital training for them." (Ocho Rios)
- "I told my husband that he will have to help me more with the housework. He looked surprised, but he thought about it and said, 'I don't mind getting my own dinner'. That's a change for him!" (Kingston)
- "The workshop was well put together. I appreciate the time spent in preparing for this workshop." (Kingston)

Recommendations for minor revisions to the training materials were made by workshop participants, and, following these amendments, in 1999, the manual *Entrepreneurial Skills for Women in Microenterprise* was published by the CGDS. A twenty-eight-minute video was developed by Hilary Nicholson, entitled *Moving Ahead: Developing and Sustaining a Successful Microenterprise*, during the course of the training workshops. The video also included clips from site visits to the business places of some participants and trainers.

A national policy seminar was held on 15 December 1999 with a view to identifying specific policy issues which impacted on female entrepreneurship and determining desirable future directions in terms of policies and programmes.

Several policy issues were identified, including the need for a counselling/resource hotline to facilitate ease of access to immediate business advice, the production of a small business directory, and closer collaboration and networking among female entrepreneurs. The meeting closed with the presentation of certificates of participation to trainers.

As a follow-up to earlier activities, phase 3 consisted of eleven one-day workshops, which catered to 205 participants; reprinting of the training manuals for distribution to relevant agencies for their use in training workshops; the production of a newsletter with networking information; establishment of a network of women entrepreneurs to facilitate exchange of information among women in microenterprises; and an impact evaluation workshop. Although it was anticipated that phase 3 would have been completed by December 2001, activities were not completed until April 2002.

As a result of the success of the Women in Microenterprise project, the RCU was invited by the Embassy of Japan to submit a further proposal, on behalf of the Government of Jamaica, to the WID Fund, administered through the UNDP. As with the Gender Differentials project, this offer created another opportunity to maximize human and financial resources as well as outputs and impacts, by partnering with other funding agencies and researchers to build on the gains realized through the project Root Causes of Gender-Based Violence funded by CIDA through the CCGEF. Activities related to the Gender, Training and Research project started in June 2003 and included the expansion, completion and publication of the *Annotated Bibliography on Gender-Based Violence in the Caribbean* started under the CCGEF project. A second annotated bibliography on gender and development in the Caribbean, developed by Lynda Quamina-Aiyejina, was also funded under this project. This bibliography was never published in hard-copy format but was uploaded to the website of the RCU at www.uwi.edu/cgds in 2005.

Funds from this project were also used to support the 2004 Gender and Development Summer Institute hosted by the Cave Hill unit of the CGDS; tuition fellowships for participants in the eighteen-month diploma programme in GDS; and a seminar/workshop on gender and trade and implications for the Caribbean, for graduate students registered in the CGDS and Faculty of Social Sciences, Mona, held in December 2005. The RCU used this opportunity of funding to expand its research on the root causes of violence, started in Jamaica, to carry out a more in-depth examination of violence in other Caribbean countries, at two levels:

1. Institutional level: with a focus on how policies and practices in educational institutions contribute to reproducing hegemonic masculinities and a culture of violence
2. Individual level: with a focus on students' experience and perceptions of violence in the home, school and community, as well as teachers' experience of violence, and ways in which these experiences influenced their views of violence in schools

The research was carried out in Dominica, Guyana and Grand Cayman and entitled "Gender Socialization, Schooling and Violence in Dominica, Guyana and Grand Cayman". Completed questionnaires from Grand Cayman, however, were misplaced by the courier service engaged to deliver the package to the CGDS in Jamaica, and they were never recovered. This resulted in a gap in the anticipated database and the absence of findings from this country in the final report.

In May 2006, a workshop, co-hosted by the RCU of the CGDS, UNIFEM Caribbean, CARICOM and UNICEF, was held in Dominica. The aim was to bring to the attention of stakeholders findings from this research and a number of other initiatives on GBV, undertaken by these entities. Findings shared at this meeting included those from "A Situational Analysis of Gender-Based Violence in the Caribbean", a CGDS research project based on various initiatives supported by UNIFEM since 1985; and "Violence against Children and the Evaluation of the Protective Environment", a project carried out in Dominica by Professor Elsie LeFranc of the Sir Arthur Lewis Institute of Social and Economic Studies as part of a larger global effort by UNICEF.

The theme of the workshop was "Strengthening Prevention Approaches to Gender-Based Violence", and a critical element was the session "An Analysis of School-Based Approaches for Addressing Gender-Based Violence: The Role of Ministries of Education", where representatives of ministries of education of ten countries shared their experiences and the limitations faced in efforts to address GBV. In the final analysis, it was agreed that what was required were national action plans which should be evidence-based, multisectoral, interdisciplinary, adequately resourced, and based on building partnerships.

Research Agenda: Campus Units

Although the campus units played a significant role in many of the research projects undertaken by the RCU, each campus unit was also individually involved in significant research activities. As with the RCU, research was often influenced by the interest and expertise of the individual heading the unit and, not least, by the inflow of funds from external funding agencies having their own specific mandates with which projects had to be aligned.

Cave Hill/NBU

Over the period under review, the research agenda of the Cave Hill/NBU was, to a large extent, constrained by the availability of both human and financial resources, and, as was the case in other units, by change of leadership. The focus of research of the unit has been on three major themes, as discussed below.

Caribbean Women: Catalysts for Change

The 2005 self-assessment report of the unit indicates that

> the major research project of the Centre is the Caribbean Women Catalysts for Change Project. The Project has three components: a research and publications aspect, a lecture series, and the establishment of a specialist collection of the papers of outstanding Caribbean women. The project was conceptualized in 1993 and began in 1994 with the aim of "documenting, analysing and disseminating – at both the popular and academic level – the contributions of Caribbean women who influenced the altering of social and economic life within their communities". The goal is to examine and locate the activities of outstanding Caribbean women in six overlapping arenas of the public domain. These are: regional and international development, politics and political participation, women organizing and the women's movement, trade unionism, education and agriculture and food production. (41)

The research aspect of the project focused on documenting the lives and work of outstanding Caribbean women. The first undertaken was that of Dame Nita Barrow of Barbados, and the resulting reader, *Stronger, Surer, Bolder: Ruth Nita Barrow; Social Change and International Development*, edited by Eudine Barriteau and Alan Cobley, was published by the UWI Press in 2001. The online comment on the publication states that the book "examines how this extraordinary Caribbean woman developed her leadership strategies to contribute to social change and shape development policy on national, regional and international levels. More than a celebration of her achievements, it analyses Barrow's career as a case study of leadership by black 'Third World' women during the turbulence of the 1930s" (http://bookshop.mona.uwi.edu/bookshop/product_info.php?cPath=73_36&products_id=12739).

In March 2002, the Cave Hill unit began researching the political leadership of Dame Eugenia Charles, under the theme "Women, Power and Politics". The output, in 2006, was a volume of essays contextualizing Dame Eugenia's contribution to Dominica and Caribbean public life, entitled *Enjoying Power: Eugenia Charles and Political Leadership in the Commonwealth Caribbean*, edited by Eudine Barriteau and Alan Cobley. The third publication in the Caribbean Women: Catalysts for Change series focuses on the public life of the Honourable Madame Justice Desirée P. Bernard, of the Caribbean Court of Justice. In the 2012 self-assessment report, it was noted that the tentative title of this publication is "Gender and Caribbean Jurisprudence", and fifteen chapters have already been submitted for inclusion.

The second aspect of this project involved the establishment of a specialist collection of the papers of outstanding Caribbean women. In February 2002, Dame Eugenia's papers were shipped from Dominica to the Cave Hill campus, and, on 19 September 2002, the unit held an official handing-over ceremony, in which Sybil Barrow and Dame Eugenia Charles presented legal documents to the university and officially donated Dame Nita Barrow's and Dame Eugenia Charles' papers to the Caribbean Women: Catalysts for Change project. This enabled the unit to move one step closer to achieving the major objective of establishing the Cave Hill campus library as a repository of the papers of outstanding Caribbean women.

This intention was realized on 15 November 2006, when the Cave Hill unit was formally renamed the NBU. Immediately after, in collaboration with the main library, the centre officially opened the Nita Barrow Specialist Collection. This housed the papers of Dame Nita Barrow and Dame Eugenia Charles and was the first specialist collection at Cave Hill dedicated to the papers of Caribbean women.

The third aspect of the project, the lecture series, is presented in chapter 10

Gender and Macroeconomic Policy

This project focused on an analysis of the impact of the stabilization and structural adjustment programme in four communities in Barbados. Funding for the project was provided by the UWI School of Graduate Studies and Research, and the intended output is a book-length manuscript on gender and macroeconomic policy in a modernizing Caribbean economy. Although the fieldwork and the coding manual was completed in January 2001, due to numerous setbacks, including the discovery, in 2003, that earlier data had been corrupted, and also due to assumption of new responsibilities following the appointment of Eudine Barriteau as deputy principal of the Cave Hill campus, the publication has not yet been produced.

Gender and Livelihoods: The Socio-Economic Impact on Women Who Are Caregivers of Chronically Ill Children

The NBU, Cave Hill, of the CGDS, in collaboration with the Hope Foundation, carried out a project on gender and livelihoods, which investigated the needs of women who are responsible for the care of children suffering from chronic diseases and the corresponding challenges they confronted with respect to their livelihoods. Through this project, the CGDS sought to provide policymakers and healthcare workers with vital information on the socio-economic challenges experienced by women who are the primary caregivers of children suffering from chronic diseases. A further intention was that the policies created would be endorsed by employers and insurance companies who were unaware of the specific needs of such women, thereby preventing such clients from falling into a poverty trap. The project was supported by UNIFEM Caribbean.

The NBU, Cave Hill, acted upon the recommendation of the Board of Studies to widen the scope of the project to include caregivers of children with intellectual, developmental and physical disabilities. In May/June 2008, the unit piloted the questionnaire towards amending the survey instrument, and, in July 2012, the findings were presented to the Hope Foundation.

Mona Unit

Over the period under review, the research projects undertaken by the Mona unit occurred under the watch of four different heads of unit. The shifting focus in the projects, no doubt, represents the unique interest and research orientation of each incumbent. Beyond 2006, with the arrival of the longest serving head, Leith Dunn, there was a sharper focus on a number of issues that were emerging in the gender and development discourse and which, at that time, had not been extensively explored in the Caribbean context.

The Making of Caribbean Feminisms

In 1994, Patricia Mohammed was appointed head of the Mona unit, where she was instrumental in shaping the early research agenda of that unit. The earliest research initiative was titled "The Making of Caribbean Feminisms", initiated in the 1998/99 academic year and carried out in collaboration with the St Augustine unit. Funding to support this project was secured from the Principal's Research Awards Committee of the Mona campus in the 2000/1 academic year.

The project encouraged the participation of graduate students of the CGDS and involved the collection of both written and oral history material throughout the Caribbean in an attempt to record the emergence of the second wave of the Caribbean feminist movement. The initial meeting was held in Trinidad in January 2002, and a common methodology and set of activities were determined. Included were biographies of women and men involved, before the 1960s, in the feminist movement in the region, with the initial focus of the project being on women in Jamaica and Trinidad. A further dimension of the project was the development of a special collection at the St Augustine main library. Work on the project at St Augustine was supported by a grant from the Campus Research and Publication Committee, in both the 2003/4 and 2006/7 academic years.

In 2002, Patricia Mohammed proceeded on a two-year research fellowship, awarded by the Office of Planning and Institutional Research of the Office of the Principal of the Mona campus, to pursue research on Caribbean iconography and the evolution of identity. In the first of those two years, she was replaced by Kamala Kempadoo, who, in the 2000/1 academic year, was one of five consultants to the United Nations Population Fund/UNICEF research project Meeting Adolescent Development and Participation Rights in Jamaica. The consultants were responsible for conducting a study to determine the factors that shaped the initiation of early sexual activity among adolescent girls and boys. The findings of the studies carried out by the consultants were published in 2002 by the funding agencies, in a book titled *Meeting Adolescent Development and Participation Rights: The Findings of Five Research Studies on Adolescents in Jamaica*.

During her short tenure, Kamala Kempadoo also had oversight of the UNESCO project Gender, Peace and Development in the Caribbean, in which the Mona unit participated along with counterparts from the St Augustine unit. The 2001 report of this project notes that the regional research project was initiated to

1. document research and development work being completed or in progress on gender, peace and development in the Caribbean;
2. identify existing areas of need and propose a programme of strategies to address these needs in gender, peace and development in the Caribbean;
3. identify potential partners from the research community; the public, private and NGO sectors; and development agencies who can collaborate in addressing the needs.

The report further states that the project was implemented in two parts:

1. An exploratory study of the organizations involved in programmes and of research completed or in progress on gender, peace and development in the Caribbean. This study was coordinated by Gwendoline Williams of St Augustine and administered by the CGDS Mona on behalf of UNESCO. Two teams of young professionals from the St Augustine and Mona campuses conducted the research. The teams were led by a project management team comprising Rhoda Reddock, Kamala Kempadoo and Claudia De Four, head of the West Indian division, UWI main library (St Augustine), who provided advice on compiling the bibliography.
2. A two-day stakeholder workshop was the second component, which was used to share with participants the results of the exploratory study; identify additional partners, strategies, documents and materials not captured in the research; and develop a draft programme of activities to address the existing areas of need.

At the end of the 2001/2 academic year, Kempadoo relinquished her temporary appointment at the Mona unit. Due to Mohammed's leave of absence and her eventual transfer to the St Augustine unit, during the period August 2002 to March 2006, Barbara Bailey, regional coordinator/university director, assumed responsibility for the Mona unit, with June Castello having responsibility for routine operational matters. During those years, the staff of the Mona unit, who, except for June Castello, were on temporary appointments, made significant contributions to the research activities of the RCU. As previously indicated, Suzanne Charles was integrally involved in the Gender Differentials project, and when, in 2003, the Mona campus research grant was awarded to the RCU, she was appointed project coordinator attached to the RCU. Althea Perkins, while still attached to the Mona unit, coordinated the Root Causes of Gender-Based Violence project, which was funded by the CCGEF.

With the appointment of Leith Dunn as head of the Mona unit in April 2006, the research agenda of the unit regained momentum, and her intention was to expand research activities to focus on the gender impact of "new and emerging" areas of concern. The three following areas are of note, with work beginning in the 2008/9 academic year.

1. Gender and trade: Leith Dunn, lead researcher, along with Anneke Hamilton, Jessica Byron of the Department of Government and Quaine Palmer, graduate student, participated in the study Gender Justice in Trade Policy: The Gender Effects of Economic Partnership Agreements, commissioned by One

World Action and the Commonwealth Secretariat and funded by the UK Department for International Development. This team had responsibility for data collection in Jamaica, which was one of three countries covered by the project, the other two being Tanzania and Mozambique. The research in these three countries revealed that job losses from import displacement were likely to be small and would not necessarily be disproportionately female. The Mona unit, along with One World Action and the Commonwealth Secretariat, co-hosted the Caribbean conference Mainstreaming Gender in Trade on 4–5 February 2009, which was attended by approximately sixty participants from seven countries. Papers from the study were also presented at trade conferences in Brussels, Belgium (Pansy Hamilton); and in Delhi, India (Leith Dunn).

2. Enhancing gender visibility in climate change and disaster risk management: This research project was commissioned by UNDP as part of the Caribbean Risk Management Initiative, an umbrella programme designed to build capacity across the Caribbean region for the management of climate-related risk. The project involved conducting five country assessments on gender mainstreaming in disaster management agencies as well as three country case studies on gender and climate change adaptation. Erika Ellis and Keino Senior, both attached to the Mona unit, presented papers on the studies carried out in Dominica and Jamaica at the fourth conference on the environment organized by the Jamaica Institute of Environmental Professionals, which was held in Kingston on May 2009. Papers from the study were also presented at the third Caribbean conference on Comprehensive Disaster Management held in Barbados in December 2009. The data derived from this project informed the development of technical reports authored by a team led by Leith Dunn and published by UNDP and the Caribbean Risk Management Initiative.
3. Gender and governance: Research on women's political participation at the highest level of decision-making focused on the experience of Jamaica's first female prime minister and gender equality in governance. This resulted in three articles published in IGDS Working Paper 5, co-published with Friedrich Ebert Stiftung, and an article published in the *JaPeople* journal of the Planning Institute of Jamaica. The research also provided input for the gender task force of Vision 2030 Jamaica, the national strategic plan coordinated by the Planning Institute of Jamaica. In addition, the IGDS Mona unit provided technical assistance to support the CIDA-funded research study

Gender and Governance: A Study of Women on Boards and Committees in Jamaica, sponsored by the Women's Resource and Outreach Centre.

St Augustine Unit

Research activities led by the St Augustine unit in Trinidad and Tobago have always had a strong interdisciplinary bias, with researchers drawn from a number of other departments and disciplines, and have not only been academic in orientation but have also often had a strong policy and activist slant. This is confirmed by remarks recorded in the 2005 external assessment review of the unit carried out by the Quality Assurance Unit of the BUS. It is noted there that "generally, the research projects are the product of cross-discipline collaboration. Academic staff from other departments/faculties as well as students are involved either as principal researchers or as part of the research teams. Notwithstanding collaboration with associate staff, the main responsibility for resource mobilization for Centre-coordinated research remains with the Centre" (UWI BUS 2005, 16).

The research agenda of the St Augustine unit addressed four themes that were partly agreed on at the regional level in the 1990s:

1. Gender, science and technology
2. The construction of Caribbean masculinities
3. The making of Caribbean feminisms
4. Gender and sexuality

Gender, Science and Technology

The Nariva Swamp: A Gendered Case Study

This project was consistent with a focus on gender and science and consisted of a gendered case study of an endangered wetland in Trinidad and Tobago, the Nariva Swamp. The objective was to examine the dynamics of male and female interactions with the biophysical environment and use of natural resources. This project was funded by the CIDA/CCGEP.

Information derived from a round table held in 2000 indicated that, at the time that the project was conceptualized, the Nariva Swamp was a centre of controversy and contestation in terms of the impact of human activities on this natural wetland environment (UWI CGDS 2000). It was identified, therefore, as a suitable site for conducting a case study in which the objective was a gender analysis of the sustainability of livelihoods and the environment. In 1998, a pilot was carried out in the Kernahan/Cascadoux community, and the project formally began in April 1999, with the major objective of empowering the community, with particular emphasis on women.

During the life of the project, two videos were produced. The first depicted the lives and livelihoods of people living in the Nariva area: *Living with the Wetlands: Women, Men and the Nariva Swamp*. Based on the success of the first video, produced during the 2002/3 academic year, additional funds were provided by the CIDA/CCGEF to produce a second video and a manual focusing on the biophysical aspect of this research, entitled *Engendering Environmental Studies and Policy: A Video Project of the Nariva Swamp*. Work on this second video began in September 2003 and ended in February 2004. This video has been used by Grace Sirju-Charran, head of the Department of Life Sciences and an associate of the CGDS, to support the gender and science course offered in that department. An interactive DVD based on the Nariva Swamp Project was also produced and was used at a theology and ecology conference to support a presentation made by Rhoda Reddock on ecofeminism.

Women, Gender and Water

This research project involved an examination of the gendered use of water and water resources in Trinidad and Tobago and the implications for policy. The project was multidisciplinary and collaborative and brought together scholars in the social sciences, natural and physical sciences and humanities. The aim of the project was to examine the multifaceted role of water in the life of women and men and the policy implications in areas such as – natural resource management, environmental management, and mitigation of the effects of natural disasters. The project was marked by the following activities:

1. Hosting of a one-day seminar "Gender, Water and Natural Resource Management", 11 March 2005
2. A mini-study of the Mount D'or and Plum Mitan Communities by Dr Diane Fox, visiting Fulbright scholar, and her research team, April 2005
3. The establishment of a multidisciplinary research group

Subsequently, the research network became involved in CAP-NET, the

Caribbean Partnership of the Global Water Alliance (Caribbean Water Net). Rhoda Reddock and Linnette Vassell presented two sessions on gender and water at a regional training course on integrated water resources management organized by the Faculty of Engineering, St Augustine.

The Construction of Caribbean Masculinities

The first conference to be held in the region on Caribbean masculinities was hosted by the St Augustine campus in 1996, establishing the UWI's leadership in this then emerging field. The publication in 2004 of *Interrogating Caribbean Masculinities: Theoretical and Empirical Analyses*, edited by Rhoda Reddock and published by the UWI Press, records ground-breaking research which explored the topic from a number of disciplinary perspectives. Despite previous attempts to observe an international men's day, Rhoda Reddock (2004) claims that International Men's Day, as now observed on 19 November, was first declared by Trinidadian Jerome Teelucksingh in 1999, while he was an undergraduate student in the course Men and Masculinities offered by the St Augustine unit. That day, his father's birthday, is now globally celebrated as International Men's Day in over sixty countries.

The Making of Caribbean Feminisms

Cultural Crossings: A Gender Image Base

In the 2004/5 academic year, Patricia Mohammed conducted a project in collaboration with Edna Bay of Emory University, Atlanta, which created a digital gender image base. This project reflected her interest in iconography and the expertise developed in this area through the DSO/UWI staff research fellowships. The database was placed on the websites of both institutions and, therefore, was made available to students and staff across the UWI sites as well as the Emory campuses.

Gender and Sexuality

Gender, Sexuality and Implications for HIV/AIDS in Trinidad and Tobago

This research project proceeded from the theoretical premise that gender profoundly influences sexuality, including the sexual conduct that places individuals at risk for HIV infection. It sought to answer questions about the influence of gender norms, expectations, attitudes, myths, ideologies and the associated power relations in sexual behaviours in Trinidad and Tobago, especially among youth. It recognized that effective intervention to change risky behaviours is almost impossible without a clear understanding of the complexities of these behaviours. The investigation was intended to bring together existing research as well as to generate new knowledge in previously unexamined areas. The findings were used to propose research-based interventions to assist in the prevention of HIV/AIDS and other STIs, as well as substance abuse. A special interest was to understand sexuality among youth between the ages of fifteen and twenty-four years, as it related to the risk of this age group to HIV infection.

Phase 1 of the project sought to identify gaps in and establish relevant approaches to this area of research. Activities included the preparation and publication of an annotated bibliography *Gender, Sexuality and the Implications for Substance Abuse and HIV/AIDS*, developed by Lirlyn Elliott in 2005; an international symposium held from 11 to 13 March 2004, which brought together regional and international experts to identify the gaps in the research in this area and to give direction for future research in this field; a preliminary research study involving St Augustine campus students entitled "Attitudes, Behaviours and Taboos Related to Gender and Sexuality among UWI St Augustine Students", which was done in 2003; and an analysis of data from the Trinidad and Tobago HIV/AIDS hotline database. As in other CGDS research projects, multi-agency funding was sought and obtained from the Caribbean Health Research Council, the CIDA/CCGEP, United Nations Population Fund and the St Augustine campus Research and Publications Fund.

Building Responsive Policy: Gender, Sexual Cultures and HIV/AIDS in the Caribbean

In the 2007/8 academic year, a similar study to that carried out in Trinidad and Tobago on sexuality, HIV and AIDS was developed and conducted in three countries: Barbados, Suriname, and Trinidad and Tobago. The proposal was jointly prepared with the University of the West Indies HIV/AIDS Response Programme at Cave Hill; York University, Canada; the foundation Ultimate Purpose, Suriname; and the UNIFEM Caribbean office; and funding was provided by the International Development Research Centre. The project was also supported by the Government of Trinidad and Tobago's Research and Development Fund.

Specific research objectives were to conduct a secondary analysis of the political economy of sexuality and HIV/AIDS in each of the selected countries and an examination of selected media and informational/advocacy campaigns on HIV/AIDS, to document and assess the underlying messages that challenge or reinforce the gender-based causes of the epidemic. In addition, it was expected that the research team working in each country would embark on at least two case studies designed to explore, in greater detail, issues related to gender, sexuality and HIV/AIDS.

Breaking the Silence: A Multisectoral Approach to Preventing and Addressing Child Sexual Abuse in Trinidad and Tobago

In the 2006/7 academic year, a proposal which focused on child sexual abuse was successfully submitted to the UNIFEM Trust Fund for Violence against Women and was also supported by UNICEF. The project started in 2007 and sought to examine the taboo subject of child sexual abuse throughout Trinidad and Tobago, and to develop interventions aimed at empowering women and children. The project utilized both qualitative and quantitative research methods, and partners included the Coalition against Domestic Violence, Caribbean Health Research Council, and Arts in Action (Theatre in Education Group) of the UWI, St Augustine.

Impact of the CGDS/IGDS Research Agenda

Several benefits have been derived from the research activities undertaken by all the CGDS units over the period under review. A major factor was the relationships forged with national, regional and international agencies and organizations mandated to address the mainstreaming of gender in development initiatives. The expected output included ensuring more equitable distribution of both material and non-material resources and more sustainable outcomes.

A significant benefit which accrued to the units and, by extension, the university from these synergies was the inflow of cash – in many instances, the result of fundraising by CGDS staff. Networking with these national, regional and international entities enabled the CGDS/IGDS to attract considerable funding, which supported research projects and academic programmes, as well as provided tangible student support. Given the fact that university budget allocations to the CGDS units were always insufficient, the funds raised were, therefore, of significant benefit not only to the IGDS but also to the UWI. The positive net result of these synergies was the building of research capacities within the CGDS/IGDS as well as among a number of disciplines across all faculties.

A logical outflow from the institutional, personal and commissioned research activities across all units of the CGDS/IGDS has been an impressive collection of readers, articles in refereed journals and books, online publications and technical reports. All of these have contributed to a burgeoning and reputable indigenous source of literature on Caribbean women, relations of gender and their influence on access to material and non-material resources which are at the core of issues of sustainable and equitable development processes. In assessing the impact of gender on UWI's evolution, Barbara Bailey (2012, 10) opined that

> a notable and inescapable impact of the gender project on the UWI academic landscape is the wide scope of the research projects undertaken by the campus units and individual faculty, embracing as they have new research and epistemological paradigms. A natural outflow from these dynamic and prolific activities has been a plethora of publications including working papers, refereed academic papers, monographs and edited readers, all of which reflect indigenous Caribbean theorizing, which have not only filled gaps in the global gender and development literature database but have been indispensable in informing national and regional policy positions. These publications have also been an invaluable resource for scholars regionally and internationally.

(See appendix 7 for a list of publications associated with CGDS/IGDS.)

Despite the generation of this vast amount of data through the varied and multifaceted research agenda of the CGDS/IGDS over a twenty-year period, and although, in some instances, dissemination activities have taken place, impact has been somewhat weak. This points to a gap that is demonstrated by academic entities such as the CGDS/IGDS, in terms of informing and influencing policy and impacting action on the ground. Project design and costing usually do not include activities and funding to carry out impact and effectiveness assessments since, invariably, a time lag of at least one year is needed to allow for implementation before such assessments can be initiated. In the absence of such follow-up, however, project beneficiaries are not motivated to carry through on agreed actions, especially where there may be deficiencies in the requisite skill sets needed for effective implementation.

CHAPTER 10

PURSUING THE MANDATE

Outreach Activities

> What has this institutional initiative meant for the betterment of the region and for its future possibilities? And what will it continue to mean? Academic achievement can be measured by the expansion of programmes, the generation of research publications and the number of students produced. It might also be gauged by the now widespread use, and misuse, of gender in common parlance. A more intangible but, in my view, vastly important benefit to the region, and to me personally, has been the emergence of this new ritual space where knowledge and experience is being traded between generations of women and across cultural boundaries. I shudder to think of how much poorer my life would have been without having seen the Caribbean through so many different eyes.
>
> —*Patricia Mohammed*

FROM INCEPTION, OUTREACH HAS BEEN A HALLMARK OF the activities of the women's/gender development studies programme across all campuses of the university. In fact, as catalogued in the earlier chapters, the WDSGs started as an externally funded programme at the UWI. Hermione McKenzie recalls that the Mona campus group, in the early years, offered an organized programme of talks and seminars on campus, with no departmental or faculty affiliation and no control systems beyond their own collective structure. This was true of all the campuses and, as GDS was a newly emerging area of discourse in the Caribbean region and at the UWI, every opportunity was used, on each campus, to host brown-bag, lunchtime or afternoon seminars on topical issues and to grasp opportunities to hear from visiting scholars working in this field. Given the freedom from faculty-defined constraints, these outreach activities were determined, for the most part, by individual interest, issues of the moment that warranted discussion and debate, and availability of speakers. These activities attracted both on-campus and off-campus audiences.

These seminars were extremely effective and successful in creating a critical interface between academics and activists and for bringing both into a mutually beneficial relationship. They created a space for exposing their audiences, many for the first time, to the use of gender as an analytical tool and as a lens through which social, economic and political phenomena could be viewed and understood. The orientation of the early seminars was, however, primarily activist-geared, as they were sharing information and building awareness of issues impacting the lives of Caribbean women.

So successful were these outreach activities that it is not surprising that, when the CGDS was formally institutionalized in 1993, its mission mirrored that of the predecessor IOP/UWI/ISS project but added outreach as the third prong to its tripartite mission, alongside teaching and research. Institutionalization, however, brought with it new imperatives – that of building and establishing the centre as a credible academic enterprise outside the established faculty boundaries, capable of offering equally rigorous interdisciplinary academic programmes at undergraduate and graduate levels. Ultimately, this would bring pressure to bear on the pre-institutionalization, free-wielding, activist-oriented outreach activities, which would eventually morph into a more structured set of activities. These were more focused on academic-oriented pursuits, such as offering technical expertise within the academy as well as to a number of national, regional and international entities.

The records show, however, that, over the years, the St Augustine unit was very successful in sustaining a strong activist orientation to its outreach activities, due, most likely, to the larger staff complement at that unit than obtained in other units. In the words of Rhoda Reddock (2014, 5), a former head of the St Augustine unit:

> Engaging with the community and building public awareness are important if any change is to be effected. Social action and activism have, therefore, always been central to the work of this unit, hence our establishment of the position of an outreach and research officer. We see our scholarship as intricately linked to the activism and advocacy of other social groups and movements working towards a better Caribbean and a better world.

At St Augustine, outreach capacity has been greatly enhanced by the creation of a position on the establishment, in 2005, of an outreach and research officer. According to the 2012 self-assessment report, "this member of staff has been primarily responsible for ensuring that there is an ongoing atmosphere of research and knowledge production at the Institute; and that there is continuous engagement with community in order to bridge connections between academia, policy and implementation" (UWI IGDS 2012a, 18).

Post-institutionalization outreach activities can be considered as belonging to two major groupings: activities internal to the academy, hosted by the units on the three campuses and directed primarily at an on-campus audience; and activities external to the academy. More often than not, requests from national, regional or international entities required technical expertise to assist in, inter alia, gender training for a variety of target audiences, project design, implementation and/or evaluation, research and policy formulation, and so on, but always including the integration of a gender perspective.

Outreach within the Academy

Staff of the CGDS/IGDS, individually and collectively, share expertise and knowledge with the UWI community through a wide variety of activities on the respective campuses, and the most significant of these activities are highlighted in this section. It should be noted, however, that all dimensions of the CGDS mission – teaching, research and outreach – are intricately interconnected, and, in activities related to any one dimension, aspects of the other two can be recognized. The inclusion and discussion of activities under the outreach rubric is, therefore, to some extent, arbitrary and could well have been subsumed under teaching and/or research.

Seminar Series

As noted previously, over the years, lunchtime seminars became a hallmark of the CGDS/IGDS, and, in this regard, the St Augustine unit has been at the forefront, maintaining a vibrant seminar series. In the space of three academic years (2005–7), thirty seminars were held, covering a range of interdisciplinary topics, many of which impacted individuals at the personal, community and national levels and were therefore geared to raising consciousness to inform social action and activism. Issues addressed included: higglering in the Caribbean, abortion law reform, Indian women and land ownership, gendering urban environment management, why men batter, women in calypso, and the Marriage Act and citizenship. Presenters included academic staff of the CGDS/IGDS and other faculties, students and local and international scholars and attracted a wide cross-section of participants from the on- and off-campus communities.

A mark of the success of the St Augustine seminar series is that it has given rise to tangible resources through which information could be further disseminated to stakeholders, which have also been used to support teaching and research. In remarks made at a twentieth-anniversary event held at the Mona campus in June 2014, Rhoda Reddock (2014, 5) noted that "[the] lunchtime seminar series led initially to the publication of a working paper series, which eventually led to the development of the respected IGDS online journal, *Caribbean Review of Gender Studies*, which was established in 2007 under the leadership of Patricia Mohammed and, later, Gabrielle Hosein, with the important support of IGDS MPhil graduate Donna Drayton".

In contrast, seminars hosted by the Cave Hill unit had a more clearly demarcated academic orientation and often were offered by visiting regional and international scholars. A sampling of speakers and topics include

- Professor Geraldine Healy and Dr Gill Kirton of the Centre for Research in Equality and Diversity, School of Business Management, Queen Mary University of London, "Professional Women as Leaders: Barriers and Opportunities";
- Professor Eudine Barriteau, deputy principal of the Cave Hill campus, "Coming, Coming, Coming Home: Applying Anna Jonasdottir's Theory of 'Love Power' to Theorizing Sexuality in Caribbean Gender Relations";
- Dr Pansy Hamilton, research coordinator of the Hugh Wynter Fertility Management Unit at the Mona campus, "Issues in Reproductive Health in the Caribbean: Implications for Development"; and
- Dr Doris Weischselbaumer, Department of Economics, University of Linz in Austria, "Sex, Gender and Sexual Orientation: Economic Studies on Labour Market Discrimination".

Over the years, the post-institutionalization seminar series at the Mona campus, introduced by Patricia Mohammed and subsequently carried on by Leith Dunn, heads of the unit, has been captioned "Conversations with Gender". The series started in 1997, and the intention was to engage the campus community, as well as the larger public, on issues pertaining to teaching, research, policy and action on gender. The 2001/2 academic year marked the sixth in the series, with each taking a somewhat different form. In that year, the seminar was entitled "A Conversation on the Making of Caribbean Feminism" and took the form of a discussion/conversation between two panels, one comprising academic staff and the other undergraduate students pursuing courses offered by that unit of the CGDS. In the previous year, the seminar was presented by Edna Bay (a visiting scholar, then an associate professor in the Graduate Institute of the Liberal Arts, Emory University, Atlanta, GA, and trained as a historian) and John Campbell, also a historian, attached to the Faculty of Humanities and Education at Mona, UWI. They addressed the theme "Women, Power and Slave Production in the Eighteenth- and Nineteenth-Century Atlantic World". In the 2006/7 academic year, the presenters were Justice Desirée Bernard, of the Caribbean Court of Justice, and Mary Clarke, children's advocate, Jamaica; and the topic addressed was GBV.

International Observances That Focus on Women

Globally, two observances are marked annually by the UN, the women's movement and some governments. International Women's Day, now celebrated on 8 March, "first emerged from the activities of labour movements at the turn of the twentieth century in North America and across Europe. The first National Woman's Day was observed in the United States on 28 February, and, in 1975, during International Women's Year, the United Nations began celebrating International Women's Day on 8 March" (http://www.un.org/womenwatch/feature/iwd/history.html).

International Day for the Elimination of Violence against Women is observed on 25 November. According to *Wikipedia*, "historically, the date is based on [the] date of the 1960 assassination of the three Mirabal sisters, political activists in the Dominican Republic; the killings were ordered by Dominican dictator Rafael Trujillo (1930–1961). In 1981, activists marked November 25 as a day to combat and raise awareness of violence against women more broadly; on December 17, 1999, the date received its official United Nations (UN) resolution 54/134". The same source indicates that "the premise of the day is to raise awareness of the fact that women around the world are subject to rape, domestic violence and other forms of violence; furthermore, one of the aims of the day is to highlight that the scale and true nature of the issue is often hidden" (https://en.wikipedia.org/wiki/International_Day_for_the_Elimination_of_Violence_against_Women).

Both these observances provide a ready-made platform for promoting outreach activities to share information, build awareness and raise consciousness, especially about violence that affects women of all ages, social classes and ethnicities. From as far back as 1995, when the Fourth WCW was held, violence against women was identified as the most critical issue facing Caribbean women. The opportunity has been seized, therefore, by all the campus units to host a variety of activities, ranging from concerts at St Augustine to collaborating with the Division of Community Development of the Ministry of Social Transformation of Barbados at Cave Hill to honour women who have given outstanding community service.

Over the years, other International Women's Day activities have included public lectures – "Between Patriarchy and Resistance: Women in Iran, Afghanistan and Tajikistan" at Cave Hill, and "Women's Reproductive Rights are Human Rights" at Mona; a panel discussion entitled "Women in the Music Industry" at Cave Hill; a concert titled "Men Who Love Women" at St Augustine; the launch of a reader, *Enjoying Power: Eugenia Charles and Political Leadership in the Commonwealth Caribbean*, by Eudine Barriteau and Alan Cobley of the Cave Hill campus; and a keynote presentation by Patricia Mohammed at commemorations hosted by the Department of Social Welfare, Social Services Division, Tobago House of Assembly.

The International Day for the Elimination of Violence against Women seems not to be as widely observed as International Women's Day and the only information received in this regard was from the Mona unit (UWI CGDS), which, inter alia, has marked the day, at various times in different ways, with

- a forum on Women in Political Leadership: What's the Difference? hosted in collaboration with the Jamaica Women's Political Caucus;
- a panel on GBV at Mona, targeting the student body and aired on Radio Jamaica;
- the mounting of a workshop for Jamaica Family Planning Association staff and associates on coping skills in relation to GBV;
- a public forum in collaboration with the Centre for Investigation of Sexual Offences and Child Abuse on survival skills and the prevention of violence against women; and
- an exhibition on women and HIV/AIDs mounted by the main library in

Plate 10.1. St Augustine campus unit protesting gender violence in the streets of Port of Spain

collaboration with University of the West Indies HIV/AIDS Response Programme.

Lecture Series and Public Lectures

A notable outreach activity was the public lecture series established by the Cave Hill and Mona units of the CGDS/IGDS. At the Cave Hill campus, the public lecture series was conceptualized in 1994 as part of the larger project on Caribbean Women: Catalysts for Change, in which it was intended that the lectures would concentrate on aspects of the work of the women who were the focus of the research and publications undertaken under the other segment of the project. This was the case of the earliest lectures, which highlighted women in health and women in political leadership, themes related to the work of Dame Nita Barrow and the Honourable Eugenia Charles respectively. Subsequently, themes were expanded to address broader gender and development issues.

By 2010, the following sixteen lectures had been successfully presented, with selected lectures published in the Cave Hill Unit Working Paper Series:

1. "The Experiences of the First Female Prime Minister in the Commonwealth Caribbean", presented by Dame Eugenia Charles, prime minister of Dominica (1980–95), 3 November 1995

2. "A Vision of Health and Development for the Twenty-First Century", presented by Dr Karen Sealy, Caribbean regional coordinator, Pan American Health Organisation, 15 November 1996
3. "Women and Political Leadership in the Commonwealth Caribbean", which should have been presented by the Honourable Portia Simpson, minister of labour, social security and sport, Government of Jamaica, on 14 November 1997, but was cancelled due to unexpected circumstances
4. "UWI: A Progressive University for Women?" presented by Dr Marlene Hamilton, PVC for administration and special initiatives, UWI, 4 December 1998
5. "Nuancing Globalization or Mainstreaming the Downstream on Reforming Reform", presented by Devaki Jain, feminist, writer and activist of Bangalore, India, and founder of DAWN, 12 November 1999
6. "The Debate on Gender and Development: An African Feminist Perspective", presented by Dr Patricia McFadden, senior programme officer, Gender Division of the South African Institute for Policy Studies, Zimbabwe, 17 November 2000
7. "Travelling Mercies", presented by Lorna Goodison, Jamaican poet, author and artist, University of Toronto, 16 November 2001
8. "Women and Islam in Africa in the Twenty-First Century: An African Feminist Perspective", presented by Dr Fatou Sow of Senegal, 15 November 2002
9. "Unsettling Masculinity in the Caribbean: Facing a Future without Guarantees", presented by Dr Linden Lewis, associate professor, Bucknell University, PA, 14 November 2003
10. "A Woman's Place in the Twenty-First Century Movement: Reflections on the Quest for Sovereignty and Unity", presented by Selma James, author, activist and widow of C.L.R. James, 12 November 2004
11. "The Promotion and Enforcement of Women's Human Rights within the Judicial System of the Caribbean", presented by the Honourable Madame Justice Desirée Bernard, judge of the Caribbean Court of Justice, 18 November 2005
12. "Economics, Power and Politics: How to Make Accountability for Human Rights and Gender Equality Part of the Picture", presented by Yassine Fall, senior policy advisor on gender equality at the UN Millennium Project, 17 November 2006
13. "Gender, Generation and Memory: Remembering a Future Caribbean",

presented by Dr Alissa Trotz, assistant professor, Women and Gender Studies Institute, University of Toronto, Canada, 16 November 2007

14. "Women's Leadership in Our Globalized Society", presented by Professor Elsa Tamez, biblical scholar and professor emerita of the Latin American Biblical University, Costa Rica, 14 November 2008
15. "Power, Labour, Pleasure: Sexuality in Everyday Life", by Professor Kamala Kempadoo, Department of Social Sciences, York University, Canada, 11 November 2009
16. "What Love Has to Do with It? Sexuality, Intimacy and Power in Contemporary Caribbean Gender Relations", presented by Professor Eudine Barriteau, UWI, 12 November 2010

At Mona, the lecture series, named in honour of Lucille Mathurin Mair, the noted Jamaican historian, politician and diplomat appointed as the first regional coordinator of the IOP/UWI/ISS Project in Teaching and Research in 1985, was initiated by Patricia Mohammed and Verene Shepherd with the

Plate 10.2. Lucille Mathurin Mair (*foreground*) visiting the CGDS Mona campus unit: (*Left to right*) Barbara Bailey, Louraine Emmanuel and Pat Mohammed

1998 inaugural lecture planning committee, including Barbara Bailey, Louraine Emmanuel and Veronica Salter. Beyond 1998, the lectures were rolled out biennially by the Mona unit.

In the 2006 report of self-assessment of the Mona unit, it is noted that

> the biennial Public Lecture was conceptualized to commemorate International Women's Day and to celebrate the work and contribution of Dr Lucille Mathurin Mair to the women's movement, locally, regionally and internationally. Dr Mair's historical study on women's experiences, as well as her work in local and international communities, have laid the foundation for academic trajectories in Caribbean women's history and have also provided a legacy for future activism. The lecture series is designed to provide a forum for all disciplinary groups on the Mona campus of the University of the West Indies to participate in the ongoing development of Gender Studies and to engage the public and the media in issues pertaining to gender in society. (UWI CGDS 2006, 34)

The lectures have all been of an interdisciplinary nature and the lecturers were either academics or activists. Lectures held between 1998 and 2010 include

- "On the Brink of the New Millennium: Are Caribbean Women Prepared?" presented by Professor Joycelin Massiah, then the regional programme advisor, United Nations Fund for Women (UNIFEM) Caribbean Office, Barbados, 6 March 1998;
- "The Rise and Fall of Feminist Politics in the Caribbean Women's Movement 1975–1995", presented by Peggy Antrobus, former tutor-coordinator, WAND, UWI, Jamaica, 9 March 2000;
- "The Angle from Which You Look Determines What You See: Towards a Critique of Feminist Politics in the Caribbean", presented by Andaiye, a feminist and activist of Red Thread, Guyana, 6 March 2002;
- "Men, Masculinities and Development", by Professor Michael Kimmel of State University, New York, 11 March 2004;
- "Confronting Gender-Based Violence in the Caribbean", presented by the Honourable Madame Justice Desirée Bernard, distinguished Guyanese jurist and judge in the Caribbean Court of Justice, 29 November 2006; and
- "The UWI Glass Ceiling: Splinters, Cracks and Scratches", by Professor Elsa Leo-Rhynie, first professor of GDS, UWI; former regional coordinator of the CGDS; and first female principal of the Mona campus, 20 November 2008.

The 2008 lecture marked the tenth anniversary of the launch of the lecture

Plate 10.3. Andaiye delivering the 2002 Lucille Mathurin Mair Lecture

series and was also used to mark the fifteenth anniversary of the founding of the CGDS as well as the sixtieth anniversary of the establishment of the UWI. Although no lecture was held in 2010, the series resumed in 2012 with a lecture entitled "Rebel Women: Engendering Transformation" by Beverley Anderson-Duncan.

During the 2007/8 academic year, Rhoda Reddock of the St Augustine unit organized and coordinated a Caribbean lecture tour, sponsored by the South-South Exchange Programme for Research on the History of Development, for Elinor Sisulu, award-winning South African writer, human rights activist and political analyst. The public lecture, "Mrs Sisulu's Husband: Gender Relations in an African Marriage", delivered on each campus, was hosted by the CGDS and provided first-hand information about the struggle of South African leaders and their families, how they had to endure and the challenges they were facing in post-apartheid South Africa. In the lecture, she shared how her husband Walter Sisulu's approach to her political and personal activities represented an inversion of traditional models of masculinity.

Mona Campus's Strategic Transformation Team

A unique outreach activity at the Mona campus was the involvement of the university director, Barbara Bailey, on a strategic transformation team, comprised of seven campus-based professors, set up by the campus principal, PVC Professor Kenneth Hall in January 2006. The principal's report indicates that the strategic transformation team undertook a number of activities intended to raise awareness of the need for strategic transformation of the campus (UWI Office of the Principal 2006). These were designed to catalyse the implementation of recommendations emanating from its precursor, the 2002 Strategic Challenges Task Force. This included, inter alia, development of policy papers; introduction of the First-Year Student Experience pilot programme aimed at improving the attitudes and broadening the social and foundation-learning skill base of students; catalysing new income-generating and performance-enhancing centres in the areas of Caribbean mental health and substance abuse, leadership and governance, and slavery research; and promoting research and teaching programmes in areas in which the Caribbean had a distinctive advantage or in which there was a clear need for policy impact.

The main area in which the CGDS made a direct contribution was in providing empirical evidence through which plans could be made to improve gender relations and reduce the incidence of gender bias. This was achieved by commissioning the CGDS to carry out the UWI's first workplace satisfaction and gender impact survey, the findings of which were intended to inform planning and policy goals aimed at promoting gender equality among staff and other stakeholders and creating an environment where opportunities and rewards were based on merit.

This initiative was congruent with efforts by the Association of Commonwealth Universities, which, through its women's programme, and in tandem with the Commonwealth Secretariat and UNESCO, had attempted to develop a comprehensive approach to address gender disparities in higher education.

Barbara Bailey served as research director and Suzanne Charles coordinated a small team of researchers. At its platform for action meeting of April 2007, the strategic transformation team was presented with a summary of preliminary findings. Complete findings pertaining to the West Indies Group of University Teachers academic and professional staff grouping were presented at the meeting of the academic board of May 2007. A report of the findings in relation to the Mona Administrative, Technical and Supervisory staff grouping was also prepared.

Outreach beyond the Academy

Between 2005 and 2006, all four units of the CGDS underwent external quality assurance reviews organized by the UWI BUS. The external team that reviewed the work of the RCU and the Mona unit in 2006 opined that "because gender issues are so critical to the future of the nation, the region and indeed globally, the occasion of this review, which fits into UWI's strategic planning process, provides a most compelling opportunity for the campus to secure its major role in gender and development initiatives" (UWI BUS 2006b, 5, 2.4).

This observation could equally apply to the reviews of the other two units, and this opportunity has not been missed. Through outreach activities, all units of the CGDS /IGDS have played a significant role at national, regional and international levels, in terms of offering expertise and providing technical assistance. In so doing, the CDGS/IGDS has increased the visibility of the university and, on its behalf, has led a number of critical initiatives, thereby making a critical contribution to development processes at national, regional and international levels.

National-Level Initiatives

National Gender Policies

A crucial area of engagement relates to the development of national policies which identify strategies for addressing inequalities that emerge from the unequal relations of gender and the imbalance of power in the personal, social, economic and political spheres of all Caribbean societies. In keeping with obligations arising from a number of binding international agreements to promote gender equality and women's empowerment, as reflected in the CEDAW Convention, Beijing Platform for Action and the third Millennium Development Goal, Caribbean governments responded by undertaking preparations of national gender policies. To this end, they sought advice and technical assistance from the CGDS/IGDS, to engage in the process of consultations, identification of strategies for pursuing equality targets and identifying indicators for monitoring implementation and tracking progress. National gender policies were developed for the following nations with assistance from the various units, as described below:

- Dominica – completed in November 2005 and presented to the cabinet in March 2006 by Patricia Mohammed, the lead consultant, supported by Deborah McFee of the St Augustine unit.
- Trinidad and Tobago – draft was completed in June 2006 in collaboration with the Division of Gender Affairs and with Rhoda Reddock, head of the St Augustine unit, as lead consultant, supported by Patricia Mohammed and Camille Antoine of that unit, as well as undergraduate and graduate students moderating workshops. Financial support was provided by the CIDA Caribbean, the UNDP and the United Nations Population Fund.
- Barbados – at the request of the Bureau of Gender Affairs, work on a national policy was started in 2006, with assistance from the Cave Hill unit.
- Jamaica – A Gender Advisory Committee was established in 2004 by the Cabinet Office, and Barbara Bailey of the RCU was appointed as chair and charged with responsibility to develop a broad-based policy, through a national consultative process, to guide the Government of Jamaica's gender portfolio. The policy was completed with financial assistance from CIDA/CCGEF, United Nations Population Fund and UN Women, Caribbean office, and published in March 2011.

In 2006, the Planning Institute of Jamaica embarked on the development of a national development plan. To achieve this end, the Planning Institute of Jamaica, through a scoping exercise, identified thematic areas that would need to be addressed and which would form the basis for developing sectoral plans that would be the foundation for developing an integrated national development plan referred to as Vision 2030 Jamaica: National Development Plan. One of thirty-one thematic areas identified was that of gender, and Barbara Bailey of the RCU was invited to chair this task force and lead activities that would result in a sector plan for promoting and achieving gender equality and women's empowerment and which could interface with the national gender policy, which was already in draft form.

Technical Support for Meeting Reporting Obligations to the UN

All Caribbean countries are signatories to a number of international conventions and instruments that require periodic reporting. In relation to issues of gender equality and the elimination of sex and gender-based discrimination, the CEDAW is of paramount importance and the most widely subscribed to by CARICOM member states. In at least three instances, technical support was sought from the CGDS in the preparation of periodic reports for submission.

Leith Dunn of the Mona unit provided assistance to the Department of Women's Affairs of the Commonwealth of the Bahamas to develop its fifth periodic report to the CEDAW committee, covering the period 1993 to 2003 and which was examined at the fifty-second session held in July 2012. Similarly, Deborah McFee of the St Augustine unit was engaged by the Gender Affairs Division, Ministry of Social Development and Family Services, to facilitate community consultations throughout Trinidad and Tobago to ensure that the reporting process was grounded in the reality of the lives of women throughout the country. Information gleaned from these consultations informed the development of the combined (fourth and fifth) periodic report of the Government of Trinidad and Tobago to the CEDAW committee.

In the case of Jamaica, the fifth periodic report was developed by the Bureau of Women's Affairs. Barbara Bailey of the RCU was invited to lead the Government of Jamaica's delegation to New York to present the report at the thirty-sixth session, in August 2006. Subsequently, she was nominated by the Government of Jamaica to serve on the CEDAW committee, and, at the fifteenth meeting of state parties who are signatories to the CEDAW, held in July 2008, she was elected to serve on the committee that monitors states parties' compliance with the convention.

Workshops and Gender Awareness Training

Building awareness of ways in which social hierarchies of gender, race, class, age, among other factors, intersect to determine differential access to material and non-material resources for members of a society, and, therefore, differential outcomes, is an important preliminary step for achieving social, economic and political transformation. Several national organizations turned to the expertise residing in the CGDS/IGDS for building this awareness through a variety of workshops targeting a range of audiences. The three interventions outlined below are indicative of the scope and unique nature of the outreach activities undertaken by the units.

In 2007, the NBU, Cave Hill, offered two dynamic writing and rapporteuring training programmes to build professional skills while sensitizing participants to gender issues and gender analysis. The programme targeted individuals who worked, or were desirous of working, as rapporteurs for national, regional and international conferences, symposia and other meetings. Participants learned technical skills and also gained an overview of the importance of accurate records generated by rapporteurs in assisting organizations to meet their planning objectives. In the first offering, the programme accepted twenty-five participants, while, in the second offering, thirty participants were trained, in response to the demand. The facilitators were Diane Cummins, an experienced rapporteur and social development consultant, and Eudine Barriteau, head of the unit.

The Mona unit's membership of the Jamaica Family Planning Association since 1997 resulted in a collaborative relationship and involvement in one of their projects, Brothers for Change, which provided counselling for "men who batter", under the supervision of court-appointed probation officers. As part of this programme, the unit facilitated a workshop on GBV and HIV/STDs on Members' Day of the Jamaica Family Planning Association. Moderated by Shakira Maxwell, the workshop was held on 25 November 2000 in Ocho Rios. In 2003, the unit continued this relationship and collaborated on the project Men against Gender-Based Violence by conducting a two-day training workshop for Jamaica Family Planning Association staff and associates. The workshop included pre- and post-evaluations of the participants' knowledge and attitudes regarding gender and also facilitated the development of coping skills in relation to issues of GBV.

The Civilian Conservation Corps Programme of Trinidad and Tobago, managed by the Ministry of National Security, targets young persons between the ages of eighteen and twenty-five and seeks to capitalize on the structure and discipline of the armed forces to enhance the lives of the young persons involved. In 2007, as a component of the orientation programme, the St Augustine unit was invited to deliver gender-sensitivity training. In 2008, the programme was extended to communities in Trinidad. A valuable, unexpected outcome of this relationship between the CGDS and these out-of-school participants is that, beyond the project, they became a readily accessible resource for research projects investigating youth-gender relations and associated issues on sexuality, gender, politics and identity.

Regional-Level Initiatives

Agencies in the Caribbean, particularly UN agencies, actively engaged in women's empowerment and gender and development issues frequently called on the expertise residing in the CGDS/IGDS to engage in a range of regional-level initiatives, some of which are outlined below.

Gender Awareness Training Programmes

The main thrust of actions to promote gender equality and women's empowerment as laid out in the Beijing Platform for Action and the CARICOM Plan of Action required integration of a gender perspective in policies and programmes related to all areas of life. As at the national level, regional training workshops were therefore in demand over the years, to equip a number of target audiences with understanding and competencies in the use of gender as an analytical tool for managing this process. At a workshop for bilateral and multilateral agencies on gender analysis in policy and planning held in Barbados in 1997, Joycelin Massiah, then regional programme advisor of the UNIFEM Caribbean office, noted in the report of the proceedings that the workshop signalled, in part, the following:

> 1. The proposal [for the workshop] had been grounded in a survey commissioned by the Canadian International Development Agency (CIDA). The findings of this survey and the recommendation for a coordinated regional approach to gender training had been endorsed by Ministers of Government.
> 2. There existed a commitment to a regional approach to training. Although there were a number of approaches to gender training as identified in the CIDA study, they are scattered and not readily accessible – hence the need for a more systematic approach. (UWI CGDS 1997, 4)

This also signalled a shift away from the model of hiring consultants to prepare materials and deliver training, with the material remaining the property of the consultant at the end of the project, to a move towards retaining copyright of the materials for publication, thereby making the material more widely available for training of similar target audiences; the net outcome was a more sustainable and cost-effective approach to gender training across the region. This thrust was led by UNIFEM, with the RCU in the role of implementing agency. Under this arrangement, material for at least three distinct target audiences was developed, with funding from different sources.

Gender Analysis in Policy and Planning

Funding for the development of the first draft of a module on gender awareness in policy and planning, prepared by Gwendoline Williams and Sonja Harris, was provided by UNIFEM Caribbean. The module was presented at a workshop for participants from bilateral and multilateral agencies in Barbados in September 1997. With further funding from the DSO/UWI project, the module was revised and used in a second regional workshop planned and carried out by the RCU for senior policymakers in government, held in Jamaica in 1999. Beyond this workshop, the module was available for use in further training.

Women in Middle Management

In response to certain training needs identified by the UN and the World Bank, which include the use of gender analysis as a strategy for bringing about change and transformation in organizational structures, the CGDS/RCU, with funding from the CCGEP (Jamaica) and the UNIFEM Caribbean, held a training workshop to enhance the skills of writers of training material for dual-mode delivery. The first draft of the material on gender and management was completed, while significant gaps were identified in the second module on gender issues in the Caribbean. Unfortunately, a complete set of these materials was not recovered from the computer files of the administrative officer of the RCU following her untimely passing.

Teacher Educators

In collaboration with the CARICOM, data were gathered from seventeen training colleges in ten Caribbean countries, including Suriname, to determine their level of gender awareness, particularly in relation to its impact on education and its processes. Selected participants attended a workshop to discuss the findings and determine what should constitute the elements of a training programme to be implemented in all regional teacher training institutions. To implement the training, CARICOM acquired CIDA funding for their capacity development programme. This was used to offset costs for the hosting of two workshops in Trinidad and Tobago and Jamaica, respectively, to prepare teacher educators from fifteen Caribbean countries to implement a module on gender issues in Caribbean education which had been developed by Barbara Bailey and Yasmeen Yusuf-Khalil of the CGDS and Monica Brown of the UWI Institute of Education. The material was published by the CARICOM Secretariat and distributed to all teacher training institutions in the region.

Women in Leadership

The website of the Caribbean Institute for Women in Leadership describes the institute as a flagship networking entity, producing high-quality research, documentation, analysis, training and advocacy to advance women's transformational leadership and increase the number of women in politics, leadership and decision-making at all levels in the Caribbean. It is supported by the United Nations Entity for Gender Equality and the Empowerment of Women (better known as UN Women), the Organization of American States, and the Commonwealth Secretariat.

The first leadership training institute, coordinated by Leith Dunn of the Mona unit, was held in Antigua and Barbuda in July 2010 with twenty-nine high-profile women from six Caribbean countries. The leadership training programme has continued under the auspices of the Caribbean Institute for Women in Leadership.

Other Regional Training Initiatives

In the 2003/4 academic year, the St Augustine unit engaged in an exercise to produce a manual and interactive CD-ROM on gender-sensitive policymaking, by facilitating the research and providing technical assistance in a regional project which was sponsored by Friedrich Ebert Stiftung, Jamaica, in collaboration with the Caribbean Policy Development Centre, Barbados. Subsequently in 2006, an intensive gender policy training course was held in Port of Spain with regional and international partners. Thirty-seven participants from across the Caribbean region came together for the workshop, which was funded by the Friedrich Ebert Stiftung Caribbean office, Jamaica; UNIFEM Caribbean office; the CIDA-funded CCGEF, Barbados; and the Ministry of Community Development, Culture and Gender Affairs, Trinidad and Tobago. As with other regional activities, this approach typifies that pursued by all the CGDS units to provide services at all levels – an inter-agency, governmental-academic collaborative approach drawing on funding and skill sets from a number of sources.

In 2005, the RCU was invited by the Americas and Caribbean Regional Office of UNICEF to engage in a similar activity and to develop an interactive learning-tool programme on CD-ROM to be used within the UN system for Latin American and Caribbean programme officers, including those of UNIFEM. This was a collaborative effort of staff from both the RCU and the Mona unit and resulted in the development of a user-friendly, interactive learning tool which covered basic gender concepts and tools for gender mainstreaming in UNICEF and UNIFEM programming. The centre anticipated that this exercise, which was a new area of endeavour for both units, would be useful for developing the capacity of the staff involved to produce similar material that could be used in their teaching programmes and other training activities.

A number of gender issues are integrally associated with the spread of HIV/AIDS globally, and the impact of the disease on the development of all countries can be devastating. In order to curb the spread of the virus, those who work in HIV/AIDS programmes need to be aware of the role that sex and gender play. In this regard, in 2006, the St Augustine unit was contracted to manage the training aspects of a project intended to mainstream gender concerns in HIV/AIDS programming in the Caribbean region. The project was coordinated by UNIFEM Caribbean and supported by the Commonwealth Secretariat, Dalhousie University, UNAIDS and the United Nations Population Fund. Other project partners included the Caribbean Coalition of National AIDS Programme Coordinators and the Caribbean Coalition of People Living with HIV and AIDS. The approach taken was the training-of-trainers workshop held in Port of Spain, which was intended to equip participants to replicate training at the national level.

CARICOM's Response to the Call for Gender Mainstreaming

Andaiye (2003) notes that, although gender mainstreaming was first evident in international texts following the third WCW in 1985, it was not until the fourth WCW in 1995 that it was explicitly endorsed as a strategy for achieving gender equality. In the Beijing Platform for Action, it is therefore specifically stated that, in addressing inequalities in each of the eleven critical issues, "governments and other actors should promote an active and visible policy of mainstreaming a gender perspective into all policies and programmes, so that, before decisions are taken, an analysis is made of the effects on women and men, respectively" (Beijing Declaration and Platform for Action 1995, 27, #79).

Two months after the Beijing meeting, the CARICOM Secretariat (1997b) initiated a process to respond to this mandate and developed the CARICOM

Post-Beijing Regional Plan of Action to the Year 2000, which called for gender mainstreaming in the culture and organization of Caribbean institutions, including their policymaking and planning, and in public debate. The plan was developed after consultations in selected countries with women's bureaux, government officials, women's NGOs and agencies. The elaboration of this plan of action was informed by work that had been undertaken by all units of the CGDS, the details of which are outlined in the 1997 CARICOM publication.

A gender awareness survey of the CARICOM Secretariat, undertaken in 1998, however, showed that, in order to be more successful in mainstreaming gender, there was need for further interventions. In response to this, in 2003, the Plan of Action to 2005: A Framework for Mainstreaming Gender in Key CARICOM Programmes was developed and adopted. This strategy was also expected to be responsive to changes that had occurred at the secretariat as well as in the social and economic environment of the region, which had impacted the operations of the secretariat and its way of doing business since the adoption of the 1997 post-Beijing plan of action.

After careful consideration of the six priority areas that had been identified, going into the Beijing conference, as being most critical for Caribbean women, it was agreed that, in its next work programme cycle, the CARICOM Gender and Development Unit should focus on three strategic areas:

1. Education, with a focus on building human capital
2. Health, with an emphasis on HIV/AIDS
3. Poverty and the economy, with a focus on the gender implications of implementing the CARICOM Single Market and Economy in the context of globalization

The December 2000 meeting where these matters were considered also saw agreement reached that a task force on gender mainstreaming should be established and tasked with identifying strategies for mainstreaming gender in the three identified areas. The RCU played a pivotal role in the process and the regional coordinator, Barbara Bailey, served as a member of a task force established for this purpose. The output of the task force was a 2003 publication of the *Framework for Mainstreaming Gender* by the CARICOM Secretariat. Barbara Bailey presented the strategy at a round table of ministers in charge of women's/gender affairs and presented the paper "Application and Implementation of the Framework: The Education Sector" in Georgetown, Guyana, in November 2003. She was also invited by the CIDA office in Guyana to make comments at the national launch of the CARICOM Plan of Action to 2005 in Georgetown and in follow-up meetings.

Although some initiatives had been undertaken to address gender differentials at various levels of Caribbean education systems, less had been achieved in the other two areas. By 2006, the secretariat determined that, as part of a 2006 grant agreement between the UNIFEM Caribbean and CARICOM, an institutional audit and a gender evaluation of the secretariat should be undertaken to ascertain the extent to which conditions and standards were present to promote the gender mainstreaming strategy that had been elaborated in 2003. A gender audit was therefore commissioned, with the overall aim to "promote organizational learning at the individual, work unit and office levels that would facilitate the promotion of gender-responsive development in the CARICOM Secretariat as a whole" (CARICOM Secretariat 2008, 43).

The review was undertaken by Barbara Bailey and Suzanne Charles of the RCU, with support from June Castello of the Mona unit. A report was submitted to the CARICOM Secretariat in October 2008. Overall, the findings indicated that gender mainstreaming had not been effective and, except for the work of the Human and Social Directorate, was not seen as central to work in other areas.

International-Level Initiatives

As at the national and regional levels, members of the various CGDS/IGDS units have provided technical assistance in the international arena, particularly in relation to monitoring compliance with internationally binding human rights instruments as well as regional and global plans of action to achieve gender equality. The CGDS/IGDS has also collaborated with international universities and scholars on projects as well as international academic conferences.

The UN Fourth WCW and Beijing +5

Bailey (2004, 632), writing on the Caribbean experience in the fourth WCW and beyond, notes that "the UN announcement of its intention to host a Beijing +5 mid-decade meeting served as an impetus for renewed effort and revitalization of the Caribbean women's movement since Member States were being called on to review and appraise progress towards the goals of gender equality, development and peace as set out in the Beijing Platform for Action".

As was the case for the 1995 Beijing conference, the Caribbean region was equally involved in preparation for and participation in the twenty-third special session of the UN General Assembly, titled "Women 2000: Gender Equality, Development and Peace for the Twenty-First Century", held in New York, 5–9 June 2000, more commonly referred to as the Beijing +5 meeting. As before, technical support was sought from the CGDS. In the Caribbean, the first marker in the review process was the Third Caribbean Ministerial Conference on Women held in Port of Spain, Trinidad and Tobago, in November 1999, hosted by the Caribbean subregional headquarters of the UN Economic Commission for Latin America and the Caribbean as well as the secretariat of the Caribbean Development and Cooperation Committee. At this meeting, panels were organized around three thematic areas. Eudine Barriteau and Barbara Bailey, representing the CGDS, were discussants on two of the panels: "Women in Power and Decision-Making" and "Human Rights, Peace and Violence", respectively. In relation to each theme, key strategies for moving towards greater gender equity in the subregion were identified and were subsequently captured in the Port of Spain Consensus coming out of that meeting.

Following close on the heels of the Port of Spain Caribbean subregional meeting was the eighth session of the Regional Conference on Women in Latin America and the Caribbean, held in Lima, Peru, in February 2000. At that regional meeting, Barbara Bailey was one of two persons contracted by CARICOM to provide advice with regard to the focus and strategy of the Caribbean's participation. She also provided, as needed, assistance to delegations in terms of making appropriate interventions and formulating language in the negotiating process consistent with the articles of the Port of Spain Consensus. In fact, many of the positions agreed in Port of Spain were acknowledged, accepted and incorporated in the Lima Consensus with little or no modification. Eudine Barriteau of the Cave Hill unit of the CGDS also participated in this meeting.

Several preparatory committee meetings related to Beijing +5 were held in New York between 13 March and 4 June. For each of these meetings, CARICOM was supported by the CGDS, and Barbara Bailey, along with Gemma Tang Nain of the CARICOM Women's Desk, assisted Caribbean delegations through the difficult negotiating process, to ensure that a Caribbean voice and position were maintained throughout the process.

The role that the CGDS played on behalf of Caribbean governments, in collaboration with the CARICOM Secretariat, leading up to the 1995 Beijing conference as well as the 2000 Beijing +5 meeting and, eventually, also the 2005 Beijing +10 meeting, should not be underestimated. The CGDS acted as consultant to CARICOM in the subregional and regional preparatory meetings as well as the major UN international meetings, thus ensuring an element of continuity. Also, the presence of a Caribbean voice at all stages of the debate proved to be essential, given the more sporadic participation of national delegations, the composition of which changed from one meeting to the next. In spite of this and other challenges, at both the Beijing meeting and subsequent meetings, the Caribbean successfully led the debate on issues such as unwaged work and the root causes of GBV and in formulating language that was eventually incorporated into the Beijing Platform for Action, thereby reflecting and being responsive to the realities of Caribbean women.

Commonwealth Secretariat Gender Equality Plan of Action

In response to the Beijing conference in 1995 and subsequent UN-related meetings, not only were national plans of action developed to address recommendations directed to governments and other groups such as the Commonwealth, a voluntary association of fifty-three countries also produced guidelines to assist member countries to progress towards the goal of gender equality. In the *Commonwealth Plan of Action for Gender Equality 2005–2015* (Commonwealth Secretariat 2005, 9), it is stated that "the [Plan of Action] reflects the Commonwealth's principles and values and incorporates its responses to the differential impacts of global changes and challenges on women and men, girls and boys. It supports and works towards the attainment of the Millennium Development Goals (MDGs) and the objectives of gender equality expressed in the 1995 Beijing Declaration and Platform for Action (BPfA) and 2000 Beijing+5 Political Declaration and Outcome Document".

In 2007, a monitoring and evaluation framework for the plan of action was adopted and it was determined that a midterm review should be undertaken to assess the extent to which member countries and the Commonwealth Secretariat's programmes, strategies and actions, as well as internal management practices, had achieved the overall goal of the plan of action to advance gender equality. The review covered the period 2007–9, and staff of the RCU gave technical support to the gender section of the Social Transformation Programme Division and, under the guidance of the Commonwealth Gender Plan of Action Monitoring Group, provided assistance at all stages of the mid-term review. The report was presented at the ninth Meeting of Minsters in Charge of Women's Affairs held in Barbados, 5–7 June 2010.

Island Sustainability, Livelihood and Equity Project

A unique and major activity in which the CGDS participated between 1995 and 2000 was the Island Sustainability, Livelihood and Equity (ISLE) Project, funded by the CIDA and involving seven academic institutions:

- Four Canadian Universities, led by Dalhousie University and including Technical University, Nova Scotia Agricultural College, University of Prince Edward Island
- Hasanuddin University, Indonesia
- The University of the Philippines in the Visayas
- The UWI

The project involved collaboration among all the partners in interdisciplinary research, curriculum development and teaching methodologies. A major aim was to develop courses that could be incorporated in a variety of graduate programmes offered by these universities. This aim was set within the broader objective of the project to enhance knowledge, respecting the unique challenges and opportunities for sustainable development of island states. The UWI's team was interdisciplinary, including staff from the CGDS and the faculties of Natural and Applied Sciences, Agriculture, and Medical Sciences.

Training workshops were held in various groupings, with participants from various disciplines, and in the report of an evaluation of the ISLE programme it is noted that "the training workshops on gender and participatory research have been well received within and outside the ISLE partnership and are leading to potentially significant changes in approaches to research and teaching of some faculty" (UWI CGDS 2000, 7). It was also noted that "as a cross-cutting theme in ISLE, gender has begun to take hold. This is reflected in strong representation of women in all aspects of ISLE work, in the creation of a Gender Advisor position on the JSC (Joint Steering Committee), in the organization of several successful training sessions and support to visibility of gender in the partner institutions" (ibid., 8).

In relation to these observations, the UWI team was integrally involved in a number of capacities. A significant activity at the UWI was a workshop held in Trinidad in February 1998 which explored ways of engendering a case study of a wetland coastal community and the kind of indicators that would need to be included in such a study. In the following year, a meeting of the Gender Group was held in the Philippines to design a proposal for development of a comparative case study format to examine gender issues in wetland communities in the participating countries. This eventually led to the *Nariva Swamp: A Gendered Case Study*, the research project in Trinidad led by Rhoda Reddock of the St Augustine unit and discussed more fully in chapter 8. In March 1999, Barbara Bailey was part of a team from Dalhousie University and the UWI that facilitated a workshop for faculty members at Hasanuddin University in Indonesia. The focus of the workshop was the development of interdisciplinary, participatory research methodologies that would be appropriate for gender-based research and analysis. In May 2000, the final All-Partners Workshop was held at the Lester Pearson International Institute, Dalhousie University, Halifax, Nova Scotia, marking the termination of the project.

African Diaspora Working Group

Barbara Bailey's involvement in an African diaspora working group, with membership drawn from scholars in the USA, Africa and Jamaica to explore issues of religion, gender and poverty in Ghana, South Africa, Kenya, Jamaica and the USA, is yet another striking example of the fact that gender is a concern that traverses all disciplines. All the scholars who participated in the study tour of these countries were theologians, except Barbara Bailey, who focused on issues of gender and its intersection with age, social class and, by extension, poverty. The project was sponsored by Princeton University's Theological Seminary and the final output was a publication, *Religion and Poverty: Pan-African Perspectives*. Barbara Bailey's contribution to the collection is titled "Feminization of Poverty across Pan-African Societies: The Church's Response – Alleviative or Emancipatory?".

International Conferences

Another form of outreach has been the mounting and hosting of international conferences which have brought together international scholars and activists to address issues related to the conference theme. Four such conferences are of note.

International Association for Feminist Economics Conference, Barbados

The International Association for Feminist Economics, a non-profit organization, seeks to advance feminist inquiry of economic issues and to educate economists and others on feminist points of view on economic issues. The International Association for Feminist Economics was formally incorporated in 1992 and, in 1997, gained NGO consultative status with the Economic and Social Council of the UN. The International Association for Feminist Economics has approximately six hundred members in sixty-four countries, and Eudine Barriteau became a member during her tenure as head of the Cave Hill unit of the CGDS. In June 2003, that unit hosted the twelfth annual conference under the theme "Gender and Globalization" and boasted the highest attendance of any International Association for Feminist Economics conference up to that time. Following the conference, the association set up a strategy committee to increase membership in countries in the south, with some success, and Eudine Barriteau was elected president of the association for the 2009/10 year.

CGDS Tenth Anniversary Conference

The annual Mona Academic Conference, instituted in 1999 by the then principal of the Mona campus, PVC Professor Kenneth Hall, was held in 2003 from 27 to 30 August, in celebration of the tenth anniversary of the establishment of the CGDS. The conference was convened under the theme "Gender in the Twenty-First Century: Perspectives, Visions and Possibilities", and the keynote address at the opening ceremony was delivered by the attorney general and deputy prime minister of Barbados, the Honourable Mia Mottley. The Honourable Maxine Henry Wilson, at that time Jamaica's minister of education, youth and culture, also addressed the audience, as did local, regional and international luminaries. The conference was well attended by a range of academics and professionals as well as new and returning students.

The papers presented at the conference served to challenge or confirm popular theories and beliefs about a variety of issues relating to gender in the Caribbean and other societies. Presentations focused on issues such as: masculinities and femininities in light of changing socialization; the impact of globalization and other factors on gender identity; interdisciplinary and pedagogical challenges; and the role CARICOM had played in promoting gender equity in the region. The output of the conference was a reader with the conference

Plate 10.4. Staff of CGDS at the centre's Tenth Anniversary Conference, 2003 *Left to right (back row)*: Els Mulder, Louraine Emmanuel, Barbara Bailey, Elsa Leo-Rhynie, Eudine Barriteau, Leith Dunn, Glenda Ottley, Rhoda Reddock, Pat Mohammed. *Left to right (front row)*: Michelle Rowley, Gabrielle Hosein, Michelle Davis, Florence Pearson

theme as its title; it was published by Ian Randle in 2004 and still provides a rich resource for supporting teaching of CGDS/IGDS courses as well as for visiting scholars and interested stakeholders.

Masculinity Research and Action Agendas

In January 2004, the St Augustine unit hosted a workshop on masculinity research and action agendas for visiting students and staff of the Center for Men's Leadership and Service, the College of Saint Benedict, and Saint John's University, Minnesota. This initiative resulted in a UWI staff member, Tyrone Ali, and a graduate, Michael Grandison, being sponsored by the St John's University and the CGDS to attend a follow-up conference. Building on a previous initiative in this area, this link was one of several that were developed by the unit in the formation of a network for teaching, research and action on masculinities.

Plate 10.5. Attendees at the Masculinities Conference organized by CGDS, St Augustine unit, 1996

The Elsa Leo-Rhynie Symposium, Fifteenth Anniversary Conference

In honour of her achievements and contributions to the CGDS, upgraded to the IGDS on 10 November 2008, the Elsa Leo-Rhynie Symposium was convened to coincide with the institute's fifteenth-anniversary celebrations. She was the first professor of gender studies at the UWI and the first regional coordinator of the GDS programme. By the time of her retirement in 2007, she had served as deputy principal of the Mona campus; PVC, BUS; and principal of the Mona campus, the first female to hold that post on any UWI campus. Some of Elsa Leo-Rhynie's areas of specialization are gender, early childhood and higher education, and the theme selected for the conference was therefore "Gender Perspectives in Education: Caribbean Impact, Global Reach".

The symposium, which was held from 9 to 11 November 2008, enjoyed participation from local, regional and international gender-studies specialists, with panels addressing issues of gender and higher education, gender and Caribbean society, and gender across the disciplines at the undergraduate and graduate levels. Round-table discussions reflected on the development of the institute over its fifteen years of existence and also examined future directions of the institution.

Plate 10.6. Opening ceremony, Elsa Leo-Rhynie Symposium, 2008: (*left to right*) Professors Eudine Barriteau (*at lectern*), Barbara Bailey, E. Nigel Harris (vice-chancellor), Elsa Leo-Rhynie, Gordon Shirley (pro vice-chancellor and principal, Mona campus), Rhoda Reddock

Serving on Regional/International Bodies

Another form of outreach at the international level has been that of serving on international bodies that engage in activities related to monitoring compliance with internationally binding instruments that establish normative standards for protecting the rights of women and eliminating sex- and gender-based discrimination. In June 2008, Barbara Bailey was elected to serve on the CEDAW committee that monitors states parties' compliance with the CEDAW. She also continues to serve on the follow-up mechanism to the Belém do Pará Convention on the Prevention, Punishment and Eradication of Violence against Women.

Heads of the campus units have also served in various capacities in the international arena. Eudine Barriteau of the Cave Hill unit served as the regional coordinator of DAWN from 1996 to 1999. Further, in 2003, she was invited to be part of the Wise Women Process, an international body of feminist scholars and activists established to revitalize the international women's movement. In that same year, as well as in 2005, she also served as an international advisor for the Institute for Women's Policy Research conferences. In July 2010, Leith Dunn of the Mona unit was invited by the Commonwealth secretary general to serve as a member of the Commonwealth observer group for the presidential elections in Rwanda, having previously served in a similar capacity for elections in Zambia in 2006. In the case of the St Augustine unit, among other positions, Rhoda Reddock served between 2004 and 2007,as an international advisor for the Global Fund for Women, founded in Palo Alto, California, by three women who were convinced that women's human rights and dignity were essential to the advancement of global agendas for social, economic and political change.

Conclusion

Outreach activities carried out by all the units have proved to be a critical dimension of the work of the CGDS/IGDS, allowing as it has interaction with the community outside the boundaries of the university. Through these interactions, all units have established enduring relationships with local, regional and international institutions and development agencies, with an agenda of promoting gender and development, providing advisory services, influencing policy direction and assisting with capacity-building in these institutions. Through these networks, the knowledge base on gender and how it impacts development has been expanded, and the visibility and influence of the university has been enhanced.

> As head of the St Augustine IGDS for fourteen years, I counted myself privileged to be able to earn my living from work in a field to which I was so committed. Despite the challenges – starting with one secretary and no space allocated – the work of establishing the St Augustine unit, as was probably the case with the others as well, was, in many ways, activist work. But, at the same time, it was necessary to establish the scholarly credentials of the field. It is my opinion that the survival of the IGDS depends on this combination as, without the continuous outreach – both on-campus and off-campus, public education and advocacy as well as links with social movements, international organizations and networks – the raison d'être and supportive environment for the IGDS disappears. This has happened in other parts of the world. We need to ensure that, if we are removed, we will be missed. (Rhoda Reddock, testimonial)

In her testimonial, Reddock alludes to the fact that outreach activities are vital to the survival of the IGDS and emphatically states that the survival of the IGDS not only depends on establishing academic credentials in the field of GDS but also in combining this with activism such as is reflected in the outreach activities undertaken by all the units of the IGDS.

CHAPTER 11

GAINING MATURITY

From Centre to Institute

> Although, initially the insertion of gender analysis in teaching and research was somewhat tentative, it is now a well refined and widely accepted art and science in the development of courses and the crafting of individual and institutional research projects across many disciplines. Beyond the academy, gender analysis is also accepted as necessary for informing equitable and sustainable development processes, and the gender and development, GAD, paradigm is now universally promoted as the means of integrating gender equality concerns in national, regional and international projects, programmes and policies. In the region, the UWI not only led the vanguard in this regard but, through its gender and development programmes, has produced a cadre of persons throughout the region with the requisite skills to engage in this critical work in their respective societies.
> —*Barbara Bailey*

Introduction

Information presented in the foregoing chapters indicates that the process of integration of gender studies in the academy was challenging and many of the obstacles encountered had to be subtly negotiated. Time has shown that, from the standpoint of the success achieved in terms of establishing the tripartite programme of teaching, research and outreach, the decision to remain autonomous and interdisciplinary has paid rich dividends, as reflected in the account of selected achievements in these three domains presented in preceding chapters.

A significant marker of the success of the CGDS/IGDS over all stages of its development and evolution has been the small size of the staff complement compared with the substantial output in all three areas of its mission – teaching, research and outreach. This phenomenon has not gone unnoticed and led an external evaluation team that reviewed the work of the RCU and the Mona unit to remark that "outputs are achieved by the creativity of the unit: contracting staff for delivery of graduate courses, hiring short-term consultants for project activities, using undergraduate student assistance and with assistance of staff from the [Mona unit]. This poses a challenge to managing the range of activities with persons from various locations" (UWI BUS 2006b, 17).

This situation was equally applicable to the Cave Hill and St Augustine units, and it is this creativity that belies the fact that, over the entire period of time under review, the units have been under-resourced; they have only been as successful as they have because of the vision and passion of all who have held the reins over the years.

Growth of Units – Expanding the Human Resources

At the time of establishment of the centre in 1993, a single academic appointment was made to each campus unit, with the appointee designated the head of the unit – Eudine Barriteau, Patricia Mohammed and Rhoda Reddock were so appointed at Cave Hill, Mona and St Augustine, respectively. Elsa Leo-Rhynie was appointed head of the RCU and coordinator of the IOP/UWI/ISS project. In each case, there was an administrative support staff appointment, and the space allocated to each unit was small and minimally equipped. Information gleaned from the annual departmental reports of the four units show that expansion of resources, both human and physical, varied across the units and was, for the most part, dependent on the funding source and "patronage" from other departments. In the main, campus units have been funded through their respective campuses, while the RCU has been funded through the University Centre.

The RCU

Between 1993 and 2010, although the volume of work of the unit increased significantly, the number of academic staff on the establishment only increased from one to three persons, despite repeated representations to the University

Grants Committee and the Technical Advisory Committee. It was not until the 2002/3 academic year, when representations were made to the vice-chancellor about the impossibility of fulfilling one of the terms of a contract with the DSO/UWI project to offer a certificate programme in GDS in that year, that a temporary appointment of an expert in instructional design, curriculum development and distance education was made. The major responsibility of the appointee was to coordinate the development and presentation of that programme, which resulted in a slight easing of the staff situation in the RCU. In 2008, however, the incumbent resigned, to take up an appointment in the Open Campus, and the post remained vacant until a new appointment was made in August 2009, with continuing responsibility for coordinating the distance-mode undergraduate diploma programme.

Beyond this appointment, it was not until 2007/8 that the unit was successful in its bid to acquire another lecturer position. This coincided with the expansion of its teaching and research programmes in accordance with the larger vision and strategic direction of the university. An appointment was made in November 2009 specifically to give support to the taught master's programme, which, until that time, had been managed and coordinated by the university director, who not only delivered and examined one of the eight courses but also acted as second marker for another four courses.

Given the breadth and scope of the research activities of the unit, the need for highly competent research assistance increasingly became a necessity, but, in spite of repeated requests for even one research assistant position in every budget submission between 1996 and 2001, the request for the position was not supported by the Technical Advisory Committee over that period. The unit, therefore, was forced to rely on ad hoc assistance for short periods of time and student help, supported by project funding. In May 2001, the situation was relieved when the unit benefited from the services of a Canadian University Services Overseas cooperant, a Canadian national and a graduate of the CGDS MSc programme in GDS, who was appointed as research assistant for a two-year period. Her employment was supported by the Canadian government, funded through the CIDA. In 2005, when the university director was invited by the principal of the Mona campus to serve on a strategic transformation team, funding was provided for the temporary appointment of a research assistant to carry out appropriate duties as assigned, and a graduate student was appointed for eighteen hours per week.

In February 2009, a two-year research fellowship was secured from the

Mona campus to support a major research project that was being undertaken by the RCU with support from the CDB, and this was used to offset the costs of the temporary appointment of a junior research fellow. However, at the same time, owing to budgetary constraints, the unit lost the services of two short-term research assistants. Furthermore, as a result of a massive cut in the Jamaican government's subvention to the UWI, the unit also lost the services of a temporary, part-time documentalist who was also responsible for maintaining the homework centre, an outreach activity of the RCU mentioned in chapter 6, which offered services for the children of staff and commuting students. The termination of the position brought to an end the specialist reference service that had been provided by the RCU to students and the academic community as well as local and visiting international researchers.

During the 2006/7 academic year, the work of the RCU was severely impacted by the sudden illness and subsequent untimely passing of Louraine Emmanuel, administrative officer attached to the unit since 1985, on 22 April 2007. The loss of institutional memory was irreparable, but, nonetheless, in November 2007, Shakira Maxwell, who had previously served in a temporary academic position in the Mona unit, was appointed as her replacement. In the interim, the senior secretary provided administrative oversight of the unit.

In July 2010, Barbara Bailey, who had held the position of regional coordi-

Plate 11.1. Professor Verene Shepherd (*centre*), university director, with Professor Eudine Barriteau (*left*) and Professor Rhoda Reddock (*right*)

nator/university director since August 1996, relinquished the post after completing a three-year post-retirement contract. On August 1 of that same year, Verene Shepherd assumed the post of university director. She is a historian who had been associated with the Mona campus WDSG from inception and who, over the years, had worked on various projects and activities of the CGDS/IGDS.

The Cave Hill Unit

The initial staff complement at Cave Hill consisted of a single academic post of head of unit, with administrative support provided by a stenographer/clerk. By the 1996/97 academic year, the staff complement had increased with the addition of three research assistants, one in a permanent post and the others in temporary appointments, as well as a documentalist. In 2000, in addition to the stenographer clerk, the position of an administrative assistant was included in the establishment. It is interesting to note that it was not only students who were impacted and influenced by programmes and activities of the CGDS. Deborah Deane, appointed as administrative assistant in the NBU/Cave Hill unit, testifies that

> working at the CGDS during the period January 2000 to July 2008 as an administrative assistant has been a very enjoyable and rewarding experience for me. Even though my job was purely administrative, my gender consciousness was raised through my exposure to the scholarship of Professor Barriteau and the other academics in the field, and also through my involvement in many of the centre's activities which I had the pleasure of coordinating.

Between 2002 and 2004, a very important and positive development was the acquisition of two new academic positions, and, while one was immediately filled, the other remained vacant until a temporary appointment was made in August 2007. These additional posts increased the academic staff complement to three, and it was expected that this expansion would facilitate the introduction of an MPhil in gender studies as well as the possibility of moving towards establishing an undergraduate major in gender studies. The first goal has been realized, but the development of the major remains outstanding. During this period, a research assistant was also appointed in a permanent position.

One of the distinctions of the CGDS is that individuals who head the units have been called to serve in senior administrative University positions. During the 2006/7 academic year, having just returned from a one-year sabbatical, the head of the NBU/Cave Hill unit, Eudine Barriteau, was appointed campus coordinator, School for Graduate Studies and Research. To compensate for the time release to manage that portfolio, a teaching assistant was appointed for a six-month period. In the following year, May 2008, the head of the unit was further elevated and appointed to the position of deputy principal at the Cave Hill campus for a three-year period, and Joan Cuffie assumed the role of acting head of the unit, with effect from August 2008. In 2009, a temporary lecturer was appointed, primarily to add support to the graduate programme. The current head of the unit is Charmaine Crawford.

The Mona Unit

In the early years, the Mona unit staff comprised the head of the unit, Patricia Mohammed, and an administrative assistant. In busy periods, undergraduate students provided clerical and research assistance. By the 2000/1 academic year, in addition to the head of unit, a temporary teaching/research assistant was added to the staff complement. In this same year, the head of the unit was awarded research fellowship leave by the Mona campus for the period August 2000 to July 2002 and handed over leadership of the unit to a visiting scholar on sabbatical, Kamala Kempadoo of the University of Colorado, who assumed an acting position but only remained for one year, between 1 August 2000 and 31 July 2001. With Kempadoo's departure, the substantive head, though still on leave, assumed responsibility for major decisions regarding the work and activities of the unit, while the regional coordinator assumed responsibility for day-to-day oversight of the unit.

At the end of the fellowship period, Pat Mohammed relocated to the St Augustine unit. At that time, the Mona campus was facing serious financial constraints due to significant cuts in the Jamaican government's subvention to the university. The regional coordinator decided, therefore, to assume oversight of the unit and to use the savings from the substantive post of head of unit to underwrite the costs of two temporary appointments, one in 2002 and the other in 2003. In 2002/3, a temporary junior research assistant also joined the staff.

This arrangement continued through to the 2004/5 academic year, but the intervening period was used to hold discussions with the deputy bursar of the Mona campus with regard to increasing the academic positions on the Mona unit establishment from one to three. The negotiations were successful, and, in 2004/5, the positions were filled, with one of the existing temporary lecturers qualifying for one of the two permanent positions and the recruitment of a permanent assistant lecturer. As a result of the exercise undertaken by the Mona campus to contain costs, the post of head/senior lecturer was not filled, and the regional coordinator continued to oversee the work of the unit. By this time, however, the responsibility of managing two units had increased, and representation was made to have the post of head of unit filled for the 2005/6 academic year. This was made possible partly by discontinuing the position of a temporary research assistant and diverting those funds to partially support this position. In March 2006, Leith Dunn was appointed head of the Mona unit. The Mona campus F&GPC also gave its approval for the establishment of a clerical assistant post, which was filled at about the same time. In order to retain the services of the other temporary research assistant, that post was reassigned to the RCU and supported by funds from a Mona campus research fellowship associated with a major research project that was then being undertaken by the RCU.

The scenario described above in relation to the staffing of the Mona unit dramatically illustrates the creativity to which external assessors referred in describing the strategy utilized for achieving outputs in spite of stringent limited human resources to adequately support programmes. These arrangements, however, came at a high non-monetary cost to staff, not only at Mona but also at Cave Hill and St Augustine, who all went beyond the call of duty to ensure the viability of the CGDS in the face of grossly inadequate human resources to manage demand which grew exponentially in all four units.

The St Augustine Unit

Although the St Augustine unit started off in the mid-1990s with a similar complement of staff as all the other units, over the years, it far outstripped them in terms of staff expansion. No doubt, this was due to the stronger economic position of Trinidad and Tobago, compared with other Caribbean economies, endowed as it is with natural oil resources.

On Patricia Mohammed's return to the St Augustine campus in 2002, in addition to her substantive post in the CGDS unit, and consistent with the pattern on other campuses, she was appointed in 2004 to serve as deputy dean, Graduate Studies and Research, for the Faculty of Social Sciences. She also acted as head of the CGDS from June 2005 to July 2006 while Rhoda

Plate 11.2. A group of CGDS staff members, circa 2005: (*left to right*) Barbara Bailey, Pat Mohammed, Eudine Barriteau, Rhoda Reddock, Yasmin Yusuf-Khalil, June-Ann Castello, Althea Perkins, Louraine Emmanuel, Michelle Rowley

Reddock went on sabbatical leave. In that same year, there were several new staff appointments, including two temporary assistant lecturers, a graduate research assistant, a clerical assistant and a teaching assistant to undertake some of the teaching assigned to Patricia Mohammed. In 2007, one of the two temporary assistant lecturer positions became permanent, while a new post of outreach and research officer was established. In the 2006/7 academic year, the full complement of permanent and temporary staff positions stood at approximately ten persons.

In August 2008, Rhoda Reddock, who had headed the St Augustine unit since its establishment in 1993, was promoted to the post of deputy principal of the St Augustine campus. This confirms that the management skills acquired and demonstrated by staff of the CGDS were in high demand on all campuses, since similar appointments had been made at both the Cave Hill and Mona campuses. By October of that same year, Piya Pangsapa was appointed head of the St Augustine unit.

Growth of Units – Expanding the Physical Resources

The gradual increase in the staff complement in all the units meant that efforts had to be made to find adequate space which could accommodate both staff and students. The CGDS having been established outside of the existing faculty structure, finding space proved to be a major challenge. Essentially, all existing space was assigned to a particular faculty/department, and the success of the quest ultimately depended on the goodwill and patronage of those sympathetic to the mission of establishing gender studies in the academy.

Over a ten-year period, 1993 to 2003, the Mona unit and RCU were first accommodated in separate locations across the campus and then provided with shared space, which quickly became inadequate. In January 2003, based on negotiations with the campus principal, brokered by the deputy principal, a former regional coordinator of the CGDS, space was secured and reconfigured to accommodate the RCU and Mona unit in the newly constructed Alister McIntyre Building mainly housing the Mona School of Business. A similar arrangement as had obtained since 1996/97, with the sharing of resources, continued, and, although the space was larger, it still remained limited for accommodating staff and students. Further, with the move, the dedicated computer-lab space established for students in the previous location was lost. An added problem faced by the two units, which was also the case with the other two campus units, was the absence of dedicated classroom and seminar rooms for undergraduate and graduate lectures and tutorials. In all instances, lecturers were at the mercy of other departments for the assignment of rooms, which, over time, became increasingly difficult.

These conditions led the external team assigned by the Quality Assurance Unit of the BUS to review the Mona unit and RCU in 2006 to observe, in their report, that "limited or no assigned permanent classroom space impacts upon the use of electronic equipment such as overhead projectors and video cassettes, as these have to be constantly transferred from room to room and stored at the end of class. When there are evening classes, it becomes onerous for administrative or academic staff to have to return to campus or work late to store equipment" (UWI BUS 2006b, 17). The team further opined that

> both the [Mona unit] and the RCU have made significant contributions in their outreach and their core programmes. It is evident, however, from all the reports and observations, that the units are grossly under-resourced, and this poses a threat

> to continued delivery of quality and timely services and information, and to the very dignity of the staff. The CGDS has continued to subsidize its need for financial resources through research and other projects, but even this ability to finance itself partially may be endangered by inadequate resources. (ibid., 15)

At Cave Hill, after ten years of being located at Hill House, in the 2002 to 2004 report of the Cave Hill unit to the regional meeting of the CGDS, it was noted that the unit was being relocated to newly designated office space near the Faculty of Social Sciences. A concern, however, was expressed that "this does not represent an expansion in office space but merely a new address. While the building is new, the actual office and storage space is smaller. We are concerned about our capacity to discharge our responsibilities in a somewhat tighter space allocation. The campus has assured us that, with expansion, the needs of the Centre will be given priority" (Report, Cave Hill Campus Unit, 2002–4, 2).

Information gleaned from the 2005 report of the external assessment of the St Augustine unit indicates that the centre was located in a section of a chemistry building secured through negotiation with that department. The external assessment team, however, opined that the unit was challenged in terms of space, and although this had already been indicated in the self-assessment report, the team reiterated the concern that "accommodation is inadequate for the existing and expanding needs of the Centre and certainly for the range of teaching methodologies it employs" (UWI BUS 2005, 10). The team suggested that the following were necessary: at least three more offices to add to the existing four for staff; an expanded reception area; reading space for researchers; a fully-resourced graduate room; and a conference room and library. Additionally, the external assessment team made several observations:

> The Head has no space for meetings that are a normal part of the running of the Centre, leaving her to juggle the use of the seminar room; and part-time staff has no space (e.g. separate desks) in which to operate, although they do not seem to be complaining but are trying to make do, some using other spaces on campus. . . . The bathrooms also need to be closer to the office staff instead of down several flights of steps. In addition, there is no disabled access; and kitchen and lounge facilities are cramped. They have used the space available creatively, but certainly comfort is desirable and achievable. The space for storage of Information Technology [IT] and other equipment and for photocopying services needs to be expanded. (UWI BUS 2005, 10)

The team noted that the deputy principal was encouraging the head of the centre to ensure that a claim be submitted so that any new construction could take the needs of CGDS into consideration. It was established that faculties had been asked to submit proposals/requests for physical expansion, but it was possible that, as an interdisciplinary entity, the CGDS may have fallen through the cracks. Even before that time, efforts had been made through the RCU to address the limited space at the St Augustine unit, particularly in light of the expansion of the staff complement, which had occurred more rapidly than in any of the other units. At the urging of the head of unit, the regional coordinator directly approached the campus principal, both in person and in writing, about the space situation of the CGDS on that campus. Although promises were made to address the situation, no concrete action materialized, and the unit has remained housed in this location.

It should be noted that, in September 2000, a meeting was held with the principal of the St Augustine campus, who, after hearing of the plight of the CGDS in terms of its limited physical resources across all the campuses, suggested that a comprehensive assessment of the needs for space and staff over the next five years be made. This was to be included as one of three infrastructure projects to be submitted to the CDB, through the Office of Planning, for consideration. Although the RCU expended significant time and effort in preparing a proposal that covered all four units, no serious consideration seemed to have been given to the submission, since no feedback was ever received. In the meantime, each unit has had to fend for itself and contend for any space that became available from time to time.

Development of an Ordinance

Although a statute governing the structure and functioning of the IGDS was not approved until 25 January 2013, several precursor events led to this decision. As far back as October 1997, a request made to the Board for Graduate Studies and Research that students pursuing graduate studies in GDS, at both the St Augustine and Mona campuses, be allocated to the CGDS and counted as part of their student enrolment was approved. The request was considered at a meeting of the Board for Graduate Studies and Research held in that same month, and the minutes reveal that there was resistance to this idea on the part of some members of the board, with one view being that "the Gender issue should be looked upon as going across disciplines and/or applied to disciplines; and that students should be registered in the department in which the discipline was being taught" (UWI BGSR 1997, minute 56.2 ii). By way of a memorandum dated January 1998 from the regional coordinator to Don Robotham, the PVC Graduate Studies, the claim that gender could be contained within discipline boundaries was challenged and a request made that the position taken at the October meeting be reconsidered, contending, inter alia, that "the University, by its recent amalgamation of Departments and Faculties, is recognizing the pedagogical value of interdisciplinarity and the need for students to learn to think and handle problems in a holistic rather than compartmentalized manner. . . . The Centre for Gender and Development Studies is leading the way in this respect." In the rebuttal, it was further contended that "the CGDS, in its Mission Statement, affirms . . . its establishment as an interdisciplinary Centre for Teaching and Research. We therefore maintain that, if students are required to focus their learning experiences within the confines of one discipline, this would run counter to the very philosophy on which the Centre has been established, as well as to current academic thought and direction."

Finally, the matter was resolved, and, by way of a memorandum dated 4 May 1998 from the secretary of the Board for Graduate Studies and Research, the CGDS was informed that, at its meeting of February 1998, the board had discussed the request for reconsideration of its position with respect to the registration and allocation of graduate students to the CGDS and had agreed that the centre could register students and develop its own curriculum. The board also laid out the routing for approval of such graduate courses.

A second marker of the move to further establish the independence of the CGDS as an interdisciplinary entity intended to offer degrees was the fact that, in 2001 a request for the assignment of a CGDS colour was made by the chair of the advisory committee of the CGDS, Elsa Leo-Rhynie, through the vice-chancellor to the senate for graduates of the CGDS to be assigned a colour (ecru) to serve as a lining of the hoods of their graduate gowns. It was intended that this colour would be unique to the CGDS and would differentiate its graduates from those of other faculties.

However, as with all other innovative steps taken by the CGDS, this request was not approved without the usual challenges. Although acknowledging that it was timely that the CGDS was asking for separate colours, in correspondence dated October 2001, PVC Errol Morrison, dean of the School for Graduate Studies and Research, informed that

> the School for Graduate Studies and Research is at this time planning to register all graduate students in centres/institutes that are not faculty-affiliated. In addition,

> the registration process will include students whose research programmes fail to fit squarely within any one faculty.
>
> This latter situation is becoming increasingly needed as research thrusts take on more and more multidisciplinary nature as well as new frontier areas which may result in candidates not fitting readily into a faculty.
>
> The CGDS, in applying for its own colours, has initiated a thrust which the [School for Graduate Studies and Research] would like to embrace by asking that you consider the proposed colours for use by graduates of the school.

Although the CGDS staff were disappointed that the ecru colour would not be unique to the CGDS, after consultations with all the staff, there was consensus that it would serve no real purpose to oppose this proposition, and a letter was sent to PVC Morrison in January 2002 agreeing to his proposal. The decision to use ecru hoods for its graduates was implemented by the CGDS, but the broader proposal seemed neither to have been accepted nor implemented.

Having taken these steps to establish the CGDS as an independent, interdisciplinary entity, it became obvious that the next logical step would be to request that an ordinance be developed to regulate the operation of the centre and to ensure that the CGDS was legally constituted within UWI structures and processes. The process was initiated, and the ordinance was drafted for consideration by the Senate Committee on Ordinances and Regulations. Based on a review of the background document setting out the mission and management structures of the CGDS to guide the drafting process, in September 2003, the university registrar, Gloria Barrett-Sobers, indicated that SCOR was of the opinion that, given the role of the consultative committee, application of the term "consultative" was misleading and asked the CGDS to identify a suitable designation for that committee.

The CGDS document was subsequently revised, and the following designation changes were submitted to SCOR:

1. The consultative committee was redesignated the management committee.
2. The regional advisory committee was redesignated the Regional Planning and Strategy Committee.
3. Head of campus unit was redesignated director of the campus unit.
4. The regional coordinator was redesignated university director, RCU.

Correspondence of January 2005 from Gloria Barrett-Sobers, university registrar, however, informed CGDS that, in light of UF&GPC's jurisdictional mandate, that committee should be asked to reconsider these redesignations and SCOR was therefore referring the draft ordinance for the consideration of F&GPC. In follow-up correspondence of February 2005, the CGDS was informed that all redesignations had been approved except for that of the head of campus unit to director of the campus unit. The UF&GPC pointed out that the change of nomenclature would be inconsistent with understandings reached in the Career Path Committee about the interpretation of "director".

This became a sticky issue, which was debated by the CGDS over an extended period of time, and, in an effort to arrive at a satisfactory solution, consultations were held with the chair of the Career Path Committee. It was finally determined that the main issue was that the title "director" implies professorship, and, although two of the current heads were professors, only the regional coordinator's post was institutionalized at the professorial level. From a budgetary standpoint, the redesignation of the heads of units would need funds to be available in the campus budgets to support a post at this level. For this reason, the UF&GPC had not approved the redesignation. Pursuant to a SCOR decision of 31 March 2005, the final text of the ordinance, reflecting the approved redesignations, was submitted to F&GPC for approval.

Beyond this, no final decision was taken by SCOR on the ordinance, and, in the interim, the request for the redesignation of the centre as an institute was approved on 10 October 2008. Subsequent to this decision, the matter of the ordinance was reopened in a letter of January 2009 to the university registrar, C. William Iton, reminding him that the matter of the ordinance had been put on hold awaiting the decision of UF&GPC on institute status. With that decision having been made, the matter now needed to be brought back to the attention of SCOR because, no doubt, there would be need for redrafting of the ordinance to accommodate the change to institute status. However, the matter was not returned to the SCOR agenda until June 2010, when information was requested for amending the ordinance based on upgrading to institute status. In response, the RCU requested that the following matters be brought to the attention of SCOR:

1. The redesignation of the centre as a university-wide institute
2. The approval of the IGDS as a degree-granting entity able to confer undergraduate and graduate degrees
3. The matter of the designation of heads of units to be reconsidered for change from head of campus unit to director, campus unit
4. The committees to remain the same as with earlier submissions, with the

regional advisory committee redesignated as the Regional Planning and Strategy Committee and the consultative committee redesignated as the management committee.

These matters were considered and approval given for all except the redesignation of heads of campus units. The matter of the ordinance was finally dispensed with in January 2013. All told, the process took ten years from initiation of the idea to adoption of the decision, illustrating again the typical time lag in the diffusion and acceptance of innovative ideas and practices.

Change of Status: Centre to Institute

In February 2009, the Office of Graduate Studies and Research issued a third edition of its *Policy for the Establishment, Operation and Governance of Units, Centres and Institutes at the University of the West Indies*. It was pointed out in the policy document that the development of this policy position had become necessary because "several Units, Centres and Institutes already exist at the University of the West Indies (UWI), and more are being continually established. However, there is little coordination and consistency in the manner in which these operational entities are established or to whom they report; and there is little consistency between the organizational structures and functions of the entities and the category to which they are assigned" (1). The policy, therefore, had been developed to ensure that these entities could readily be identifiable in terms of consistency of nomenclature, mode of establishment, scope of work, reporting and governance within the UWI multi-campus system. To this end, definitions were set out for campus/faculty units, campus/faculty centres and university institutes.

On reviewing the criteria for identifying an entity as a university institute, it became evident that the CGDS was much more closely aligned with a university institute than a university centre, as it was then designated. The defining features of an institute as outlined in the document were examined, and several parallels emerged in relation to expected characteristics and activities, governance structures, reporting and accountability requirements and procedures for review of its operations. In terms of the identified characteristics, the centre was already engaged in university-wide teaching and intramural and commissioned research. The fact that the centre was already engaged in a wide range of national, regional and international collaborations and had established linkages, commitments and relationships with external research institutions, business and government groups and national, regional and international stakeholders with a focus on gender and development initiatives was highlighted. Further, it was pointed out that, on all three campuses, the CGDS had developed a tradition of receiving visiting extra-regional scholars and researchers who sought attachments with the centre, while academic staff of the centre had, on several occasions, been invited to be visiting scholars at a range of well-recognized institutions.

In terms of both structure and operation, the existing structures of the CGDS also satisfied the governance structure requirements of an institute as set out in the policy document. The CGDS already had a Regional Planning and Strategy Committee, which met once per year and which could be expanded to satisfy the requirement for external members, and there was also an internal management committee, which met bimonthly by teleconference via UWI Distance Education Centre. The financing of the units was, also, already in keeping with the guidelines for university institutes. The RCU was administered by the university bursar in the Office of Finance, and by the campus bursaries, in the case of the campus units, arrangements which could remain in place under institute status.

In terms of reporting and accountability requirements, it was recommended in the policy document that university institutes would report to their advisory boards and the vice-chancellor. Again, this requirement had already been met, given that each of the four units tabled a report at the annual Regional Planning and Strategy Committee and was already compliant with the requirements and timelines for the *Vice-Chancellor's Report to Council*, departmental reports, principal's report to campus council and also reported to the BUS as well as to the Board for Graduate Studies and Research. It was also recommended that institutes should be reviewed every three years to determine status and continuity. The CGDS was already a part of the review system under the Quality Assurance Unit of the BUS and, at the time of the request, all units had already been subjected to an external review.

Based on this review of the defining features of an institute as well as a process of consultation with all the heads of units, in March 2008, a justification for a change of status from centre to institute was prepared and submitted for consideration through the relevant channels. In response, on 14 October 2008, the university director received a memorandum from the university registrar, William Iton, advising that the university F&GPC, at its meeting on 10 October

2008, approved the redesignation of the CGDS as an institute of the UWI. In January 2009, the university registrar was asked to alert centre and campus offices (registry, bursary, student records and so on), including those of the Open Campus, of the need to incorporate the change of status in all systems and procedures in matters pertaining to staff and students of the institute. This plea, however, was largely unheeded.

The welcomed redesignation notice communicated in the memorandum from the registrar, however, also stated that "the UF&GPC asserted that the issuance of degrees must be done in collaboration with a Faculty as the Institute may not issue its own degrees". An appeal of this decision was immediately prepared, in light of the history of the establishment of the CGDS as an interdisciplinary centre, its approval as a degree-granting entity outside of a faculty, and its functioning as such, since its inception in 1993. Four critical points were raised in the appeal submitted by the IGDS in May 2009:

1. The IGDS, in its previous designation as the CGDS, was deliberately designed and accepted as a unique body within the university system to reflect its mandate to function as an interdisciplinary centre.
2. The model, which was approved and which has been successfully implemented, involved the establishment of boards of studies which are equivalent to faculty boards, and which are chaired by the heads of the campus units.
3. The arrangement for boards of studies and for the inclusion of unit heads on academic boards was an important aspect of the approval of the IGDS as a distinct entity, equivalent to a faculty in terms of its academic objectives, including the granting of degrees.
4. In response to increasing demand, a major in gender studies had been approved at the Mona campus.

Based on these justifications, it was felt that it was especially important that the independence of the redesignated institute be preserved so that its interdisciplinary nature and emphasis could be sustained. An appeal was, therefore, made for the UF&GPC to reverse the directive, thereby allowing the IGDS to have degree-granting status.

In June 2009, correspondence was received from the university registrar indicating that the UF&GPC had considered the request. The committee had, however, agreed that, since the matter of degree-granting was the purview of the senate, it would rescind its ruling on the matter and refer it to the BUS and the Board for Graduate Studies and Research. Finally, the IGDS welcomed a memorandum dated 20 October 2009 from the university registrar advising that "the UF&GPC, at its meeting on October 9, 2009, at the St Augustine Campus, having received the endorsement of the Board of Undergraduate Studies and the Board of Graduate Studies and Research, approved, without reservation, the assertion by the Institute of Gender and Development Studies that it was eligible to deliver interdisciplinary academic programmes and to issue its own degrees".

Even while clarification of the matter of degree-granting status was in train, the request was made to the university registrar, in January 2009, to alert centre and campus offices about the change of status to institute. Finally, a news release was sent out, but, from all accounts, this seemed to have very little effect. Few adjustments have been made to existing systems to accommodate the IGDS as a degree-granting entity; and, although approvals were given at the highest levels of the university, the IGDS has continued to move against the tide in terms of gaining recognition and moving seamlessly through academic systems and processes.

Maturity: An Unfinished Task?

The institutionalization of GDS at the UWI has had an indisputable impact on both the academic landscape of the institution as well as on the development agenda of the wider Caribbean and international community. The former is evidenced by the scholarly output from the centre/institute through the publication of readers, inclusion of papers authored by staff of the units in refereed journals, the introduction of an online journal at St Augustine, the production of working papers by all the campus units, the hosting of lecture series and public lectures of visiting scholars, the mounting of significant international conferences and the conducting of personal, institutional and commissioned research, the findings of which have informed national and regional policy positions. Much of this was only possible through the acquisition and infusion of significant financial resources from a range of sources. The impact at the regional and international levels is evidenced by the fact that the staff of all the units have offered a wide range of advisory and technical services to national governments and regional and international agencies as well as served on regional and international bodies addressing gender and development issues.

The most striking testimony of the impact of the gender project at the UWI on the Caribbean community is the signal honour of having six of those who, over the years, had been closely associated with the project being awarded the CARICOM Triennial Award for Women for "dedication and determination in broadening the parameters of existence for women and improving their economic, social, political, cultural and legal status". Included in this group are: Dr Peggy Antrobus, 1990; the Honourable Dr Lucille Mathurin Mair, 1996; Professor Joycelin Massiah, 1999; Professor Rhoda Reddock, 2002; Professor Barbara Bailey, 2008; and Professor Eudine Barriteau, 2011. The outstanding contributions of these individuals and others have also been recognized and honoured at the national level.

As significant as these achievements in the academic sphere have been, Bailey (2012, 12) notes that

> Gender Studies is not only a legitimate academic pursuit but dissemination and acquisition of this body of knowledge is also intended to bring into question long accepted ideologies of power, status and control and to challenge gender-based stereotypes and norms. At the institutional level, the political agenda of a gender project should therefore be concerned with challenging inequitable power relations as well as changing normalized patriarchal attitudes, values and behaviours.

In this regard, she conceded that "from inception, the drivers of the gender project have been moving upstream against the current of long accepted institutional norms and, at best, success in changing the political landscape of the institution has been minimal" (ibid.).

Over the twenty years covered by these recollections and reflections, the balance of power between the genders has shifted little in the academy and currently remains firmly in the hands of a male hierarchy; this is in spite of the fact that the demography of the institution has changed dramatically from being a male preserve in the 1960s to being, at the turn of the twenty-first century, a female-dominated institution in terms of student enrolment (69 per cent female, 31 per cent male, in 2010), while, in terms of academic staff, men had a slight numerical advantage (53.1 per cent) and women accounted for 46.9 per cent of all academic staff. The disparity in the sex ratio between those at the top of the ladder of academic hierarchy and those at the bottom continued to reflect the classic pattern of male advantage, with the male/female ratio among appointments at the professorial level being in favour of men (72.2 per cent), while, at the other end of the spectrum, women accounted for 57.4 per cent of all assistant lecturers. Bailey (ibid.) further notes that, "although over the years there has been some ebb and flow in terms of appointment of females to senior governance positions as pro vice-chancellors, a principal in one instance, deputy principals and deans, as of now, save for the Open Campus, these positions are held by males".

It is not without significance, therefore, that, after some twenty years and more of the existence of a gender project within the academy, women in the institution continue to find themselves on the fringes of the power structures. Bailey, therefore, conceded that she had no choice but to conclude that "all told, the impact of the gender project on UWI's evolution has been profound in terms of ways in which it has shaped and altered research and epistemological paradigms and the academic structure of the institution. The governance structures, however, have been altered little in terms of yielding male exercise of power and authority to females" (ibid., 13).

In a nutshell, the evidence presented in this review leaves little doubt that, in terms of the introduction of the gender project on the landscape of the UWI, academic maturity has not only been achieved, it has been stellar. However, the political imperative of shifting the balance of power between and among the sexes, which is an integral part of any gender project, remains unfinished and is still a work in progress.

Section 5

CONTINUITY

JOYCELIN MASSIAH, ELSA LEO-RHYNIE
AND BARBARA BAILEY

CHAPTER 12

LOOKING TO THE FUTURE

The Journey Continues

> The IGDS was formed in a moment that held (and still holds) both incredible promise and tremendous challenge.
> —*Alissa Trotz, keynote address, opening ceremony of the IGDS Twentieth Anniversary Conference, 2013*

AN INITIATIVE SPANNING THIRTY-FIVE YEARS NECESSARILY PRODUCES ACHIEVEMENTS to be applauded, lessons to be learned, and challenges to be addressed. In the mid-1970s, when women at the UWI undertook the journey to establish a programmee in women/gender and development studies, it was not clear what would be found, where the journey would go and the path the journey would follow. By the second decade of the twenty-first century, new knowledge, new programmes, new institutions, new structures, new friendships and more have been created. Indeed, women have stretched inward and moved outward, tapping into their ability and creativity and, in the process, influencing individuals and groups throughout the Caribbean and beyond. From this experience, many lessons have been learned, which can be shared with those continuing the journey.

In this chapter, a number of the achievements at each stage of this fascinating gender journey in UWI are examined in order to identify major lessons learned along the way. To accomplish this, two of the four stages of innovation as proposed by Rogers and Shoemaker (1971) – *initiation* and *institutionalization* – were used as reference points and extended to include a *consoli-*

dation stage. Actions taken during each of these stages were also considered in terms of the two categories proposed by Rowland (1982) – *pragmatic* and *political*. Pragmatic actions are those needed to introduce a women's studies programme/course in institutions of higher learning which, as Rowland puts it, "are usually hierarchical, autocratic and male-dominated", whereas political actions are those intended to confront and overcome any obstruction which may be encountered. Rowland's categories mirror those proposed by Caroline Moser (1989) in describing needs to be addressed in respect of development projects – *practical* and *strategic gender needs*. Reflecting on the experience of the WDS/GDS programme with which this volume is concerned, however, it was clear that many of the actions and results were simultaneously *pragmatic/practical* and *political/strategic*, using the definitions of these terms by the stated authors. The vocabulary of these frameworks provided a useful mechanism for categorizing and describing the activities and actions at each stage of the programme over the past thirty-five years.

Thus, initiation (which involved women's NGOs, WAND, WICP and the WDSGs), institutionalization (typified by the formation and establishment of the CGDS) and consolidation (which details the growth and development of the centre, following institutionalization, and its transition to the IGDS) all involved actions which could be considered practical/pragmatic and/or political/strategic. Use of the frameworks allowed for more precise definition of the kind of achievements recorded as well as lessons learned at successive stages of the journey.

Achievements and Lessons

Three major themes or categories were used to summarize the achievements during each of the stages – initiation, institutionalization and consolidation; and for each theme, attempts have been made to extract the main lessons learned, in the hope that the cadre of young leaders who comprise the next generation will benefit.

Theme 1: Creating Academic Validity

In an academic setting, expectations of a newly introduced discipline are development of teaching courses and related materials as well as the design and conduct of research projects. This innovative programme, however, eventually combined teaching and research with outreach activities. The programme raised gender awareness in the academy; it promoted what Bailey calls feminist pedagogy, creating a space for the emergence of indigenous theorizing; it encouraged young academics by deliberately creating opportunities for capacity-building; and it significantly enhanced the promotion potential of staff. Perhaps most importantly, the programme strongly defended the notion of interdisciplinarity, insisting that accommodation within the faculty structure would undermine its validity. Instead, successful negotiation led to the programme's location in the University Centre and to the devising of a mechanism which was unique to the university, to ensure that the accountability demanded of disciplinary faculties was also adhered to by the interdisciplinary CGDS.

At the initiation stage, the very fact that the university was willing to establish WAND implies an admission that the subject of WAD was a valid issue for inclusion on the academic agenda, even if that inclusion extended only to outreach activities. But WAND demonstrated that it was possible to combine research – admittedly, not necessarily academic-type research – with the design and implementation of outreach activities. The WICP demonstrated that women were willing to talk about their lives and their understandings of the positive and negative aspects of the socio-economic, political and cultural issues which affected them. The fashioning of research methodologies which allowed for the sharing of these issues while adhering to the requirements of rigour in the research process was a major achievement of the WICP.

It was these two initiatives which facilitated the introduction of a WDS programme at UWI and gave validity to women's issues as an academic concern, thus laying the foundation for the introduction of the WDSGs. They, in turn, created new ways of working together in an academic environment, successfully raised funds which helped to build capacity of staff, extended the debate across faculties and generally raised gender awareness in the academy. The WDSGs also introduced the initial WDS undergraduate interdisciplinary course, and courses in other disciplines, without the benefit of a "blessing" from the university administration. It was the institutionalized CGDS, however, that implemented curriculum development activities resulting in continued expansion of course offerings at the undergraduate level, the introduction of postgraduate degree programmes, extension of the research programme and an increasing number of seminars, symposia and publications. The summer certificate programme offered to participants from all the countries of the region, including those of the Eastern Caribbean, ensured that the discourse was not limited to campus audiences but also engaged others who could exert influence on policy in the region.The distance-mode diploma programme was not only designed to meet the objective of creating awareness and building skills in gender analysis among women and men in the Caribbean, but also to provide a route for their matriculation into degree programmes. All of these activities, conducted within the prevailing university rules and procedures, represented full integration of GDS into the academic agenda of the university. In the course of these developments, many lessons were learned.

Lesson: Rome Was Not Built in a Day

One of the often overlooked, or underestimated, aspects of this *gender journey* is that it has been an effort aimed at transforming attitudes, relations, behaviours and practices which are entrenched. As a general goal, this takes time. In an academic setting, it takes time to create and nurture a core of persons willing to undertake the journey, to garner support from colleagues, to persuade the administrators to take the effort seriously and make the necessary administrative accommodations, to develop and implement teaching, research and outreach activities and to find the necessary resources. The journey is now thirty-five years old; much has been achieved, yet much more needs to be done. Several lessons have been learned along the way, perhaps the most important being to take time to build carefully towards the envisaged goal. Out of this general lesson, a number of others follow.

Be Patient

One of the main lessons which the initiators of this programme learned was the need to curb their impatience and to take time to solidify gains. It took five years for the idea of introducing WDS in the UWI academic curriculum to emerge; another two years for the emergence of the WDSGs; another ten years before the university was willing to appoint a professor of WDS; one more year to establish the CGDS; and another fifteen years to convert the CGDS to the IGDS: a total of thirty-five years to get to the point of having similar status, if not similar recognition, to other comparable UWI entities. The quantity and quality of the achievements over these many years suggest that there was wisdom in proceeding slowly and carefully, rather than speedily, in addressing the many challenges faced at all stages of the process. Indeed, as an old Caribbean proverb proclaims, it is better to "take a little and live long".

Be Vigilant: Struggle to Preserve Gains

In her keynote address at the opening ceremony of the IGDS Twentieth-Anniversary Conference, Professor Alissa Trotz draws attention to the virtually unchanged situation of women, despite the years of activism throughout the region. On the one hand, public policy continues to espouse strategies which undermine the value of women's work to society, generate increasing income inequality and foster increased domestic violence. On the other hand, gains which women have made, such as increased educational attainment and higher positions in the public service, private sector and political spheres, continue to be minimal, in terms of their impact on the overall position of women and on the prevailing levels of gender inequality. She calls it the "paradox of visibility and marginalization" (Trotz 2013). This is an interesting observation when, for the past two decades, the women's movement has been attempting to address the theory of male marginalization, even as the issue of women's marginalization is explored. The debate has forced the question: if men say they are being marginalized by women, and women say they are being marginalized by men, who really is being marginalized and by whom (Massiah 2006, 75). The answer must lie in the fact that there has been no significant disruption of the gender system and the associated social mores which, therefore, have not accommodated to the notion of gender equality which programmes such as those of the IGDS hold as their ultimate goal. This lesson points to the need to be vigilant in the use of the lens of gender to constantly review and analyse circumstances, to use new knowledge to understand ongoing changes and to persist in finding ways to preserve gains which reflect the quest for gender justice.

Sustain the Vision

Particularly during the institutionalization and consolidation stages, there have been strenuous efforts to expand and increase the relevance of teaching courses, teaching techniques, research topics and methodologies, outreach strategies and administrative practices, all with the aim of strengthening the academic programme within parameters set by the administrative authorities.

Plate 12.1. Continuing the journey – IGDS faculty and staff, 2013: Verene Shepherd, university director (*centre back*), Leith Dunn, head, Mona unit (*second from left*), Dr Charmaine Crawford, head, NBU, Cave Hill (*standing next to Dunn*); Piya Pangsapa, head, St Augustine unit, Rhoda Reddock and Eudine Barriteau (*extreme right, front row*)

In most cases, these efforts have yielded substantial returns, but constantly changing circumstances have demanded changes in the academic programme. The lesson here has been, and will continue to be, the need to maintain ongoing monitoring of societal changes, upgrade pedagogical techniques and revise curricula in order to keep the programme both academically sound and culturally relevant.

> A feminist agenda of social change is not won overnight, and I believe that the NBU has a vibrant, young academic staff that has the intelligence, tenacity, skills and will power to do what is needed to build on, and also continue, the legacy that was established decades ago. Some things may look, and be done, differently compared to our predecessors, but the NBU's commitment to academic excellence and social justice remains the same. I can unequivocally say that I am proud to be a part of IGDS family and tradition. (Charmaine Crawford, testimonial)

Be Assertive in the Face of Obstacles/Hurdles

Over the thirty-five years of its existence, this gender journey has faced many obstacles and/or crossed many hurdles. At several points in this narrative, reference has been made to experiences of negativity or opposition to some aspect of the programme or, indeed, to the programme itself. In the early days, this was a constant obstacle, which has diminished appreciably but is still alive and well. Reference has also been made to the various ways in which individuals on the programme have dealt successfully with such opposition. The lesson must be to remain calm in the face of such opposition, to assess the content and quality of the specific obstacle and to determine whether or how best to confront it. All of this takes time and patience as well as assertiveness.

A constant hurdle has been that of fundraising. Despite the inability and/or unresponsiveness of the UWI, due to its own financial difficulties, to provide the necessary resources for the activities envisioned and undertaken by the CGDS/IGDS, the centre/institute has progressed and even flourished because of the external funding it has been able to garner. Always a problem, obtaining such funding has become even more difficult in recurring periods of recession. Time-consuming and stress-inducing, this hurdle has constituted an integral aspect of the journey, which had to be faced and overcome. Confidence in the goals and strategies of the programme helped to develop the assertiveness which was often required to persuade donors to provide the requested support. Perhaps more importantly, assertiveness was vital in maintaining the independence of the programme in the face, sometimes, of donor demands which conflicted with the overall goals of the programme.

Theme 2: Successful Programme Management

From its inception, the *gender journey* at the UWI has been marked by strong recognition of the need for action to implement the ideas which women had generated and action to confront the resistance which they anticipated. Thus, the practical achievements included what was accomplished by reinforcing the idea of collaboration and widening the network of partners, as done by the early women's organizations and WAND; by developing a strong database through innovative research, as was done by the WICP; by building the capacity of staff, as was done by WAND, WICP and the WDSGs; by being prepared to take risks, as was demonstrated by each of these early players. The practical actions/activities during the initiation stage reflected not only a high degree of creativity but also produced important strategic advantages. Thus, for example, the thrust of WAND's work catalysed the thinking of women's NGOs, forcing them to think creatively, thus enabling them to be more confident in their discourse on development issues. The work of the WICP created a vehicle which empowered women to speak about their own lives and encouraged the researchers, mainly female, to experiment with unfamiliar methodological strategies and theoretical explanations. The work of the WDSGs strengthened the ability of women in the academy to work with the administration and enabled them to be more assertive in pursuing their goals in keeping with their desired position within the institutional structure.

These practical actions were continued through the institutionalization and consolidation stages. However, it was at the institutionalization stage – that is, at the stage of establishing the CGDS – that the leaders of the programme became more assertive, by carving out a space for the centre on the academic agenda. During this stage, the focus was on attracting and ensuring the appointment of appropriate staff, establishing offices and strengthening teamwork across the three campuses, as well as working closely with donors. The CGDS developed the political ability to seize the moment, particularly in respect of fundraising; learned to manoeuvre within academic bureaucracy; insisted on its own proposals for an appropriate institutional structure and developed new, creative ways of working with its various partners. Especially important was its ability to maintain its own autonomy within an institutional structure which was not only hierarchical but also extremely patriarchal. At this stage, the programme accomplished a number of strategic goals, including creating a new relationship between the university and the community through outreach activities as well as collaborating with new partners, notably the UN. The collaboration with UN agencies was evident in the key roles played by various staff in the Caribbean preparations for the 1995 Beijing conference and participation at the NGO forum at that conference. Another important achievement was the establishment of a mechanism for institutionalization, thus facilitating the eventual thrust towards being designated as an institute of the UWI.

The transition of the CGDS to IGDS built on these achievements by facilitating the development of additional course offerings at both undergraduate and postgraduate levels. It was the political action at this stage, however, that helped to strengthen the public profile of the programme. This was evident in the continuation of the process of collaboration on UN activities – in this case, the Beijing+5 Conference – and the increased ability to provide expertise to a widening range of stakeholders, both within and outside the region. Strategically, it was at this stage that the unflagging efforts of the CGDS brought to fruition the process of institutionalization which resulted in the transformation of the CGDS into the IGDS.

Out of these achievements and results, a number of critical lessons were learned.

Lesson: Leadership Is Crucial

Collective action may be powerful, but being effective requires skilled, committed and creative leadership. Such leadership must be inclusive, sensitive to differences, firm and dedicated to the principles of social justice and gender equity. Some years ago, the then UNIFEM Caribbean office (now UN Women) hosted a workshop focusing on the issue of leadership. By the end of the workshop, participants had produced a definition of transformational leadership, which, in part, stated that "it is a leadership that begins with transformation at the individual level and leads to the redefinition of gender and power relations in a process that fundamentally changes the structures, organizing principles and operational practices of institutions and society. It is a leadership that is technically competent, politically aware and culturally sensitive" (Massiah 2001, xii). While this definition may not necessarily have been a guiding principle of the WDS/GDS programme, there are certainly elements in the management of the programme which suggest that critical elements of good leadership as conceived by this definition did exist in the programme. Five such may be identified, and they are expanded on below.

Know Your Strengths

To operationalize the programme, it was necessary to have leaders at a number of points – regional unit leaders, campus group leaders, leaders of committees, leaders of outreach activities. It would be fair to say that, initially, few of these persons had any real experience as leaders. In fact, several may have had little knowledge of women and gender issues, except perhaps a general interest in the subject. Bridget Brereton explains: "I've always had an unarticulated interest in women's affairs, since I was probably a teenager. In a quiet and unobtrusive way I've always cherished some feminist principles, although I'm not a natural activist or natural joiner, but I've always been intellectually interested in what we now call gender issues" (quoted in Kaminjolo 1993).

Therefore, the question of self-transformation did not yet arise. However, these were highly educated, professional women, and, as the journey progressed, many of them quickly acquired considerable competence in the discipline, guided by their own perception of the need for self-education, by the interdisciplinary and disciplinary seminars which were part of the capacity-building intent of the IOP/UWI/ISS project and by the staff training exercises devised by those to whom leadership responsibility was given. They also developed remarkable leadership skills, which helped the groups to grow from strength to strength. They all committed to ongoing strengthening of the academic programme through continual assessment of theories and practices, and to fostering an all-inclusive environment by maintaining and upgrading the level of teamwork, cultivating student support and including men in the programme. They were all also committed to ensuring that the structure and operational practices of the new programme would have a positive impact on the administration.

Know Your History, Culture, Environment

In order for the programme to be culturally relevant, it was important to know and understand the historical heritage of the region, to draw strength from what was positive and to find ways to mitigate the negative. The framers of the programme understood this and were particularly careful to design components which took the social, economic, political, cultural and geographic environment into account. Thus, they organized research, seminars and conferences which spoke to many of these factors, drawing out the gender implications (for example, Engendering History Conference, Nariva Swamp Research Project) and highlighting possible policy responses. During the preparations for the Fourth WCW, governments of the region identified five critical areas of concern – poverty, violence against women, health, leadership and institutional mechanisms. For Beijing+5, the themes education, health (with an emphasis on HIV/AIDS), globalization, gender and trade were added to the original five. Following Beijing +5, migration, child protection and gender mainstreaming were included as further concerns. These issues therefore provided a framework within which research and teaching of direct relevance to the governments and peoples of the region could take place. The leaders of the programme have understood the necessity for these kinds of linkages, as an examination of the research undertakings and seminar topics over the years indicates.

Learning from Predecessors and Passing On to the Next Generation Is Critical

All leaders of the programme had to be aware of two key obligations. One was concerned with finding more creative ways of sharing information and experiences by engaging with young people to address issues of importance to them and facilitating research and training links between students in academic institutions, between women's groups and individual women, between men's groups and individual men. The other was the young people themselves, about them being willing to commit to building on what had gone before rather than trying to reinvent the wheel; being creative about advocacy; and being receptive to new ideas, approaches and circumstances. It was about respect for one's elders, an important aspect of the culture of peace which is integral to our cultural context, despite the evidence of growing incidence of violence in our societies. Leaders of the programme have had to learn how to honour those who had gone before while, at the same time, respecting those who were coming on stream, perhaps with new ideas and new ways of operating.

Be Prepared for the Unexpected

Working with gender and development issues is not a static process. Most circumstances and issues are constantly changing, while some remain static. One of the fascinating features of Caribbean society has been the profound and rapid change which has taken place in a variety of areas over the past generation. Constant pressure has been placed on these societies to adjust their institutions, relationships and systems to accommodate the changes, as well as to anticipate new ones. Among the specific factors which have affected the operation of the gender system in the region must be included the limited availability of financial resources to improve the situation of women and men; the constant reordering of global economic ideologies and practices; and the emergence of a scholarship on men and masculinity which has had both positive and negative impact. Thus, if an academic programme on gender and development is to be relevant, it is crucial to address the contextual, conceptual, thematic and operational issues on an ongoing basis. It is also crucial to recognize that these analyses and any action they produce may be met with objections and resistance, sometimes from totally unexpected quarters. Grace Sirju-Charran, a former coordinator of the St Augustine WDSG, recalls that, at the time when she joined the group, "the group was at a stage in its development when its members were viewed by a large percentage of the academic community as activists, belonging to the Faculty of Arts and General Studies or Social Sciences, having a chip on the shoulder, or being 'men-haters' or lesbian. I discovered this very quickly from the reaction of colleagues and relatives when they heard I had become a member" (quoted in Kaminjolo 1993).

As a good leader, the possibility of backlash must be anticipated, and strategies to deal with whatever form it takes should be readied.

Be Willing to Take Risks

In the final analysis, the entire venture was a major risk – to the women involved and to the university. Those women in the academy who chose to get involved stood the risk of being ridiculed, being maligned, having their progress through the system slowed down, or even curtailed altogether, and their achievements minimized. Had the programme failed, the university itself could have been in an embarrassing position in higher education circles. It is to the credit of the women involved that, although some of this negativity did occur, they had enough self-confidence to move forward, to be patient yet assertive, to cultivate student support and to continually seek ways of attracting support from high-ranking men in both the faculties and the administration. They were willing to experiment with project design, as in WAND; with research methodologies, as in the WICP; to initiate WDSGs; to negotiate for a CGDS with unique features and, later, for an IGDS. These were all examples of risk-taking designed to confront university conservatism, to counter negativity from various sources and, ultimately, to lead to the success of the programme.

Theme 3: Maintaining Visibility

In order to ensure that the outcomes of the *gender journey* were recognized and appreciated, it was necessary that, at every stage, efforts be made to design and implement suitable communication activities. Thus, from the earliest stage, such efforts were an integral aspect of the programme. In the days of the early women's NGOs, CARIWA was the only regional women's organization and was one of the entities which successfully lobbied for the establishment of WAND. The visibility of CARIWA was evident through their biennial conferences, at which members reported on activities, developed proposals for a programme of work for the next biennium and produced recommendations to be taken forward to their respective governments. At the national level, members held press interviews which were given wide publicity, leaving no doubt about concerns facing women, programmes to address these, and the role of governments in providing the necessary resources.

WAND went further and introduced a comprehensive, region-wide publication programme, which not only provided information on their activities and those of their partners but also encouraged critical discussions on development issues and approaches. WICP, more concerned with providing information about the actual research project, chose a more formal dissemination package, using a variety of formats suitable for different audiences. In both cases, these efforts were highly successful in terms of the response across the region from a variety of stakeholders, ranging from governments to women in small communities.

At the institutionalization stage, the visibility achievements centred on a large number of seminars, conferences, formal and informal publications and addresses/speeches to a wide variety of audiences. Further, the extensive range and volume of these outreach activities led to increased demand for the services of staff as consultants. Perhaps more importantly, the range and volume of these exercises served to expose many persons, including staff, students and the general public, to the myriad issues pertaining to gender.

These issues included, for example: the impact of structural adjustment policies on the regional population, especially its women; the evidence of ever widening income inequality across class and gender; and the increasing incidence and brutality of violence, especially against women and children. In each of these instances, and many others, the analyses carried out by the gender and development programme gained national, regional and international recognition, both for the programme and the university. A major example of this is how individual countries and agencies throughout the region sought out the involvement of the centre, through its academic staff, in national and regional preparations for and representation at the UN Fourth WCW.

Lesson: Communication Is Vital

Keeping all those involved in the initiative informed, at all stages of the journey, requires careful attention to ways of communicating about routine matters, about plans for the future and about ongoing activities. Absence of strategies for implementing internal communication channels can sometimes lead to unnecessary misunderstandings and confusion. Such channels are particularly necessary where groups are geographically scattered, as are the three UWI campuses.[1] Even where efforts were made to hold periodic meetings among group leaders, information needed to be shared within groups. In 1990, independent management audits on the three campuses drew attention to the need for improving communication within and among the groups, as well as between the groups and the regional office (see Addae and Williams 1990; Chaderton and McClean 1990; Crick 1990). Techniques such as sharing minutes of meetings, newsletters and representation at each other's staff meetings were all tried, as was special staff training, such as the "Andaiye School" hosted by WAND in an attempt to introduce staff to gender and development issues. The lesson here is that specific efforts need to be made to create effective internal communication tools and those efforts must be constant and consistent.

External communication initiatives between the campuses and groups beyond the campuses were imperative in a gender and development programme as both informational and educational tools. Such initiatives must target different audiences, use language appropriate to the particular audience and must demonstrate the benefits of the gender programme to the wider community and not simply to the particular audience. The experience of this programme as it endeavoured to make its work known yielded a number of lessons, as discussed below.

Apply the Lessons Learned from Strengthening Project Management

This refers to the admonitions to know one's strengths, know one's environment, learn from one's predecessors, be prepared for the unexpected and be willing to take risks. These lessons have particular resonance in the area of communication since, in many cases, the target audience has been the general public and not simply a limited group of academics. It has been necessary, therefore, to be extremely careful in determining the method and content of any communication strategy being contemplated.

Develop a Wider Range of Outreach Activities with a Variety of Partners

Even a cursory glance at a list of the partners cultivated throughout the life of the *gender journey* demonstrates a recognition of the intrinsic value of gender analysis in understanding the development issues of the region. Initially, the main partners were women's organizations, primarily through what was, at the time, a vibrant women's movement. Within a relatively short period, the range of partners increased substantially to include government agencies, regional and international agencies, UN agencies, funding agencies, voluntary organizations (including women's and men's organizations) and educational institutions. All of these agencies were willing to partner with the centre/institute at different stages of the initiative, thus endorsing the validity of the work and also its relevance to the objectives of the partner agencies. It was important, therefore, to keep these partners informed of the progress of the programme and to do so in ways which directly addressed the concerns of each partner. One strategic result of this approach has been the securing of allies who have been willing to reinforce the message of the programme in arenas to which the programme may not have had direct access. In addition, it generated demand for the services of programme staff as consultants in several areas, thus providing opportunities to extend the work of the programme. This lesson has been learned and applied successfully over the years and should be continued into the future.

Involve Communication Specialists

While individual staff members may have some knowledge, even skill, in communication strategies, it is the specialist knowledge of trained communicators which will bring the greatest results in the design and implementation of an integrated communications strategy. This was certainly the experience of WAND, which actually employed such a specialist full-time on their staff, and of WICP, which collaborated with the Caribbean Institute of Mass Communications to develop its dissemination package. In both cases, the results were far greater than if regular staff had attempted to apply such a strategy on their own. Of course, much depends on the availability of funds, but if the idea is to spread information and knowledge about this innovative programme, then all avenues for doing so need to be explored.

Maintain a Vision of Social Justice, Peace and Gender Equity

In a region which has embraced the UN themes of social justice, peace and gender equity, gender analysis has to be conceptualized beyond the mere compilation of data. The analysis of that data must be applied to the social, economic and political issues of the day and to an understanding of how to achieve and maintain the vision/goals which society claims to embrace. Sustained analysis and constant reminders of what has been achieved and what remains unchanged, despite the rhetoric, must continue to be the focus of the communication strategy. This change must start within the university. Few women are to be found at the highest levels of governance, though the numbers have improved somewhat in recent times. In effect, the institution remains fundamentally patriarchal, despite the greater number of female students enrolled at undergraduate level, the greater number of women graduating, the greater number of postgraduate students who are women and the greater number of women on the administrative staff. If the gender and development programme is to be relevant to the wider society where similar situations exist, then it must address the situation in its own system. It can do so with a suitable and ongoing communication exercise framed by the themes of social justice, peace and gender equity. The lesson here is about the need for the CGDS programme to intensify its efforts in working with the UWI, to ensure that the attributes advocated over the years through WAND/WICP/WDSGs/ CGDS/IGDS initiatives are reflected in the culture and structure of the UWI.

Looking to the Future: Needs/Challenges

> Institutionalization did not necessarily produce a "happy ever after" ending. Indeed, the gender issues in the society and the university continue to be challenging.
> —*Hermione McKenzie, "Shifting Centres and Moving Margins: The UWI Experience"*

Thirty years after initiation of what was, in retrospect, a revolutionary step in bringing to the academy an exciting new area of scholarship which needed to prove itself, many challenges remain. At that time, the quest was for academic recognition and acceptance as well as investment in the concept of a new way of viewing the lives of individuals, adding another dimension – gender – to the accepted analytical categories of social class and race. The complex issue of gender has enriched the intellectual discourse by incorporating new perspectives and allowing for the development of new theoretical frameworks. Institutionalization of GDS allowed for this evolution and also for recognition and inclusion of gender as both an interdisciplinary field of learning and as an integral part of the disciplinary scholarship of the academy. Over the twenty years of the IGDS (formerly CGDS), significant achievements have been recorded and a range of lessons learned. Looking to the future, however, and the importance of sustainability of the work, many needs can still be identified. These needs have been identified within three major areas, scholarship, outreach and visibility, while actions required to satisfy the needs are suggested using the definitions outlined in the previous section: practical/pragmatic and/or political/strategic. The challenges facing the IGDS in light of the vision for and expectations of the institute in the three categories are discussed.

Scholarship

Needs

The need which immediately springs to mind is for a continuing search for knowledge and transformation of existing knowledge through the generation and analysis of new paradigms, and new theories which seek to elucidate the complex relationships of gender in relation to Caribbean history, culture, technology and science and its economic, social and political realities. It is the research, the analysis and the theorizing which will strengthen the foundation on which the academic credibility of GDS will continue to grow and flourish. The IGDS is well placed to achieve this objective.

In doing so, the institute must recognize the continuing gender bias and discrimination in Caribbean societies, which can only be successfully addressed once a critical mass of the population, including policymakers and planners, become conscious of the inequity and are committed to bringing about change. Development of minors and a major in GDS has provided an avenue for undergraduate students to register for and pursue courses which explore the theoretical and conceptual issues surrounding gender and which employ gender pedagogy. This must continue. Initiatives such as the diploma in GDS, offered via distance mode by the UWI Open Campus, must be reinstated and aggressively promoted across the Caribbean so that the number of individuals with the necessary exposure to gender concepts and gender analysis skills is increased and their expertise made available to the region. Graduate students should also be targeted through offerings developed in conjunction with faculties and by addressing specific issues of importance and priority in the society. Thus, design and implementation of masters programmes in gender and health, gender and science, gender and education, gender and psychology, gender and media, and so on need to become strategic objectives of the IGDS along with rigorously designed and executed policy-oriented research in a variety of areas. What is needed are increased registrations and involvement of a wide range of students from all faculties in gender courses, as electives, minors or majors, so that gender analysis will be one of the skills acquired and employed by most UWI graduates in whatever professional sphere they operate. Acquisition of this intellectual capacity is usually accompanied by an attitude shift resulting from expanded perceptions which recognize and appreciate the importance of gender equality and equity. This shift usually involves support for the integration of this understanding in everyday activities and in policy statements and action, whether at domestic, organizational, national or regional levels. Development of interest in and commitment to gender equality and equity at the undergraduate level is a major strategy to increase the numbers of students pursuing graduate study in this area.

These political and strategic outcomes require a funding base for the IGDS which can allow for increased staff as well as expanded and improved accommodation for this staff, and the IGDS will have to intensify its efforts to lobby the administration and seek external funding to obtain the necessary resources to achieve its vision.

Challenges

The reduction in available resources to the university as a whole presents the institution with challenges which seriously affect the IGDS and the continued excellence of its scholarship. Gender is not one of the priority areas identified for financial investment, and the institute will have to make well-designed and convincingly argued proposals to the university grants committees as well as to external funding agencies to overcome the constraints imposed by the limited resources it currently has available. Increased resources, in the form of human capacity and physical space, are needed if the IGDS is to satisfy the stated needs. The demand for policy-oriented research speaks to the importance of a vibrant graduate programme as well as of the generation and use of data based on explorations of a range of issues. Collaboration with departments within faculties will be essential.

Faculties, however, also have reduced funding, and their focus is on areas of student demand and programmes which are seen as providing a clear pathway towards employment. The integration of gender in such proposed programmes as psychology and gender, science and gender, media and gender will need to have strong justification and convincing evidence of their validity and viability in the workplace to attract students, whose priorities increasingly align with the employability criterion when choosing their degree programmes. As Wieringa pointed out in 2004, however, there is "need for theoretically well-trained gender experts . . . to engage in critical gender analysis in a range of disciplinary areas e.g. gender and human rights, gender and livelihoods, gender dimensions of HIV/AIDS etc. and in cultural contexts" (391–92). This need is even more critical in 2016 when the international development agenda is demanding integration of gender and gender mainstreaming and when the agencies responsible are seeking individuals with the knowledge and skills to undertake this task.

Outreach

Needs

One of the major needs identified consistently over the twenty years of the existence of the CGDS/IGDS is the revitalization of the women's movement in the region. There is the expectation that the development of scholarship in the academy will be accompanied by action to improve the lives of women. The activism of the WDSGs, which was the stimulus for the establishment of the CGDS, unfortunately waned once the goal of institutionalization had been realized. Linnette Vassell (2004, 696) commented that

> the fear was that feminist discourse and political engagement, which had unmasked the gender system of patriarchy and its encasement in the cultural, economic, political and social system, would be undermined by gender professionalization and that, as a consequence, gender studies would lose the activist mission that women's studies had established that we wanted to understand the world in order to change it . . . the question we should ponder is this – is there a disconnection of Gender Studies from its feminist and activist roots?

"Regrets: we never did bridge the perceived gap between academics and our other sisters on campus. Also, as the programmes became more numerous and successful, activism almost ceased. Many of our members were recognized for their contributions and promoted into positions where activism was not the way to go" (Veronica Salter, testimonial).

Issues which adversely affect women's lives have highlighted the need for and expectation of increased activism on the part of the IGDS. The seeming loss of that aspect of the work of the WDSGs has been decried, and there are calls to reinstate links which had been loosened and to establish the network needed to build a regional "gender community". This would involve reshaping the work with NGOs and participating in activities which include "hands-on" programmes with women in our communities. The need for this is evident in the face of the dire economic situation in the countries of the Caribbean and the impact of this on women's lives as well as the prevalence of issues such as skin bleaching and domestic violence, which are current subjects of heightened debate and concern. Public education and active intervention to address such issues are usually outside the realm of academia except as topics of research, analysis and commentary, but the political nature of GDS demands deeper involvement and action. This will be needed as a strategic move to counter the "backlash" expressed through comments made by many persons in the Caribbean who note the advances which women have made over the years and consider that issues associated with gender no longer have any currency in Caribbean societies. These comments are made despite research which highlights the exploitation of girls and women and despite newspaper reports which disclose the brutal acts of violence to which women are subjected in many communities. Systems which oppose gender equality and equity, and institutions which hinder progress in this regard also have to be confronted and resisted.

> I remember the discussion about the exploitative work in the free zone, but some hold the view that going to work empowered thousands of women with a new identity, independence and new opportunities. Unfortunately, those who were opposed to the free zone development have not articulated viable alternatives. While we have been good at the diagnostics, we have failed on the prescriptions. I look ahead for the new generation to learn from the work of the previous generations, to solve what seem to be our intractable problems. (Hilary Robertson-Hickling, testimonial)

There is need for IGDS to apply its influence strategically, at both grass-roots and policy levels, and to lobby for reinstatement of important structures such as the CARICOM Women's Desk and refocusing the work of national women's/gender bureaux. The time may well be ripe for revitalization of the WDSGs as their members would then be able to be advocates both on and off the campuses. The linkage with WAND, a powerful and influential one in the institute's history, is one that could be explored for revitalization, particularly since that group continues to have strong ties with NGOs. Re-establishment of the work of the WDSGs with influential entities such as the Women's Political Caucus in Jamaica and regional NGOs such as CAFRA is also critical in the revival of the activism needed.

An important critique of *gender* studies/action is that it prioritizes women and pays insufficient attention to situations affecting boys and men. Involvement of men as partners in research and programmes, and inclusion of the needs and issues affecting the lives of boys and girls, women and men in research and analysis emanating from the IGDS are now expectations of the institute.

> There was controversy over the move to the moniker *gender*. Leo-Rhynie made the point that she was addressing gender and said something like: we cannot be comfortable with the educational performance of our boys. I was not firmly with her on this point, as I was concerned about everything surrounding what came to be the powerful marginalization slogan, which I distinguish from the body of (Errol) Miller's work even while, mainly, disagreeing with him. In addition, while I have always sought to clarify that gender affects everyone, it is not six for one sex and half dozen for the other.
>
> I have been increasingly concerned about the failure of gender studies to get to the point (here I speak primarily of Mona/Jamaica, which I know better). For example, although not recently, I have heard a gender presentation on health (by an expert) which covered only female dimensions, when men's weak, "health-seeking" behaviour is a very gendered problem, with morbid consequences. There is also a tendency for some male scholars to move into the gender zone from a somewhat masculinist approach. Meanwhile, gender problems of hegemonic male masculinity do not seem to be addressed in a way that is sufficiently visible by the mainstream genderists, in ways which can help to deflect the masculinist backlash. It's for that reason that I started writing on gender. The face of gender studies is still overwhelmingly female. Is anyone concerned about the demographics? I am not sure how, or to what degree, all of this can be addressed. (Mark Figueroa [UWI professor and former WDSG (Mona) member], testimonial)

Challenges

The scholarship and activism link is one which has to be faced by academics in this area of study because of the asymmetrical power relationships which persist in different forms in societies of the Caribbean and which define, therefore, the political nature of the discipline. Interrogation of issues such as those raised in Figueroa's testimonial, encouraging the research which can assist in finding answers to these concerns and others, such as those expressed by Robertson-Hickling, and finding the resources needed for both research and intervention are major challenges.

The IGDS has become an influential voice in national and regional gender affairs. The challenge is to use this influence strategically to ensure that gender equity is promoted through community-based, national and regional programmes which advance human rights, economic and social equity and reduce gender gaps. Research which focuses on the impact of such programmes, in terms of identifying and satisfying the priorities and needs of women and men, can guide and accelerate the progress of national development.

> I think, also, there has been an awareness that the issue of outreach and activism and work with social movements and communities has been one of the hallmarks of the IGDS. I believe that, in recent times, we may have lost that a bit, but I think that there is a recognition that gender studies programmes cannot be like any other academic programme. They emerged out of a need for transformation in gender relations, and social and economic transformation, more generally, and, if we lose that, we will almost be losing our raison d'être. So part of our work, in addition to transforming knowledge, is to revitalize, invigorate, encourage, excite a new generation to continue this work, wherever they may be located. (Reddock 2014)

Visibility

Needs

The vision and expectations evident in the needs expressed and the challenges which have been identified demand that the work of the IGDS be expanded. Such expansion, in an environment of limited resources, is largely dependent on the recognition of the unique and vital role played by the institute in addressing social problems and in national affairs. The visibility of the institute, based on its achievements over the past two decades, has to be sustained and increased by practical initiatives which continue to emphasize the value of the IGDS to both the UWI and the Caribbean region and also by solutions and strategic action to challenge existing power structures and change entrenched gender ideologies and practices.

Strategically, the IGDS needs to establish a better interface between gender-based research, policy and programmes as a sure way of catalysing change in economic and social priorities, identifying gender needs and shifting focus to consider how these can be met in the context of national, regional and global developments.

> IGDS is very unique . . . it was the ringleader in the idea of a real institute that fosters not only teaching, and teaching of new knowledge, but research and activism. At present, all our universities are being asked to demonstrate to stakeholders what our relevance is, and I think the IGDS has been doing that from day one. Our mandate from day one was teaching, research and outreach. (Pat Mohammed [UWI professor, first head of CGDS Mona unit, now head of IGDS St Augustine unit], in conversations recorded at the IGDS twentieth-anniversary conference)

Challenges

To satisfy the broad agenda of sustaining visibility, resources are needed to initiate and carry out research, analysis, policy determination and programme implementation. The resources required are significant, and, in the present economic climate, obtaining them is a monumental challenge. Efforts must, however, be made.

Another major challenge is the UWI itself, where the governance structure of the institution does not reflect an ongoing commitment to gender equity in leadership. The visibility of women in leadership in the latter part of the 1990s and early 2000s has now been lost. In 2008, of three women who had been appointed as PVCs, two were replaced, on their retirement, by men. Of three women appointed as campus principals, one had retired and another was serving in an interim arrangement – both were replaced by men. The only female university registrar ever appointed was succeeded by a man, on her retirement. Noteworthy, however, was the fact that the principal, deputy principal, registrar and bursar of the Open Campus were all female (Leo-Rhynie 2008). We must heed the warning of Drayton (1993) that "what we have learned (over the past ten years) is that gains must be protected and defended or you lose them. The way is long and the wind is sometimes cold, but the journey must go on."

Inclusion of women in leadership at campus, national and regional levels is important politically, as it is then more likely that gender aspects of development issues will be considered and, possibly, given priority. Women's presence, messages and initiatives also have an impact on the self-concepts and attitudes of young women and can be a strong motivating force in encouraging both women and men to become engaged in gender scholarship, with the potential for revitalizing and reconstituting the women's movement of the region.

Wieringa (2004, 391) noted that her observations of UWI indicated that it "has a strong and committed student body, highly qualified younger staff, and a very supportive group of 'older wise women' who have always supported the Gender Studies Centre". The maintenance of such a balance is critical to the continued success of the institute. A number of the leadership roles in UWI management and administration during the 1990s and since 2000 were assumed by women who had been involved in the WDSGs and the CGDS/IGDS, but, with their retirement, posts held by these and other women have reverted to men. A challenge is for the IGDS to engage in succession planning, not only for the leadership of the institute, but also to ensure that new generations of women who are assertive and can be effective gender advocates are represented at the highest levels in the UWI governance structure.

> On reflection, I realized I worked hard because I really enjoyed and liked what I did; in fact, I was passionate about it. I was fortunate to work with strong colleagues, assets really, inside and outside of CGDS. I was very willing to make mistakes and apologize if I had to. In fact, a former registrar said to me, "Don't try that again, Dr Barriteau – you do exactly what you want to do for CGDS and then apologize profusely after getting your way". It was an effective way, at times, to circumvent bureaucracy. More critically, I felt I had been entrusted with an important responsibility and therefore could not fail. There were times I felt daunted but never discouraged. There were times I irritated others or felt irritated by them, but, throughout, I maintained a profound respect for the pioneers and partners and was determined that CGDS and its staff would understand its particular responsibility to the university and the region. Looking back, I am surprised by how much work I did. It was not because I was motivated to get to another space or seek promotion. Rather, it grew out of feeling blessed to acquire a job in an area I felt passionate about and being awed by the responsibility of institutionalizing gender studies at the Cave Hill campus. (Eudine Barriteau, testimonial)

There are signs that the innovative and resourceful spirit continues. Tonya Haynes, the first PhD graduate of the NBU, Cave Hill, was interviewed by Michelle Springer for *CHILL News* (issue 14, May 2013) and reported that she and fellow classmates from the first cohort of graduate students on the Cave Hill campus had formed a group, Code Red for Gender Justice, an online community of feminist activists dedicated to addressing current affairs issues using feminist modes of analysis. Out of this has come CatchAFyah, which is described as "a regional gathering of young/ish feminists from across the region who came together for a 2 day session of feminist 'reasonings' in May 2012".

Using the strategies of the current generation to engage in what is being called cyber-feminism, the group is supposedly very active and involved in addressing, in novel ways, issues adversely affecting the lives of women in the region. Interestingly, the meeting of the group in 2012 was largely funded by the DAWN network, and the group treasured the "privilege of interacting with celebrated Caribbean and transnational feminist thinkers/activists Andaiye and Peggy Antrobus" (ibid.). The intergenerational cycle continues, and linkages with such a group have the potential to renew and expand the range of influence of the IGDS and the impact of its work. Such initiatives are important in ensuring continuity of the IGDS programmes and influence within and outside the academy.

> The women's movement however is at an important crossroads. It is facing problems of backlash, generational transition and the negative impacts of economic neoliberalism and a new conservatism. One of the strengths of this era of the movement however has been the establishment of a legacy of institutions, scholarship and policy interventions at governmental and community level which may serve to make the gains of this important period of history more long-lasting. More specifically the emergence and institutionalization of formal programmes of women's and gender studies at universities, colleges and other institutions of higher education have been a significant development. Throughout the world feminists within universities and colleges lobbied, strategized and created alliances in order to establish these programmes which now exist in countries throughout the world. (Reddock 2009)

Looking to the Future: What Next?

Our world has changed, and much of the optimism of the 1970s and 1980s has been replaced by a more gloomy outlook and reversals of fortunes in our region. We are currently having to grapple with our understandings and relationships with the emerging powerhouses in Brazil, India, China, South Africa and Russia. How is gender playing out in these countries and their academies? The leaders of the gender

> movement must become engaged in partnerships with groups involved in economic development, the environment, justice, human rights and other critical issues.
> —*Hilary Robertson-Hickling, testimonial*

The lessons learned and the challenges confronted in establishing and consolidating the tripartite programme of GDS across the three main campuses of the UWI, as well as in the UWI 14, point to the pitfalls to be avoided in the future, in the continued evolution of the IGDS. This involves further consolidation of the gains made over the thirty and more years since the initiation, development and institutionalization of the programme; any move in this direction should be informed by the lessons learned and should seek to confront and alleviate the challenges encountered as well as others which will undoubtedly occur in the future. Continuity, however, will involve preserving valuable aspects of the past and creating new paths for the future.

The needs identified in the previous section point to the many challenges which the IGDS has to face in the continuing gender journey. Expansion of the teaching agenda to include double-focus degrees, such as gender and psychology, gender and media, may trigger new modalities of teaching delivery such as distance offerings of a minor in gender, which could be pursued by students in the various departments who elect to follow such programmes. The units may consider rationalization of the offerings, with different units developing and offering different courses but together providing the credits necessary for a gender minor (or major) by mixed-mode delivery. Collaboration with the Open Campus and adaptation and inclusion of the courses developed for the diploma programme may be part of such an initiative. In this way, the IGDS could once again be a trailblazer in the area of teaching.

The relevance of the content of courses in gender also demands contact with individuals who function at the grassroots level. This could be achieved through the revival of linkages with the NGO community and other civil-society organizations, which will assist in ensuring that the analysis and discussion associated with the developed and offered courses are grounded in lived realities. By so doing, the IGDS, through the units, would remain true to its origins. The academia/activism link may take novel forms, as technology now allows for different modes of connection and interaction and the new generation of women may be more comfortable in using the tools familiar to them to engage and effect the needed change. The example of CatchAFyah is instructive.

By the middle of the decade of the 2000s, even before gaining institute status, it had become evident that the CGDS had gained significant national, regional and international recognition and was well positioned to play a leading role in gender and development initiatives in all of these arenas. An obvious contribution was the pushing of the boundaries of the discourse, particularly by viewing it through a unique Caribbean prism, reflected in the plethora of publications, research reports, bibliographies and databases produced by the various units of the centre, as well as through making available the technical expertise in gender analysis, gender mainstreaming, gender evaluations and audits, project design and execution, and policy formulation that resided in staff attached to all units of the centre.

Based on past achievements, the assessment of future needs and an evolutionary vision, a proposal for establishing the CGDS as a regional centre of excellence was developed, which could address some of the various challenges facing the units and also meet a need identified by Caribbean gender specialists, who are constantly seeking relevant data on a variety of issues.

During the consolidation stage of institutionalization, each of the campus units had assumed specific roles within the institute, and their engagement with teaching, research and outreach was being effectively carried out on the campuses. The RCU, as the coordinating unit, recognized how critical the need was for a central clearing house for national and regional documentary material related to issues of gender and development and social equity. The concept of "excellence" was embedded in the vision, and the aim of the proposal was to create a hub located at the RCU to which all units, including the RCU, would contribute based on their ongoing agendas and from which they would benefit. This would be achieved by intentionally

- establishing a clearing house for data sources on gender and development themes and issues;
- enhancing the capacity of the centre to play an advisory role to governments and other national and regional institutions, in terms of formulation of evidence-based, gender-sensitive policy and programmes related to gender and development concerns and issues; and
- serving as a link between scholars, professionals, activists and development/funding agencies whose work centres on intersections of gender with issues of national and regional significance, who would access the resources and services of the centre through mutually agreeable arrangements.

Over the years, engagement in and management of regional research projects and various national initiatives by the units of the CGDS had clearly highlighted the need for improved access to information on gender and development discourse. More specifically, access to data sets disaggregated, at a minimum, by sex and location, as well as to annotated bibliographies was needed to inform a gendered analysis of national and regional gender and/or development issues. Provision of such access and information would not only serve the academy through consolidation of the existing CGDS mission but would also provide a readily accessible platform to serve as a regional clearing house on gender and development concerns. In addition, it would be a training hub for individuals and organizations engaged in the advancement of gender equality and social equity. The resources of the proposed RCH would also be available, through all the units, to academics, undergraduate and graduate students, visiting scholars, the range of national, regional and international organizations engaged in gender and/or development issues and would provide products that could inform the three prongs of the CGDS mission – teaching, research and outreach.

This expansion of the reach and enhancement of the impact of the IGDS would allow it to be more effective in responding to challenges related to the three major categories of need identified in the preceding section: scholarship and the need to transform existing knowledge and generate new theories and paradigms which elucidate complex relations of gender in relation to Caribbean realities; providing data and analyses to inform outreach and activism on the part of individuals, NGOs and/or women's organizations; and increasing the visibility of the CGDS and the UWI through engaging in initiatives aimed at addressing critical economic and social, national and regional priorities.

This vision of the expansion of the role of the then CGDS was grounded in UWI priorities as derived from the UWI Strategic Plan (2002–7) in force at the time. The following strategic priorities, as set out in that plan (UWI Office of Administration 2002, 10–11), were considered to be congruent with the envisioned RCH:

- The need to make the university research agenda more responsive to regional needs and to promote the highest standards of scholarship and professional excellence.
- The need to achieve a better alignment of the research efforts of the university with regional, societal and developmental needs.

In the plan, it was also stated that "the strategy of establishing and strengthening research centres has been visibly advanced" and that "specialized units and centres have been active in researching fields such as environment and sustainable development, gender and development", which had helped to build critical mass in areas of great relevance to the region and "also serve to foster multidisciplinarity and improve research focus and coordination". The challenge, at the time, however, was to "ensure that the centres achieve their full potential to raise the quality, quantity and impact of the University's research effort" (ibid., 12–13).

The vision was endorsed by the team that conducted the external evaluation of the RCU and Mona unit in 2006, who recommended that the idea be given full support and opined that such a development would "enhance the alignment of the research efforts of the University to regional, national and societal needs, and will facilitate the availability and accessibility of data sources and data sets on gender and development themes and issues. In addition it will enhance the capability of the centre to play an advisory role to the government/s and other national and regional institutions" (UWI BUS 2006b, 20).

Although the RCH would be managed by the RCU, given its regional placement and coordinating function, it would have distinct benefits for all units of the IGDS, including the RCU itself. The synergistic interface that all units would develop with the clearing house would ensure that there is a mutually agreeable flow of products from units into the RCH and vice versa. In turn, these products, grounded as they would be in a uniquely Caribbean perspective, would be invaluable for informing future developments in the three areas of need identified: scholarship, outreach and visibility.

The products housed in the RCH would be an invaluable source of information for designing a wider spectrum of interdisciplinary and/or disciplinary specializations at undergraduate and graduate levels, in areas of specific relevance to the Caribbean, such as gender and health, gender and psychology, gendered disaster management, gender dimensions of poverty reduction and economic empowerment as well as gender mainstreaming and gender budgeting. This was identified as a critical need.

Revitalization of the academic/activist outreach agenda of public education, awareness raising, community-based research and active debate and interventions on critical issues, such as intimate-partner violence, grounds for legal abortion, teenage sexuality and the politics of gender relations in home, community and nation, would also be readily facilitated. Creation of the RCH and the undertaking of these initiatives, in turn, would enhance the visibility of the IGDS as well as that of the UWI and significantly boost the reputation of the UWI as being the primary institution of higher learning in the region.

Despite the fact that the vision was not considered a priority when it was proposed at the 2005 Regional Strategic Planning Meeting, the acquisition of institute status in 2008 makes the conceptualization even more critical to its relevance. The policy document developed by the UWI School for Graduate Studies and Research (2009, 4) states that a university institute "should display significant multidisciplinary activity, facilitated by national, regional and international collaborations". A major intention envisaged was that moving in this direction would facilitate a more targeted approach to engaging all units of the IGDS in the goal of development of a centre of excellence in keeping with the above-stated mandate.

Pursuit of this trajectory would satisfy many critical criteria that delineate a university institute:

- University-wide teaching, research, consulting or other service activities
- A level of activity that is generally greater than that of a centre; for example, in research publications, the generation of income, consultancies, graduate projects and research supervision
- International and regional recognition, as evidenced by the attraction of regional and extra-regional graduate students, staff and researchers or visiting scholars
- Extensive links with external research institutions, business and government groups, and other regional and international stakeholders with a similar focus
- Revenue derived from a variety of sources, including competitive grants, industry, international donors, fees, endowments, inter alia

It is bold initiatives such as this, which reflects the collaborative spirit of the pioneers of the IGDS and engages the interest, skills and objectives of the current staff of the units, that will propel the IGDS into being a regional and international hub of expertise and competence in gender research, analysis and policy formulation. An essential part of this initiative will be the assembly of data using participatory methodologies grounded in the lived realities of those most affected by such issues and policies. All units of the IGDS will play a vital role through their practical and strategic initiatives, which would not only serve their own agendas but also contribute to this visionary goal and ultimately improve their scholarship and outreach and enhance their visibility.

The constant need for vigilance on the part of IGDS to counteract "backlash" and ensure that all activities undertaken by the institute subscribe to the goals of gender equality and equity, which are crucial in the ongoing journey, is critical. This is particularly so at the UWI, where gains in leadership are now reversed. The appointment to posts at the highest levels of governance and influence within the university community, on all four campuses, of women who were pioneers in the establishment of the CGDS/IGDS is testament to their leadership qualities – displayed and recognized within the university community. The need to ensure that such leadership is sustained demands that the unit heads engage in succession planning, so that the IGDS can continue to be visible within the academy and be seen as a focal point of innovation and excellence.

The opportunities are boundless. In terms of the gender journey at the UWI, the path winds onward. The IGDS must remain totally committed to its mission of ensuring that the institution is a space renowned not only for its academic excellence but also for its passion for the promotion of gender justice and social equity, both within and beyond the academy. That has been the vision for thirty years. Academics and activists must continue, through collaborative action, to direct their energies to making the extraordinary vision of the pioneers a reality and to giving substance to renewed vision and as yet uncharted paths.

Note

1. *Groups* here refers both to the former WDSGs and to the current body of staff involved in teaching, research or outreach activities of the programme.

POSTSCRIPT

Reflections of the Future

EDWARD GREENE*

AS THE UWI IGDS CELEBRATES ITS TWENTIETH ANNIVERSARY, it is worthy to reflect on the pioneers on whose shoulders rest the visionary process of articulating and actioning a programme of research and outreach on WAD in the Caribbean. I recall the pioneering studies spearheaded by Joycelin Massiah in collaboration with Peggy Antrobus and Lucille Mathurin Mair. They marshalled the intellectual fabric of a group of women. They ushered in an era that placed women and gender as cross-cutting elements of academic significance, which gave substance to the claims by ordinary women for greater attention to the social and economic challenges they faced. Policy, advocacy and militancy were backed by evidence. I was privileged to be part of the ISER leadership at the time, to witness the unfolding of this dynamic movement that connected the university to the wider society. New ways of arriving at solutions were stimulated through the proliferation of consultations and seminars and the fashioning of rigorous yet creative methods of investigation. There was a seismic shift in understanding the challenges of women in the workplace, in politics, in entrepreneurial ventures and, in particular, the discrimination and disadvantages they encountered in a value chain resistant to change. By the time the programme morphed into having a focus on gender, the groundwork

*Former director, ISER; professor emeritus and PVC, UWI; now UN secretary general's advisor on HIV and global health.

had been laid, solidly embedded in the culture of the university, with vibrant reverberations throughout the region. The recognition of the leadership of this movement in the form of the Triennial Award for Women by the CARICOM Heads of Government is only one illustration. That, from its onset, the programme reached out to women of all walks of life, involving them not only as subjects of research but as participants in shaping their future, is an attribute worth emulating. The alliances across the national, regional and international spectrum that IGDS has formed are to be celebrated. So too is the tremendous impetus the programme has given to charting the course towards achieving gender equity. This reflection of the future requires that the struggle for social justice be sustained, not only for achieving the appropriate millennium development goals, but also for ensuring that gender retains a prominent place in the post-2015 development agenda.

APPENDIX 1

Organizational Links: 1982–2010

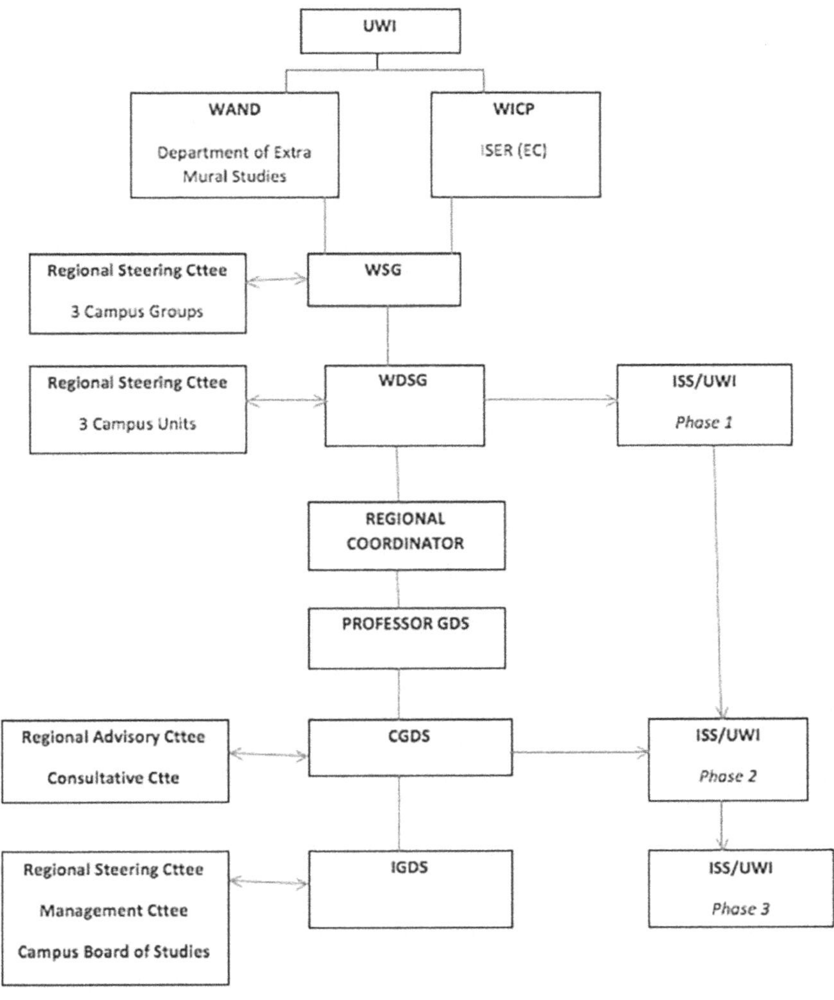

APPENDIX 2

List of WICP Publications

Bibliography

Massiah, Joycelin. 1979. *Women in the Caribbean: An Annotated Bibliography; A Guide to Material Available in Barbados.* With the assistance of Audine Wilkinson and Norma Shorey. Mimeo. Occasional Bibliography Series, no.5. Barbados: Institute of Social and Economic Research (Eastern Caribbean), University of the West Indies, Cave Hill.

Books

Massiah, Joycelin, ed. 1986. "Women in the Caribbean". Special issue, *Social and Economic Studies* 35 (2–3).

Senior, Olive. 1991. *Working Miracles: Women's Lives in the English-Speaking Caribbean.* London: ISER, UWI, Cave Hill, Barbados/James Curry; Bloomington: ISER, UWI, Cave Hill, Barbados/Indiana University Press.

Phase 1 Research Monographs

The following six volumes are all published by the Institute of Social and Economic Research, University of the West Indies, Cave Hill, Barbados.

Vol. 1. Forde, Norma. 1981. *Women and the Law.*

Vol. 2. Durant-Gonzales, Victoria, Jean Jackson, Joycelin Massiah and Dorian Powell. 1982. *Women and the Family.*

Vol. 3. Duncan, Neville, and Kenneth O'Brien. 1983. *Women and Politics in Barbados, 1948–1981.*

Vol. 4. Brodber, Erna. 1982. *Perceptions of Caribbean Women: Towards a Documentation of Stereotypes.*

Vol. 5. Cole, Joyce, and Patricia Mohammed. 1982. *Women and Education.*

Vol. 6. Gill, Margaret, and Joycelin Massiah. 1984. *Women, Work and Development.*

Reports

Massiah, Joycelin. 1983. *Report of the Conference on the Role of Women in the Caribbean, September 12–16, 1982*. Barbados: Institute of Social and Economic Research, University of the West Indies, Cave Hill.

APPENDIX 3

WDSG Coordinators

(Listed in alphabetical order)

Cave Hill

Eudine Barriteau
Christine Barrow
Jean Callender (acting for a short period)
Kathleen Drayton
Elaine Fido
Maxine McClean

Mona

Barbara Bailey
Carolyn Cooper
Kamala Dickson
Elsa Leo-Rhynie
Hermione McKenzie
Hilary Robertson-Hickling
Veronica Salter
Alafia Samuels

St Augustine

Bridget Brereton
Jeanette Morris
Helen Pyne-Timothy
Carmen Redhead
Grace Sirju-Charan
Marjorie Thorpe
Rosina Wiltshire

APPENDIX 4

List of Seminars under IOP/UWI/ISS Project Phase 1

Interdisciplinary

"Gender, Culture and Caribbean Development", Mona, 8–19 June 1987
"Women, Gender and Development Studies: The Theoretical and Methodological Challenges", St Augustine, 7–18 September 1987
"Women Studies: Interdisciplinary Readings", Cave Hill, 15–29 September 1987

Disciplinary

"Gender Issues in the Humanities", Faculty of Arts and General Studies, St Augustine, September 1988
"Alternative Strategies for Agricultural Development: An Analysis of Women and Gender Issues", Faculty of Agriculture, St Augustine, January 1990
"Women, Development Policy and the Management of Change", Faculty of Social Sciences, Cave Hill, April 1989
"Engendering Justice: Gender and the Rule of Law in the Commonwealth Caribbean", Faculty of Law, Cave Hill, December 1990
"Women and Health", Faculty of Medical Sciences, Cave Hill, October 1992
"Gender and Education", Faculty of Education, Mona, November 1989
"Engendering History", partially funded by Department of History, November 1993
"Gender, Science and Technology", partially funded by Faculty of Natural Sciences, Mona, February 1994

APPENDIX 5

Consultative Process for Academic Approval of Gender Studies Undergraduate and Graduate Courses and Programmes (1993–1996)

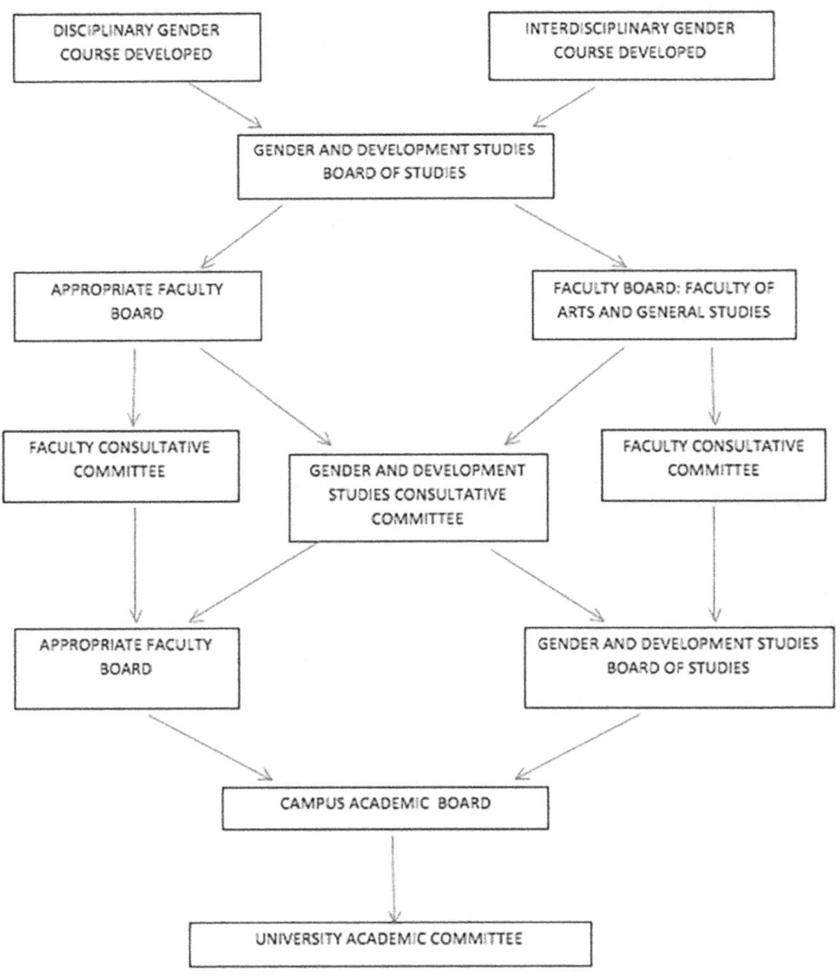

APPENDIX 6

Consultative Process for Academic Approval of Gender Studies

Undergraduate/Graduate Courses and Programmes (1996–2010)

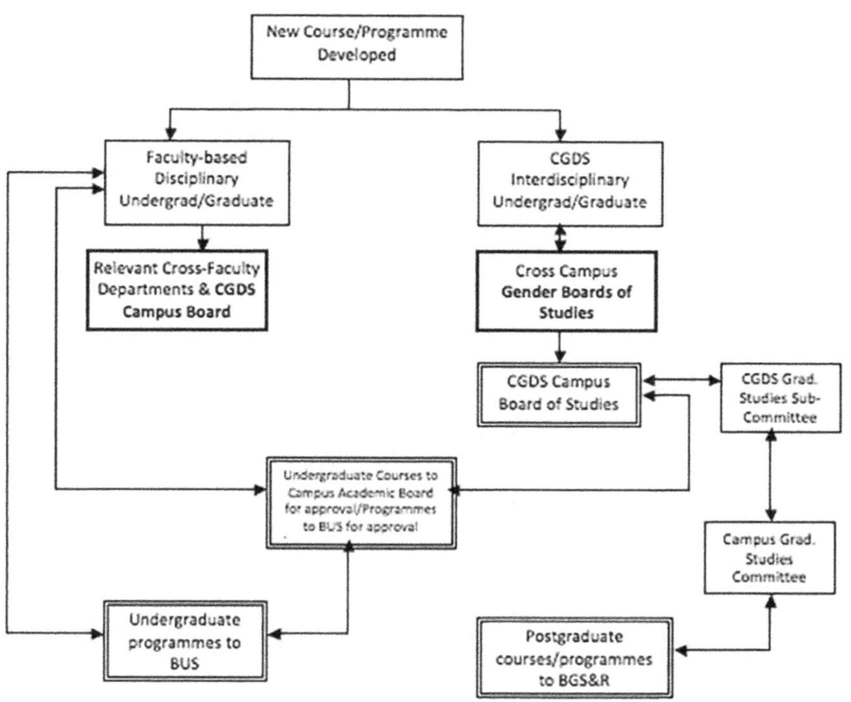

APPENDIX 7

Books Published in Association with CGDS/IGDS

Bailey, Barbara, ed. 2007. "Gender in Education". Special issue, *Caribbean Journal of Education* 20 (April).

Bailey, Barbara, and Joan Browne. 1999. "Entrepreneurial Skills for Women in Microenterprise: A Training Manual". Kingston: Centre for Gender and Development Studies, University of the West Indies.

Bailey, Barbara, and Elsa Leo-Rhynie, eds. 2004. *Gender in the Twenty-First Century: Caribbean Perspectives, Visions and Possibilities.* Kingston: Ian Randle.

Barriteau, Eudine. 2003. *Confronting Power, Theorizing Gender: Interdisciplinary Perspectives in the Caribbean.* Kingston: University of the West Indies Press.

Barriteau, Eudine, and Alan Cobley, eds. 2001. *Stronger, Surer, Bolder: Ruth Nita Barrow – Social Change and International Development.* Kingston: University of the West Indies Press.

———, eds. 2006. *Enjoying Power: Eugenia Charles and Political Leadership in the Commonwealth Caribbean.* Kingston: University of the West Indies Press.

Barrow, Christine, ed. 1998. *Caribbean Portraits: Essays on Gender Ideologies and Identities.* Kingston: Ian Randle/Centre for Gender and Development Studies, University of the West Indies.

Carby, Barbara, and Vilma McClenan, eds. 1997. *Readings in Gender, Science and Technology.* Kingston: Centre for Gender and Development Studies and the Faculty of Natural Sciences, University of the West Indies.

Leo-Rhynie, Elsa, Barbara Bailey, and Christine Barrow, eds. 1997. *Gender: A Caribbean Multidisciplinary Perspective.* Kingston: Ian Randle/Centre for Gender and Development Studies, University of the West Indies/ Commonwealth of Learning.

Mohammed, Patricia, ed. 2002. *Gendered Realities: Essays in Caribbean Feminist Thought.* Kingston: University of the West Indies Press.

Mohammed, Patricia, and Catherine Shepherd, eds. 1988. *Gender in Caribbean Development.* Kingston: UWI, Women and Development Studies Project.

Morgan, Paula, and Youssef, Valerie. 2009. *Writing Rage: Unmasking Violence through Caribbean Discourse.* Kingston: University of the West Indies Press.

Quamina-Aiyejina, Lynda. 2007. *Gender and Education in the Commonwealth Caribbean.* Institute of Education Publication 3. Kingston: Institute of Education and the Centre for Gender and Development Studies, University of the West Indies, with support from UNESCO.

Quamina-Aiyejina, Lynda, and Joan Braithwaite. 2005. *Gender-Based Violence in the Commonwealth Caribbean.* Barbados: Centre for Gender and Development Studies/UNIFEM Caribbean Office.

Reddock, Rhoda, ed. 2004. *Interrogating Caribbean Masculinities: Theoretical and Empirical Analyses.* Kingston: University of the West Indies Press.

Shepherd, Verene, Bridget Brereton, and Barbara Bailey, eds. 1995. *Engendering History: Caribbean Women in Historical Perspective.* Kingston: Ian Randle.

APPENDIX 8

List of Persons Who Submitted Testimonials (in Alphabetical Order)

Every effort was made to ensure that extracts from all testimonials submitted were included throughout the text.

1. Dr Peggy Antrobus, retired tutor/coordinator, WAND
2. Professor Barbara Bailey, professor emerita and retired university director, IGDS
3. Professor Eudine Barriteau, first head, CGDS NBU, Cave Hill; now principal, Open Campus, UWI
4. Professor Sir Hilary Beckles, vice-chancellor, UWI
5. Jeanette Bell, former project officer, WAND
6. Margaret Bernal, former research assistant, WICP
7. June Castello, former lecturer, CGDS Mona; now programme officer, Open Campus, UWI
8. Roberta Clarke, former research assistant, WICP; currently regional director, UN Women (South East Asia)
9. Professor Carolyn Cooper, former coordinator, WDSG Mona, UWI
10. Dr Charmaine Crawford, head, IGDS NBU/Cave Hill, UWI
11. Diane Cummins, former research assistant, WICP; now a gender consultant
12. Deborah Deane, former administrative assistant, CGDS NBU/Cave Hill, UWI
13. Dr Leith Dunn, head, IGDS Mona, UWI
14. Professor Mark Figueroa, university professor and former member WDSG Mona, UWI
15. Margaret Gill, former research assistant, WICP; now lecturer, UWI Cave Hill
16. Dr Edward "Eddie" Greene, former director, ISER; professor emeritus and PVC, UWI

17. Professor Marlene Hamilton, professor emerita, retired PVC, UWI
18. Professor E. Nigel Harris, vice-chancellor (2004–15), UWI
19. Sir Alister McIntyre, vice-chancellor (1988–98), UWI
20. Hermione McKenzie, retired senior lecturer, UWI; former coordinator, WDSG Mona, UWI
21. Professor Patricia Mohammed, first head, CGDS Mona, UWI; now head, IGDS St Augustine, UWI
22. Professor Rhoda Reddock, first head, CGDS St Augustine, UWI; now deputy principal, UWI St Augustine
23. Rose Ann Richards, Summer Certificate programme participant; now an attorney-at-law
24. Tereza Richards, librarian, UWI; member, WDSG Mona, UWI
25. Dr Hilary Robertson-Hickling, lecturer, UWI; former coordinator, WDSG Mona, UWI
26. Dr Veronica "Ronnie" Salter, lecturer, UWI; former coordinator, WDSG Mona, UWI
27. Dr T. Alafia Samuels, medical practitioner; former coordinator, WDSG Mona, UWI
28. Professor Verene Shepherd, university director, IGDS
29. Norma Shorey, former project officer, WAND
30. Faith Webster, former executive director, Bureau of Women/Gender Affairs, Jamaica
31. Dr Rosina Wiltshire, former coordinator, WDSG St Augustine, UWI

APPENDIX 9

Tributes/Citations on Honourees of the Tenth Anniversary of the CGDS, August 2003

The University of the West Indies Centre for Gender and Development Studies Salutes Peggy Antrobus: Visionary, Enabler, Facilitator

One of the earliest lessons we learned in our exposure to women's studies is the decline of the midwife. Although, in some parts of the world, they continue to have pride of place, yet, in our own country, midwives were slowly losing their hold on that most sacred of professions – mediating and facilitating the birth of a new life.

It is not often then that we talk today about the midwife, but the figure of the midwife is an apt metaphor to describe the *one* important aspect of Peggy Antrobus's contribution to the Caribbean women's movement and the Caribbean vision for change. Peggy has been a midwife in that for close to three decades; she has been associated with, often playing the role of facilitator and enabler to, almost every institution related to women's and gender issues in the anglophone Caribbean. As first director of the Jamaica Women's Bureau, Peggy led the Jamaica delegation to the 1975 International Women's Year Conference. In 1974, Jamaica became one of the first countries in the world to establish what we now know as national machineries for women's affairs, and Peggy was there in those formative years. As first director, she established a tradition for autonomy and action which has continued to the present.

Between 1977 and 1978, Peggy, as secretary of the Caribbean Coordinating Committee for Women's Affairs, presided over the implementation of the recommendations of the 1977 Caribbean Coordinating Committee for Women's Affairs/CARIWA/UWI subregional conference on the integration of women into the development process. This led to the establishment of WAND – The Women and Development Unit of the Extra-Mural Department (now School of Continuing Studies) of the University of the West Indies, the Women's Desk in the CARICOM Secretariat and the Women's Desk at The United Nations Economic Commission for Latin America and the Caribbean (UN/ECLAC).

During Peggy's tenure as tutor-coordinator at WAND between 1978 and 1995, WAND became a central force around which activities related to women and gender in the region coalesced. It was Peggy who in 1981, invited Rhoda Reddock to Barbados to meet with her and invited her to prepare a position paper on the Introduction of a Programme of Women and Development Studies at the University of the West Indies. That paper was presented to the regional meeting in March 1982 which led to the establishment of Women's Studies Groups on each of the UWI's campuses coordinated by a regional steering committee led by Joycelin Massiah. The work of these groups, supported by funding from the Netherlands government and the Ford Foundation, led to the establishment of the Centre for Gender and Development Studies in September 2003.

After years of discussion and planning for the establishment of a regional feminist network, it was Peggy Antrobus who brought together the founding members to begin concrete planning to launch the CAFRA, on the day after the UN end-of-decade Caribbean celebration in April 1985. That organization became a focal point for feminist activism in the entire region, going beyond the traditional boundaries of the anglophone region to include the other linguistic and cultural regions of the Caribbean.

As a visionary, Peggy would often see what was necessary and seek immediately to put it into place. There were many who would be drawn into her net – willingly or unwillingly – and be inspired by her indomitable enthusiasm. Who could forget the day she got the idea to develop a network of networks? Once again, it was Peggy Antrobus who came up with the idea of establishing the Caribbean Policy Development Centre as a mechanism to facilitate collaboration among Caribbean networks and federations and strengthen their influence on policy in the region.

Extending beyond the Caribbean, in 1984, Peggy was also a founding member of DAWN and served as its general coordinator from 1990 to 1996. Every one of these organizations to which Peggy helped give life still exists. After facilitating its birth, like a true midwife, she would remain as long as necessary to ensure that the newborn was safe and healthy before moving on to the next case. This time period could range from seven to the seventeen years she spent as tutor/coordinator of WAND.

The Centre for Gender and Development Studies, UWI, as indeed the women's movement and gender studies community in the Caribbean and the world, is grateful for the contribution of Peggy Antrobus. We are honoured to have been associated with her life and work over the past decades and look forward to a continued association in the years to come.

The University of the West Indies Centre for Gender and Development Studies Salutes Louraine Emmanuel: Loyal, Committed Administrator

In 1986, when Dr Lucille Mathurin Mair agreed to direct the first project of cooperation between the Netherlands government and the UWI, which eventually led to the establishment of the CGDS, she needed a competent and knowledgeable assistant to work with her in developing this new area of scholarship within the university. Louraine Emmanuel was the person selected, and she left her post in the UWI library at Mona to take on this new assignment. Since then, she has been constantly and consistently involved in the work of the Women and Development Studies Groups, of the RCU, of all three campus units, and has been administrator of the projects with the Netherlands government as well as other projects. As administrative officer in the RCU of the CGDS, she has provided unwavering support to the units on all three campuses and has been our financial guide, our administrative prod, our collective memory and our most invaluable support. Els Mulder of the ISS, who has worked closely with Emmanuel over the years, sums up the feelings of us all in her message to this conference when she notes

> there is only one person who has been there throughout the whole process and who is still assisting the regional coordinator, and that is Mrs Louraine Emmanuel. She has the institutional memory. She was the one who always patiently explained to me how the rather complex management structure of UWI worked and what I could, and what I certainly could not, write and say. I have learned a great deal from her. She was the one who was always running around to get all matters settled in time for progress and financial reporting and to get all details from three campuses in order to make consolidated reports for the sponsor – not an easy task. She has done a lot of work for the projects, the centre and all the regional coordinators, who each had different priorities. I am grateful to her for all her contributions, her friendship and, last but not least, her humour.

We salute and honour Mrs Emmanuel this afternoon and ask her to come forward to receive an award from the CGDS for her commitment, loyalty and contribution to the growth and development of the centre.

The University of the West Indies Centre for Gender and Development Studies Salutes Joycelin Massiah: Trailblazer, Innovator, Leader

Joycelin Averil Massiah is part of the generation of leaders who came of age in the post-independent Caribbean. With the Caribbean as her background, Joycelin Massiah carved her space in the academy and in Caribbean society. Between 1972 and 1992, she was the director of the ISER (Eastern Caribbean) of the University of the West Indies Cave Hill campus, and, for ten years, 1992–2002, she served the Caribbean as UNIFEM's regional programme advisor.

For the three decades most critical to the growth and maturation of Caribbean feminist scholarship, activism and advocacy, Joycelin Massiah occupied key leadership positions. There, she used her intellect, influence and unwavering concern for Caribbean women to generate knowledge about women's lives and generate funding for programmes that would improve basic socio-economic conditions and improve the lives of women as well as men and children.

Between 1979 and 1982, she conceptualized and coordinated the Women in the Caribbean Project (WICP). The WICP was the first multidisciplinary regional research project to centralize women's lives as the subject matter of investigation. In her own words, the study was "multidisciplinary in design, consultative in outlook and innovative in intent". Women became visible, when they were not before, and the project established a benchmark for research on women in the anglophone Caribbean. Although the methodology and findings are still open to interrogation and debate, there is no research that can be legitimately undertaken on Caribbean women, there is no course that can or should be taught in Caribbean women's studies that does not take the contributions of the WICP into consideration. It highlighted the need for development of research capability and new methodological tools to adequately address the issues affecting women's lives and to influence policy to bring about change.

Joycelin, along with Peggy Antrobus, convened a now historic meeting in 1982, where a proposal for introducing a women's studies programme in the University of the West Indies, developed by Rhoda Reddock, was presented. This was the stimulus for the establishment of Women and Development Studies groups within the university. Her role as coordinator of the steering committee of these groups provided the consultative and innovative leadership that was so important in developing the project and negotiating the funding which facilitated the work of the groups and ensured their survival during the early years. The Centre for Gender and Development Studies is a direct outgrowth of the work of these groups.

As a woman and leader, as a catalyst for change, Joycelin Massiah achieved a number of firsts in the academy. Here is a sampling: She is the first female to head a department at the UWI, Cave Hill; the first female director of a research institute at the university; the first female professor at the Cave Hill campus; the first female professor in the Faculty of Social Sciences at the UWI. In 1992, Massiah left the university for another first: to establish and manage the first-ever regional office of the UNIFEM, which office covers twenty-six countries. Her post as regional programme advisor involved her in the organization, coordination and chairing of regional conferences, diplomatic representation and liaison with partner organizations, including UN agencies and governments.

The awards and honours for Joycelin's exemplary and trailblazing service have been many. A few are highlighted here. In 1998, she was named one of the University of the West Indies' distinguished graduates during its fiftieth-anniversary celebrations. In that same year, she was awarded the Gold Crown of Merit by the Government of Barbados, and, in 1999, she was awarded the CARICOM Triennial Award for Women, the region's highest award for women. She continues to serve the region with dedication and commitment in a wide range of national, regional and international organizations and committees, and she is actively involved in both central and campus-based university committees and decision-making bodies.

Scholarship, advocacy, service – Joycelin Averil Massiah, a twentieth-century woman and leader.

The University of the West Indies Centre for Gender and Development Studies Salutes drs Elisabeth "Els" Mulder: Committed, Effective Professional

There was a long period of gestation, some of it quite painful, before the birth of the Centre for Gender and Development Studies as a part of the institutional structure of the University of the West Indies (UWI). During that period, many persons played roles of varying importance and made their contributions, over time, to the process of establishing the centre. Chief among these were the women and men in the women's studies groups on each campus and the campus coordinators of those groups, who, with commitment and dedication but very few financial or human resources, kept the movement going. A breakthrough came when major funding was secured from the Government of the Netherlands to conduct a project of cooperation in teaching, research and outreach in women and development studies. This project was designed to build the institution's capacity to develop and teach gender studies and conduct gender-focused research and outreach. It was the first of its kind to be financed by the Netherlands Ministry of Foreign Affairs' Directorate General for International Cooperation under its International Education Programme and was done in collaboration with the ISS. What is not generally known is the part played by a very quiet, very efficient and very generous-spirited woman called Elisabeth Mulder, senior project officer and head, Project Management Unit of the ISS, who is more generally and affectionately known as Els.

Drs Els Mulder became involved in the writing and submission of that project proposal at its inception in the early 1980s, a period when gender was gradually becoming a focal point at the ministry and the ISS. Her input and interventions during the stages of the proposal, through two or three incarnations to a successful completion, cannot be overstated. Between 1986 and 1998, she visited Jamaica and developed an understanding of how the UWI system worked, and she helped to keep things clear by being the liaison person between the ministry and the university. For example, she arranged, in 1988, for the administrative officer of the project to have an interview with the officer responsible for the project at the ministry, to discuss matters related to its administration. Her professionalism, help and support over the two phases of the project were invaluable, and life would have been very much more difficult without her willing and uncomplaining interventions from time to time. She has facilitated the visits of a number of fellowship recipients, faculty and graduate students from the UWI to the ISS and patiently helped them overcome the myriad challenges arising in transferring from one educational system to another. All have reported on her kindness and the level of courtesy with which they were treated during their visits.

For these and many other reasons, the Centre for Gender and Development Studies extends its thanks and appreciation to you, Els, in recognition of your significant contribution, and that of the ISS and the Government of the Netherlands, to our having achieved institutional status and establishing a record of which we can all be proud.

The University of the West Indies Centre for Gender and Development Studies Salutes Dr Saskia Wieringa: A Woman of Controversy

Saskia Wieringa's work in the development of women and gender studies, and in the feminist movement, spans over two decades. It also spans many continents – both geographic and ideological, for she is as intrepid as she is controversial; as a scholar, policymaker, institutional builder and activist. She is equally energetic in uniting all of these.

The University of the West Indies has been fortunate to have benefited from Saskia's energy in the Caribbean. I have a memory of her visit to the Mona campus to lecture to our students in the MSc programme, stirring up their ideas and creating a great deal of vibrant discussion. One of her public lectures delivered here, entitled "Essentialism versus Constructivism: Time for a Rapprochement", was timely in the region, providing those of us who disagreed with the artificial divide between nature and nurture, between biological and social gender, with cogent arguments for defending our own views. This lecture, later transformed into a paper, is the first in the edited book *Gendered Realities: Essays in Caribbean Feminist Thought,* a publication which came out of the Mona campus unit, Centre for Gender and Development Studies in 2001, a signal of our respect for her scholarship.

As sound as her academic production is, so also does Saskia's work provoke controversy, keeping the already contentious area of women and gender studies bubbling with a not unacceptable prurient interest. Saskia is never hesitant to address issues, such as female homosexuality, which she thinks need to be highlighted – sometimes ignoring the norms acceptable in society, whether that society is the Netherlands, Namibia or Jamaica.

It is this same quality of directness, of confronting challenges, that Saskia has, which has worked in favour of the Caribbean. In her responsibility, for many years, as the project coordinator for the ISS, The Hague, in the UWI/ISS Project of Cooperation in Teaching and Research in Women and Development Studies, she has been steadfast in her defence of its specific needs. She was always ready to fight for its continuation and for what was right for this project, always there to assist in putting justification to the appropriate Dutch ministry official in the right words to demand the lioness's share for us, just as we are ready today to say where Saskia stands with us. Saskia Wieringa, your colleagues at the University of the West Indies: Mona, Cave Hill and St Augustine, thank and honour you for your valuable contribution to our programme.

REFERENCES

Addae, H., and G. Williams. 1990. "Management Audit of the Women and Development Group". Women and Development Group, UWI, St Augustine.

Andaiye. 2003. *Plan of Action 2005: Framework for Mainstreaming Gender into Key CARICOM Programmes.* Georgetown: CARICOM Secretariat.

Anderson, Patricia. 1986. "Conclusion: Women in the Caribbean". In "Women in the Caribbean: Part I", edited by Joycelin Massiah. Special issue, *Social and Economic Studies* 35 (2): 291–330.

Anderson-Duncan, Beverley. 2012. *Rebel Women: Engendering Transformation.* Lucille Mathurin Mair Lecture, no. 7. Kingston: Institute for Gender and Development Studies, UWI/Friedrich Ebert Stiftung.

Antrobus, Peggy. 2000. "The Rise and Fall of Feminist Politics in the Caribbean Women's Movement, 1975–1995". The Lucille Mathurin Mair Lecture, CGDS, UWI, Mona, 9 March.

———. 2004. *The Global Women's Movement: Origins, Issues and Strategies.* Kingston: Ian Randle.

Bailey, Barbara. 2003. "Innovation and Change at the University of the West Indies: The Establishment of a Women's/Gender Studies Programme". Unpublished paper prepared for presentation at VI Encuentro de Centros y Programas de Estudios de la Mujer y de Genero En Instituciones de Educacion Superior deAmerica Latina y el Caribe, Cuernavera, Mexico, October.

———. 2004. "The Caribbean Experience in the International Women's Movement: Issues, Process, Constraints and Possibilities". In Bailey and Leo-Rhynie 2004, 636–54.

———. 2012. "The Impact of Gender on UWI's Evolution". Paper presented on a panel on The Evolution of the UWI since Independence, at the SALISES 50/50 Conference 2012, Jamaica Pegasus Hotel, Kingston, Jamaica.

Bailey, Barbara, and Elsa Leo-Rhynie, eds. 2004. *Gender in the Twenty-First Century: Caribbean Perspectives, Visions and Possibilities.* Kingston: Ian Randle.

Beckles, Hilary McD. 1988. *Afro-Caribbean Women and Resistance to Slavery in Barbados.* London: Karnak House.

———. 1989. *Natural Rebels: A Social History of Enslaved Black Women in Barbados.* London: Zed Books.

Biervliet, W.E., and P. McPherson-Russell. 1990. "Evaluation Report: Mission to Evaluate the Project of Cooperation in Teaching and Research in Women and Development Studies in the Caribbean". NUFFIC.

Blank, Lorraine. 1998. "Project in Support of Teaching, Research and Outreach in Gender and Development Studies at the University of the West Indies". Commissioned by the Netherlands Embassy, Kingston, Jamaica.

Bush, Barbara. 1990. *Slave Women in Caribbean Society.* Bloomington: Indiana University Press.

CARICOM Secretariat. 1983. "Report of Second Meeting of Ministers with Responsibility for the Integration of Women in Development". Georgetown: CARICOM Secretariat.

———. 1997a. Charter of Civil Society for the Caribbean Community. Georgetown, Guyana, CARICOM Secretariat.

———. 1997b. *Gender Equality, Social Justice and Development: The CARICOM Post-Beijing Regional Plan of Action to the Year 2000.* Georgetown: CARICOM Secretariat.

———. 2003. "Plan of Action to 2005: Framework for Mainstreaming Gender into Key CARICOM Programmes". Prepared for the CARICOM Secretariat by Andaiye. Georgetown, Guyana.

———. 2008. "Gender Audit". Prepared by B. Bailey, S. Charles and J. Castello. Univeristy of the West Indies, Centre for Gender and Development Studies.

Commonwealth Secretariat. 2015. *Commonwealth Action Plan for Gender Equality 2005–2015.* London: Commonwealth Secretariat.

Chaderton, Robertine, and Maxine McClean. 1990. "Report of the Management Audit of the WDSG, UWI, Cave Hill Campus". University of the West Indies, Cave Hill, Barbados.

Crick, Anne P. 1990. "Management Audit of the Mona Campus Women and Development Group and Project". University of the West Indies, Mona, Jamaica.

Drayton, Kathleen. 1982. "Introduction: Women in Education". In *Women and Education*, edited by Joyce Cole and Patricia Mohammed. WICP Research Papers, Phase 1. Cave Hill, Barbados: Institute of Social and Economic Research (Eastern Caribbean), University of the West Indies.

———. 1997. "White Man's Knowledge: Sex, Race and Class in Caribbean English Language Textbooks". In *Gender: A Caribbean Multidisciplinary Perspective*, edited by Elsa Leo-Rhynie, 159–81, Barbara Bailey and Christine Barrow. Kingston: Ian Randle.

———. 1993. "Women and Development Studies: The Cave Hill Experience". Paper presented at Tenth Anniversary Symposium, Cave Hill.

———. 2010. "A Call to Freedom and Justice: Lessons from My Life". Address commemorating International Women's Day, Barbados. UWI, Cave Hill, IGDS, NBU.

Ford-Smith, Honor. 1989. Ring Ding in a Tight Corner: A Case Study of Funding and Organizing Democracy in Sistren, 1977–1988. Toronto: Women's Program, International Council for Adult Education.

Great Britain. 1945a. *Report of the West India Royal Commission (Moyne Commission).* Cmd. 6607. London: HMSO.

———. 1945b. *Report of the West Indies Committee on Higher Education in the Colonies. (The Irvine Report).* Cmd. 6654, no. 22. London: HMSO.

Hamilton, Marlene. 1998. "Women and Higher Education in the Commonwealth Caribbean: UWI: A Progressive Institution for Women?" Fourth lecture in the series *Caribbean Women Catalysts for Change* dedicated to the memory of Dame Nita Barrow, CGDS, NBU, UWI, 12 December.

hooks, bell. 1989. *Talking Back: Thinking Feminist, Thinking Black.* Boston: South End Press.

IOP/UWI/ISS. 1985. "Project of Cooperation on Teaching and Research in Women and Development Studies, October 1985–September 1990". UWI and ISS. April. Rev. ed., August. Page references are to the revised edition.

———. 1990. "Project of Cooperation in Teaching, Research and Outreach in Women and Development Studies, Phase 2". Government of the Netherlands/ University of the West Indies/ Institute of Social Studies.

Kaminjolo, Althea. 1993. *A Decade of Development, 1982–1983.* St Augustine, Trinidad and Tobago: WDSG, UWI.

Kamphuis, Eric B. 1997. "Evaluation of the Second Phase of the ISS/UWI Project of Cooperation in Teaching and Research in Women and Development Studies". Activity Number 7221 91 BB/91/950, 24 March 1997. ETC Foundation.

Leo-Rhynie, Elsa. 1992. "Women and Development Studies: Moving from the Periphery?" Inaugural professorial lecture presented at the Women and Development Studies Tenth Anniversary Symposium, UWI, Mona, 8–10 December. Edited version in Mohammed 2002, 147–63.

———. 1999. "The Story of the Centre for Gender and Development Studies". Opening address at the conference "Theoretical Approaches to Gender in the Caribbean: Interdisciplinary Perspectives", CGDS, UWI, Cave Hill, 2 June.

———. 2003a. "Gender and Power in Contemporary Society: A Case Study of Student Government". In *Confronting Power, Theorizing Gender: Interdisciplinary Perspectives in the Caribbean,* edited by Eudine Barriteau, 283–99. Kingston: University of the West Indies Press.

———. 2003b. "Gender Studies: Crossing Boundaries, Charting New Directions". Tenth Anniversary Lecture, CGDS, UWI, St Augustine, 3 December.

———. 2004. "Gender Studies: Interdisciplinary and Pedagogical Challenges". In Bailey and Leo-Rhynie 2004, 419–36.

———. 2008. "The UWI Glass Ceiling: Splinters, Cracks and Scratches". The Lucille Mathurin Mair Lecture, CGDS, Mona Unit, UWI, Mona, 20 November.

Leo-Rhynie, Elsa, Barbara Bailey, and Christine Barrow, eds. 1997. *Gender: A Caribbean Multi-Disciplinary Perspective.* Kingston: Ian Randle.

Massiah, Joycelin. 1979. *Women in the Caribbean: An Annotated Bibliography – A Guide to Material Available in Barbados.* With the assistance of Audine Wilkinson and Norma Shorey. Occasional Bibliography Series, no. 5. Cave Hill, Barbados: ISER, UWI, Cave Hill.

———. 1983. *Report of the Conference on the "Role of Women in the Caribbean": Barbados, September 12–16, 1982.* Barbados: ISER, UWI, Cave Hill.

———. 1986a. "Establishing a Programme of Women and Development Studies in the University of the West Indies". *Social and Economic Studies* 35 (1):151–97.

———, ed. 1986b. "Women in the Caribbean". Special issue, *Social and Economic Studies* 35 (2–3).

———. 1993. "Vashti or Esther? The Choice Is Yours". Feature address at symposium celebrating the tenth anniversary of the WDS programme, UWI, Cave Hill, 2 December 1993.

———. 1998. "On the Brink of the new Millennium: Are Caribbean Women Prepared?" Inaugural Lucille Mathurin Mair Lecture. 6 March.

———. 2001. Foreword. In *Stronger, Surer, Bolder: Ruth Nita Barrow -Social Change and International Development,* edited by E. Barriteau and A. Cobley. Kingston: University of the West Indies Press.

———. 2004. "Feminist Scholarship and Society". In Bailey and Leo-Rhynie 2004, 5–34.

———. 2006. "Ten Years after Beijing: What More Do Caribbean Women Want . . .?" *Journal of Eastern Caribbean Studies* 31 (1): 55–79.

Mathurin Mair, Lucille. 1975. *Rebel Woman in the British West Indies during Slavery.* Kingston: Institute of Jamaica Publications.

———. 1988b. "Women's Studies in an International Context". In Mohammed and Shepherd 1988, 1–9.

———. 2006. *A Historical Study of Women in Jamaica, 1655–1842.* Edited, with introduction, by H.McD. Beckles and V. Shepherd. Kingston: University of the West Indies Press/Centre for Gender and Development Studies.

McKenzie, Hermione. 2004. "Shifting Centres and Moving Margins: The UWI Experience". In Bailey and Leo-Rhynie 2004, 397–416.

McPherson-Russell, P. and G.W. Peters. 1988. "Report of the Mid-term Evaluation of the Project of Cooperation in Teaching and Research in Women and Development Studies". IOP/UWI/ISS, Kingston. May.

Mohammed, Patricia. 1989. "Women's Responses in the 70s and 80s in Trinidad: A Country Report". *Caribbean Quarterly* 35 (1–2): 36–45.

———, ed. 2002. *Gendered Realities: Essays in Caribbean Feminist Thought*. Kingston: University of the West Indies Press.

———. 2011. "Gender-Based Violence in Calypso". Keynote address at the breakfast seminar to commemorate the International Day for the Elimination of Violence against Women, held by the Ministry of Gender, Youth and Child Development, Trinidad and Tobago. 25 November.

———. N.d. "Reflections on the Women's Movement in Trinidad and Tobago: Calypso, Changes and Sexual Violence". Typescript.

Mohammed, Patricia, and Catherine Shepherd, eds. 1988. *Gender in Caribbean Development*. Kingston: UWI, Mona, Women and Development Studies Project.

Mondesire, Alicia, and Leith Dunn. 1995. *Towards Equity in Development: A Report on the Status of Caribbean Women in Sixteen Commonwealth Countries*. Georgetown, Guyana: CARICOM Secretariat.

Moser, Caroline. 1989. "Gender Planning in the Third World: Meeting Practical and Strategic Gender Needs". *World Development* 17 (11): 1799–825.

Mulder, Els. 2003. "Gender in the Twenty-First Century: Caribbean Perspectives, Visions and Possibilities". Message to the UWI Mona Academic Conference. 29–31 August. Published in the conference progamme.

Nettleford, Rex. 1989. "Caribbean Crisis and Challenges to the Year 2000". *Caribbean Quarterly* 35 (1&2): 6–16.

———. 1993. *Inward Stretch, Outward Reach: A Voice from the Caribbean*. New York: Caribbean Diaspora Press at Caribbean Research Center, Medgar Evers College, CUNY.

Rathgeber, Eva. 1990. "WID, WAD, GAD: Trends in Research and Practice". *Journal of Developing Areas* 24 (4): 489–502.

Reddock, Rhoda. 1994. "Women's Studies at the University of the West Indies: A Decade of Feminist Education?" *Women's Studies Quarterly* 3 (13): 103–15.

———, ed. 2004. *Interrogating Caribbean Masculinities: Theoretical and Empirical Analyses*. Kingston: University of the West Indies Press.

———. 2009. Opening Address to the Fifteenth Anniversay Lecture of the IGDS, St Augustine, and to commemorate the International Day for the Elimination of Violence against Women. UWI Trinidad and Tobago. 20 November.

———. 2014. "Greetings to the IGDS at 20: An Exhibition and Cocktail Reception". Regional Headquarters, UWI, Jamaica. 3 June.

Rogers, E.M. 2003. *Diffusion of Innovation*. 5th ed. New York: Free Press.

Rogers, E.M., and F.F. Shoemaker. 1971. *Communication of Innovation: A Cross-Cultural Approach*. New York: Free Press.

Rowland, Robyn. 1982. "Women's Studies Courses: Pragmatic and Political Issues concerning Their Establishment and Design". *Women's Studies International Forum* 5 (5): 487–95.

Senior, Olive. 1991. *Working Miracles: Women's Lives in the English-Speaking Caribbean.* London: James Curry.

Shepherd, Verene, Bridget Brereton, and Barbara Bailey, eds. 1995. *Engendering History: Caribbean Women in Historical Perspective.* Kingston: Ian Randle.

Snyder, Margaret. 1995. "Towards a New Development Paradigm: WAND in the Caribbean". In *Transforming Development: Women, Poverty and Politics*, 143–50. London: Intermediate Technology Publications.

Trotz, Alissa. 2013. "Inescapable Entanglements: Notes on Caribbean Feminist Engagement". Keynote address at the opening ceremony of IGDS Twentieth Anniversary Conference, UWI, St Augustine, Trinidad and Tobago, 6–8 November.

UNDP (United Nations Development Programme). 1995. *Human Development Report, 1995.* New York: Oxford University Press.

———. 1997. *Human Development Report, 1997.* New York: Oxford University Press.

———. 2007. *Human Development Report, 2007/2008.* New York: Palgrave Macmillan.

———. 2013. *Human Development Report, 2013.* http://hdr.undp.org/en/2013-report.

———. 2015. *Human Development Report, 2015.* http://hdr.undp.org/en/2015-report.

United Nations. 1995. Fourth World Conference on Women. Beijing Declaration and Platform for Action. http://www.un.org/womenwatch/daw/beijing/platform

UNESCO and UWI CGDS. 2001. "Report: Gender, Peace and Development in the Caribbean". http://www.unesco.org/cpp/uk/projects/projectfinalreport.pdf. September

UWI AB (Academic Board). 1997. "Report of the Academic Board, St Augustine, December 1997". IGDS (M) P.3 1997/98.

UWI BGSR (Board for Graduate Studies and Research). 1997. "Minutes of the Meeting of the Board for Graduate Studies and Research held on October 8, 1997". Board for Graduate Studies and Research.

———. 2009. *A Policy for the Establishment, Operation and Governance of Units, Centres and Institutes at the University of the West Indies.* 3rd ed. Kingston: BGSR, UWI.

UWI BUS. 2005. "Review of the Centre for Gender and Development Studies, St Augustine Campus. Trinidad & Tobago". Quality Assurance Unit, Office of the Board for Undergraduate Studies.

———. 2006a. "Review of the Centre for Gender and Development Studies, 2005/2006". Quality Assurance Unit, Office of the Board for Undergraduate Studies, UWI Mona. 30 January–2 February.

———. 2006b. "Review of the Centre for Gender and Development Studies (Mona and Regional Coordinating Unit)". Office of the Board for Undergraduate Studies, UWI, Mona. April.

UWI CGDS. 1996. "Project Evaluation, Phase 2, Project of Cooperation in Teaching and Research in Women and Development Studies Project". BB/91/950. July.

———. 1997. "Gender Analysis in Policy and Planning: A Workshop for Bi-lateral and Multilateral Agencies: Report of Proceedings". Hotel PomMarine, Barbados, 23–25 September.

———.1999. "Report on the Section of the Project Women and Micro-Enterprise Development in Jamaica funded by the Government of Japan". Centre for Gender and Development Studies, Regional Coordinating Unit. Prepared by Joan Browne. April.

———.2000. "Report on Research/Action Project 'Building Gender Approaches Towards Sustainable Livelihoods: The Nariva Swamp, A Gendered Case Study". Hotel Normandie, Port of Spain, Trinidad. 14 December.

———. 2005. "Self-Assessment Report". Centre for Gender and Development Studies, UWI, Cave Hill, Barbados. 18 November.

———. 2006. "Self-Assessment Report". Prepared by the Mona Unit, Centre for Gender and Development Studies, UWI Mona, Jamaica. Submitted to the Quality Assurance Unit, Board for Undergraduate Studies, February 2006.

UWI IGDS. 2012a. "Self-Assessment Report 2012". Quality assurance review. Trinidad & Tobago: St Augustine Unit.

———. 2012b. "Self-Assessment Report. Institute for Gender and Development Studies, Nita Barrow Unit". Cave Hill: University of the West Indies, Cave Hill campus. November.

UWI Office of Administration. 1990. *The University Centre Development Plan 1990–2000 AD*. Kingston: Office of Administration, UWI.

———. 1994. *A New Structure: The Regional University in the 1990's and Beyond: Report of the Chancellor's Commission on the Governance of UWI, July 1994*. Kingston: Office of Administration, UWI.

———. 1998. *The Charter, Statutes and Ordinances*. Vol. 1 (excluding Ordinance 8). Kingston: Office of Administration, UWI.

———. 2002. *The UWI Strategic Plan. 2002–2007*. Kingston: Office of Administration, UWI.

———. Various years. *UWI Statistical Review*. Kingston: Office of Administration.

UWI Office of the Principal. 2006. *Principal's Report 2006*. Kingston: Office of the Principal, UWI, Mona.

UWI University Academic Committee. 1993. "The Proposal for the Establishment of a Centre for Gender Studies to Be Established on the Mona Campus of the University of the West Indies". WDS-AC2.

UWI WDS. 1987. WDS Project. "Composite Report of the Interdisciplinary Seminars in Women and Development Studies at the University of the West Indies". ISER, UWI St Augustine, Trinidad.

———. N.d. [1992?]. "Caribbean Women in Transition: a Research Programme on Women, Gender and Caribbean Development". WDS, UWI St Augustine, Trinidad.

University Women's Group Mona. 1994. "Minutes of Extraordinary General Meeting, University Women's Group (Mona), September 22, 1994".

Vargas, Virginia, and Saskia Wieringa. 1998. "The Triangle of Empowerment, Processes and Actors in the Making of Public Policy for Women". In *Women's Movements and Public Policy in Europe, Latin America and the Caribbean,* edited by Geertje Lycklama, Virginia Vargas and Saskia Wieringa, 3–25. New York: Garland.

Vassell, Linnette. 2004. "Feminisms, Gender Studies, Activism: The Elusive Triad". In Bailey and Leo-Rhynie 2004, 687–705.

WAND. 1982. "Report of Meeting to Discuss the Introduction of Women's Studies into the UWI, Barbados, March 22–23".

———. 1988. "Report of WAND's Women's Studies Activities for Inclusion in the UWI WDS Project Report to the ISS, The Hague".

———. 1993. *A Historical Profile of the Women and Development Unit.* Cave Hill, Barbados: WAND

———. n.d. *The Story of WAND.* Cave Hill, Barbados: UWI, Extra-Mural Department.

Wieringa, Saskia. 2004. "Shifting Centres and Moving Margins: The ISS Experience". In Bailey and Leo-Rhynie, 373–96.

Yudelman, Sally. 1987. "Women and Development Unit". In *Hopeful Openings: A Study of Five Women's Development Organisations in Latin America and the Caribbean,* by S. Yudelman, 77–92. West Hartford, CT: Kumarian Press.

INDEX

www.ingramcontent.com/pod-product-compliance
Lightning Source LLC
Chambersburg PA
CBHW030835300326
41935CB00036B/91
9789766405823